Modes of Therapeutic Action

Other books by Martha Stark

A Primer on Working with Resistance

Working with Resistance

About the Author

Martha Stark, M.D., a graduate of the Harvard Medical School and the Boston Psychoanalytic Institute, is a psychiatrist/psychoanalyst in private practice in Newton Centre, Massachusetts. Dr. Stark is on the faculty of both the Boston Psychoanalytic Institute and the Massachusetts Institute for Psychoanalysis. She is also a Clinical Instructor in Psychiatry at the Harvard Medical School, has a teaching appointment at the Massachusetts Mental Health Center, and is on the faculty of the Center for Psychoanalytic Studies at the Massachusetts General Hospital.

Modes of Therapeutic Action

ENHANCEMENT OF KNOWLEDGE, PROVISION OF EXPERIENCE, AND ENGAGEMENT IN RELATIONSHIP

Martha Stark, M.D.

JASON ARONSON INC.
Northvale, New Jersey
London

This book was set in 11 pt. Fairfield Light by Alpha Graphics of Pittsfield, NH and printed and bound by Book-mart Press, Inc. of North Bergen, NJ.

10 9 8 7 6 5 4 3 2 1

Library of Congress Cataloging-in-Publication Data

Stark, Martha.
Modes of therapeutic action : enhancement of knowledge, provision of experience, and engagement in relationship / by Martha Stark.
p. cm.
Includes bibliographical references and index.
ISBN 0-7657-0202-9
1. Psychotherapist and patient. I. Title.
RC456.S725 1999
616.89'14—dc21 98-54402

Printed in the United States of America on acid-free paper. For information and catalog write to Jason Aronson Inc., 230 Livingston Street, Northvale, NJ 07647-1726, or visit our website: www.aronson.com

To Mom and Dad—

With deep love and gratitude

You have always been the wind beneath my wings

Contents

Foreword

NO THEORY IS AN ISLAND

In our postmodern climate of deconstruction, the mythically comprehensive intellectual framework of classical psychoanalysis has been shaken by a number of compelling and insightful challenges. The different terrain of mental life mapped in these theories perplexes clinicians toiling in the irrefutably diverse fields of clinical reality. Each theory unabashedly claims primacy of importance in understanding human nature. And, examined individually, each theory presents a valid, key piece of the human dilemma. How does one integrate these worthy views in a theoretical and clinical package that makes sense?

Martha Stark's synthesis does not presume to encompass all new theories that have developed, but draws from several of the most influential. The reader will quickly realize from the candid nature of the clinical examples in this volume that these perspectives are especially consonant with her personality and clinical practice. In staying with what she knows best, Dr. Stark offers us keen empirical evidence for her amalgam. Accordingly, her accrued clinical experience will speak to others struggling to harmonize discordant elements of training, evolving theories, and practice.

Classical psychoanalysis spent many years engaged in exploration of a mental world separated from the external world, a world of innate fantasy trends and patterns. The nature/nurture dilemma was heavily weighted in the direction of a programmed psychological nature. The attention to intrapsychic determination of behavior was a swing of the pendulum toward appreciation of unconscious psychological life. The shadow of this gigantic intellectual object was long cast on our rational ego.

Striking in contemporary thinking is a return to fascination with the impact of external reality on personality, particularly the reality of culture. Respect for relativity of experience has emerged. Issues such as class, race, gender, or trauma have complicated formulations of personality development and therapeutic interventions. Sociosomatics, the impact of culture on the body and personality, offers reasonable intellectual challenges to the older outlook of psychosomatics. Within the dreamlike, social psychological microcosm of psychotherapy, Dr. Stark has awakened to a special reality, that of the therapist.

The co-construction of the therapeutic process (reality) between patient and therapist is an essential understanding for Dr. Stark in describing the healing power of what she terms an authentic relationship. In Hegelian dialectical fashion, she builds a picture of the creative, dynamic interchange of therapist and patient personalities. Only attention to the subjective and objective realities of both parties can provide comprehension of the therapeutic process as well as discovering solutions to its dilemmas. I am reminded of certain views of dream life wherein meaning creates a dream, which then possesses new meaning. Dr. Stark describes many long, hard-traveled clinical roads to reach these conclusions. The reader will find recognizable, down-to-earth therapeutic realities, which put experiential meat on these concepts that may read here as bare-bone words.

Working at the intimate edge of authentic engagement in these interactive terms is intensely demanding. A therapist is pushed to anxious limits of personality, knowledge, professional ability—and, often, fate—as they step out into the bare space of imagination and unknown self. Dr. Stark catalogues, case by case, elements of her personality that have been unpredictably unsettled in her dedicated pursuit of understanding and healing. Readers will resonate in empathic recognition or uneasy anticipation.

While reaching into the unmapped zone of the active participant-observer, Dr. Stark acknowledges the complicated presence of other theories embodied in her most valued clinical abilities. This wise integration is fostered by undeniable clinical experiences in intensive, transference-driven psychotherapy, and culls enduring truths from past theory and practice. In particular, the labyrinthine domains of classical psychoanalysis's insight through interpretation, self-psychology's empathy, and the interpersonal dances of object relations are sifted and sorted for value. The delightful dexterity and perspicacity of these scholarly probings might easily be subtitled: "The Re-analysis of Guntrip's Re-analysis with Fairbairn by Winnicott plus the Re-analysis of the Two Analyses of Mr. Z. (Kohut) by Martha Stark."

A multiplicity of theoretical guides is understandable, given the range of human nature that comes to life in the consulting room. Oscillation of attitude and technique, nimbly and humbly, is emphasized as a realistic response to types of patients, stages of treatment, and growth of the therapist's awareness. Weaving through all these concepts, however, is the omnipresent, emotional growth vitamin of grief and sadness. Each theory or technique must come to grips with the ubiquitous human tension between real or fantasized gratification and loss—the search for love always involves pain. The pain of loss decides many a psychic fate. Regardless of theoretical shepherd, a piece of Martha Stark's vision gauges the emotional level of grief and sadness.

The search for love, importantly, is what motivates and sustains a therapeutic relationship. In this libidinous realm, Dr. Stark offers what she feels is her most unique and valuable contribution: the displacive transference. Analogous to free-floating attention, Dr. Stark has cultivated openness to free-floating role-responsiveness to patients' unconscious and conscious efforts to shape her personality. The interpersonal, transformative powers of projective identification are described creatively, as is the linked therapeutic detoxification of the projected pathogenic bad object. Additionally, Dr. Stark has discovered the transference/countertransference tightrope of being shaped as the desired, good love object. With courageous integrity of purpose and understanding, she elaborates on the therapeutic quicksand of the seductive therapist, which also entails the mysterious path between hope and disillusionment. Yet, she explains how assuming the risks and surmounting the therapeutic dangers holds the reward of an otherwise unattainable, profound transformation for the patient. It is fitting that a book on modes of therapeutic action should conclude by leaving the reader with the quandrous dilemma of love, since it is ultimately love that patients are seeking—and love that heals.

Sheldon Roth, M.D.
Training and Supervising Psychoanalyst,
Psychoanalytic Institute of New England
Assistant Clinical Professor of Psychiatry,
Harvard Medical School

Introduction

Over the past decades, numerous attempts have been made to address what it is about the psychotherapeutic process that is healing. I have found one such effort, Stephen Mitchell's 1988 book *Relational Concepts in Psychoanalysis*, to be the most intellectually satisfying and clinically useful conceptualization of the different modes of therapeutic action. The theory he advances synthesizes three different perspectives: the drive-conflict model, the deficiency-compensation model, and the relational-conflict model.

Drawing upon Mitchell's ideas (as well as the ideas of others), I have developed an integrative model of therapeutic action that takes into consideration many different schools of thought. It is my belief that most psychotherapeutic models boil down to advocating either knowledge, experience, or relationship—that is, either enhancement of knowledge, provision of experience, or engagement in relationship—as the primary therapeutic agent.

In this Introduction, I will attempt to summarize what I present in a much more elaborated form in Parts I and II. As will soon become clear, although there is significant overlap among the three perspectives, each one contains elements that distinguish it from the other two. The models of therapeutic action are therefore not mutually exclusive but mutually enhancing.

The first model is the interpretive model of classical psychoanalysis. Structural conflict is seen as the villain of the piece, and the goal of treatment is thought to be a strengthening of the ego by way of insight. Whether expressed as (1) the rendering conscious of what had once been unconscious (in topographic terms); (2) where id was, there shall ego be (in structural terms); or (3) uncovering and reconstructing the past (in genetic terms), in Model 1 it is "the truth" that is thought to set the patient free.

Interpretations, particularly of the transference, are considered the means by which self-awareness is expanded.

How do interpretations lead to resolution of structural conflict?

As the ego gains insight by way of interpretation, the ego becomes stronger. This increased ego strength enables it to experience less anxiety in relation to the id's sexual and aggressive impulses; the ego's defenses, therefore, become less necessary. As the defenses are gradually relinquished, the patient's conflicts about her sexual and aggressive drives are gradually resolved.

The Model 1 therapist sees herself not as a participant in a relationship but as an objective observer of the patient. Her unit of study is the patient and the patient's internal dynamics. The therapist conceives of her position as outside the therapeutic field and of herself as a blank screen onto which the patient casts shadows that the therapist then interprets.

Model 1 is clearly a one-person psychology.

In some ways it is not surprising that Freud would have been reluctant to recognize the importance of the actual relationship, because Freud never had any "relationship" whatsoever with an analyst. His, of course, was a self-analysis. By way of a meticulous analysis of his dreams, he was able to achieve insight into the internal workings of his mind, thereby strengthening his ego and resolving his intrapsychic conflicts.

But there were those analysts both here and abroad who found themselves dissatisfied with a model of the mind that spoke to the importance not of the relationship between patient and therapist but of the relationships among id, ego, and superego. Both self psychologists in the United States and object relations theorists in Europe began to speak up on behalf of the individual as someone who longed for connection with others.

In fact, Fairbairn (1943), writing in the 1940s, contended that the individual had an innate longing for object relations and that it was the relationship with the object and not the gratification of impulses that was the ultimate aim of libidinal striving. He noted that the libido was "primarily object-seeking, not pleasure-seeking" (p. 60).

Both the self psychologists and the European (particularly the British) object relations theorists were interested not so much in nature (the nature of the child's drives) but in nurture (the quality of maternal care and the mutuality of fit between mother and child).

Whereas Freud and other classical psychoanalysts conceived of the patient's psychopathology as deriving from the patient (in whom there was thought to be an imbalance of forces and, therefore, internal conflict), self psychologists, object relations theorists, and contemporary relational analysts conceived of the patient's psychopathology as deriving from the parent (and the parent's failure of the child).

How were such parental failures thought to be internally recorded and structuralized? Interestingly, some theorists (Balint 1968) focused on the price the child paid because of what the parent did not do; in other words, "absence of good" in the parent–child relationship was thought to give rise to structural deficit (or impaired capacity) in the child. But other theorists (Fairbairn 1954) focused on the price the child paid because of what the parent did do; in other words, "presence of bad" in the parent–child relationship was thought to be internally registered in the form of pathogenic introjects or internal bad objects—filters through which the child would then experience her world.

But whether the pathogenic factor was seen as a sin of omission (absence of good) or a sin of commission (presence of bad), the villain of the piece was no longer thought to be the child but the parent—and, accordingly, psychopathology was no longer thought to derive from the child's nature but from the nurture the child had received during her formative years. No longer was the child considered an agent (with unbridled sexual and aggressive drives); now the parent was held accountable—and the child was seen as a passive victim of parental neglect and abuse.

When the etiology shifted from nature to nurture, so, too, the locus of the therapeutic action shifted from insight by way of interpretation to a corrective experience by way of the real relationship (that is, from within the patient to within the relationship between patient and therapist).

No longer was the goal thought to be rendering conscious the unconscious so that structural conflict could be resolved; now the goal of treatment became filling in structural deficit and consolidating the self by way of the therapist's restitutive provision.

With the transitioning from a one-person to a two-person psychology, sexuality (the libidinal drive) and aggression took a back seat to more relational needs—the need for empathic recognition, the need for validation, the need to be admired, the need for soothing, the need to be held.

The therapist was no longer thought to be primarily a drive object but, rather, a selfobject (used to complete the self by performing those functions the patient was unable to perform on her own) or a good object–good mother (operating in loco parentis).

To repeat, the deficiency-compensation model—embraced by the self psychologists and by those object relations theorists who focused on the internal recording of traumatic parental failure in the form of deficit—conceived of the therapeutic action as involving some kind of corrective experience at the hands of a therapist who was experienced by the patient as a new good (and, therefore, compensatory) object.

In Model 2, then, the patient was seen as suffering not from structural conflict but from structural deficit—that is, an impaired capacity to be a good parent unto herself. The deficit was thought to arise in the context of failure in the early-on environmental provision, failure in the early-on relationship between parent and infant.

Now the therapeutic aim was the therapist's provision in the here-and-now of that which was not provided by the parent early-on—such that the patient would have the healing experience of being met and held.

Of note is that some deficiency-compensation theorists (most notably the self psychologists) focused on the patient's *experience* of the therapist as a new good object; others (the Model 2 object relations theorists) appeared to focus more on the therapist's *actual participation* as that new good object.

But what all the deficiency-compensation models of therapeutic action had in common was that they posited some form of corrective provision as the primary therapeutic agent.

It was then in the context of the new relationship between patient and therapist that there was thought to be the opportunity for a "new beginning" (Balint 1968)—the opportunity for reparation, the new relationship a corrective for the old one.

But although relationship was involved, it was more an I–It than an I–Thou relationship—more a one-way relationship between someone who gave and someone who took than a two-way relationship involving give-and-take, mutuality, and reciprocity.

It is for this reason that self psychology, which is a prime example of a deficiency-compensation model, has been described as a one-and-a-half-person psychology (Morrison 1994)—it is certainly not a one-person psychology, but then it is not truly a two-person psychology either.

Let us return to the issue of what constitutes the therapeutic action. There are an increasing number of contemporary theorists who believe that what heals the patient is neither insight nor a corrective experience. Rather, what heals is interactive engagement with an authentic other; what heals is the therapeutic relationship itself.

Relational (or Model 3) theorists who embrace this perspective conceive of patient and therapist as constituting a co-evolving, reciprocally mutual, interactive dyad—each participant initiating and responding. For the relational therapist, the locus of the therapeutic action always involves this mutuality of impact.

Unlike Model 2, which pays relatively little attention to the patient's exerting of pressure on the therapist to participate in certain ways, Model 3 addresses itself specifically to the force field created by the patient in an effort to draw the therapist into participating in ways specifically determined by the patient's early-on history—ways the patient needs the therapist to participate if she (the patient) is ever to have a chance to master her internal demons. In other words, in Model 3, the patient with a history of early-on traumas is seen as having a need to re-find the old bad object—the hope being that perhaps this time there will be different outcome. In order to demonstrate the distinction between a theory that posits unidirectional influence (Model 2) and a theory that posits bidirectional (reciprocal) influence (Model 3), I offer the following:

As we know, self psychology (the epitome of a corrective-provision model) speaks to the importance of the therapist's so-called "inevitable" empathic failures (Kohut 1966). Self psychologists contend that these failures are unavoidable because the therapist is not, and cannot be expected to be, perfect.

How does relational theory (Model 3) conceive of such failures? Many relational theorists believe that a therapist's failures of her patient are not just a story about the therapist (and her lack of perfection) but also a story about the patient and the patient's exerting of interpersonal pressure on the therapist to participate in ways both familial and, therefore, familiar to the patient (Mitchell 1988).

Relational theory believes that the therapist's failures do not simply happen in a vacuum; rather, they occur in the context of an ongoing, continuously evolving relationship between two real people—and speak to the therapist's responsiveness to the patient's (often unconscious) need to be failed so that she can achieve belated mastery of her internalized traumas.

In Model 3, then, the patient is seen as an agent, as proactive, as able to have an impact, as exerting unrelenting pressure on the therapist to participate in ways that will make possible the patient's further growth. The relational therapist, therefore, attends closely to what the patient delivers of herself into the therapy relationship (in other words, the patient's transferential "activity"); by the same token, ever aware of how telling her own response is to that activity, the therapist also remains very much centered within her own experience (in other words, her countertransferential "reactivity").

In fact, relational theory conceptualizes the patient's activity in relation to the therapist as an *enactment*, the unconscious intent of which is to engage (or to disengage) the therapist in some fashion—either by way of eliciting some kind of response from the therapist or by way of communicating something important to the therapist about the patient's internal world. In fact, the patient may know of no other way to get some piece of her subjective experience understood than by enacting it in the relationship with her therapist.

I will be using the word *provocative* to describe the patient's behavior when she is seeking to re-create the old bad object situation (so that she can rework her internal demons), *inviting* to describe her behavior when she is seeking to create a new good object situation (so that she can begin anew), and *entitled* to describe her behavior when, confronted with an interpersonal reality that she finds intolerable, she persists nonetheless—relentless in her pursuit of that to which she feels entitled and relentless in her outrage at its being denied.

If the Model 3 therapist is to be an effective container for (and psychological metabolizer of) the patient's disavowed psychic contents, the therapist must be able not only to tolerate being made into the patient's old bad object but also to extricate herself, by recovering her objectivity and, thereby, her therapeutic effectiveness, once she has allowed herself to be drawn into what has become a mutual enactment.

The therapist must have both the wisdom to recognize and the integrity to acknowledge her own participation in the patient's enactments; even if the "problem" lies in the intersubjective space between patient and therapist, with contributions from both, it is crucial that the therapist have the capacity to relent—and to do it first.

Patient and therapist can then go on to look at the patient's investment in getting her objects to fail her, her compulsive need to re-create with her contemporary objects the early-on traumatic failure situation.

If the therapist never allows herself to be drawn into participating with the patient in her enactments, we speak of a failure of engagement. If, however, the therapist allows herself to be drawn into the patient's internal dramas but then gets lost, we speak of a failure of containment—and the patient may be retraumatized.

Although initially the therapist may indeed fail the patient in much the same way that her parent had failed her, ultimately the therapist challenges the patient's projections by lending aspects of her "otherness," or, as Winnicott (1965) would have said, her "externality" to the interaction—such that the patient will have the experience of something that is "other-than-me" and can take that in. What the patient internalizes will be an amalgam, part contributed by the therapist and part contributed by the patient (the original projection).

In other words, because the therapist is not, in fact, as bad as the parent had been, there can be a better outcome. There will be repetition of the original trauma but with a much healthier resolution this time—the repetition leading to modification of the patient's internal world and integration on a higher level.

It is in this way that the patient will have a powerfully healing "corrective relational experience," the experience of bad-become-good.

In the relational model, it is the negotiation of the relationship and its vicissitudes (a relationship that is continuously evolving as patient and therapist act/react/interact) that constitutes the locus of the therapeutic action. It is what transpires in the here-and-now engagement between patient and therapist that is thought to be transformative.

And so this third model of therapeutic action is the relational (or interactive) perspective of contemporary psychoanalytic theory. No longer is the emphasis on the therapist as object—object of the patient's sexual and aggressive drives (Model 1), object of the patient's narcissistic demands (Model 2), or object of the patient's relational need to be met and held (Model 2). In this contemporary relational model, the focus is on the therapist as subject—an authentic subject who uses the self (that is, uses her countertransference) to engage, and to be engaged by, the patient.

Unless the therapist is willing to bring her authentic self into the room, the patient may end up analyzed—but never found.

By way of review: Whereas Model 1 is a one-person psychology and Model 2 is a one-and-a-half-person psychology, Model 3 is truly a two-person psychology.

And whereas the Model 1 therapist is seen as a neutral object (whose focus is on the patient's internal process) and the Model 2 therapist is seen as an empathic selfobject or good object–good mother (whose focus is on the patient's moment-by-moment affective experience), the Model 3 therapist is seen as an authentic subject (whose focus is on the intimate edge between them).

In Model 1, although the short-term goal is enhancement of knowledge, the ultimate goal is resolution of structural conflict. In Model 2, although the immediate goal is provision of (corrective) experience, the long-range goal is filling in structural deficit. In Model 3, although the short-term goal is engagement in relationship (and a deepening of connection between patient and therapist), the ultimate goal is development of capacity for healthy, authentic relatedness.

And, finally, whereas Model 2 is about offering the patient an opportunity to find a new good object, so that there can be restitution, Model 3 is about offering the patient an opportunity to re-find the old bad object, so that the traumatogenic early-on interactions can be worked through in the context of the patient's here-and-now engagement with the therapist.

Along these same lines, Jay Greenberg (1986b) has suggested that if the therapist does not participate as a new good object, the therapy never gets under way; and if she does not participate as the old bad one, the therapy never ends—which captures exquisitely the delicate balance between the therapist's participation as a new good object (so that there can be a new beginning) and the therapist's participation as the old bad object (so that there can be an opportunity to achieve belated mastery of the internalized traumas).

Indeed, psychoanalysis has come a long way since the early days when Freud was emphasizing the importance of sex and aggression. No longer is the spotlight on the patient's drives (and their vicissitudes); now the spotlight is on the patient's relationships (and *their* vicissitudes).

And where once psychoanalysis focused on the relationship that exists between structures within the psyche of the patient, contemporary psychoanalysis focuses more on the relationship that exists between the patient and her objects—or, more accurately, the intersubjective relationship that exists between the patient and her subjects. In Jessica Benjamin's (1992) words: "where objects were, subjects must be" (p. 44).

In the chapters that follow, I will elaborate on the three models of therapeutic action—the interpretive model, the corrective-provision model, and the relational model. In Part I, entitled "The Therapist's Choices," I will develop the three models in much greater depth, making special note of those features distinguishing each model. In Part II, entitled "Clinical Applications," I will demonstrate (by way of numerous examples and clinical vignettes) translation of the theory into the clinical situation; and I will revisit some of the thornier (and more intriguing) conceptual issues raised in Part I.

A particular issue with which I have been struggling involves the following discrepancy: Although much attention has been paid in the literature to the patient's need to be failed and her active efforts to recreate—with her therapist—the old bad object situation (by way of projective identification), scant attention has been paid in the literature to the patient's equally powerful need to find what never was and her active efforts to create opportunities for such restitution.

As Steven Stern (1994) has astutely observed, "there has been no systematic effort to define a . . . counterpart to projective identification, that is, the patient's unconscious efforts to evoke in the therapist specific responses that are different from those of the traumatizing figures of the past" (p. 320).

In Part II, I will be addressing this and other compelling theoretical (as well as clinical) conundrums.

Throughout the book, my intent will be to demonstrate the clinical usefulness for the therapist of thinking in terms of enhancement of knowledge, provision of experience, and engagement in relationship as the three primary agents for therapeutic growth and change. I will hope to show that if the therapist is to be optimally effective, then she must be able to work comfortably within all three models of therapeutic action—sometimes using first one approach, then another, sometimes using two or three approaches simultaneously.

In any event, at each point in time, the therapist must tolerate the necessary uncertainty that comes with the holding open of different possibilities for the therapeutic action, while avoiding the temptation to jump to premature closure in order to ease the anxiety and the strain—all in the interest of being able to enhance the therapeutic potential of each moment.

Author's note: In what follows, for the sake of simplicity, I will be using the pronoun "she" instead of the more cumbersome "he/she." In addition, although I will usually refer to the parent as the "mother," I intend this to encompass the broader category of mothering person, caregiver, father, and so on.

PART I

The Therapist's Choices

CHAPTER

1

The Therapeutic Action

What is it that enables patients to get better? How do we conceptualize the process by which patients grow and change?

I have found it clinically useful to think in terms of three different models of therapeutic action. I will later be defining terms and elaborating more extensively on the ideas I am here introducing.

Model 1 speaks to the importance of knowledge or insight; as we will see, it is a one-person psychology, because its focus is on the patient and the internal workings of her mind.

Model 2 speaks to the importance of experience, a corrective experience; it has been described by some as a one-and-a-half-person psychology because its focus is on the patient and her relationship with a therapist whom she experiences as either an empathic selfobject (when our frame of reference is self psychology) or a good object–good mother (when our frame of reference is object relations theory). In any event, in Model 2 the therapist is considered to be a half person—because it is not who she is that matters but rather what she provides.

Model 3 speaks to the importance of relationship, the real relationship; it is a two-person psychology because its focus is on patients and therapists who relate to each other as "real" people. In Model 3 the therapist is considered to be a whole person.

Let us begin by thinking about how the therapist positions herself moment by moment in relation to the patient. My intent is to provide the therapist with a way to conceptualize the options available to her as she sits with her patient—with respect both to how she arrives at understanding and to what she then says or does.

With respect to how the therapist arrives at understanding of the patient, my contention is that the most effective listening stance is one in which the therapist achieves an optimal balance between positioning herself as object, as selfobject, and as subject.

1. As a neutral object, the therapist positions herself outside the therapeutic field in order to observe the patient. Her focus is on the patient's internal dynamics.
2. As an empathic selfobject, the therapist joins alongside the patient in order to immerse herself in the patient's subjective reality. Her focus is on the patient's affective experience.
3. As an authentic subject, the therapist remains very much centered within her own experience, using that experience (in other words, the countertransference) to deepen her understanding of the patient. Her focus is on the here-and-now engagement between them.

To this point, the therapist is simply gathering information; she has not yet done anything with what she has come to know.

With respect to how the therapist then intervenes, my belief is that the most effective interventive stance is one in which the therapist achieves an optimal balance between formulating interpretations, offering some form of corrective provision, and engaging interactively in relationship.

1. The therapist formulates interpretations with an eye to advancing the patient's knowledge of her internal dynamics. The ultimate goal is resolution of the patient's structural conflicts.
2. The therapist offers some form of corrective provision with an eye either to validating the patient's experience or, more generally, to providing the patient with a corrective experience. The ultimate goal is filling in the patient's structural deficits and consolidating the patient's self.
3. The therapist engages the patient interactively in relationship with an eye to advancing the patient's knowledge of her relational dynamics and/or to deepening the connection between the two of them. The ultimate goal is resolution of the patient's relational difficulties and development of her capacity to engage healthily and authentically in relationship.

Of course, it will be impossible for the therapist, with every intervention, either to promote the patient's insight, to offer the patient some form of corrective provision, or to engage the patient interactively in relationship. It is possible, however, for most of the therapist's interventions to be designed with an eye toward the ultimate achievement of one or another of these therapeutic goals. For example, before the therapist can intervene in a way that will advance the therapeutic process, she may need to do some preliminary work (perhaps in the form of asking questions to obtain further details about a particular situation or to gather more specific historical data).

But whether the therapist is attempting to lay the foundation for future change or is striving to effect change in the moment, the therapist can optimize her effectiveness if she has the capacity to hold in her mind an intuitive sense of whether the therapeutic action in the moment involves *knowledge*, *experience*, or *relationship*.

With each patient, whatever her diagnosis, whatever her underlying psychodynamics, the optimal therapeutic stance is one that is continuously changing. In fact, moment by moment, the therapist's position shifts.

The stance the therapist assumes is sometimes spontaneous and unplanned, sometimes more deliberate and considered. In other words, there are times when the therapist finds herself unwittingly drawn into participating with the patient in a particular way because the intersubjective field has "pulled" for that form of participation. But there are other times when the therapist makes a more conscious choice, based on what she intuitively senses the patient most needs in the moment in order to heal.

How the therapist decides to intervene, therefore, depends on both what she has come to understand about the patient by virtue of the listening position she has assumed and what she believes the patient most needs—whether enhancement of knowledge, a corrective experience, or interactive engagement in relationship.

At any given point in time, the therapist is also profoundly affected by what has come before—in the moments leading up to the current moment. Past and present are always inextricably linked; no point in time stands on its own. And so it is that the way the therapist chooses to intervene in the moment depends not only on what she is hoping will transpire in the moments ahead but also on what has already transpired in the moments preceding.

I believe that the three modes of therapeutic action (knowledge, experience, and relationship) are not mutually exclusive but are mutually enhancing. The model I am offering here is a synthetic one that integrates three perspectives:

1. The interpretive perspective of classical psychoanalytic theory;
2. The corrective-provision (or deficiency-compensation) perspective of self psychology and those object relations theories emphasizing the "absence of good"; and
3. The relational (or interactive) perspective of contemporary psychoanalytic theory and those object relations theories emphasizing the "presence of bad."

As I will later demonstrate, some object relations theorists—like Michael Balint (1968)—speak to the price the child pays (in the form of internal absence of good) because of what the parent does not do, and others—like W. R. D. Fairbairn (1954)—speak to the price the child pays (in the form of internal presence of bad) because of what the parent does do. As a result, some object relations theorists conceive of the therapeutic action as involving the therapist's corrective provision and others conceive of the therapeutic action as involving negotiation at the "intimate edge" (Ehrenberg 1974) between patient and therapist—which enables a reworking, in the context of the here-and-now engagement between patient and therapist, of the patient's internalized traumas.

The impetus for my effort to integrate the three models stems from my belief that none of the three is sufficient, on its own, to explain our clinical data or to guide our interventions. Although there is of course some overlap, each model contains elements lacking in the other two.

Obviously, no model can begin to do justice to something this complex and multifaceted, but my hope is that the integrative model I am proposing will prompt therapists to become more aware of the choices they are continuously making about how they listen to the patient and how they then intervene.

CHAPTER

2

Insight versus Experience

Numerous papers have been written about the so-called therapeutic action of psychoanalytic psychotherapy, and many authors have attempted to conceptualize what they consider to be the primary therapeutic agent.

From the earliest days of psychoanalysis, the relative merits of insight by way of interpretation, on the one hand, and a corrective experience by way of the real relationship, on the other, have been heatedly debated. In fact, the Freud–Ferenczi controversy (Hoffer 1991) boils down to Freud's advocacy of insight and Ferenczi's (1930) advocacy of a corrective experience as the primary therapeutic agent.

Interestingly, most authors in the psychoanalytic literature come down on the side of either insight or experience/relationship—that is, they emphasize either what takes place within the patient or what takes place between patient and therapist; but very few theorists have presented the advantages of both perspectives and fewer still have attempted an integration of the two.

Classical psychoanalytic theorists who conceive of the patient's psychopathology as deriving from the patient (in whom there is thought to be an imbalance of forces) understandably designate the locus of the therapeutic action as residing within the patient. In contradistinction to this perspective are self psychologists, object relations theorists, and contemporary psychoanalytic theorists who conceive of the patient's psychopathology as deriving from the parent (and the parent's failure of the child), and who therefore designate the locus of the therapeutic action as residing within the relationship between patient and therapist.

In other words, as the etiology of psychopathology has shifted from nature to nurture, so, too, the locus of the therapeutic action has shifted from insight to experience/relationship.

I would now like to elaborate upon these two therapeutic agents—insight and experience/relationship. For many decades, these were the two most widely accepted modes of treatment. As we will see, only in the past decade or so have theorists come to appreciate that there are important clinical distinctions between experience and relationship as therapeutic agents. As these distinctions have come to be recognized, some theorists have begun to posit the existence of not just two, but three modes of therapeutic action—insight (or knowledge), experience, and relationship.

But I would like first to highlight the distinction between a drive-conflict model of therapeutic action that conceives of insight as the treatment of choice for the patient's structural conflicts and a deficiency-compensation model of therapeutic action that conceives of experience/relationship as the treatment of choice for the patient's structural deficits.

STRUCTURAL CONFLICT AND INSIGHT

For patients with structural conflict, insight by way of interpretation is thought to be curative. Patients are said to have structural (or neurotic) conflict when there is internal tension between id impulse pressing for yes and ego defense countering with no (with the superego coming down usually on the side of the ego).

For such patients, the therapeutic action is thought to involve enhancement of knowledge. Whether expressed as (1) the rendering conscious of what had once been unconscious (in topographic terms), (2) where id was, there shall ego be (in structural terms), or (3) uncovering and reconstructing the past (in genetic terms), insight is believed to be the primary therapeutic agent.

Interpretations, particularly of the transference, are considered the means by which such insight is acquired.

Paula Heimann (1956) once suggested that the therapist must repeatedly ask herself the following question: "Why is the patient now doing what to whom?" (p. 307). The answer to this question constitutes the transference interpretation. And as the patient comes to understand, deeply, why she is now doing what to whom, she gains insight into the internal workings of her mind.

How is it that interpretations lead to resolution of structural conflict?

As the ego gains insight by way of interpretations, it becomes stronger. This increased ego strength enables the ego to experience less anxiety in relation to the id; the ego's defenses therefore become less necessary. As the patient begins to relinquish her defenses, she becomes less conflicted—and we speak then of the patient's structural conflict as having been resolved.

A drive-conflict model of therapeutic action therefore posits insight by way of interpretation as the primary therapeutic agent. Classical psychoanalysis is a prime example of such a model.

The interpretive therapist sees herself not as a participant in a relationship but as an objective observer of the patient. Her unit of study is the patient and the patient's internal dynamics. The therapist conceives of her position as outside the therapeutic field and of herself as a blank screen onto which the patient casts shadows that the therapist then interprets.

How the patient experiences the therapist—that is, the transference—is thought to be primarily a story about the patient (not the therapist), primarily a story about the patient's there-and-then (not the here-and-now of the therapeutic situation).

If the therapist remarks to her colleagues that she has a patient who is in the throes of an intensely negative transference, she usually intends this to be a statement about the patient's "distorted" perception of her, not about how she (the therapist) has indeed failed the patient.

To the patient she might interpret this negative transference by directing the patient's attention inward and backward—encouraging her to observe her tendency to experience new objects as old ones. For example, the therapist might offer the patient the following formulation: "Your assumption is that I will disappoint you in much the same way that your mother used to disappoint you."

Whereas a relational therapist (as we will later see) conceives of the patient's experience of the therapist as co-constructed, as co-determined by patient and therapist, as ultimately a story about the contributions of both, an interpretive therapist conceives of the patient's experience of the therapist as determined primarily by the patient, as ultimately a story about the patient and her unresolved past.

And so it is that in a drive-conflict model of therapeutic action, what is thought to be curative for the patient is the ferreting out of the truth. Jacques Lacan (1977) captures the essence of this first model with his wry suggestion that in classical psychoanalysis the patient is cured once the patient has come to know all that the therapist knows—which is what the patient had (unconsciously) known all along.

Freud, and those who followed in his footsteps, believed that "the truth" would set the patient free, that strengthening the patient's ego by way of making her more aware of the internal workings of her mind would enable her to become less constricted, less defensive, less neurotic.

STRUCTURAL DEFICIT AND CORRECTIVE EXPERIENCE

Let us now shift from the drive-conflict model of therapeutic action embraced by those who focus on insight as the primary therapeutic agent to the deficiency-compensation model of therapeutic action embraced by those who focus on experience/relationship. No longer is structural conflict in the limelight; now structural deficit assumes center stage.

Self psychology and those object relations theories that emphasize the internal recording of traumatic parental failure in the form of deficit (or absence of good) are prime instances of deficiency-compensation models.

First of all, what do we mean by deficit? Self psychology defines *structural deficit* as impaired capacity—or limited ability to regulate self-esteem internally. The patient with structural deficit is unable, on her own, to feel good about herself. The patient's deficit creates a need; the need is for an object (a selfobject) to provide external regulation of self-esteem. More generally, the need is for an object to complete the self.

In a deficiency-compensation model, the patient is therefore seen as suffering not from conflict but from deficit. The deficit is thought to arise in the context of failure in the early-on environmental provision—failure in the early-on relationship between infant and caregiver (or "mothering person"). Now the therapeutic aim is the provision of that which was not provided consistently and reliably by the mother early on. It is in the context of the relationship between patient and therapist that there is thought to be an opportunity for reparation—with this new relationship a corrective for the old one.

What is curative for the patient with structural deficit is the experience not of the truth (which is thought to be the curative agent in the drive-conflict model of therapeutic action) but of being provided for in the way that a good mother provides for her young child. When the frame of reference is self psychology (a theory about deficit), the therapist is described as an empathic selfobject who offers the patient validation of experience. When the frame of reference is an object relations theory that focuses on the price the child pays (in the form of deficit) because of the good the parent does not do, the therapist is described as a good object–good mother who—operating in loco parentis—offers the patient a corrective emotional experience.

But whether the frame of reference is self psychology or an object relations theory that emphasizes the absence of good (and, as we will later see, whether the focus is on the patient's experience of the therapist as a new good object or the therapist's actual participation as that new good object), making good a deficiency is at the heart of what heals. The healing requires an experience in the present with a new object that compensates for damage sustained early-on at the hands of the infantile object. This deficiency-compensation model conceives of the therapeutic action as involving the filling in of deficit and the consolidation of the self.

In such a model, it is thought that part of what enables the therapist to be deeply effective is that she comes (by way of the patient's regression) to assume the importance of the original parent. When the therapist has been vested with such power, then and only then is the therapy relationship able to serve as a corrective for damage sustained during the patient's formative years.

Interestingly, because parents in the here-and-now no longer have the same power they once had, the parent now has much less power to heal than the parent once had power to hurt. It is therefore not so much the contemporary parent who can make a difference in the patient's life as it is the therapist, who operates in the place of the original parent.

Edgar Levenson (1988) has captured well the essence of the stance the therapist assumes in a deficiency-compensation model with the following: "To the extent that we believe something real was done to the patient, we tend to believe that something real must be done to correct it" (p. 137).

INTERPRETATION VERSUS EMPATHIC RESPONSE

In a drive-conflict model, the emphasis is on the therapist's ability to offer the patient the truth, which she does by way of interpretations. In marked contrast to this is the deficiency-compensation model (particularly self psychology), where the emphasis is on the therapist's ability to validate the patient's truth, which she does by way of empathic responses.

Whereas an interpretive response focuses on what is outside the patient's consciousness (that is, what is experience-distant), an empathic response focuses on what is within the patient's consciousness (that is, what is experience-near).

In order to demonstrate the distinction between a theory that focuses on the therapist's experience of the truth and one that focuses on the patient's experience of the truth, I offer the following vignettes.

Clinical Vignette—The Customer Is Always Right

Let us imagine the situation in which a therapist has said to her patient: "I wonder if you are upset with me because I have increased your fee."

If the therapist's intent is to make the patient aware of upset that the therapist believes is there but with which the patient is out of touch, then the therapist's remark is an interpretive intervention.

If, however, the therapist's intent is to resonate empathically with the patient's experience of upset—upset with which the therapist believes the patient is in touch, then the therapist's remark is an empathic intervention.

In other words, it is the therapist's intent that makes it either an interpretation or an empathic response.

Whereas in the interpretive model the therapist is thought to be in the know, in the deficiency-compensation model the patient is thought to be the ultimate authority on "the truth."

In fact, it has been suggested that in the interpretive mode, "the customer is always wrong" (Abend 1989); by the same token, it could be said that in the empathic mode, the customer is always right.

Clinical Vignette—Who Has the Inside Track on the Truth?

Let us now consider the situation of a patient who comes to his session five minutes late and insists, with some vehemence, that his lateness had nothing to do with ambivalent feelings about being there—that he had very much wanted to come.

The therapist knows that the previous session had been very difficult for the patient and that despite the patient's protests to the contrary, the patient must on some level still have feelings about this.

The interpretive therapist is interested in ferreting out these negative feelings. To that end, she might formulate the following interpretation: "I wonder if your lateness has anything to do with the difficult session we had last time?" or "Given how difficult our session was last time, I wonder if you found yourself having mixed feelings about coming here today," or even, "Perhaps you have some residual feelings of anger from our last session."

In contrast to this is the empathic therapist, who believes it is important to take the patient at his word and therefore does not insist that the patient admit to having negative feelings from the previous session.

The empathic therapist recognizes that (in the moment) the locus of the patient's affect is in his distress, his concern that he will not be believed—thus his vehement insistence that it was important to him to be there on time.

And so the empathic therapist says, "It's important to you that I understand just how much you wanted to be here today—and on time." The therapist resonates with the patient's need (albeit a defensive one) to have the therapist believe that the patient's lateness was not an acting out of his upset from the previous session.

The empathic therapist recognizes that there will be time enough, perhaps later in this session, perhaps in a subsequent session, to explore with the patient the mix of feelings that he might well have had from the previous difficult session (a mix of feelings against which he is defending himself)—but only once the patient has signaled his readiness to explore these feelings.

As it happened, the patient was so relieved to have been taken seriously that he heaved a deep sigh of relief and, interestingly, then began to talk—with much heartfelt affect—about how devastated he was feeling as he anticipated his therapist's upcoming vacation (two months thence).

Although the interpretive therapist (who suggests that the patient might have some residual feelings of anger from their last session) would seem to be addressing an affect, in the moment it is not an affect with which the patient is in touch. The intervention is therefore more interpretive than empathic, because its intent is to render conscious something in the patient's unconscious, not to resonate empathically with the patient's "felt" experience.

More generally, if an intervention addresses something of which the patient is unaware, if it addresses something the patient is wanting not to have to feel or to know, then it is an interpretation. But if an intervention addresses the patient's affective experience (affect of which the patient is aware—or at least partially aware), then it is an empathic response.

In the first instance, the therapist is thought to be in the know; in the second instance, it is the patient who is thought to be in the know.

Clinical Vignette—On Being Taken Seriously

The end of the session has arrived. The patient, disappointed and frustrated, says: "I don't feel that I used my time in here very well today." The therapist, gently: "I think you did. This is difficult, painful material, and it takes a lot of courage to be doing what you are doing." Who is right? The therapist or the patient? Was it a good session or not?

The empathic therapist would say that the patient has the inside track on the truth and that if the patient says she feels she didn't use her session very well, then that's what matters and it is for the therapist to join her there, resonating empathically with the patient's experience of disappointment and upset.

The interpretive therapist, however, would say that the therapist has the inside track on the truth and that if the therapist believes it was a good session (which the patient is needing, for whatever reason, not to know), then that's what matters, and it is for the therapist to start there.

In the example above, it would seem that the therapist is more interested in his own perception of the session than he is in his patient's perception of it. He believes that it took courage for the patient to do what she did in the session and that if the patient is needing to deny this truth, then she must be protecting herself in some way.

Although the therapist may be attempting to provide the patient with positive reinforcement, her intervention is clearly at odds with the patient's experience and the potential danger is that the patient may well end up feeling not heard.

As it happened, in this particular example, the patient had come to me for a consultation around her therapy because she felt that her therapist, although well-meaning and kind, did not always take what she was saying seriously.

HOMEOSTATIC VERSUS DISRUPTIVE ATTUNEMENT

As we have seen, empathic therapists (who embrace a deficiency-compensation model) focus the patient's attention on what is inside her awareness in an effort to validate the patient's experience; interpretive therapists (who embrace a drive-conflict model) focus the patient's attention on what is outside her awareness in an effort to advance the patient's knowledge of her internal process.

Along these same lines, I would like to suggest that we think in terms of the therapist's interventions as either speaking to where the patient is (which is what an empathic response does) or directing the patient's attention elsewhere (which is what an interpretive response does).

The empathic therapist speaks to where the patient is in an effort to validate the patient's experience; in so doing (if the therapist is accurate in her empathy), she offers the patient the opportunity to feel understood. The interpretive therapist directs the patient's attention elsewhere in an effort to enhance the patient's knowledge; in so doing (if the therapist is accurate in her interpretation), she offers the patient the opportunity to understand.

Relevant here, I think, is the distinction James Herzog (1984) has made between homeostatic attunement and disruptive attunement. The therapist is homeostatically attuned when she joins the patient where the patient is (which is what the empathic therapist does) and disruptively attuned when she asks that the patient join the therapist where the therapist is (which is what the interpretive therapist does). In both situations, patient and therapist connect—although, in the first instance, the therapist joins the patient and, in the second instance, the patient joins the therapist.

To demonstrate the distinction, Salman Akhtar (1994) has offered the following: Imagine the situation of a young child playing by himself with his toys on the floor of the living room. Mother comes in, sits down on the floor beside her son, and joins him in his play; the little boy gurgles with pleasure and delight. Homeostatic attunement. Now let us imagine that it is not mother who enters the room but father. Father, let us say, does not sit down on the floor beside his son but instead goes over to sit on the couch, beckons to his son to join him there, and then playfully swoops his son up in his arms and swings him back and forth in the air; the little boy gurgles with pleasure and delight. Disruptive attunement. Although demonstrated in different ways, both mother and father are attuned to their child and the child's gurgles of pleasure and delight attest to how much he appreciates that attunement.

The therapist must decide from moment to moment whether to be with the patient where she is or to direct the patient's attention elsewhere—in other words, whether the patient is primarily interested in being understood or primarily interested in gaining understanding.

There are times when the therapist senses that the patient is open to the possibility of acquiring insight. There are other times, however, when the therapist senses that what the patient wants is, simply, empathic recognition of who she is and what she is feeling. It is for the therapist, moment by moment, to use her intuition to assess whether the patient wants insight or recognition, whether she wants to understand or to be understood. The therapist must be ever attuned to—and respectful of—the tension, the delicate balance within the patient between her need to be as she is and her capacity to consider therapeutic change.

I believe that there is a corresponding tension within the therapist between her awareness of who the patient is in the present and her sense of who the patient could become at some point in the future, were she to be open to change.

In any event, when the therapist is with the patient where the patient is, she eases the patient's anxiety. When the therapist directs the patient's attention elsewhere, she raises the patient's anxiety—at least in the moment. I propose, therefore, that the therapist can titrate the level of the patient's anxiety by doing either one or the other—or first one and then the other.

In sum, if the therapist's intervention addresses affect of which the patient is aware, then the therapist is said to be responding empathically. Empathic responses are directed to what is experience-near (what is inside the patient's awareness); the intent of an empathic response is to validate the patient's experience. The patient usually responds to an empathic intervention with a decrease in her anxiety.

But if the therapist's intervention addresses affect of which the patient is unaware (affect against which the patient is defending herself), then the therapist is said to be responding interpretively. Interpretations are directed to what is experience-distant (what is outside the patient's awareness); the intent of an interpretation is to enhance the patient's knowledge of her internal process. The patient usually responds to an interpretive intervention with an increase (at least momentarily) in her anxiety.

It has been suggested that the artist of modern sensibility should spend her time trying to see what is visible and, more importantly, trying not to see what is invisible. Perhaps the same could be said of the empathic therapist, who deals with the overt (not the covert). When the therapist dons her empathic hat, she takes the patient at her word. The empathic therapist must not attempt to gain access to what she senses may be lurking beneath the surface; she must avoid trying to discover hidden meanings and what is "really going on"—that is, what the patient is really feeling or really thinking, what is invisible, what is being defended against.

When the therapist dons her interpretive hat, on the other hand, her intent is to see beneath the surface. The classically trained therapist is interested in the reality underneath the appearance of things; the surface is thought to conceal a deeper core of truth. It is this reality that the interpretive therapist assiduously attempts to unearth.

Only somewhat with tongue-in-cheek has it been suggested that in classical psychoanalysis, things are never what they would seem to be. If the patient arrives late to a session, it must be because she is ambivalent about being there. If the patient arrives early, it must be because she is anxious about being there. And if she arrives on time, it must be because she is compulsive.

ENHANCED KNOWLEDGE VERSUS CORRECTIVE PROVISION

Whereas the drive-conflict model considers the child an agent (with unbridled sexual and aggressive drives), deficiency-compensation models see her as a passive victim of parental failure. The villain of the piece is no longer the child but the parent; psychopathology is no longer thought to derive from the child's nature but from the nurture the child received.

In a deficiency-compensation model, the goal of treatment is not to tame the id, strengthen the ego, and mitigate the severity of the superego so that structural conflict can be resolved. Rather, the goal is filling in structural deficit by way of some form of corrective provision. Concepts like corrective emotional experience (Alexander 1946), corrective symbiotic experience (Mahler 1967), new beginning (Balint 1968), benign regression (Balint 1968), therapeutic dependence (Guntrip 1973), facilitating environment (Winnicott 1965), holding environment (Winnicott 1965), symbolic gratification (Modell 1984), empathic ambience (Kohut 1971), and selfobject matrix (Kohut 1971) speak to what is involved in a model of therapeutic action that posits, as the primary therapeutic agent, some kind of corrective experience at the hands of the therapist.

No longer a drive object, the therapist is now considered a selfobject (used to complete the self by performing those functions the patient is unable to perform on her own) or a good object–good mother (offering the kind of holding provision the patient was denied as a child).

These deficiency-compensation models of therapeutic action, embraced by self psychologists and by those object relations theorists who focus on the internal recording of traumatic parental failure in the form of deficit, conceptualize the patient–therapist relationship as involving the provision now of that which was not provided early on. It is then, in the context of the patient's relationship with a new good object, that the patient is given an opportunity to begin anew, to "start over" (Winnicott 1955).

To review, for classical psychoanalytic theorists, structural conflict is seen as the villain of the piece and the goal of treatment is thought to be a strengthening of the ego by way of enhanced knowledge. This drive-conflict model of therapeutic action posits insight by way of interpretation as the primary therapeutic agent.

For self psychologists and those object relations theorists who emphasize the absence of good, structural deficit is seen as the villain, and the goal of treatment is thought to be the making good of deficiency by way of some form of corrective provision. This deficiency-compensation model of therapeutic action posits a corrective experience by way of the real relationship as the primary therapeutic agent.

CHAPTER

3

Three Modes of Therapeutic Action

Let us now look more specifically at what it is that ultimately heals the patient with structural deficit. When it is said that the therapeutic action involves a corrective experience by way of the real relationship, the implication is that experience and relationship are flip sides of the same coin. I would like to suggest, however, that a corrective experience is one thing but that the real relationship is something quite different.

When we say that the therapist provides the patient with a corrective experience, we are suggesting that the therapist offers the patient something that the patient should have received reliably and consistently as a child, but never did.

Although relationship is involved, it is more an I–It than an I–Thou relationship—more a one-way relationship between someone who gives and someone who takes than a two-way relationship involving give-and-take, mutuality, and reciprocity.

It is for this reason that self psychology (a prime example of a deficiency-compensation model) has been described by Morrison (1994) as a one-and-a-half-person psychology—it is certainly not a one-person psychology, but then it is not truly a two-person psychology either.

Balint (1968)—also an advocate of the corrective-provision approach—speaks directly to the I–It aspect of the patient–therapist relationship with the following:

> It is definitely a two-person relationship in which, however, only one of the partners matters; his wishes and needs are the only ones that count

> and must be attended to; the other partner, though felt to be immensely powerful, matters only in so far as he is willing to gratify the first partner's needs and desires or decides to frustrate them; beyond this his personal interests, needs, desires, wishes, etc., simply do not exist. [p. 23]

In other words, the emphasis in a deficiency-compensation model is not so much on the relationship per se as it is on the filling in of the patient's deficits by way of the therapist's corrective provision.

But this relationship between a person who provides and a person who is the recipient of such provision is a far cry from the relationship that exists between two "real" people—an intersubjective relationship that involves two subjects, both of whom contribute to what transpires at the intimate edge between them.

And so it is that theorists, in the past ten years or so, are beginning to make a distinction between the therapist's provision of a corrective experience for the patient and the therapist's participation in a real relationship with the patient. They are differentiating between the therapist's participation as a generic good object and the therapist's participation as an authentic (and, therefore, more individualized) subject.

INTERACTIVE ENGAGEMENT

Let us return to the issue of what constitutes the therapeutic action. An increasing number of contemporary psychoanalysts believe that what heals the patient is neither insight nor a corrective experience.

Rather, what heals is interactive engagement with an authentic other; what heals is the therapeutic relationship itself—a relationship that involves not subject and drive object, not subject and selfobject, not subject and good object, not subject and good mother, but, rather, subject and subject, both of whom bring their authentic selves to the therapeutic interaction—both of whom influence and are influenced by the other.

Theorists who embrace this relational (or interactive) perspective conceive of patient and therapist as constituting a co-evolving, reciprocally mutual, interactive dyad—like a ping-pong game being played with two balls simultaneously (each participant both proactive and reactive, both initiating and responding).

It is now the negotiation of the relationship and its vicissitudes that constitutes the locus of the therapeutic action. It is what transpires in the here-and-now engagement between patient and therapist that is thought to be most profoundly transformative. Although the short-term goal is to advance the patient's understanding of what she is playing out in the therapy relationship and (as part of that process) to deepen the level of engagement between patient and therapist, the longer-term goal is, more generally, to develop the patient's capacity for relatedness.

Whereas the interpretive therapist strives to enhance the patient's understanding of her internal dynamics, the relational therapist strives to enhance the patient's understanding of her relational dynamics—that is, those aspects of her internal dynamics that she delivers into her relationships, particularly the relationship with her therapist.

For example, if the patient reports a dream, the relational therapist would want to explore not only its content and what that might reveal about the patient's internal dynamics but also what might be transpiring in the relationship between patient and therapist. Perhaps the patient, eager to please her therapist and knowing that her therapist loves to interpret dreams, is presenting the dream to her therapist as a gift; perhaps the patient, in an attempt to avoid talking about something more emotionally charged that would make her feel too vulnerable in relation to her therapist, uses the dream to keep distance between them; or perhaps the patient, concerned about the intensity of her underlying rage, reports a terrifying dream to her therapist in order to see how comfortable the therapist is with the patient's aggression.

In each such situation, the patient is delivering some aspect of herself into the here-and-now engagement with her therapist; in each such situation, the patient's reporting of her dream is seen as an attempt to engage (or to disengage) the therapist in some particular way.

In fact, the relational (or interactive) therapist pays particular attention to all that the patient delivers of herself into the therapy relationship—in other words, the patient's "activity" with respect to the therapist. This activity is seen as an *enactment*, the unconscious intent of which is to engage the therapist—either by way of eliciting some kind of response from the therapist or by way of communicating something important to the therapist about the patient's internal world. In fact, the patient may know of no other way to get some piece of her subjective experience understood than by enacting it in the relationship with her therapist.

What the patient enacts in the therapy relationship is thought to derive from the patient's relational dynamics; in turn, the patient's relational dynamics are thought to derive from her internal dynamics.

With respect to the therapist's enactments, when the therapist allows herself to be drawn into participating countertransferentially in the patient's transferential enactments, then we speak of the therapist's activity as an enactment—the unconscious intent of which may be to provoke a particular response from the patient or to convey something to the patient about the therapist's response to the patient's activity.

At the point when the therapist becomes a participant in the patient's enactment, we speak of a *mutual enactment*.

Included in the group of theorists who conceive of the relationship itself—and the negotiation of its vicissitudes—as the locus of the therapeutic action are relational theorists (Miller et al. 1991, Mitchell 1988), intersubjectivists (Stolorow et al. 1987), social constructivists (Hoffman 1992), relational perspectivists (Aron 1996), interpersonalists (Ehrenberg 1984, Levenson 1991), interactive theorists (Bollas 1987, Casement 1985, Sandler 1987), and developmentalists (Beebe and Lachmann 1988, Stern 1985).

No longer is the emphasis on the therapist as object—whether object of the patient's sexual and aggressive drives, object of the patient's narcissistic demands, or object of the patient's relational needs. In this contemporary relational model, the focus is on the therapist as subject—an authentic subject who "uses" the self (that is, uses her countertransference) to find, and to be found by the patient.

And so it is that whereas it was once thought that the therapeutic action involved either insight or experience/relationship, in recent years it has come to be understood that experience and relationship cannot be telescoped.

I am positing, therefore, the existence of not just two modes of therapeutic action—namely, insight and experience/relationship—but three modes: insight, experience, and relationship.

I am further suggesting that it will be the focus of the therapist's attention in the moment that will determine whether the therapist thinks in terms of insight, experience, or relationship as the primary modes of action.

Moment by moment, this focus will shift.

Sometimes the therapist positions herself outside the therapeutic field: she dispassionately observes the patient; teases out recurring themes, patterns, and repetitions; formulates hypotheses about the patient, her internal dynamics, and the impact of her past on the present; and, in order to advance the patient's knowledge of herself, offers the patient interpretations. I will be referring to this drive-conflict model of therapeutic action as Model 1—an interpretive model.

At other times the therapist positions herself alongside the patient: she decenters from her own experience; immerses herself empathically in the patient's experience; resonates with what is experience-near for the patient; and, in order to give the patient a corrective experience, meets the patient where she is—be it in the form of either empathic recognition of the patient's need or its actual gratification. I will be referring to this deficiency-compensation model of therapeutic action as Model 2—a corrective-provision model.

At still other times the therapist remains very much centered within her own experience: she focuses on the here-and-now engagement or intimate edge between the patient and herself; is ever attuned to what each brings of herself to the therapeutic encounter and its impact on the other; and, in order to deepen the connection between them, uses her authentic self to participate with the patient in an intersubjective relationship that involves mutuality and reciprocity. I will be referring to this model of therapeutic action as Model 3—a relational (or interactive) model.

And so it is that whereas Model 1 is a one-person psychology and Model 2 is a one-and-a-half-person psychology, Model 3 is truly a two-person psychology.

INTERDEPENDENCE OF THE THREE MODES

Before I go any further, I would like to clarify that although Model 1 emphasizes interpretation, obviously the interpretation is offered in the context of a relationship in which the therapist is experienced as generally empathic. As Fred Pine (1990) has suggested, interpretations work only in the context of a deeply personal relationship that matters to both participants.

In Model 1, then, a good relationship is thought to be necessary—but, on its own, is not considered to heal the patient; the relationship simply provides a backdrop for the more important interpretive work that is the cornerstone of the classical model.

I would also like to clarify that although Model 2 emphasizes empathy and corrective provision, obviously such responses are offered in the context of a relationship and may well have interpretive (and/or clarifying) elements. The focus, however, is always on the patient's affective experience in the moment, and not so much on making conscious the patient's unconscious (Model 1) or clarifying the ongoing here-and-now engagement between patient and therapist (Model 3).

Finally, although Model 3 emphasizes engagement and relationship, patient and therapist cannot effectively negotiate at the intimate edge between them unless they have some kind of empathic connection. Furthermore, the therapist's use of self (that is, the use of her countertransference) to engage the patient may well involve interpretive interventions. But whereas the therapist's interpretations in Model 1 direct the patient's attention to her internal dynamics, the therapist's interpretations in Model 3 direct the patient's attention to her relational dynamics—that is, those aspects of her internal dynamics that she actually plays out (or enacts) in her relationships.

In sum, the three models of therapeutic action—interpretation, provision, and interaction—are intended to provide the therapist with a way to conceptualize the options available to her. They are not intended to be a formula for what the therapist should do, but rather a highlighting of the choices the therapist is always making with respect to how she listens and to how she then intervenes. In other words, they are not a prescription for what the therapist should do, but rather a description of what the therapist already does do (Greenberg 1981).

The position the therapist assumes affects both what she comes to know about the patient and the way she then intervenes. In order to demonstrate that impact, I offer the following hypothetical clinical situation.

Clinical Vignette—Do You Love Me?

Let us imagine a situation in which the patient, with some urgency, tells her therapist, "I need to know that you love me!" Let us also imagine that a little earlier in the session the patient had expressed some dissatisfaction with the therapy and, by extension, with the therapist. Also relevant is the fact that this is not the first time the patient has demanded to know that her therapist loves her.

Let us first look at what the therapist might come to know based on the position she assumes in relation to the patient.

Model 1. As a neutral object watching the patient, the therapist focuses her attention on the patient's internal process. The therapist makes a note to herself that the patient might have become anxious after the patient talked about her dissatisfaction with the therapy.

Model 2. As an empathic selfobject joining alongside the patient, the therapist focuses her attention on the patient's affective experience in the moment. The therapist is able to feel the patient's anxiety and the urgency with which she is asking for reassurance that things are still all right between them.

Model 3. As an authentic subject using her countertransferential response to the patient, the therapist focuses her attention on her own experience of what it is like to be seated opposite someone who repeatedly demands reassurance that she is loved. The therapist becomes aware of feeling impatient, annoyed. The patient knows (from her experience, over the course of some months, of being in therapy with her therapist) that the therapist is not someone who tends to offer reassurance; but, even so, the patient periodically presses for reassurance. In fact, well known to both patient and therapist is the patient's history of having alienated many of the people in her life through her demanding insistence that she be reassured again and again that she's okay.

Let us now look at what the therapist might choose to do with what she has come to know about the patient.

Model 1. Intent upon calling to the patient's attention the relationship between having articulated her dissatisfaction with the therapy and her consequent anxiety about having so expressed herself, the therapist might formulate the following interpretation: "You appear to have become anxious shortly after you spoke about your dissatisfaction with the therapy."

Perhaps the therapist goes on to say: "I wonder what it is that makes it difficult for you to feel comfortable expressing your dissatisfaction."

Model 2. Intent upon letting the patient know that the therapist understands how anxious the patient feels and hoping thereby to encourage the patient to elaborate further on what she is actually feeling in the moment, the therapist might decide to validate the patient's experience as follows: "You are feeling anxious and, at such times, find yourself wanting reassurance that things are still all right between us."

Note that a Model 2 intervention does not necessarily involve actual gratification of the patient's request for reassurance; there are times when the therapist deems it sufficient to provide, simply, empathic recognition of the patient's need. The therapist's hope is that the patient, now feeling understood, will feel safe enough to delve more deeply into her actual experience of anxiety.

Note also that this particular intervention, although directly addressing the patient's experience of anxiety, speaks indirectly to the relationship between her anxiety and her need for reassurance. Had the therapist's intent been both to resonate empathically with the patient's wish to be reassured and to direct the patient's attention to the possible relationship between her expression of angry disappointment with the therapy and her anxiety-driven need for reassurance, then we would say of the therapist's statement that it was both a Model 2 and a Model 1 intervention.

The following intervention addresses directly both the patient's experience of anxiety and the relationship between that anxiety and her need for reassurance: "When you let yourself express something negative about either the therapy or me, you appear to become anxious that something bad might happen. At such times, it's important to you to be reassured that things are still all right between us."

Model 3. The therapist, recognizing that her own experience (in relation to the patient) of feeling pressured to deliver may be similar to the patient's experience (in relation to her mother) of feeling such pressure, offers the patient the following: "When you press me to reassure you that things are still all right between us, you may be trying to convey to me something of what it was like for you to be feeling so often pressured by your mother to reassure her that you still loved her," or, alternatively, "I think I am coming to understand a little better what it must have been like for you, all those years, to be so often in the position of feeling that your mother needed you to bolster her self-esteem."

The therapist is here suggesting that a projective identification might have taken place, in which the patient is enacting with the therapist what the patient's mother was wont to enact with her. The therapist is able to understand something of what it must have been like for the patient growing up with such a mother by virtue of the therapist's ability to recognize her own negative reaction to the patient's demanding insistence that she be repeatedly reassured.

Please also note that unlike the Model 2 therapist, the Model 3 therapist does not always strive to be empathic. Her interest is primarily in calling the patient's attention to what she is enacting in the relationship with the therapist (and perhaps in most of her relationships)—something the therapist suspects speaks to unresolved feelings the patient has about having been at the receiving end of her anxiously insecure mother's plaintive cries for reassurance.

The net result of this intervention, as with many Model 3 interventions, may be that the patient comes to understand more about what she plays out in her relationships and what is still unresolved in her relationship with her mother—in other words, the intervention may have far-reaching ramifications. By understanding what she is enacting in the relationship with her therapist (and how that speaks to unresolved issues she still has in relation to her mother's anxious insecurity and demandingness), the patient's relationship with her therapist (as with others in her world) may improve.

CHAPTER

4

Corrective Provision

The emphasis in a deficiency-compensation model is not so much on intellectual understanding (the goal in a drive-conflict model) as on emotional experiencing.

As we have seen, both self psychology and those object relations theories emphasizing the internal absence of good (that is, Model 2 object relations theories) speak to the importance of the therapist's offering the patient some form of corrective provision to compensate for damage sustained early-on.

Self psychology speaks to the importance of (1) the patient's experience of the therapist as a new good object, (2) the therapist's empathic recognition of the patient's need, and (3) the therapist's validation of the patient's affective experience. Model 2 object relations theories speak to the importance of (1) the therapist's actual participation as a new good object, (2) the therapist's actual gratification of need, and, more generally, (3) the therapist's provision of a corrective (emotional) experience for the patient.

But whether the emphasis is on the patient's experience of the therapist as a new good object or the therapist's actual participation as that new good object, the focus in Model 2 is on the healing power of the therapist's corrective provision. Meeting the patient involves sometimes empathic recognition (in self psychology), sometimes an actual response (in Model 2 object relations theories).

What form does this responsiveness take?

Winnicott (1960) writes about the importance of the good-enough mother's meeting of her child, that is, she recognizes and responds to the child's developmental needs. Winnicott suggests that this may involve either gratification or frustration—as happens, for example, when the child is having a tantrum and the good-enough mother recognizes that what her infant most needs from her in the moment is the provision of loving restraint. The mother understands that the most therapeutic response is a restraining one, although her child may experience such restraint as maddeningly frustrating.

So, too, there are times when it is thought that what the patient most needs is containment—that is, external containment in the form of limits—because the patient lacks the capacity to be internally self-containing. Again, such containment may be experienced by the patient as more frustrating than gratifying, but it is necessary, and ultimately it demonstrates the therapist's recognition of the patient's underlying need for containment.

In other words, although the patient may not experience the therapist's response (of loving restraint or containment, say) as particularly gratifying, the therapist's response is nonetheless thought to constitute a therapeutic response because it offers the patient the corrective experience of being held.

And so it is that whereas self psychology speaks to the importance of empathic recognition of the patient's need, Model 2 object relations theories conceive of the therapeutic action as involving both recognition of, and responsiveness to, that need—whether such responsiveness takes the form of gratification or frustration.

By the same token, whereas self psychologists conceive of the therapist as an empathic selfobject (performing those selfobject functions assigned to it), Model 2 object relations theorists conceive of the therapist as a good object, a good mother, a holding environment, a facilitating environment. And whereas self psychology speaks to how important it is that the patient be able to experience the therapist as the good mother she never had (an experience that is thought to involve some illusion), Model 2 object relations theories speak to how important it is that the therapist actually participate as that good mother.

But whether the emphasis is on the validation of affective experience or the provision of a corrective experience, on recognition or responsiveness, on gratification or frustration, in a deficiency-compensation model the therapeutic action always involves some form of corrective provision. The Model 2 therapist is therefore ever attuned to the patient's affective experience in the moment (those points of emotional urgency that are experience-near for the patient) and ever intent upon meeting the patient where she is.

Although both self psychology and Model 2 object relations theories embrace the idea that some form of corrective provision is necessary in order to make good the deficiencies acquired early-on by the patient, there are some further distinctions between the two schools of thought upon which I would now like to elaborate.

SELF PSYCHOLOGY

Although self psychologists speak of gratification and frustration, their use of the word gratification usually suggests that the therapist's response is experienced by the patient as empathic, and their use of the word frustration usually suggests that the therapist's response is experienced by the patient as unempathic.

How does self psychology conceive of the therapeutic action?

Some self psychologists believe that what is compensatory and ultimately healing is the experience of gratification. But many believe that it is the experience of working through frustration against a backdrop of gratification that promotes structural growth. In other words, they believe that nontraumatic frustration or optimal disillusionment is the occasion for building new healthy structure. These self psychologists contend that if there is no frustration of need, no thwarting of desire, then there is nothing that needs to be mastered and therefore no impetus for internalization and the laying down of psychic structure.

Growing up (the task of the child) and getting better (the task of the patient) have to do with learning to master the disenchantment that comes with the recognition of just how imperfect (yet good-enough) the world really is. Moving from infantile need to mature capacity has to do with coming to terms with the loss of illusions about the perfection or the perfectibility of the world. It has to do with transforming the need for one's objects to be other than, better than, who they are into the capacity to accept them as they are.

I am here reminded of a *New Yorker* cartoon in which a gentleman, seated at a table in a restaurant by the name of The Disillusionment Cafe, is awaiting the arrival of his order. The waiter returns to his table and announces, "Your order is not ready, nor will it ever be."

According to the self psychologists, when the selfobject therapist has been experienced as gratifying (or "good") and is then experienced as frustrating (or "bad"), the patient deals with her disappointment by taking in the good that had been there prior to the introduction of the bad, which enables her to preserve internally a piece of the original experience of external goodness. The patient must both master her disillusionment with the therapist and make her peace with having been failed—in other words, she must grieve.

An inevitable accompaniment of this grieving process will be the patient's internalization of those psychological functions her selfobject therapist had been performing prior to the latter's failure of her. These transmuting internalizations (Kohut 1966) are the process by which internal structure is built—because internalized selfobject functions become psychic structures.

By way of grieving, the patient is able to work through the therapist's empathic failures; and by way of internalizing aspects of the selfobject, the patient is able to accrete internal structure and to fill in structural deficit.

By way of example, if in relation to her therapist a patient has had the experience of being always understood (illusion) and then one day finds herself feeling misunderstood (disillusionment), then the patient—by way of grieving—is thought to internalize the "understanding" that the therapist had offered the patient prior to failing her. It is by way of internalizing the selfobject function (of understanding) that the patient will transform her need for external understanding into a capacity to provide such understanding internally. More generally, it is by way of transmuting internalizations that the patient transforms need into capacity, energy into structure (Stark 1994a,b).

In other words, according to self theory, good is internalized not so much as a result of being gratified but more as a result of working through frustration, disappointment, and loss—against a backdrop of gratification. Good is internalized as a consequence of surviving the experience of being failed. Transmuting internalization and accretion of internal structure accompany the experience of having something good, losing it, and then mastering the grief one feels about its loss.

As part of the grieving she must do, the patient must come to accept the fact that she is ultimately powerless to do anything to make her objects, both past and present, different. She can, and should, do things to change herself; but she cannot change her objects—and she will have to come to terms with that painful reality. The patient does this by feeling, to the very depths of her soul, her anguish and her outrage that her infantile objects were as they were, her contemporary objects are as they are, and the transference object is as it is. Such is the work of grieving—and mastering the experience of having been failed; such is the work of making one's peace with reality—and moving on.

As Sheldon Kopp (1969) writes, "Genuine grief is the sobbing and wailing which express the acceptance of our helplessness to do anything about losses" (p. 30).

The patient gradually replaces her illusion that the therapist will be for her the good parent she never had, with a reality—namely, that she will have to become for herself the good parent she never had. Her need for illusion will be gradually replaced by a capacity to tolerate reality.

My claim is that both patient and therapist must ultimately face the reality that the therapist will never be (for the patient) the good parent they would both have wished she could be. Both patient and therapist must eventually confront that sad truth and grieve it.

In its barest bones, self psychology is a theory about grieving, grieving the loss of illusions about the perfection (or the perfectibility) of the self and/or the object. It is about paradise lost and never refound—it is about having illusions, losing them, and then recovering from their loss.

OBJECT RELATIONS THEORY

In self psychology, the emphasis is much more on empathic recognition of the patient's need than on its actual gratification. Such recognition is thought to validate the patient's experience. In object relations theory, the therapeutic action is thought to involve not so much gratification as meeting the patient where she is—in the way that a good mother recognizes and responds to her young child's needs. Such a response is thought to constitute a corrective experience for the patient. As we saw earlier, it may involve either gratification of the patient's need or its frustration.

The object relations theorist must therefore continuously ask herself which of the patient's needs should be gratified and which frustrated.

Ego Needs and Id Needs

Winnicott (1965) makes an interesting distinction. He suggests that we think of the patient as having different kinds of needs: (1) id needs, which relate to the patient's need for instinctual gratification, and (2) ego needs, which relate to the patient's need for objects—her need for connection with, and recognition by, objects.

Winnicott puts forth the idea that id needs can be frustrated but that ego needs must be gratified.

If an id need is frustrated, the patient experiences rage. The rage the patient experiences in the here-and-now belongs in part to the current frustrating situation, but in larger part to the original traumatic failure situation. There is thus an opportunity for the patient to rework the original environmental failure situation by working through the rage she experiences in the here-and-now relationship with her therapist.

If an ego need is frustrated, however, the patient experiences not rage but retraumatization—a reinforcement of the original traumatic failure.

Winnicott never really makes explicit how the therapist determines whether the patient's need is an id need or an ego need, other than to say that the therapist must use her intuition to assess whether the patient must be given the experience of having her need met or whether the patient can tolerate the experience of having her need thwarted.

An example of an ego need is the patient's need to be able, at least for a while, to feel that she can be the center of someone's world. If as a child the patient's developmental need for omnipotent control was consistently frustrated or challenged, then the patient may never have had the opportunity to feel that she could have an impact on the world.

It is therefore crucial that the therapist be able to provide a space within which the patient can experience herself as important, can believe that she matters, and can feel that she creates her objects.

In fact, early on in life it is crucial that the "helplessly dependent" infant have a mother who responds so readily to the infant's every need that the infant can have the experience of omnipotent control of her surrounds. She then has the experience of willing something to happen—and it does.

Winnicott (1958, 1965) suggests that during the infant's earliest months, the mother's adaptation to her infant should be as close to perfect as is humanly possible. The infant cries when she's hungry;

pronto, the devoted mother—recognizing and even having anticipated her infant's need—is there with her breast. The good-enough mother meets the omnipotence of her infant. The infant hallucinates; the mother presents. And the mother does this repeatedly.

Over and over she brings the world to her child. In so doing, the mother reinforces her infant's illusions of omnipotence and belief in the goodness of the world.

In this way, the infant has the experience, at least for a while, of being able to exercise omnipotent control over the world—her so-called sphere of omnipotence.

The good-enough mother will be able to give such an experience to her infant, and the good-enough therapist will be able to give such an experience to her patient.

One of my patients needed me to close my eyes whenever she told me about things that made her feel shame. So I would do that. And then when she was ready, she would tell me that it was now time for me to open my eyes. Which I would also do. It was profoundly empowering for her to be able to feel that she could make me do things according to her wish.

Clinical Vignette—The Need for Omnipotent Control

I worked with a latency-age girl, Amy, for two years. Her mother had brought her in originally because she was a "behavior problem" in school. Her mother was seen by a colleague of mine; I saw the daughter.

Every week, in the therapy sessions, Amy would have us play "school." She was the teacher, and I was her student. Actually, it seemed to me that she was a rather strict teacher, but then she seemed to feel that I was a rather naughty student.

In fact, Amy was really quite a stern taskmaster, quite a tough disciplinarian—and, I might add, not always very nice about it. I did the best that I could to be very good, to respond as well as I could to each and every one of her many commands; but she was relentless and very punitive.

Sometimes Amy would demand that I sit at the desk, a tiny little thing into which I could barely fit at all. Whenever I would complain about how small the desk was, she would tell me that it only seemed that way because I was so fat and that I should be quiet.

Periodically, she would tell me to stand up beside my desk and, as soon as I had struggled to my feet, she would insist that I be promptly seated. Up and down, up and down, again and again and again.

If I didn't react quickly enough, she would send me to the corner of the room, where I was to stand by myself in order to think about how bad I had been.

It also gave her particular pleasure to make me write my name on the blackboard over and over again—when she was mad at me or thought I had been misbehaving and therefore needed to be punished. I would write my name over and over on the doggone blackboard, though I kept telling her that I didn't like chalk or the blackboard—but she would make me do it anyway. So I would make a face as I was doing it, which I knew she saw.

Amy would give me homework assignments that I was to do between sessions. I did each and every one of them, with great care and very neatly. But she usually gave me a bad grade even so. When I would complain that the grade was not fair, she would tell me that it was because I was so dumb.

Indeed, she was a tough little tyrant. But I never once challenged her authority, and I always did the very best I could to accommodate myself to every single one of her imperious commands.

Amy just loved bossing me around. And, as it happens, I didn't really mind either, except for the part about the chalk on the blackboard.

Interestingly, Amy never once asked me to do something that I really would not have been able to do. In other words, she never once put me in the position of having to say no to her.

Over the course of our two years together, I did basically everything she asked. I offered her no resistance. I did not interpret her need to be in control: I did not, for example, suggest that perhaps her need to have omnipotent control was compensatory for underlying feelings of impotence and inadequacy in relation to her mother.

I wanted Amy to have the experience, in her relationship with me, of being able to exercise omnipotent control over her surrounds—an experience I sensed she had been denied as an infant and was now being denied as a latency-age girl in the relationship with her domineering mother.

Meanwhile, I was beginning to hear from her mother's therapist that Amy was behaving herself much better in school and was no longer engaging in the negative attention-getting behaviors that had originally brought her to treatment.

And there came a time in our own work when my little friend appeared to need less and less for me to accommodate myself to her every need. As she developed confidence in her ability to control her surrounds, she no longer had the same need to be constantly demonstrating such power and, in Winnicott's (1958, 1965) words, was able gradually to abrogate some of her omnipotence. In our sessions, she became less tyrannical, less bossy, less controlling—more vulnerable, more accessible.

Sometimes, to reward me when she thought I had been particularly obedient or when she was especially pleased with me, she would give me a little pat on my back. One time she even told me that something I had done was "very good."

Amy also started to give me *A*s on my homework assignments. One day she even brought me in a little gold star for my homework because I had done such a good job with it.

My little friend and I certainly did other things over the course of our two years together (including some interpretive work), but I believe that what was most healing for her was my willingness to provide her with consistent gratification of her need for omnipotent control of her environment, a need that had been traumatically thwarted early-on by her mother.

This example demonstrates a patient's use of her therapist as a new good object, as a stand-in for the infantile object, as someone who is able to provide for her in a way that her own mother was never quite able (or willing) to do. The therapist's successful provision enables the patient to regress to the point of the original environmental disruption and to start over, to begin anew.

This is an example, then, of gratifying a patient's ego need.

Clinical Vignette—A Gift from My Analyst

I remember an incident from my own analysis, a time when I told my analyst that I thought his waiting room was arranged the wrong way. I told him that I thought the chair was too close to the door of his office and that the bookcase shouldn't be there at all. Rather boldly and probably somewhat obnoxiously I suggested an alternative arrangement for his waiting room that I thought would be much better.

You can imagine my surprise (and delight) when upon my return the next day, I discovered that he had rearranged his waiting room furniture in accordance with what I had suggested the previous day.

What a generous gift he gave me in that. It was all the more powerful in that it happened at a time in our work when I felt that he was not really hearing what I was saying. That he was able to "hear" what I wanted him to do with his waiting room, that he was willing to respond in the gratifying way that he did, was a wonderfully affirming and healing experience for me.

RESPECTING THE PATIENT'S EXPERIENCE

Both self psychologists and Model 2 object relations theorists believe it is important that the therapist be able to decenter from her own experience in order to enter empathically into the patient's experience, so that the therapist can come to know where the patient is and what she wants. By decentering from her own experience, the therapist is able to be affectively attuned to what is emotionally real for the patient in the moment.

But whereas the Model 2 object relations theorist emphasizes the importance of responding to the patient in a way that will enable the patient to feel met (as happened in the two vignettes above), the self psychologist emphasizes the importance of responding to the patient in a way that will enable her to feel seen and heard.

Therapists who are not particularly well-versed in the art of empathy sometimes protest that a listening perspective involving the therapist's decentering from her own subjectivity must surely make patients feel that their therapist is using a technique and is not genuinely present.

In fact, any therapist skilled at using the empathic approach knows that there are many times when all the patient wants is to know that what she is putting out there is being heard, registered, and understood by a therapist who takes the patient at her word, offers the patient no resistance, and does not impinge by having her own judgments, her own biases, her own interpretations. At these times, the patient is not interested in knowing how a therapist more centered in her subjectivity might be responding to what the patient is saying—that is, whether the therapist is in agreement or disagreement, is approving or disapproving, is pleased or displeased, is interested or uninterested.

In other words, the empathic listening stance is not about the therapist; it is about the patient. It is not about how the therapist really feels, it is about how the patient really feels.

Interestingly, Carl Rogers (1961), widely known as a staunch proponent of the empathic approach, is purported to have readily agreed with a patient who noted (approvingly) that Rogers' empathic perspective was actually rather "impersonal."

I would like now to demonstrate what we mean when we say that the self psychologist responds empathically to "where the patient is."

If, for example, the patient expresses her concern that no one could love her were that person to know just how awful she really is, the empathic therapist does not challenge the patient's perception by protesting otherwise. Rather, the empathic therapist must be able to hear the patient out and to tolerate the patient's "awfulness"—perhaps the patient does indeed have a lot of ugly feelings that really are not all that appealing. The therapist must not need the patient to be "nice" and "lovable." The patient may be trying to tell the therapist that she needs a safe space into which she can deliver some not-so-nice feelings. The therapist who jumps too quickly to offer the patient pat reassurances about her lovableness may deprive the patient of the opportunity to deliver all of who she really is into the therapy relationship.

Or if the patient says that she is afraid she will fall apart, the empathic therapist does not remind the patient of all the ways in which the patient is resourceful and resilient. It may well be that the patient has tremendous internal reserves but if, in the moment, the patient is in her fear, then to remind the patient of her capabilities is for the therapist to direct the patient's attention away from where she affectively is—away from the point of emotional urgency for the patient. The empathic therapist needs to be able to sit with the patient in her fear—without trying to talk her out of it.

Or if the patient acknowledges through reluctant tears that she is sad, the empathic therapist does not (even gently) encourage the patient to say more. Let us assume that the patient's reluctant tears speak to the patient's conflict about having accessed the depths of her sadness and to her need, in the moment, not to say anything further. The therapist who encourages the patient to say more is probably responding more to her own need (to be helpful) than to the patient's need. The empathic therapist respects the patient's reluctance to be in her sadness; she may therefore offer the patient an empathic utterance that demonstrates to the patient that the therapist appreciates both the patient's sadness and her distress about finding herself in it. The patient may then elaborate further upon either just how sad she is or how hard it is for her to be in her sadness—or the patient may remain quiet, secure in her knowing that her therapist is with her.

By the same token, if the patient says that she is filled with suicidal despair and does not know how she can keep going, the empathic therapist does not suggest that she believes in the patient, that she has faith in the patient. Rather, the empathic therapist enters into the patient's experience, feels the patient's despair as if it were her own, and responds in a way that demonstrates to the patient that the therapist understands just how desperate and just how hopeless the patient is feeling. In the process, the therapist also conveys to the patient that she is not entirely alone in her despair.

More generally, if the patient is in a state of need, the empathic therapist offers empathic recognition of the patient's need; if the patient is in a state of frustrated need, the empathic therapist offers empathic recognition of the patient's disappointment, upset, and anger; if the patient is in a state of confusion (and not knowing whether she wants recognition of her desire or of her thwarted desire), the empathic therapist resonates empathically with the patient's experience of confusion.

It is important to remember that the therapist is not being empathic when she resonates with where she thinks the patient would be were the patient to allow herself to be in touch with what she is "really" feeling. There may well be times when the therapist opts to name an affect that she senses is there but is not being acknowledged; doing so, however, constitutes a Model 1 interpretation, the intent of which is to make the patient aware of something against which she has been defending herself.

Empathy, then, is not about what the therapist thinks some hidden part of the patient must be feeling (if the patient could but admit it). Nor is empathy about what the therapist thinks some hidden part of the patient would want to hear—empathy is not about being "supportive" to the patient. Empathy is about being with the patient where she is, taking her at face value, trusting that what she is saying is her truth.

In order to be truly empathic, the therapist must be able to enter into the patient's internal experience and be willing to experience the world as the patient does. The empathic therapist must be able to let go of her own ways of experiencing the world, her own subjectivity, her own biases, her own preconceptions, so that she can enter into the patient's experience uncontaminated by her own perspective. The therapist must let go of what is her own in order to embrace the patient's perspective.

Furthermore, the therapist must attempt to understand not only what the patient is feeling but also why she is feeling it—that is, its context. For example, it is usually not enough that the therapist be able to understand that the patient is experiencing a particular affect; rather, the therapist must also be able to contextualize the patient's affective experience. I believe that the empathic therapist can arrive at such understanding by way of (1) feeling her way into the patient's experience, (2) attending very closely to what seems particularly emotionally charged for the patient, and (3) listening very intently to all that the patient is saying and to how she is saying it. It is important that the empathic therapist not become distracted by her own feelings, her own thoughts, her own formulations.

The empathic therapist, as we know, is ever busy "tracking" the patient's affect. But it is not just that the therapist must be empathically attuned to the affect the patient is experiencing; the therapist must also have entered so deeply into the patient's affect that the therapist will have been able to grasp something about its meaning for the patient and/or its context.

Let us imagine, for example, that the patient is speaking with flat affect about something insignificant in his current life when he suddenly becomes very sad. The empathic therapist not only resonates with the patient's experience of sadness but also attempts to understand what has given rise to that sadness. I am speaking here to the distinction between the empathic therapist's ability to resonate empathically with the patient's affect and the empathic therapist's ability to understand, in addition, the context in which that affect has arisen.

In the example above, it may well be that the patient's sadness is about his mother's insensitivity, something about which he had spoken with much heartfelt anguish earlier in the session but had then gotten away from because it was too painful for him to sit with for long. The empathic therapist, ever attuned to the patient's affect, recognizes that the patient's distress about his mother is still very much unresolved. But the therapist is also respectful of the patient's (defensive) need to get some distance from his heartbreak by shifting to talk about something more neutral. As soon as the patient slips back into his sadness, however, the therapist, who has never lost sight of just how deeply disturbed the patient had been at the beginning of the session about his mother's insensitivity, is able to understand the context in which the patient's sadness has arisen.

Were the therapist to offer her patient an empathic response, it might take the form therefore of either "You find yourself feeling suddenly very sad" (which simply names the sadness), or "It's hard to get away from the sadness you feel about your mother" (which attempts to provide a context for the patient's sadness). In other words, the empathic therapist may either acknowledge the simple fact of the patient's affect or frame that affect in the context of the meaning it would seem to have for the patient.

By way of other examples, please note the distinction between "You are angry," and "You are angry about how abusive your father was." Or the distinction between "It makes you sad," and "It makes you sad to think about how alone you have always felt."

It is relatively easy for the therapist to empathize with people like herself, much harder to empathize with people unlike herself. When the patient experiences the world as the therapist experiences it and reacts as the therapist reacts, it is not too difficult for the therapist to enter into the patient's experience in order to be with her in that. But when the patient is different from the therapist, then it is a lot more difficult for the therapist to enter into the patient's experience and to understand, deeply, why the patient feels as she feels and does what she does.

For example, it is not too hard to be empathic with a patient who is in a great deal of distress because her boyfriend physically abuses her. It is much more difficult to be empathic when she tells us that she cannot leave him. This latter situation requires of us that we let go of our investment in thinking that things should be a certain way; it means being willing to put ourselves in her place so that we can deeply understand why she needs this man in her life. Even though there are times when he makes her feel horrible, it may well be that at other times she feels loved by him in a way that she has never before felt loved. Perhaps when he is loving her he makes her feel special. Perhaps she feels that she is deeply unlovable and should be grateful for whatever love she can find. Perhaps she does not realize that it could be different.

Perhaps being in the relationship with this man enables her to hold on to her hope that maybe someday, if she is good enough, she may yet be able to get him (perhaps a stand-in for her father) to love her as she so desperately yearns to be loved. She does not like the abuse but is willing to put up with it if it means being able to hold on to her hope that someday she may be able to get what she has craved for so long.

How do we understand the relentlessness of the patient's hope? When people have had the early-on experience of abuse, they are not usually satisfied with simply finding in the present a good (loving) object who treats them well. Their investment is in finding—re-finding—a bad (abusive) object whom they can make into a good object. The empathic therapist will be able to appreciate this and will understand that part of what fuels the patient's hope is her belief that perhaps, this time, things will indeed be different.

With respect to the example cited above about the patient with the abusive boyfriend, the therapist may either decrease the patient's anxiety by resonating with where the patient is (which is what the empathic therapist attempts to do), or increase the patient's anxiety by directing the patient's attention to elsewhere (which is what the interpretive therapist might attempt to do).

Were the therapist to respond interpretively, she might offer the patient something like: "It would seem that you experience your boyfriend in much the same way that you experience your father—namely, as someone who cannot love you as you would want to be loved. I wonder if part of what makes it so hard for you to let go of your boyfriend has to do with how painful it would be were you to give up on getting your father's love?" or "It occurs to me that some of the pain you are now experiencing in relation to your boyfriend is related to the pain you once experienced in relation to your father." Here the therapist, in an effort to advance the patient's understanding of the internal workings of her mind, directs the patient's attention to the connection between her past and her present (an instance of disruptive attunement).

Alternatively, were the therapist to respond empathically, she might say something like: "Although you hate it that your boyfriend hurts you in the ways that he does, you stay with him because he makes you feel very special," or "Although it bothers you that your boyfriend can be so abusive at times, perhaps you stay with him because you are hoping that maybe, someday, he will change." Here the therapist, in an effort to provide the patient with the experience of being understood, speaks to where the patient is (an instance of homeostatic attunement).

In any event, the empathic therapist must be deeply respectful of the patient's need, even if it is a defensive one, to be as she is and to believe as she does. The empathic therapist must be able to understand deeply why the patient needs the defenses that she has, why the patient protects herself in the ways that she does, why the patient is immobilized in the ways that she is, and why the patient keeps repeating that which she would rather not and cannot let herself do that which she would rather (Russell 1980, 1982).

It is this respect for the patient and what motivates her that informs the interventions the empathic therapist then makes.

When the patient feels understood, then she may well elaborate upon her internal experience, may well delve more deeply, and in a more heartfelt manner, into whatever she is really feeling in the moment—and why. Within the context of safety provided by her relationship with a therapist whom she knows really does understand, the patient may then be able to feel the pain, the anger, the disappointment, and the hurt against which she has spent a lifetime defending herself.

A Personal Experience

I had an experience recently that highlights the distinction between a response that resonates with where one is and a response that attempts to direct one's attention elsewhere. I had had a mammogram on a Friday morning and, that afternoon, just before five, had received a message on my voice mail from the radiology department at the hospital informing me that they had discovered something "suspicious" in my left breast and asking that I give them a call on Monday morning to schedule another set of x-rays.

That weekend was certainly one of the most difficult weekends I have ever experienced. Although I knew that the x-ray report did not necessarily mean that I was going to die of cancer, I did feel that I had suddenly been forced to confront the reality that I might indeed have breast cancer and might conceivably die from it. I had been brought face-to-face with my own mortality.

I can count on the fingers of one hand the number of my friends and colleagues who were able to tolerate being with me in my fear and in my anguish. Most people tried to reassure me that everything would be all right. Some people suggested that the radiology report might have been a false positive anyway and then everything would turn out just fine; others reminded me that there are now very effective treatments for breast cancer detected early on.

I understood that such responses were intended to offer me support and hope, but they ended up making me feel more anxious than comforted. I felt, somehow, that these friends were fighting me; I was in a quiet panic, but they were wanting me not to be feeling that panic. What I needed was to be able to talk about how frightened I felt and to have someone be with me in that, so that I would not be so alone in my fear. I did not need to be reminded of what, on some level, I too knew—namely, that it might turn out to be nothing at all.

Only Gunnar (my partner) and two or three others were able to enter into my fear in such a way that I was able to feel truly held and comforted—and not so alone.

As it turns out, I was tremendously relieved when the repeat x-rays on Monday demonstrated that the original ones had been misread and that there was no cause for concern whatsoever.

I present this personal example because it highlights the importance of being with someone where she is. Although there are times when it may be more useful to the patient for the therapist to direct the patient's attention elsewhere (perhaps to some underlying theme, pattern, or repetition, perhaps to some reality that the patient has, in the moment, lost sight of or possibly never knew), there are nonetheless many times when the patient is needing simply to have her experience understood and appreciated.

THE THERAPIST'S TECHNICAL TASK

Often the patient is simply feeling her experience and needs to have the therapist be with her in that—and not to fight her. The empathic therapist is able to do just that.

At other times, however, the patient can step back from her experience and become curious about her internal process. At such times, she brings to bear her observing ego and is then willing to have the interpretive therapist direct her attention elsewhere.

The technical task for the therapist is to decide when the patient is needing the therapist to be where she (the patient) is, and when the patient is open to having the therapist direct her (the patient's) attention in another direction.

I think that the most effective game plan is one in which the therapist alternates back and forth, between being with the patient where she is and directing the patient's attention elsewhere, back and forth, between engaging the patient's experiencing ego and engaging the patient's observing ego, back and forth, between offering the patient an opportunity to feel understood and offering the patient an opportunity to understand.

CHAPTER

5

Empathy versus Authenticity

As we have just seen, the therapist is continuously shifting back and forth between responding empathically (Model 2) and responding interpretively (Model 1).

I would like now to highlight an important distinction between the empathic attunement of the Model 2 therapist and the authentic engagement of the Model 3 therapist and then to present some clinical vignettes that speak to that difference.

Whereas the empathic (Model 2) therapist decenters from her own experience, the authentic (Model 3) therapist remains very much centered within her own experience.

(1) I am suggesting that empathy involves a kind of selflessness on the therapist's part, which she is able to achieve when she steps aside (decenters) from her own experience of self.

(2) I am suggesting that authenticity involves the therapist's use of self (that is, the use of her countertransference), which she is able to do when she remains very much present—centered—within her own experience of self.

In other words, I am suggesting that the therapist's empathy is about decentering from her own experience, entering into the patient's experience, and taking it on "as if" it were her own. I am suggesting that the therapist's authenticity is about remaining centered within her own experience, allowing the patient's experience to enter into her, and taking on the patient's experience "as" her own.

Thus it is by way of the Model 2 therapist's empathy that she is able to become attuned to the patient, and by way of the Model 3 therapist's authenticity that she is able to become engaged with the patient.

KNOWING THE EXPERIENCE OF ANOTHER

Those theorists who speak to the importance of an empathic decentering from one's own perspective are repeatedly asked by theorists who speak to the importance of a more authentic centeredness: "Can you really know another's experience without actually experiencing it yourself?"

One way to answer this somewhat provocative question is with the following: "But even if you do actually experience it yourself, can you even then ever really know another's experience?" In other words, How can a therapist ever really know that what she's experiencing is the patient's experience?

So let us consider the pros and cons of each listening perspective.

As an empathic selfobject, the therapist decenters from her own experience and immerses herself empathically in the patient's experience. The bad news is that the therapist takes on the patient's experience only as if it were her own, although it never really becomes her own. The good news is that what the therapist comes to know about the patient's internal experience is relatively uncontaminated by her own subjectivity—at least to the extent that she is able to decenter from it.

As an authentic subject, the therapist remains very much centered within her own experience—ever attuned to her own subjectivity and the patient's impact on it. The good news is that by allowing herself to be permeated by the patient's experience, the therapist is able to take on the patient's experience as her own. The bad news is that what the therapist comes to know about the patient's internal experience is, at least in part, always contaminated by her own subjectivity.

In sum, as an empathic selfobject, the therapist takes on the patient's experience only as if it were her own—but at least it is relatively uncontaminated by the therapist's subjectivity. Conversely, as an authentic subject, the therapist takes on the patient's experience as her own—but it is always contaminated by the therapist's subjectivity.

Although empathic attunement and authentic engagement may sometimes go hand in hand, they involve (as we have just seen) a different positioning of the therapist and, therefore, a different use of the therapist's self.

Let me now offer clinical vignettes that clearly demonstrate the distinction.

Clinical Vignette—I Wish I Had Cancer

Many years ago I was seeing a chronically depressed and suicidal patient who had just been diagnosed with breast cancer. Shortly thereafter she came into a session having learned that her axillary lymph nodes had tested "negative" (that is, no cancer). Through angry tears, she told me that she was upset about the results because she had hoped the cancer would be her ticket out.

I had to think for a few moments but then I managed to say softly: "At times like this, when you're hurting so terribly inside and feeling such despair, you find yourself wishing that there could be some way out, some way to end the pain."

In response to this, she began to cry much more deeply and said, with heartfelt anguish, that she was just so tired of being so lonely all the time and so frightened that her (psychic) pain would never, ever go away. Eventually she went on to say that she realized now how desperate she must have been to be wishing for an early death from cancer.

What I managed to say was, I think, empathic; but to say it, I needed to put aside my own feelings so that I could listen to my patient in order to understand where she was coming from. And so my response, although empathic, was not at all authentic, because what I was really feeling was horror. What I was really feeling about my patient's upset with her negative test results was "My God, how can you think such an outrageous thing!" To have said that would have been authentic—but not particularly analytically useful!

Although the response I offered my patient was not authentic, it was empathic. And I think it enabled her to feel understood and then to access deeper levels of her pain and her anguish—and, eventually, her own horror that she would have been so desperate as to want cancer.

Now had I been able to process my countertransferential response of horror more quickly, I might have been able to say something that would have been both authentic and analytically useful, something to the effect of: "A part of me is horrified that you would want so desperately to find a way out that you would even be willing to have (metastasizing) cancer, but then I think about your intense loneliness and the pain that never lets up—and I think I begin to understand better."

I present this example because it highlights the distinction between an empathic response and a more authentic response. Both are important dimensions of the patient–therapist interface, but the two stances involve a different use of the therapist's self.

Clinical Vignette—Holding the Patient's Ambivalence

The patient, Kathy, has been involved with a man, Jim, who appears to be very attached to her but, nonetheless, periodically has affairs with other women. It is always devastating for Kathy when she finds out, but each time Jim resolves to do better in the future and Kathy takes him back.

One day, however, Kathy discovers that Jim has had a one-night stand with someone she had considered to be her best friend. To her therapist, she reports her outrage that Jim would be doing this to her—yet again, and with her best friend! Kathy tells her therapist that the relationship with Jim is definitely over.

The therapist is easily able to be empathic with how Kathy feels.

But it is much harder for the therapist to empathize when Kathy comes to the next session with a report that she and Jim have had a good talk and have reconciled. Kathy explains that Jim is beginning to recognize that he has a problem and so has promised to get himself into therapy. Jim has told her that he feels awful about having done what he did and begs her forgiveness.

The therapist, knowing that this is neither the first time Jim has promised to get himself into therapy nor the first time Jim has promised things will change, finds herself feeling skeptical; she is also aware of feeling horrified that Kathy would actually be willing to give Jim yet another chance. To herself the therapist thinks, "Heavens, when is Kathy going to get it!? Jim is never going to give her what she wants. Why can't Kathy just let him go!?"

The therapist considers the possibility of sharing with Kathy some of her sentiments (or, at least, a modified version of them). She decides, however, that for now her feelings are so raw and so unprocessed that she does not really trust herself to say something that would be therapeutically useful to Kathy, something that would further the therapeutic endeavor.

And so the therapist decides to respond more empathically to Kathy by trying, as best she can, to decenter from her own feelings of outrage at Jim's provocative behavior and of horror at Kathy's refusal to confront that reality. The therapist therefore offers Kathy the following: "You are outraged and devastated by what Jim has done but want very much to believe that this time Jim has finally understood that his behavior is unacceptable. You are encouraged by his decision to enter therapy, and you are feeling that he is finally beginning to take some responsibility for his actions."

Clearly feeling understood and supported by the therapist's empathic recognition of where she is, Kathy responds as follows: "Jim makes me feel loved in a way that I have never before felt loved. He makes me feel very special, and that means a lot to me." Later, Kathy goes on to admit, "I do know that Jim could always do it again. He has done it many times in the past. But I guess I need to believe that this time he will come through for me."

The therapist's empathic response creates a space for Kathy within which she can feel safe enough, and nondefensive enough, that she can delve more deeply into acknowledging her need for Jim—that is, Kathy elaborates upon the positive side of her ambivalence about Jim. Later, she is able to get in touch with the negative side of that ambivalence, which she must be able to do if she is ultimately to work through her conflictedness about Jim.

In other words, for Kathy to be able, in time, to let go of Jim, she must come to understand both the "gain" (that is, what her investment is in staying with Jim) and the "pain" (that is, the price she pays for refusing to let go). In order to understand the gain, Kathy must be given the opportunity to expound upon the positive side of her ambivalence about Jim; in order to understand the pain, Kathy must get to a place of being able to recognize the negative side of her ambivalence about Jim.

The therapist's empathic response frees Kathy up to talk about how it serves her to be with Jim. Once Kathy has had an opportunity to do this, she is then able, of her own accord and at her own pace, to let herself remember just how painful the relationship has been for her.

Now had the therapist, instead of being empathic, been able to process her own feelings of outrage and of horror a little more quickly, she might, alternatively, have used aspects of this experience to offer Kathy the following: "On the one hand I find myself feeling horrified that you would be willing to give Jim yet another chance (given how much he has hurt you), but then I think about how important it is for you to be able to feel loved (because of how unloved you felt by your father)—and I think I begin to understand better why you might be willing to give him one more chance."

The therapist, by bringing together both sides of her own ambivalent response to Kathy, is here offering herself as a container for Kathy's disavowed conflictedness. Although (in the moment) Kathy might have lost sight of the negative side of her ambivalence, the therapist is remembering and carrying (on Kathy's behalf) both sides of the ambivalence.

We would say of the therapist that she has capacity where Kathy has need: the therapist has the capacity to sit with and to hold in mind simultaneously both sides of her ambivalence, whereas Kathy, in those moments when she is expressing her desire to give Jim another chance, would seem to have the capacity to remember only the positive side of her ambivalence and to have the need not to remember the negative side.

The therapist's capacity to tolerate what the patient finds intolerable is the hallmark of a successful projective identification (Stark 1994a,b). The therapist takes on Kathy's conflict and, after processing it psychologically, makes a modified version of it available to Kathy for re-internalization. In time, Kathy herself may well be able to acknowledge simultaneously both sides of her conflictedness—that is, both the gain and the pain.

I present this example because I think it shows how effective both an empathic response and an authentic response can be, even though they involve a different use of the therapist's self.

Although (as in the two examples above) the therapist's hypothetical authentic response may be reasonably empathic, an authentic response need not be empathic at all. In fact, it may well be confrontative, critical, or judgmental, as the next example demonstrates.

Clinical Vignette—Great Tan, Bitch!

The patient, Janet, is a 31-year-old married woman who has a history of difficult relationships with almost everyone in her life; she is particularly troubled by her lack of close women friends. Janet has been working hard in the treatment, has made substantial gains in her professional life, and has very much improved the quality of her relationship with her husband.

Janet and her therapist (a woman) have had a good, relatively unconflicted relationship; Janet clearly likes, and is respectful of, the therapist.

Upon the therapist's return from a week-long vacation in Florida, Janet, at the end of the session, just as she is leaving, turns back to her therapist and, as her parting shot, blurts out: "Great tan, bitch!"

The therapist, taken aback, says nothing, smiles wanly, and nods goodbye.

The therapist (after discussing the situation with a colleague) opens the next session with the following: "We have talked a lot about how upsetting it is for you to have so few women friends. I think that now, in light of what happened at the end of our last session, I am coming to understand something I had never before completely understood. When you left last time, your parting words were 'Great tan, bitch!' I wonder if by saying that, you were trying to show me what sometimes happens for you when you feel close to a woman and then find yourself feeling competitive?"

Here the therapist is using her experience of self, that is, her countertransferential reaction, to inform an intervention that is reasonably authentic—although not particularly empathic. Her intent is not to resonate empathically with the patient's affective experience in the moment; rather, her intent is to enhance the patient's understanding of what she enacts in her relationships with women when she begins to feel close (and, therefore, competitive) with them.

CHAPTER

6

Empathy versus Intersubjectivity

Earlier we distinguished between experience and relationship, although the two terms are often (and unfortunately) used interchangeably. We have just now seen how empathy and authenticity represent a different positioning of the therapist in relation to the patient, although here, too, the distinction between these two concepts is often (and unfortunately) blurred.

I would like now to suggest that we consider the relationship between empathy and intersubjectivity. Just as experience and relationship and just as empathy and authenticity are often used synonymously in the literature, so, too, empathy and intersubjectivity are often equated in ways that obscure important clinical differences.

Empathy, as Heinz Kohut (1971) originally conceived it was thought to involve the therapist's immersion in the patient's internal experience by way of the therapist's decentering—as best she could—from her own experience.

I believe that Robert Stolorow (Atwood and Stolorow 1984) also originally conceived of empathy as speaking to the therapist's capacity to come to know from a position within, uncontaminated by the therapist's perspective. Stolorow (1978), in his earlier writings, made several references to the therapist's need to decenter from her own subjectivity in order to immerse herself empathically in the patient's subjectivity. In fact, he specifically described the stance the empathic therapist assumes in relation to the patient as a "decentered perspective" (Atwood and Stolorow 1984, p. 49)—a stance the therapist must adopt in order to empathize with the patient's immediate conscious experience.

At one point, Stolorow (Atwood and Stolorow 1984) made reference to "the analyst's reflective self-awareness and capacity to decenter from the organizing principles of his own subjective world and thereby to grasp empathically the actual meaning of the patient's experience" (p. 47). He went on to suggest that "When such reflective self-awareness on the part of the analyst is reliably present, then the correspondence or disparity between the subjective worlds of patient and therapist can be used to promote empathic understanding and analytic insight" (pp. 47–48).

It would appear, however, that over time Stolorow began to experience this definition of empathy as somewhat limiting and so expanded it to include the therapist's attentiveness to her own subjectivity. In other words, Stolorow gradually extended his definition of empathy to include the therapist's participation in the therapeutic interaction not just as an empathic selfobject but as a subject (as someone with her own subjectivity).

In fact, Stolorow's coining of the term *intersubjectivity* to describe his stance clearly speaks to his vision of the therapeutic field as involving two subjects (the patient and the therapist), not subject (the patient) and selfobject (the therapist).

If one reads between the lines of Stolorow's (1988) later writings, one gets the sense that he now conceives of the therapist's stance as involving a dialectical interplay between the therapist as an empathic selfobject (ever straining toward a prolonged empathic immersion in the patient's internal world) and as a co-participating subject (very much centered within herself and ever attuned to her own experience)—a dynamic tension between the therapist as decentered and the therapist as very much centered.

My contention is that Stolorow's unacknowledged dissatisfaction with the more restrictive definition of empathy and his subtle broadening of the concept, over time, to include the therapist's own experience of self (or subjectivity) accounts, in large measure, for some of the current confusion about the relationship between empathy and intersubjectivity.

My own belief is that there is still a place for a pure (even if limited) definition of empathy that involves, as Richard Geist (1995) has suggested, an effort to put aside one's own theoretical bias so that what one comes to see in the patient (whether one is a classical analyst, a self psychologist, or an interpersonalist) will be the same from therapist to therapist.

But there must also be a place for the therapist's subjectivity, her remaining ever attuned to her own internal process, her own internal experience.

Indeed, when the therapist's subjectivity is taken into account (as it is in the more recent writings of Stolorow) and the therapeutic encounter is seen as an interaction between two subjectivities, then we have moved way beyond the original (more restrictive) definition of empathy. Now we are talking about intersubjectivity—with both patient and therapist bringing their authentic selves into the relationship.

In sum, just as there appears to be, in the literature, an abiding confusion about the relationship between (corrective) experience on the one hand and (real) relationship on the other and between empathy on the one hand and authenticity on the other, here, too, we are seeing that there has been confusion about the relationship between empathy and intersubjectivity.

I believe that the confusion in all three instances is a result of the transitioning (for the most part unacknowledged) from a conception of the therapeutic relationship as involving a therapist who gives and a patient who takes to a conception of the therapeutic relationship as involving give-and-take by both participants.

CHAPTER 7

Authentic Engagement

I am suggesting that the term intersubjective be used to describe the relationship that exists in Model 3 between patient and therapist—both of whom are thought to contribute, by virtue of their participation as authentic subjects, to what transpires at the intimate edge between them.

SUBJECTIVE AND OBJECTIVE COUNTERTRANSFERENCE

Whereas Model 1 conceives of the therapist's countertransference as primarily a story about the therapist, Model 3 introduces the idea that it is a story about not only the therapist but also the patient (by virtue of her impact on the therapist). In other words, in a relational model the countertransference is thought to be co-constructed, with contributions from both participants; the therapist's contribution is referred to by Winnicott (1965) as subjective countertransference, and the patient's contribution is referred to as objective countertransference.

By way of illustration, let's imagine the situation of a therapist who finds herself annoyed by her patient's repeated references to how good her friend's therapist is—and, by implication, how disappointing her own.

What might be the therapist's contribution to this scenario? Perhaps the therapist, because of unresolved issues about her worth as a therapist, is particularly sensitive to (and easily injured by) criticism—

thus her immediate and intense reaction of annoyance. Subjective countertransference.

What might be the patient's contribution? The patient is being provocative and the invidious comparison she is making between her friend's therapist and her own would probably elicit some kind of negative response, like annoyance, from any therapist. Objective countertransference.

The therapist's countertransferential response of annoyance, therefore, has elements of both the subjective (a story about the therapist's unresolved past) and the objective (a story about the impact of the patient's provocativeness on the therapist).

More generally, in Model 3, the countertransference is always thought to have aspects that are subjective, aspects that are objective. As such, it provides crucial information about the internal workings of the minds of both.

But this way of conceptualizing the countertransference is, of course, very much at odds with one that conceives of it as an impediment to the analytic process and therefore as something to be overcome.

How do we understand these two very different ways of conceptualizing the countertransference?

In fact, when countertransference is thought to be primarily a story about the therapist, it is being used as it was originally conceived in the classical psychoanalytic literature. My claim will be that this classical definition of countertransference is the province of both Model 1 (in which countertransference is thought to interfere with the therapist's objectivity) and Model 2 (in which it is thought to interfere with the therapist's capacity to decenter from her own subjectivity so that she can be truly available to the patient as an empathic selfobject).

By the same token, when countertransference is thought to be a story about both therapist and patient, it is being used as it is currently being used in the contemporary psychoanalytic literature. My claim will be that this contemporary definition of countertransference is the province of Model 3 (in which countertransference is thought to be an important source of data about both therapist and patient).

In a relational model, the therapist's countertransference is thought to offer much that is therapeutically useful but, even so (and particularly if not worked through in a timely fashion), it may sometimes be implicated in the premature demise of a treatment—as it is in the case that follows.

Clinical Vignette—The Gun

I worked for six months with Cindy, a 50-year-old, highly successful attorney whose specialty was domestic violence. She presented to treatment after a devastatingly painful breakup with a man, Scott, who had abused her both emotionally and physically. As a child Cindy had been abused by her alcoholic mother, a woman who would periodically fly into murderous rages. Cindy, terrified, would run from her mother, her only refuge a little space in the corner of the attic, beside an old bureau. Her father, a quiet, ineffectual man, was often absent and, when present, offered Cindy little protection from the ravaging effects of her mother's impulsive destructiveness.

In our early work together, I attempted as best I could to immerse myself empathically in Cindy's experience and came to understand both how important Scott had been to her (despite his abusiveness) and why she had been so devastated by the loss of him. It was by way of positioning myself alongside Cindy that I was able truly to appreciate why she felt she could not live without Scott in her life. Even though there were times when he made her feel awful, there were other times when he would do things for her to show her how deeply and how passionately he loved her—and she would feel so cherished. In fact, he let her know that he had never before allowed himself to get this close to anyone.

There were other moments when I would step back from Cindy, the better to observe her and to piece together some of the recurring themes and patterns in her life. I was able to interpret the loneliness she felt in present-time as the loneliness she must have felt as a child in relation to her mother, whom she had wanted so desperately to love her. I was able to see that being with Scott had enabled her to cling to her hope that maybe someday, somehow, someway, were she to try hard enough, she might yet be able to get him (a stand-in for her mother) to love her right. Clearly, Cindy did not like Scott's abusiveness, but she was willing to put up with it if it meant being able to hold on to her hope that perhaps she might eventually be able to get from him the nonabusive love for which she had been searching her entire life.

Some months into our work, Cindy began to grieve the loss of Scott, belatedly grieving as well how unloved and how unprotected she had always felt in relation to her parents. It was excruciatingly difficult, painful work—but Cindy demonstrated an incredible courage and willingness to deal with her outrage and her devastation, particularly with respect to her mother.

But in a session at the end of the half-year mark, Cindy one day made passing reference to her gun. I thought I must have misheard her and so asked her to repeat what she had just said. Rather awkwardly, I'm sure, I pressed her for details and found out that, indeed, she had a gun which she carried at all times—as she had for years now. Somewhat haltingly I asked her where the gun was right then. She pointed matter-of-factly to the jacket resting on the floor beside her chair.

I didn't tell her that I had suddenly become afraid, but I had—and she knew it. Knowing that she had a loaded gun beside her made me very anxious.

In the short time that was left in the session, I tried as best I could to propose a compromise with respect to her gun. I said I understood that she wanted to be able to feel safe but wondered if she would be willing, during her time with me, to dismantle her gun, perhaps leaving the bullets in her car. But she said that she did not feel comfortable with that arrangement, that she felt the need to have her gun with her at all times.

Unfortunately, we were unable to reach any kind of resolution by the time the session was over. At one point near the end, I said I understood that Cindy, defenseless as a child, had obviously found now a way to feel protected, to feel safe; I said I appreciated that having the gun with her at all times felt empowering to her. She said that I was absolutely right.

As she was leaving, I said something to the effect that I was sure we would be able to figure out a solution that would work for us both—but my "reassurance" rang hollow even to my ears.

That was the last session we ever had.

Cindy called before her next appointment to say that she was not going to be coming back. In the message she left for me on my answering machine, she reiterated her need for the gun and said that even were I to agree that she could have the (loaded) gun in the sessions, she did not at this point think that it would be fair to subject me to that.

I called her back several times and, unable to reach her, ended up finally leaving a message on her answering machine. I acknowledged the anxiety I had felt in the session, but I also shared with her my equally intense desire to be able to negotiate some kind of resolution to our dilemma, so that we would both feel safe and our work could continue. I suggested that while we were in the process of trying to reach an agreement between us, we consider doing our sessions by phone.

Several days later, Cindy left me another message in which she said that she appreciated my effort to negotiate a compromise but that doing the sessions by phone would not work because she had liked being able to see me in person. She thanked me, more generally, for the work we had done and said that she thought she would be fine.

It makes me very sad that I was not able to contain the fear I felt about Cindy's gun, that I was so drawn into her internal drama that I was not able to wend my way out by providing some kind of containment that would have enabled us both to feel safe. I knew it was important that I be able to contain my fear in relation to Cindy—something Cindy had never been able to manage in relation to her mother; but I couldn't quite pull it off in time.

I believe that, by way of projective identification, Cindy had been unconsciously communicating to me something very important about what her experience as a child must have been like; she was getting me to feel (in relation to her) the fear that she must have felt in relation to her mother. Had I done a better job of containing my own fear, then I might have been able to demonstrate to Cindy how fear could be mastered. But in the time that we had left at the end of our session, I was not able to control the fear that I felt.

I wish I had not failed Cindy in the way that I did. I have the feeling that I brought something of my own subjectivity to the interaction, which made it particularly difficult for me to recover my balance in time. I was not exposed to violence as I was growing up, but perhaps the presence of the loaded gun tapped into fears I have about losing control. I was not aware of being concerned that Cindy would suddenly, impulsively, angrily, pick up her gun to shoot me, but I do remember fearing that the gun might simply go off of its own accord.

I think that another therapist might have done a better job than I did of containing the fear and the uncertainty in the room during that last session. Although there have been clinical situations (one such situation involving a patient's suicidality) that I was able to tolerate that colleagues of mine have told me they would never have been able to tolerate, in this instance (with the gun) I was not able to have my wits about me enough to intervene in an analytically useful way—whether interpretively, empathically, or authentically.

I see the failure of the treatment as having resulted, in large part, from my difficulty containing the fear the patient had induced in me by way of her provocative behavior. I think that, on some deep level, she was desperately hoping that I would figure out a way to deal with my fear, which unfortunately I was not able to do. Although there was certainly a significant component of my countertransferential reaction of anxiety that was objective and might therefore have been felt by anyone in my shoes, it is the element that was subjective that still haunts me.

SUBJECTIVE AND OBJECTIVE TRANSFERENCE

Let us now move now from a consideration of the therapist's experience of being in relationship with the patient to a consideration of the patient's experience of being in relationship with the therapist.

Just as Model 1 conceives of the patient's experience of the therapist (namely, the transference) as primarily a story about the patient, Model 3 introduces the idea that it is a story about not only the patient but also the therapist (by virtue of her impact on the patient). In other words, in a relational model the transference is thought to be co-constructed, with contributions from both participants; thus I will be referring to the patient's contribution as *subjective transference* and I will be referring to the therapist's contribution as *objective transference*.

The focus in Model 1 is on the subjective transference (because the patient's experience of the therapist is here thought to be a story about the patient's unresolved issues); the focus in Model 3 is on both the subjective transference and the objective transference (because the patient's experience of the therapist is here thought to be a story about both her unresolved issues and the "reality" of who the therapist is).

What I am referring to as the objective transference is described by Irwin Hoffman (1983) as the patient's interpretation of the therapist's experience (an interpretation that is thought to be at least a "plausible construction" of the therapist's participation in the here-and-now) and by Lewis Aron (1991) as the patient's experience of the therapist's subjectivity. Both Hoffman and Aron are addressing themselves to those aspects of the patient's experience that are "realistic" or "objective."

In Model 3, then, the patient's experience of the therapist is thought to have elements of both realistic and unrealistic perception—that is, the transference is thought to be a story about not only the reality of who the therapist is (objective transference) but also the meaning the patient makes of that reality (subjective transference).

Let us imagine a situation in which the patient has just said that she is experiencing her therapist as critical. In order to encourage the patient to elaborate upon her experience, the Model 1 therapist might ask the patient: "Could you say more about your experience of me as critical?"

Because the Model 1 therapist conceives of herself as an anonymous, blank screen onto which the patient casts shadows that the therapist then interprets, the therapist's underlying assumption is that the patient's experience of her as critical is "distorted"—that is, that the patient's experience speaks more to negative experience the patient had as a child in relation to a critical parent than to "real" experience the patient is now having as an adult in relation to her neutral therapist.

The Model 3 therapist, on the other hand, thinks first in terms of eliciting information from the patient about her actual experience of the therapist and the therapist's participation. To that end, the Model 3 therapist might ask the patient: "Is there something in what I said or didn't say, something in what I did or didn't do, that led you to believe I might be feeling critical of you?" The Model 3 therapist is hoping to convey through both her words and, more generally, her open attitude that she is prepared to receive feedback about her behavior.

The Model 3 therapist is giving the patient permission to elaborate upon her actual experience of the therapist as critical, the therapist's underlying assumption being that the patient's experience of her as critical is at least a plausible interpretation of some aspect of the therapist's participation. There will then be time to pursue that part of the patient's experience which reflects her early-on experience at the hands of a critical parent.

The important distinction here is the therapist's intent. Whereas the Model 1 therapist's intent is to encourage the patient to look inward and backward (in order to reflect upon experiences she might have had as a child in relation to a pathogenic parent), the Model 3 therapist's intent is to encourage the patient to look outward (in order to reflect upon what she is experiencing as an adult in the here-and-now). The

Model 3 therapist takes seriously the patient's perception of her as critical—and is prepared to reflect carefully on her own participation.

In my books on resistance (Stark 1994a,b), I speak to the distinction between the patient's experience of the therapist, as informed by the past, and the patient's knowledge of the therapist, as informed by the present. I am now reframing that distinction: the subjective transference is informed by the patient's past and the objective transference is informed by the present.

CO-CREATION OF MEANING

In Model 3, then, not only are the therapist's countertransference and the patient's transference thought to be co-constructed, but all experience (all meaning, all reality, all that transpires in the intersubjective field at the intimate edge) is thought to be co-determined, with contributions from both participants in the therapeutic dyad.

Let us now look more closely at the co-construction of meaning—the making (or constructing) of meaning by both patient and therapist.

Winnicott's (1958) squiggle game is a good metaphor for the way patient and therapist are thought (by the Model 3 therapist) to participate in the therapeutic encounter. Winnicott would draw a line on a piece of paper, and the child would turn the line into something. Then the child would draw a line, and Winnicott would turn it into something.

Whose squiggle was it? Was it the child's or Winnicott's? Like a transitional object, it belonged neither inside nor outside. Rather, it emerged from the space between them.

The relational therapist believes that both patient and therapist participate in the creation of experience and in the ascribing of meaning to it. Again, in Model 3, all experience is thought to be co-constructed, with both its shape and its meaning determined by the contributions of each.

As Paul Wachtel (1980) has observed: "We are always constructing reality every bit as much as we are perceiving it" (p. 62).

The patient comes with a story to tell and to enact; the therapist both interprets the patient's story and participates with the patient in the making of it. "Reality" is not merely discovered; it is created on a moment-by-moment basis.

I present the following four vignettes by way of illustration.

Clinical Vignette—Was She Really Serious?

A mutual flirtation has been going on for months now between my patient, Bob, married, and a colleague of his, Sally, also married. Bob and Sally have plans for lunch. When they run into each other earlier that day, Sally says to Bob: "Maybe we shouldn't go to lunch. Maybe we should go somewhere else." Bob, smiling, responds: "Naughty! Naughty!"

In the session with me, Bob says: "I wonder what she really meant when she said that maybe we should go somewhere else. Did she really mean it?"

What Bob and I came to realize was that had he responded by saying, "Good, let's go," without skipping a beat she might well have proposed the Marriott—in which case it could certainly be said that yes, she had really meant it.

But by responding with a playfully dismissive "Naughty! Naughty!" Bob made Sally's suggestion, which might otherwise have been serious, into something much less serious—and the whole thing was dropped.

Clinical Vignette—When Was He Killed?

Tom, with murderous intent, stabs Adam in the heart with a knife. Adam is rushed to the hospital where, two days later, he dies. When did Tom kill Adam?

In the moment of the stabbing, Tom's intent was to kill Adam. But inasmuch as Adam did not immediately die, Tom was not (at least initially) successful in his effort to kill Adam.

It was only two days later, when Adam did finally die, that Tom was charged with murder—and his intent was actualized. Prior to Adam's actual death, Tom's action did not constitute murder.

In other words, the meaning made depends on both the intent and the response—and evolves over time.

Clinical Vignette—Interpretations That Hurt

Let us imagine a situation in which the therapist offers her patient the following interpretation: "You would seem to be choosing men who (like your father) are emotionally unavailable." The patient, even as she grants that there may be some truth in the therapist's interpretation, becomes upset because she thinks the therapist is being critical of her.

The interpretive therapist, who sees herself as an observer, not as a participant, conceives of the patient's experience of her as deriving primarily from the patient's internal dynamics. The Model 1 therapist may therefore be tempted to assume that the patient's reaction is much more a story about the patient (and her tendency to experience others as critical) than a story about the therapist (and her actual participation as a critical other).

By contrast, the relational therapist, who sees herself as very much a participant in the intersubjective field, conceives of the patient's experience of her as deriving from both the patient's internal dynamics and the therapist's actual participation. The Model 3 therapist therefore recognizes that the patient's reaction is at least a plausible construction of the situation—that is, that the patient's reaction may well be the response anybody would have to an interpretation that, although clarifying, is not particularly flattering.

Whereas the interpretive therapist conceives of the patient's transferential reaction as primarily a story about the patient (subjective transference), the relational therapist conceives of the patient's transferential reaction as a story about both patient and therapist (subjective and objective transference).

In response then to the question of who decides if the therapist's interpretation is critical or not, the answer really depends on how the patient experiences it—not just on how the therapist intends it.

More generally, the meaning of something is determined on the basis of both what is intended and how it is responded to; it is co-determined, a joint creation, with contributions from both participants.

In a relational model, there is no inherent meaning in something. Rather, its meaning evolves over time—by virtue, in part, of the response it elicits.

Clinical Vignette—I Was Only Kidding

On a humorous note, I once saw a movie, the title of which I have long since forgotten, in which a young man says something provocative to his girlfriend, who is understandably hurt and angered. She, in her turn, reciprocates with something equally provocative, to which the young man responds with, "You didn't have to take it so seriously; I was only kidding!" His girlfriend, without missing a beat, quips, "So was I!"

Both participants in an encounter define the meaning ultimately made of a particular interaction.

MUTUALITY OF IMPACT

A relational model of therapeutic action posits not only that the therapist has an impact on the patient but also that the patient has an impact on the therapist. In other words, a relational therapist believes that there is always mutuality of impact—a prime instance of which is projective identification.

Clinical Vignette—Disavowed Grief

A patient's beloved grandmother has just died. The patient, unable to feel his sadness because it hurts too much, recounts in a monotone the details of his grandmother's death. As the therapist listens, she feels herself becoming intensely sad. As the patient continues, the therapist finds herself uttering, almost inaudibly, an occasional "Oh, no!" and "That's awful!" As the hour progresses, the patient himself becomes increasingly sad.

In this example, the patient is initially unable to feel the depths of his grief about his grandmother's death. By reporting the details of her death in the way that he does, the patient is able to get the therapist to feel what he cannot himself feel; in essence, the patient exerts interpersonal pressure on the therapist to take on as the therapist's own what the patient does not yet have the capacity to experience. This is clearly an instance of the patient's impact on the therapist.

As the therapist sits with the patient and listens to his story, she finds herself becoming very sad, which signals the therapist's quiet acceptance of the patient's disavowed grief. We could say of the patient's sadness that it finds its way into the therapist, who takes it on as her own. The therapist's sadness is therefore co-created—it is in part a story about the patient (and his disavowed grief) and in part a story about the therapist (in whom a resonant chord has been struck).

The therapist, with her greater capacity (in this instance, to experience affect without needing to defend against it), is able both to tolerate the sadness that the patient finds intolerable and to process it psychologically. It is the therapist's ability to tolerate the intolerable that makes the patient's previously unmanageable feelings more manageable for him. The patient's grief becomes less terrifying by virtue of the fact that the therapist has been able to carry that grief on the patient's behalf.

A more assimilable version of the patient's sadness is then returned to the patient in the form of the therapist's heartfelt utterances—and the patient finds himself now able to feel the pain of his grief, able to carry that pain on his own behalf. This is clearly an instance of the therapist's impact on the patient.

For the relational therapist, the locus of the therapeutic action always involves this mutuality of impact; both patient and therapist are continuously changed by virtue of being in relationship with each other.

INEVITABILITY OF EMPATHIC FAILURE

Whereas Model 2 addresses itself to the therapist's impact on the patient but pays relatively little attention to the patient's impact on the therapist, Model 3 addresses itself not only to the therapist's impact on the patient but also to the patient's impact on the therapist. In fact, in Model 3, the patient is thought to exert pressure on the therapist to participate in ways specifically determined by the patient's early history (Casement 1985).

In order to demonstrate the distinction between a theory that posits unidirectional influence (Model 2) and a theory that posits bidirectional influence (Model 3), I offer the following.

As we know, self psychology (Model 2) speaks to the importance of the therapist's so-called "inevitable" empathic failures (Kohut 1966). Self psychologists contend that these failures are unavoidable because the therapist is not, and cannot be expected to be, perfect.

How does relational theory (Model 3) conceive of such failures? Many relational theorists believe that a therapist's failures of her patient are not just a story about the therapist (and her lack of perfection) but also a story about the patient and the patient's exerting of pressure on the therapist to participate in old, familiar ways. In other words, the Model 3 therapist believes that the therapist's failures do not simply happen in a vacuum; rather, they occur in the context of an ongoing, continuously evolving relationship between two real people, and speak to the therapist's responsiveness to the patient's (often unconscious) need to be failed.

As with every "repetition compulsion," the patient's need to re-create the early-on traumatic failure situation in the here-and-now engagement with her therapist has both unhealthy and healthy aspects.

(1) The unhealthy component has to do with the patient's need to have more of the same, no matter how pathological, because that's all the patient has ever known. Having something different would create anxiety because it would highlight the fact that things could be, and could therefore have been, different; in essence, having something different would challenge the patient's attachment to the infantile (parental) object.

(2) But the healthy piece of the patient's need to be now failed as she was once failed has to do with her need to have the opportunity to achieve belated mastery of the parental failures—the hope being that perhaps this time there will be a different outcome, a different resolution.

And so it is that, in Model 3, the therapist's failures of her patient are thought to be co-constructed, both a story about the therapist (and what she brings to the therapeutic interaction) and a story about the patient (and what she brings to the therapeutic interaction).

Again, in the relational model, there is always this mutuality of impact. Not only is the therapist thought to influence the patient (as happens in Model 2), but also the patient is thought to influence the therapist. Each participant is therefore both shaping and being shaped, influencing and being influenced.

Moreover, in Model 3, the concept of mutuality refers not to mutual disclosure but to mutual influence. It is believed by the relational therapist that the patient must be able to know that she can affect the therapist; can have an impact on the therapist; and, ultimately, can change the therapist.

CHAPTER

8

The Therapist as Old Bad Object

Before I say more about the relational (or interactive) model, I would like to return, for a moment, to the deficiency-compensation model in which it is thought that the locus of the therapeutic action involves the therapist's offering the patient some form of corrective provision.

VALIDATION VERSUS CONFIRMATION

The empathic therapist conceives of the therapeutic action as involving empathic recognition of the patient's experience (often referred to in self psychology as "validation" of the patient's experience). But what does it really mean when self psychology suggests that the therapist seeks to provide validation of the patient's affective experience or subjective reality?

Although validation of experience would seem to suggest "confirmation" of the reality of that experience or, even, "agreement" with the patient, what self psychologists usually mean when they make reference to the importance of validation is simply a response that indicates (as we have seen) the therapist's affective attunement to where the patient is in the moment.

When it is said that the therapist validates the patient's experience, the emphasis is usually more on the therapist's empathic recognition of the patient's need than on her actual gratification of that need.

In other words, if the patient wants the therapist to tell her that she will get better, when we say that the empathic therapist provides validation of the patient's experience, we mean that the therapist resonates empathically with the patient's need to be reassured—not that the therapist actually provides that reassurance.

Or if the patient wants the therapist to tell her that she is special, the empathic therapist validates the patient's experience by conveying to the patient her understanding of just how important it is to the patient that she be able to feel special, not by telling the patient that she is, in fact, special.

Finally, if the patient wants the therapist to understand that she is being exploited in her current job, when we say that the therapist validates the patient's experience we mean simply that the therapist resonates, say, with the patient's experience of outrage at being in a position where she finds herself feeling used, not that the therapist "agrees" with the patient's assessment of her job situation.

Evelyne Schwaber (1979, 1981, 1983), who has written extensively about the empathic mode of listening, suggests that the more insistently demanding the patient, the more actively responsive the therapist must be—but, as she clarifies, this does not mean actually doing something. The therapist may feel pressured to do something to alleviate the patient's distress, but Schwaber advises that what is truly empathic is the therapist's search for the meaning that underlies the urgency of the patient's demanding insistence.

In other words, despite pressure from the patient to gratify her need, the empathic therapist believes that what is most transformative for the patient is the experience of having her need recognized—and its genetic underpinnings revealed. The therapist's empathic recognition of where the patient is in the moment enables the patient to delve more deeply into what it feels like to be there.

A noteworthy exception involves situations of trauma and abuse, where the therapeutic action may well lie in providing the patient with the experience of having her reality not just understood but actually confirmed by the therapist.

I will now present a case vignette by way of illustration.

Clinical Vignette—Confirming the Reality of Abuse

A patient of mine had been emotionally abused in a previous treatment. In order to trust me, she felt she needed to know that I understood deeply just how damaged she had been by that abuse.

In addition, however, she felt she needed to know that I believed not just that the abuse had been her "experience" but that it had "really happened"—that her perception of her therapist as abusive had been "accurate." In other words, in order to be able to feel safe with me, she felt she needed to have me confirm her reality, not just understand it.

More generally, there are times when a patient may need the therapist to appreciate that not only did she (the patient) experience herself as having been failed, but she actually had been failed. In other words, validation may sometimes require not just empathic recognition of the patient's reality but its actual confirmation.

The following vignette poignantly speaks to this point.

Clinical Vignette—The Letter

My patient, Mary, had been telling me for years that her mother did not love her. Again and again she would complain bitterly about all the attention her mother showered on her other daughters. Mary claimed that she, on the other hand, was treated by mother with either indifference or actual disdain.

Of course I believed her; that is, of course I believed that this was her experience of what had happened as she was growing up. I wanted to be very careful not to condemn Mary's mother as unloving. My fear was that were I to agree with her that her mother did not love her, I would be reinforcing a distorted perception, which might then make it much more difficult for Mary to reconcile with her mother at some later point, were she ever to decide to do that.

And so I was always very careful never to say things like: "Your mother clearly did not love you," "Your mother obviously favored your sisters over you," or "Your mother had very little to give you."

Instead, I would frame my "empathic" interventions in the following way: "And so your experience was that your mother did not love you—and that broke your heart." Or I would say something like, "How painful it must have been to have had the experience of wanting your mother's love so desperately and then feeling that you got so little of it."

In retrospect, it makes me sad to think that I said these things and that Mary let me. Part of her problem was that she allowed people to say these kinds of things to her.

But one day she came to the session bearing a letter from her mother. She began to read it to me, and I was horrified. It was totally clear, beyond a shadow of a doubt, that for whatever the reason, her mother really did not love her in the way that she loved her other daughters. It was a horrible letter and my heart ached for Mary; now I really understood what she had meant all those years. And I felt awful that I had thought my patient's perceptions of her mother might be distortions of reality.

When Mary had finished reading one of the saddest letters I have ever heard, I said, "Oh my God, your mother really doesn't love you as much as she loves the others, does she? I'm so sorry that it took me so long to get that."

Mary then hung her head and said quietly, with a mixture of anguish and relief, "You're right. My mother really doesn't love me very much." She began to sob in a way that I had never before heard her sob. I am sure that she was crying both about how unloved she had always been by her mother and about how disappointed she was now in me, that it had taken me so long to understand something so important.

On some level, unconsciously I had been defending her mother. I think I was having trouble believing that her mother would have been so heartless as to favor her other daughters over my patient; I was so fond of my patient that I could not imagine any mother not loving her.

The reality is that I had not really taken Mary seriously when she had told me that her mother did not love her. I understood that she had felt unloved as a child, but I could not bear to think that she had actually been unloved. And so I did her a grave disservice in assuming that she was inaccurately perceiving the reality of the situation. In doing this, I was blocking some of the grieving that she needed to do about her mother.

By the way, as Mary grieved the reality of how unloved she had actually been by her mother, she and I came to discover something else: although she had not been loved by her mother, she had in fact been deeply loved and cherished by her father, a man who, although severely alcoholic and often absent from home, was nonetheless very deeply attached to Mary and proud of her. We might never have gained access to the special connection with her father had I persisted in my belief that Mary's mother had to have loved her.

Let me add, at this point, that another way to understand what happened between Mary and me is to think in terms of my patient as having needed me to fail her as she had been failed in the past, so that she would have the opportunity to achieve belated mastery of her old pain about not being taken seriously.

Were we to conceptualize the situation in this way, then we might say about my failure of Mary that it was not just a story about me (and my difficulty coming through for her) but also a story about Mary (and her difficulty letting me come through for her).

More generally, such a perspective has it that there are times when the patient needs the therapist to participate not just as a good object but also as a bad object (the old bad object)—so that there can be an opportunity for the patient to revisit the early-on traumatic failure situation and perhaps, this time, to achieve mastery of it. Mitchell (1988) has aptly described the therapist's participation in this way as the "familial and therefore familiar" object.

Greenberg (1986b) has suggested that if the therapist does not participate as a new object, the therapy never gets under way; if she does not participate as the old one, the therapy never ends—which captures exquisitely the delicate balance between the therapist's participation as a new good object (so that there can be a "starting over" or a "new beginning") and the therapist's participation as the old bad object (so that there can be a reworking of internalized traumas).

INTERNAL RECORDING OF PARENTAL FAILURE

As we mentioned earlier, classical psychoanalytic theorists think in terms of the patient's psychopathology as deriving from the patient (in whom there are unbridled sexual and aggressive drives); self psychologists, object relations theorists, and contemporary psychoanalytic theorists think in terms of the patient's psychopathology as deriving from the parent (and the parent's failures of the child).

How are such parental failures thought to be internally recorded and structuralized? Interestingly, some theorists focus on the price the child pays because of the "good" the parent does not do (which produces an internal absence of good, in the form of structural deficit) and some theorists focus on the price the child pays because of the "bad" the parent does do (which produces an internal presence of bad, in the form of pathogenic introjects or internal bad objects).

But whether the pathogenic factor is thought to be a sin of omission (the focus in Model 2) or a sin of commission (the focus in Model 3), the villain of the piece is seen as the parent, not the child.

Model 2 theorists focus on the internal registering of traumatic parental failure in the form of structural deficit or impaired capacity. The deficit creates a need; the need is for an empathic selfobject—or a good mother—to complete oneself.

Such a patient is thought to be relatively unconflicted in her search for new good relationships; when the therapist is able to meet the patient where she is, the patient embraces this "new good object" unambivalently. The locus of the therapeutic action therefore involves the therapist's participation as a new good object.

Model 3 theorists, however, focus on the internal registering of traumatic parental failure in the form of internal bad objects, or pathogenic introjects, that become filters through which the patient experiences her world.

There are three ways in which these internal bad objects can make their presence known: (1) the patient may choose a good object and then, by way of projection, come to experience her as bad; (2) the patient may choose a good object and then, by way of projective identification, draw her into participating as a bad object; or (3) the patient may simply choose a bad object. In any event, the patient's internal bad objects make her afraid and create what I refer as "relational difficulties"—that is, an impaired capacity for healthy, authentic relatedness.

Such a patient is thought to be very conflicted about finding new good relationships because of her fear—fear that she will be now failed as she was once failed, fear that her heart will be now broken as it was once broken.

Many (but not all) Model 3 theorists use the conceptual framework of internal bad objects to understand the patient's fear. In other words, they conceive of the patient's interpersonal difficulties as stemming from the presence of internal bad objects.

Some Model 3 theorists, however, attribute the patient's relational difficulties to her fear of being retraumatized by some kind of unempathic response. Such fear is not thought to be specifically mediated by way of internal bad objects but is thought, more generally, to be the result of early-on traumatic experiences that make the patient particularly vulnerable to subsequent retraumatization.

Absence of Good versus Presence of Bad

A deficiency-compensation model is embraced by both self psychologists and those object relations theorists who emphasize the absence of good.

The locus of the therapeutic action in Model 2 is then thought to involve either the patient's experience of the therapist as a new good object (in self psychology) or the therapist's actual participation as a new good object (in Model 2 object relations theories).

Whether the therapist is simply experienced as a new good object or actually participates as a new good object, it is believed that the corrective provision offered by the therapist enables the patient's deficits to be filled in and her "self" to be consolidated.

I am now suggesting that a relational or interactive model is embraced both by contemporary psychoanalytic theorists and those object relations theorists who emphasize the presence of bad.

Thus locus of the therapeutic action in Model 3 is thought to involve either the therapist's participation as an authentic subject (in contemporary psychoanalytic theory) or the therapist's actual participation as first old bad and then new good object (in Model 3 object relations theories), such that the patient's experience will be of bad-become-good. It is then in the context of the here-and-now engagement between patient and therapist that the patient's internal bad objects can be gradually reworked, modified, and detoxified—the therapist lending herself as a container for and psychological processor of the patient's disavowed psychic contents (such as overwhelming grief, anxiety-provoking conflictedness).

Whether the therapist participates as an authentic subject or participates as first old bad and then new good object, it is the interactive engagement between patient and therapist that is thought to enable the patient, in time, to overcome her fear and to develop the capacity for healthy, authentic relatedness.

I would like to explore in greater detail how such a transformative process takes place.

THE FEAR OF BEING FAILED

The patient who is afraid of being failed (because of the bad that happened early-on) either brings about that which she most fears or avoids authentic engagement altogether. In other words, the patient's fear is such that she either re-creates the old bad traumatic failure situation—to which Mitchell (1988) refers as relational conflict—or finds herself unable to bring her authentic self into relationship—to which I refer as relational deficit.

With respect to the patient who demonstrates relational conflict: although consciously the patient has a fear of being failed, underlying that fear is a need to be failed—a need that is fueled by the patient's intense attachment to her internal bad objects. There is something so compelling for her about these old bad objects that a part of her is ever in search of new objects whom she can make over into the old objects—her (unconscious) need to be failed is ultimately greater than her (conscious) fear of being failed. The country rock song by Warren Zevon entitled "If You Won't Leave Me I'll Find Someone Who Will" speaks directly to the patient's need to be failed in the old, familiar ways.

With respect to the patient who demonstrates relational deficit: it is the patient's fear of being failed that prevails—a fear that makes it difficult for her to engage with others. Unlike the patient with relational conflict whose attachment to her internal bad objects is such that she is ever intent upon recreating that dynamic externally, the patient with relational deficit decathects from all objects, both external and internal.

The first group of patients would seem to need the old bad object; in W. R. D. Fairbairn's (1943) words, "a bad object is infinitely better than no object at all." The second group of patients would seem to need to avoid relationships entirely; as Harry Guntrip might have said, better to have no object at all than to run the risk of encountering a bad object.

In both situations, the patient's fear is enacted in such a way that it has a profound effect on how she actually engages in relationship.

Although in Model 2 it is understood that here, too, the patient is afraid of being failed, this fear is not thought to affect how she actually engages in relationship. The Model 2 therapist believes that even though the patient fears being failed, she deeply longs for gratification of her thwarted developmental needs. Here the emphasis is on the patient's need for good (and her embracing of that good when it presents), not her fear of bad.

On the other hand, the Model 3 therapist, whether she embraces a relational-conflict or a relational-deficit model, believes that the patient is conflicted about being in relationship because—on some level—she fears being failed. Although it is thought that the patient also longs to be gratified, it is the patient's fear of being failed and the effect that fear has on how she engages in relationship (or disengages from relationship) that is the focus of the therapist's attention.

Whereas the deficiency-compensation model conceives of the therapeutic action as involving correction for the internal absence of good by way of working through disruptions of the positive transference (wherein the therapist is experienced as the good parent the patient did not have), both the relational-conflict and the relational-deficit models conceive of the therapeutic action as involving correction for the internal presence of bad by way of working through the negative transference (wherein the therapist is experienced as the bad parent the patient did have). By comparison, the second model conceives of working with the positive transference in order to fill in structural deficit, and the third model conceives of working with the negative transference in order to detoxify the patient's pathogenic structures.

It will be only when the patient's internal bad objects have been reworked that the patient's fear will be overcome and she will be able to enter healthily (particularly relevant for the patient with relational conflict) and authentically (particularly relevant for the patient with relational deficit) into relationships.

Incidentally, the deficiency-compensation model pays little attention to the internal presence of bad; in fact, self psychologists have no place in their theory for pathogenic introjects. Reinforced need, increased vulnerability, and impaired capacity, yes—but no pathogenic introjects or internal bad objects. It is to the third model (with its emphasis on the internal presence of bad) that we must look in order to understand (1) the patient's intense attachment to the internal bad object and her compelling need to re-create with the therapist the interactional dynamic that had characterized the early-on relationship with the traumatizing parent and (2) the patient's reluctance to engage at all for fear of being devastated by the response she imagines she will encounter.

Problems with Relatedness

When Mitchell (1988) introduced his three models of therapeutic action in *Relational Concepts in Psychoanalysis*, he spoke of the first as a drive-conflict model, the second as a deficiency-compensation (or developmental-arrest) model, and the third as a relational-conflict (or relational) model. He appeared to use the terms relational conflict and relational almost interchangeably.

I would like now to make a distinction between the two terms.

1. I will limit Mitchell's concept of *relational conflict* to those patients who would seem to have a need to re-create the early-on traumatic failure situation—that is, a need to be failed.
2. I will use my concept of *relational deficit* to describe those patients who would seem to have a need to avoid relationships altogether for fear of being failed.
3. I will employ Mitchell's concept of the *relational model* to encompass the therapeutic work that needs to be done with the patient who has relational conflict, the patient who has relational deficit, and any patient who would seem to lack the capacity to engage healthily and authentically in relationship because of what she brings from her past.

In my schematization, this third model of therapeutic action, the relational (or interactive) model, focuses on the patient's relational difficulties; its goal is to facilitate development of the patient's capacity to overcome her fear so that she can engage with others both healthily and authentically.

Fairbairn and Guntrip

Interestingly, both Fairbairn (1943, 1954, 1958) and Guntrip (1961, 1969, 1973) write about schizoid personalities, but I think the way each conceptualizes the underlying endopsychic situation captures in a nutshell the distinction between the patient with relational conflict and the patient with relational deficit.

Intense Attachments to Internal Bad Objects

Earlier I had suggested that the patient who presents with relational conflict has an unconscious need to be failed that ultimately triumphs over her conscious fear of being failed. I would like now to draw upon the ideas of Fairbairn (1943), who writes about the patient's "intense attachments" to her internal bad objects, to help us understand more specifically how it comes to pass that the patient (with relational conflict) would be so tenaciously attached to her internal bad objects and so intent upon recreating in the here-and-now the early-on traumatic failure situation.

Over the years many psychoanalysts have written about internal bad objects (or pathogenic introjects) that become the filters through which the patient experiences herself and her world of objects, but very few of them have addressed the issue of the patient's attachment to (or investment in) these objects.

Freud (1923), for example, wrote about superego introjects, but nowhere did he write about the nature of the patient's attachment to these introjects. Melanie Klein (1964) wrote about internal bad objects that persecute, terrorize, and destroy, but she too had little to say about the actual nature of the patient's attachment to these "savage beasts" (p. 143). Roy Schafer (1968) wrote at length about pathogenic introjects but said almost nothing about the patient's ties to these internal "felt presences" (p. 38).

And William Meissner (1974, 1976, 1980) has written extensively about so-called introjective configurations—negative interactions between parent and child that are internally recorded and structuralized in the form of pairs of introjects. Such introjects exist in a state of internal turmoil and conflict; what once had been external conflict between parent and child now becomes internal conflict between the poles of the introjective pairs.

As an example, imagine the situation of a mother who repeatedly puts her daughter down. Over time, this dynamic becomes internally registered in the form of a superior introject in the daughter's ego ideal and an inferior introject in the daughter's ego, such that the ego experiences shame in relation to the ego ideal and the ego ideal experiences contempt or disdain for the ego.

But even here the focus is on the nature of the relationship between the poles of the introjective pairs—and not on the nature of the patient's attachment to these introjective configurations.

It is to Fairbairn (1943, 1954) that we must look in order to understand the nature of the patient's attachment to her internal bad objects, an attachment that makes it difficult for her both to separate from the infantile object and to extricate herself from her compulsive repetitions—an attachment that is at the very heart of her relational difficulties.

Let us review what Fairbairn has to say about how "bad" experiences at the hands of the infantile object are internally recorded and structuralized.

Says Fairbairn, when the child's need for contact is frustrated by her mother, the child deals with her frustration by internalizing the bad mother. It is as if the child finds it intolerably painful to be disappointed by her mother. And so the child, to protect herself against the pain of having to know just how bad her mother really is, introjects (both defensively and adaptively) her mother's badness—in the form of an internal bad object. Basically, in order not to have to face the pain of her grief, the child takes the burden of her mother's badness upon herself.

The child's introjection of the mother's badness is both defensive (in that it protects the child from the pain she would have to feel were she to let herself know the truth about her mother) and adaptive (in that it enables her to preserve at least some semblance of a relationship with her mother—a relationship that might otherwise have been intolerable).

Introjection of the parental badness happens all the time in situations of abuse. The patient will recount episodes of outrageous abuse at the hands of her mother (or her father) and will then say that she does not feel angry at the mother but she does feel guilty—for having gotten in the way, or even for being alive. It is easier to experience herself as bad (and unlovable) than to experience the mother as bad (and unloving), easier to experience herself as having deserved the abuse than to confront the intolerably painful reality that the mother should never have done what she did.

More generally, a child whose heart has been broken by her mother will defend herself against the pain of her grief by taking on the mother's badness as her own, thereby enabling her to preserve the illusion of her mother as good and as ultimately forthcoming if she (the child) could but get it right. In essence, by internalizing the bad mother, the child is able to maintain an attachment to her actual mother and, as a result, is able to hold on to her hope that perhaps someday, somehow, someway, if she is but good enough, she may yet be able to get her mother to love her.

In other words, the child internalizes the bad mother in order not to have to separate from her and in order not to have to confront how alone she really is.

And so it is that a relationship with a bad object, says Fairbairn, is infinitely better than no relationship at all, because the child can at least still have hope. Were she to disengage herself entirely from the (now internalized) infantile object, were she to renounce her dependence upon the object, such renunciation would be tantamount, in her eyes, to forfeiting all hope of ever securing gratification of her unsatisfied longing for connection, acceptance, and love.

Fairbairn contends, therefore, that the child's unrelenting hopefulness is what fuels the intensity with which she remains attached to the internal bad object.

But what does Fairbairn suggest is the nature of the child's attachment to this internal bad object?

As we have just seen, the child who has been failed by her mother takes the burden of the mother's badness upon herself. Introjection is, therefore, the first line of defense.

Splitting is the second line of defense. Once the bad object is inside, it is split into two parts, the exciting object that offers the enticing promise of relatedness and the rejecting object that ultimately fails to deliver. Both the enticing (or exciting) mother and the depriving (or rejecting) mother are bad mothers.

Earlier I had implied that, according to Fairbairn, a bad mother is a mother who frustrates her child's longing for contact. But, says Fairbairn, a seductive mother—who first offers her child the enticing promise of something good and then fails to deliver—is a very bad mother.

Fairbairn's interest is in seductive mothers. When a child has been failed by a mother who is seductive, the child introjects this bad mother. Once inside, this bad (seductive) mother is split.

Splitting of the ego goes hand-in-hand with splitting of the object. The so-called libidinal ego attaches itself to the exciting object and longs for contact, hoping against hope that the object will come through. The antilibidinal ego, which is the repository for all the hatred and the destructiveness that have accumulated as a result of frustrated longing, attaches itself to the rejecting object and rages against it.

So what, then, is the nature of the patient's attachment to the bad object? It is, of course, ambivalent; it is both libidinal and antilibidinal (or aggressive) in nature. The bad object is both needed (because it excites) and hated (because it rejects).

Repression is the third line of defense, repression of the ego's attachment to the exciting/rejecting object.

The patient, unconscious of her compulsion to re-create the early-on situation of seduction and betrayal, is then ever in search of love objects who excite but then reject, who promise but never deliver. And the drama is recapitulated again and again, in the hope that perhaps this time the outcome will be different, perhaps this time she will find the love for which she has been searching all her life.

According to Fairbairn, then, at the core of the repressed is not an impulse, not a trauma, not a memory; rather, at the core of the repressed is a "forbidden" relationship—an intensely conflicted relationship with a bad object who is both loved and hated. Such a relationship involves both longing and aversion, desire and revulsion—although, because the attachment is repressed, the patient may be unaware that both sides exist.

As it happens, Fairbairn was more interested in the exciting/rejecting object (the parent who offers the enticing promise of relatedness and then reneges) than he was in any other kind of bad object, but I think we can use his idea that there is an ambivalent attachment to the internalized exciting/rejecting object to inform our understanding of the child's attachment to all manner of internal bad objects—that there is both longing for the bad object to be good and hatred of the object for being bad.

Even though the patient's attachment to her internal bad objects is ambivalent, it is nonetheless very intense by virtue of the hope that accompanies it—an intensity that fuels the patient's compulsion to find the old bad object. It is this compulsion to re-create in the here-and-now the early-on traumatic failure situation that gives rise to the patient's relational conflict—that is, her conflict about finding new good objects.

Compare what Fairbairn is saying here to what Kohut says about how the child attempts to master her experience of disappointment at the hands of the parent. Kohut (1966, 1971) suggests that when the parent has been good and is then bad, the child attempts to master her disappointment by taking in the good parent (that is, the good that had been there prior to the introduction of the bad). Fairbairn (1943, 1954), on the other hand, suggests that when the parent has been good and is then bad, the child attempts to master her disappointment by taking in the bad parent. These are obviously two entirely different conceptualizations of the process by which the child attempts to master her experience of disappointment at the hands of the frustrating parent.

Perhaps a way to reconcile these two opposing perspectives is to consider Kohut and Fairbairn to be addressing different clinical situations.

Let us think about the distinction Kohut (1966) makes between frustration that is nontraumatic (or optimal) and frustration that is traumatic. If a frustration can be worked through by way of grieving, then it is called a nontraumatic frustration; if it cannot—for whatever the reason—be worked through and resolved, then it is called a traumatic frustration.

Kohut's belief is that nontraumatic frustration (that is, frustration properly grieved) prompts the child to internalize the good parent. Interestingly, in situations of traumatic frustration, Kohut's belief is that nothing is internalized—which is why there are no internal bad objects in self psychology. In situations of traumatic frustration, the child simply develops structural deficit because of what does not happen (namely, internalization of the good parent).

We can then use Fairbairn's ideas about the child's internalization of the bad parent to help us understand what happens in situations of traumatic frustration. The child, unable to master her experience of disappointment, takes the burden of the parent's badness upon herself, which is why the child who has suffered at the hands of a parent has internal bad objects to which she is intensely attached. As we have just seen, it is thought to be these attachments that fuel the patient's conflict about finding new good objects—that is, fuel her relational conflict.

Renunciation of Object Seeking

Earlier I had suggested that the patient who presents with relational deficit has taken flight from all relationships, both external and internal. I would like now to draw upon the work of Guntrip (1969), who is best known as the author who drew attention to Fairbairn's contributions by making the latter's theories more comprehensible, but who also had his own theory about the endopsychic situation of the schizoid personality. I think Guntrip's ideas about the "final split" in the libidinal ego can help us understand more clearly how it comes to pass that the patient with relational deficit would have chosen to withdraw from all relationships.

Although Fairbairn conceives of the schizoid personality as someone who has withdrawn from external objects but has established intense attachments to internal bad objects, Guntrip conceives of the schizoid personality as someone who has detached from all objects.

Fairbairn's libidinal ego yearns for contact with the exciting object; Guntrip, however, postulates that the libidinal ego undergoes a final split: Part of it remains attached to the exciting object and continues its relentless search for relatedness, but another part of it (the regressed ego or self) splits off and becomes even more withdrawn, renouncing object seeking altogether.

It is this avoidance of all objects that gives rise to the patient's relational deficit—that is, her impaired capacity to engage authentically in relationship.

Tenacity versus Withdrawal

Let me now highlight some of the distinctions between the Fairbairnian patient (who demonstrates relational conflict) and the Guntripian patient (who demonstrates relational deficit).

Whereas Fairbairn writes about patients for whom attachments to objects, even bad objects, are absolutely essential, Guntrip (1969) writes about patients for whom attachments to objects are intolerable.

Whereas Fairbairn's patient is entangled with, and compulsively attached to, her objects, Guntrip's patient has abandoned relationships with all objects, both external and internal.

For Fairbairn the patient's regressive longings relate to a desire to remain attached to her bad objects, but for Guntrip the patient's regressive longings relate to a desire to retreat from all relationships and to withdraw into total isolation.

For Fairbairn the greatest resistance in therapy is the patient's tenacious attachments to her bad objects, but for Guntrip the greatest resistance in therapy is the patient's terror of being in relationship and, especially, her refusal to engage with the therapist.

In addition to Fairbairn, a relational-conflict perspective is put forth by such theorists as Joseph Sandler (1976), Thomas Ogden (1979, 1982a,b, 1983), Arthur Malin and James Grotstein (1966), Jay Greenberg (1991), and—of course—Stephen Mitchell (1988) himself.

In addition to Guntrip, a relational-deficit perspective is embraced by such theorists as Winnicott (1960), Modell (1975, 1980), and the Stone Center (Miller 1988, Stiver 1990).

But whether the patient is thought to have relational conflict or relational deficit, the relational (or interactive) perspective has it that what is curative for the patient is the experience of finding and of being found by an authentic other, of engaging and of being engaged by another and of negotiating at the intimate edge between patient and therapist.

RELATIONAL CONFLICT

When the patient is seen as having relational conflict, the therapist must be able to make herself available as a container for the patient's projective identifications. It is important that the patient have the experience of delivering all of herself (including what she has difficulty owning) into the therapy relationship—and of then discovering that both she and her therapist survive. In fact, ultimately their engagement will be both deeper and more authentic for having weathered the storm together.

The essence of what is therapeutic for the patient lies in the therapist's ability to receive the patient's projections, to use aspects of herself to process the projections, and to return the metabolized (and now slightly detoxified) projections to the patient.

When the therapist uses herself to contain the patient's projective identifications, the experience for the patient is one of containment and, ultimately, of greater integration.

The patient with relational conflict will have the profoundly healing experience of having been contained; what had once been not-me (and therefore not owned) will now be integrated into what is me. The patient will feel more alive, more real, more whole.

I offer the following in order to demonstrate the relational-conflict model in action.

Clinical Vignette—Relentlessly "Empathic"

This vignette speaks to a patient's need to be failed by her therapist. It is a story about Nancy, a patient with whom I worked for many years.

Periodically Nancy would fault me for being unempathic. I would take seriously her claim that I was being unempathic and would ask, specifically, about what I might have done or said that was unempathic. Nancy, however, was never quite able to come up with any real evidence of empathic failure on my part. So it would be clear to us both that it was a case of "mistaken identity"—that she was inaccurately perceiving me as her bad, unempathic mother. Once she understood that we were talking about distortion, not reality, that the real object of her anger was her mother, not I, then she would dutifully rail against her mother.

Over the course of the first few years of our work together, Nancy frequently faulted me for lacking empathy but never was she able to provide any real proof to support this. I would therefore offer her genetic interpretations of her transference distortions—namely, that her misperceptions of me as unempathic must speak to how unresolved she still was about her mother.

I was failing to recognize that the negative transference kept emerging because I was not doing something quite right. Whenever a patient complains again and again about a specific something with respect to the therapist, then the therapist is probably doing something wrong—if not the specific something about which the patient is complaining, then something else.

In this particular situation, I was not fully appreciating Nancy's investment in getting me to be her unempathic mother. I was not fully appreciating her need to have me fail her. Over and over again, Nancy was delivering into the treatment situation her need to be failed; over and over again, I was thwarting her. Perhaps it could be said that by being so unflinchingly "empathic," I was actually thwarting her.

In any event, as long as I refused to accept Nancy's projections, as long as I refused to participate with her in her transferential enactments, I could not really be available to her as an effective transference object. I had my own need—to be "empathic" no matter what!—and so, unwittingly, was not really letting Nancy use her here-and-now engagement with me to work through the unresolved relationship with her toxic mother.

As Wachtel (1986) has observed, "it is in the very act of participating that the analyst learns what it is most important to know about the patient" (p. 63). By remaining more observer than participant, I was, in effect, denying myself access to important information about just how attached my patient was to her unavailable mother.

And so things continued in this way for several years. In the meantime, of course, we were getting other kinds of work done, but we were not making any real headway in terms of Nancy's repeated experience of the objects in her world as "not understanding."

At the end of our third year, however, there came a session in which something different happened. As usual, Nancy began to fault me for being unempathic; as usual, we looked at what I might have done or said that would be making her experience me in this way.

But this time, unlike previous times, Nancy did have evidence—which I will recount in a moment. Let me first say, however, that as soon as Nancy protested my lack of empathy, I realized that indeed I had been incredibly unempathic. Furthermore, as I thought about it, I recognized that I felt strangely elated, even glad that I had said what I had.

Nancy had been talking about how upset she was about her parents' sudden announcement that they were getting a divorce. Not only was I not with her in her obvious upset, but I was absolutely delighted that her parents were finally getting out of what had been an absolutely horrid, mutually destructive relationship.

And so instead of "Oh, that's terrible," I blurted out something to the effect of "Wow, that's great!"

Now what was really happening?

First, I was probably carrying, on Nancy's behalf, the pleasure she felt but could not acknowledge about the fact that her parents were at last getting their long-awaited divorce; Nancy could not let herself experience pleasure about that because it made her feel too guilty, too disloyal. Second, and more important, I was finally willing to let myself be drawn into Nancy's internal drama, willing to let myself become a player on her stage.

And so Nancy had finally succeeded in getting me to become her bad, unempathic mother, thereby recreating with me—in fact, not just in fantasy—the early-on relationship with her mother.

I am, of course, speaking of projective identification, in which the patient exerts pressure on the therapist to accept her projections and to participate as the old bad object.

But now there was opportunity, where before there was not, opportunity for the patient to have, ultimately, the experience of bad-become-good.

I immediately apologized to Nancy for having been so outrageously unsympathetic at a time when I knew that a part of her desperately wanted my support. By acknowledging my error and by apologizing to her for it, which is something her mother had never done, I was introducing something new. Nancy had never before had the experience of being wronged and then of having that wrong acknowledged and an apology offered.

In short, by allowing myself to be made bad, I was accepting Nancy's projection. But by demonstrating my willingness to own my unempathic behavior and by offering her an apology for having been so unsupportive, I was showing her that I was not, in fact, as bad as she had feared I might be. I was providing a form of "corrective feedback."

Remember that when there is the internal absence of good (in the form of deficit or impaired capacity), the patient must be given the opportunity to deliver her need for good into the relationship with her therapist. Gradual internalization of the good encountered there is the process by which the internal absence of good is corrected for (Stark 1994a,b).

When, however, there is the internal presence of bad (in the form of pathogenic introjects), the patient may not be able to experience the object as good because of her conflict about being in relationship with new good objects. When the patient's traumatic history has been internally recorded and structuralized in the form of internal bad objects, the patient must be given the opportunity to detoxify these pathogenic structures before she will be able to experience new good (Stark 1994a,b).

This can be done when the patient is able to re-create with the therapist the interactional dynamic that had characterized the original relationship with the toxic parent. A negative transference will emerge in which the therapist will either be experienced as the old bad parent (if just projection is involved) or be made to become the old bad parent (if projective identification is involved).

It is by working through the negative transference that the patient's internal bad objects will be gradually detoxified, her intense attachment to them will be gradually relinquished, her relational conflict will be gradually resolved, and her need to experience her therapist as the old bad object will become gradually transformed into the capacity to experience her as a new good object. It is this working-through process that will enable the patient to master the original trauma and to transform it into healthy structure and capacity.

In order to make my point about how important it is that the therapist allow herself to respond to unconscious cues from the patient, I suggested in the vignette above that my relentlessly "empathic" behavior during the first three years of my work with Nancy might actually have been "unempathic." I went on to suggest that it was only when I "failed" Nancy that I was finally being empathic. In essence, I was putting forth the idea that by being empathic I was actually being unempathic and that by being unempathic I was actually being empathic.

In fact, I think that Nancy had both a conscious need to be understood (to which I was initially responding) and an unconscious need to be failed (to which I eventually responded).

I am not entirely sure that my empathy during the first three years of Nancy's treatment was entirely unempathic. I was responding to that part of Nancy that was needing me to be with her where she was.

But, as it turned out, the other part of Nancy began, over time, to emerge in the treatment—a part of Nancy that was needing to be able to re-create with me the interactive dynamic that had characterized the relationship with her difficult mother.

Had I not responded at all to the pressure Nancy was exerting on me, then I might have denied Nancy the opportunity to engage me in the way that, on some level, she was needing to. I think the important thing is that I did eventually allow myself to be acted upon by Nancy and to be drawn into participating countertransferentially with her in her transferential enactment. An interesting question has to do with whether I could have responded earlier and could then have spared Nancy some unnecessary anguish.

In other words, using a deficiency-compensation model to understand the therapeutic action does not capture the richness of what transpired between Nancy and me. In order to capture that richness, one must call upon a model of therapeutic action that takes into consideration the patient's unconscious exerting of pressure on her therapist to participate as the old bad object—in essence, one must call upon a relational-conflict model.

From the perspective of Model 3, my failure to respond to the patient's pressure to be failed would not be seen as unempathic but then neither would my responsiveness to such pressure be seen as empathic. Rather, my ability to allow myself ultimately to be drawn in as a player on her stage would speak to my ability to use my authentic self to give Nancy what she most needed in order to work through her relationship with her internal bad mother.

As for Nancy, after we came to understand the dynamic that had been played out between us (which included her recognition of the part she had played in its creation), she was able, finally, to separate from her mother and, at last, to relinquish her investment in being failed. As her conflict about being in relationship with good objects was gradually resolved, her need to be misunderstood became transformed into a capacity to tolerate having someone really be there for her.

Interestingly, never again has Nancy mistakenly experienced me as unempathic.

Re-creation of the Original Traumatic Failure Situation

The relational-conflict therapist, then, believes that on a conscious level the patient fears being failed but on a deeper level needs to be failed—so that she will have an opportunity, belatedly, to work through the internalized traumas. The patient is thought to use the therapist's failures to rework early parental failures.

In a relational-conflict model, the patient is thought to be not just a passive victim of a bad parent or a bad therapist (deficiencies for which she must be compensated) but also an active initiator of what she needs in order to resolve her conflict about being in a good relationship. What a patient with relational conflict brings to the relationship with her therapist is the need to be failed in ways specifically determined by her developmental history so that she can rework (and master) her internal demons.

Let us begin by considering the patient who, as a child, was traumatized (whether emotionally, physically, or sexually) by a parental figure. These early-on traumatic interactions are internally recorded and structuralized in the form of introjective configurations—pairs of internal bad objects or pathogenic introjects (victimizer–victim, criticizer–criticizee, and so on)—that become part of the patient's repertoire of internalized object relationships.

Under the sway of the repetition compulsion (some aspects of which are unhealthy, some healthy), the patient re-creates in the here-and-now the original environmental failure situation. By exerting pressure on the therapist to accept her projections, she draws the therapist into participating countertransferentially with her in her transferential enactments.

Although initially the therapist may indeed fail the patient in much the same way that her parent had failed her, ultimately the therapist challenges the patient's projections by lending aspects of her "otherness," or, as Winnicott (1965) would say, her "externality," to the interaction—such that the patient will have the experience of something that is "other-than-me" and can take that in. What the patient internalizes will be an amalgam, part contributed by the therapist and part contributed by the patient (the original projection).

In other words, because the therapist is not, in fact, as bad as the parent had been, there can be a different outcome. There will be repetition of the original trauma but with a much healthier resolution this time, as the repetition leads to modification of the patient's internal world and integration on a higher level.

It is in this way that the patient will have a powerfully healing "corrective relational experience," the experience of bad-become-good—which is the hallmark of a successful projective identification.

Clinical Vignette—No Wonder No One Loves You!

A student of mine recounted the following story. She had a patient, Maria, who could not stand it when her therapist was nice to her. Repeatedly, Maria would tell her therapist that she hated her therapist for being nice to her, that it always felt so much better when people were mean to her, that she could only really feel cared about when people were abusive to her.

As you might well have guessed, Maria is someone who had grown up knowing, on some level, that she was hated by her mother; Maria, in turn, had hated her mother. In all her subsequent relationships, she was comfortable only when she was able to recapitulate that mutually hateful dynamic.

In the therapy, Maria was ever busy exerting interpersonal pressure on her therapist to become impatient with her, to be frustrated with her, to be annoyed with her, even to hate her, by insisting with rageful vehemence that she (Maria) was worthy of nothing but the therapist's utter contempt, that she (Maria) was a bad, awful, hateful person, that the therapy was a waste of time, that she hated coming, that the therapist was a bad, awful, hateful person, that the therapist would never be able to help her, and so on and so forth.

And so Maria devoted all her efforts toward drawing her therapist into her internal drama, all her efforts toward getting her therapist to participate with her in a dramatic re-enactment of that early-on hateful relationship between herself and her mother.

For a long time, the therapist steadfastly refused to participate in Maria's drama, steadfastly refused to hate Maria.

But there came a time when Maria succeeded at last in getting the therapist to fail her, to fail her just as her mother had failed her; finally, Maria got her therapist to say something hateful. One day, in utter exasperation, the therapist blurted out: "My God, you'll never be able to get anybody to love you as long as you're like this!"

As soon as the therapist had said it, she was horrified. She was also dumbfounded; she could not imagine that she could have said something so awful to her patient. She could not reconcile the hateful thing she had said with her view of herself as a compassionate, caring, sensitive therapist and human being.

But Maria, in response to the therapist's hateful words, was neither horrified nor dumbfounded. In fact, Maria was visibly relieved. This was something familiar, known, safe; this was something she could live with. Now she was able to feel connected, involved, engaged with the therapist in a way that she had never before felt before her therapist's outburst.

In the aftermath of her therapist's "failure" of her, the two were then able to work together to understand Maria's intense need to re-create in the transference and in all her relationships the early-on hateful dynamic between herself and her mother.

Once the power of Maria's repetition compulsion was made explicit, the therapist was easily able to recover her loving feelings for Maria. And over the course of the next years, Maria's self-esteem improved considerably; her need to hate and to be hated became transformed into a capacity to engage warmly with people who cared about her.

Maria's experience of first bad and then bad-become-good was profoundly healing and proved to be the turning point in her relationship with her therapist—it was truly a corrective relational experience.

Negotiation of the Relationship and Its Vicissitudes

The therapist must be able not only to tolerate being made into the bad object but also to extricate herself once she has allowed herself to be drawn in as the bad object.

The therapist must have the wisdom to recognize and the integrity to acknowledge her own participation in the patient's enactment; even if the "problem" lies in the intersubjective space between patient and therapist, with contributions from both, it is important that the therapist have the capacity to relent—and to do it first.

Patient and therapist can then go on to look at the patient's investment in getting her objects to fail her, her compulsive need to re-create with her contemporary objects the early-on traumatic failure situation.

If the therapist never allows herself to be drawn into participating with the patient in her enactment, it is a failure of engagement. If, however, the therapist allows herself to be drawn into the patient's internal dramas but then gets lost in what has become a mutual enactment, it is a failure of containment.

In sum, the relational-conflict therapist appreciates the patient's need for good (in order to compensate for early-on failures) but is particularly attuned to the patient's need for bad (in order to achieve belated mastery of those failures).

RELATIONAL DEFICIT

The relational-deficit therapist believes that the patient is so fearful of being failed that she either keeps those parts of herself that are most authentic out of relationship or avoids relationships altogether. The patient is thought to deal with her conflict by not engaging authentically with others.

Guntrip (1969) believes that it is the fear of being failed that motivates the patient to detach herself completely from objects and to renounce all hope. Because of intolerably painful early-on disappointments and heartache, the innermost self of the patient has secretly withdrawn. The patient attempts to cancel relationships, to want no one, and to make no demands. The resolve is to live in a detached fashion, aloof, untouched, without feeling, keeping others at bay, avoiding (at whatever the cost) commitment to anyone. The fear is of being found and disappointed; the need is to remain hidden, not seen.

Although the patient with relational deficit may not demonstrate such an extreme avoidance of relationships, she is reluctant to deliver all of herself into any relationship, including the therapy relationship. Or if she does dare to deliver herself into a relationship, she may quickly retreat if she encounters disappointment, frustration, or loss.

The following is an excerpt from a session I had with a patient of mine, very dear to me, just before my upcoming vacation:

> *I feel lost and alone and like I'll never find my way. I feel like I've fallen into an abyss, and there is no one there. I am screaming, but all I can hear is an echo. I imagine being a baby, crying in my crib—but my mother doesn't come. I know she won't come. And even if*

she did, she wouldn't understand what it is like to be me and how I feel inside. It's like this absolute panic that no one can understand—that I am so different. And it's such a horrible experience. I have this incredible feeling of disconnection and aloneness all the time. I don't think I have an existence. It is so terrifying. I feel I could be dead. I feel completely detached, like there is no me, there is no you, there is no one.

Let us now think about other theorists (Miller et al. 1991, Modell 1975, 1980, Winnicott 1963a,b) whose interest is in patients who are unable to engage authentically with others for fear of being failed—that is, patients with a relational deficit and therefore an impaired capacity to engage in authentic relationship.

Winnicott's (1958, 1965) false self is a patient with relational deficit.

Such a patient never had the experience of a good-enough mother who was able to provide a protective envelope within which her infant's "inherited potential" could become actualized. In other words, when the mother is not good-enough, she does not provide her infant with the necessary protection from impingement—and may herself be impinging. The infant cannot therefore act spontaneously but must be ever reacting to the mother's impingement.

Reacting, however, interrupts being; and when there is no continuity of being, the true self cannot come into existence. It gets split off, becomes isolated, and atrophies over time. The little peapod true self, the source of spontaneity and creativity, goes into hiding, avoiding at all cost the possibility of exposing itself without being seen or responded to. In other words, the child's true (or authentic) self never comes into being.

Not only does such a mother not meet her infant's needs—but she asks of her infant that the infant meet hers. The infant, in order to preserve the connection with her mother, must therefore accommodate herself to her mother's needs. The infant does this through the development of a chameleon-like mantle, which crystallizes out over time into a false self.

The false self comes into existence, then, as the child's way of being in relation to the mother—that is, the false self becomes consolidated around the child's reactivity to the impinging object.

Winnicott (1960) likens the experience of having a mother who is not good-enough to the experience of looking in a mirror and seeing nothing.

The child will live, but the existence will be hollow, not genuine. It will be one based on compliance—the child doing and being what she senses is expected of her by others, responding and adapting to the needs of others, always reacting, no longer acting spontaneously, creatively, and in accordance with her own needs. The child will make a show of being real, but she will only be "as if" alive because it will all be a sham, a charade, a part she is playing, a borrowed identity assumed for the occasion.

The child will live, but the existence will be false. It will be one based on conformity, not on authenticity.

Modell (1975) describes the narcissistic defense against affects as a defense employed by the patient with relational deficit. Modell uses the metaphor of a cocoon to describe such a patient's internal experience of affective nonrelatedness. He speaks to the patient's need (present to some extent in all of us) to protect the self from the other, to protect the self from being shattered (or "fractured") by an unempathic response from the other. Modell believes that for such patients it is intolerable to communicate affect because to do so would be to betray desire—the desire for some kind of response from the other.

To defend herself against the possibility of further traumatic disappointment and heartache, the patient keeps important parts of herself out of relationship. Even as she longs to be known and understood, she must keep herself hidden—in order, Modell suggests, to preserve the integrity of a vulnerable self.

Finally, Miller (1988) believes, as do Guntrip and Modell, that at the core of human experience is the paradoxical yearning for connection even as there is the fear of being failed. The patient longs to make contact but keeps important parts of the self out of real engagement. Because of past hurts, disappointments, and violations, the patient has lost authenticity; she has learned that being herself is too risky.

Miller believes that both patient and therapist experience this same paradox about connection and disconnection. Patient and therapist must therefore struggle to understand the forces within each of them that stand in the way of mutual empathy and mutual empowerment.

In fact, Miller (and others at the Stone Center) believe that the basic process of therapy occurs because not only can the patient be moved by the therapist but also the therapist can be moved by the patient.

The goal of treatment is movement of the patient out of disconnection and isolation to connection and empowerment. It is an interactive process that involves empowering the patient so that she dares to risk exposure of her vulnerabilities and to acknowledge her underlying longing for connection. In order to accomplish this movement, the therapist must also dare to be authentic, vulnerable, and emotionally present.

In sum, the relational-deficit therapist understands the patient's impaired capacity to be in relationship as speaking to her fear of being now failed as she was once failed.

The Fear of Being Found

When the patient is seen as having relational deficit (perhaps the very same patient who, a moment earlier, had been seen as having relational conflict), the therapist must be willing to put herself out there and to make herself vulnerable in her pursuit of a patient who wants desperately to be engaged but is terrified of being found.

Modell (1975, 1980) speaks to the conflict such patients bring to the treatment situation when he suggests that the therapist must use her intuition to assess whether the patient wants to be found or is needing, in the moment, to remain hidden, not found. Modell reminds us that there are times when the patient does not want to be engaged by the therapist—and the therapist must respect this.

Along these same lines, Winnicott (1960) speaks to what is required of a good-enough mother. When her child is in an excited state and clamoring to have her needs met, the mother must be able to recognize and to respond to such needs. But there are times when her child is in a quiescent state and asking nothing of her mother but that she be there; at such times, the mother must be able to provide a nondemanding presence. In other words, the mother must be able to tolerate her child's needing nothing from her and, furthermore, must be able to be with her child without asking that the child accommodate herself to her mother.

So, too, the good-enough therapist must both meet her patient's needs when her patient is excited and be nondemandingly present when her patient is quiescent.

But Brian Bird (1972) cautions that, even so, the therapist should beware of allowing the patient to go unfound for too long. The ultimate abandonment of a patient may take place, Bird warns, when the therapist does not make "sufficient claim" on the patient and, instead, allows the patient to "destroy" her by rendering her therapeutically useless.

In the face of the patient's retreat, the therapist must demonstrate resilience and durability; she must be willing and able to fight for the relationship, to go out on a limb on the patient's behalf—because the patient is afraid and truly does not know how to bring herself into the room.

The patient with relational deficit will then have the profoundly healing experience of having been found.

I present the following in order to demonstrate the relational-deficit model in action.

Clinical Vignette—Impassioned Pursuit

Several years into my work with a patient whom I was seeing three times a week, the following occurred. One Saturday morning around 9:00 A.M., my patient (who had never before called me between sessions) left a message on my machine, in which she said that she really wanted to speak with me—if I could get back to her at some point within the next three hours.

As it happens, I did not pick up her message until Saturday afternoon. I tried then, and numerous other times over the course of the weekend, to reach her at the number she had given me (as well as at her home number), but to no avail.

When I saw her for our regularly scheduled appointment on Monday, she told me that she had called me because something important had come up for her that she had wanted very much to discuss with me, but that she had intentionally placed a time limit of noon on Saturday because, if I could not get back to her by then, she did not want to bother me during my weekend.

These years later, I do not remember the specifics of what prompted my patient to call me, but what I do still remember was my upset and my anger that she would have made it so difficult for me to come through for her—which had been the story of our three-year relationship. When I received her urgent call, I was deeply touched that she would have let herself reach out to me and I found myself wanting very much to be able to be there for her—indeed, she had been very much on my mind the entire weekend. And, yes, of course I knew that with respect to the time limit she had imposed, she had done the best she could—that it was very deeply a part of who she was that she would have needed not to presume upon anyone.

Even so, I was upset and angry that she had made it so hard for me to reach her. During our session on Monday, I remember pounding my fist on the arm of my chair and, in my frustration, practically shouting at her, "How could you not know that of course I would have wanted to be able to respond to your call!?"

She looked at me in surprise—partially, I'm sure, because of my somewhat uncharacteristic outburst and, partially, I believe, because I had caught her attention with what I was saying. Her response to my little meltdown was that she was truly amazed that it would have mattered to me that I be able to get back to her. She then began to cry softly because now, she said, she understood—in a way that she had never before understood—that I really did care about her.

I offer the above in order to demonstrate the power of the therapist's willingness to go out on a limb in order to make contact, even if it involves letting the patient see that the therapist is vulnerable and that something the patient has done has had an impact.

In fact, letting the patient see that she has had an impact empowers the patient; it enables her to know that she can affect someone.

I think that my reaction (particularly the pounding of my fist and my raised voice) was somewhat inappropriate for the occasion, but it was heartfelt and it was authentic. Furthermore, I think it both enabled my patient to experience just how deeply committed I was to her and highlighted the extent to which she had never really been able to register, internally, the fact of my love for her.

Clinical Vignette—Do You Fear My Being Attracted to You?

A supervisee of mine presented the following, which also speaks to how powerful it can be when the therapist is willing to go out on a limb in pursuit of a patient.

The patient was an attractive young man who had been coming to treatment because of his difficulty tolerating sustained intimacy with women. Of note was his unusually close relationship to his controlling mother. With respect to his therapist, he appeared to feel good about her, although he always kept himself somewhat at a remove from her.

Over time, the therapist became aware of a sexual charge in the air between them. The therapist therefore decided to be bold. With her heart in her throat, she asked him if he had ever found himself having any sexual feelings about her. The patient, with some hesitation, responded that he did not feel sexually attracted to her because she was not his type.

The therapist, able to preserve her good feelings about herself even in the face of her patient's "rejection" of her, managed somehow to get said: "Do you ever imagine that I might have sexual feelings about you?"

As it turns out, the patient had long feared that his therapist, like his mother before her, had a sexual hunger for him and wanted to control him. Prior to this point, he had never dared to tell the therapist of his fear.

Once this fear had been exposed to the light of day by his therapist's courageous intervention, the patient was freed up to talk about how frightened he had always been that the women in his life would want to devour him with their desire for him, and how diminished he had always felt in the face of their need to control him in this way.

Once the patient's fear had been named, it became easier for him to deliver his authentic self into the relationship with his therapist and the level of their engagement deepened considerably. Furthermore, as the patient got more and more in touch with just how outraged he was by his mother's intrusiveness, he became better able to sustain intimate contact with the other women in his life.

This example demonstrates the transformative power of a therapist's willingness to put herself out there on behalf of a patient who, frightened and angry, initially rebuffs her. The therapist's ability to pursue the patient, even so, enables the two of them to get to the bottom of what had been interfering with his ability to commit to the therapy relationship—namely, his fear that his therapist might try to possess him. It was this fear that had made it difficult for him to engage authentically in the therapy relationship (and, more generally, with women)—it was this fear that had fueled his relational deficit.

Clinical Vignette—Refusal to Be Daunted

I offer the following by way of further demonstrating the Model 3 therapist's use of herself to pursue a patient who wants desperately to be found, but who is afraid.

The patient, Marion, is a woman who had been in treatment for five years. Although over the course of that time the patient had made considerable progress in certain areas of her life, her major concern (namely, what amounted to a phobia about having sex) had never been effectively addressed and understood. Her therapist asked that I see Marion in consultation because the therapist was feeling that although she and Marion had a good relationship, there was a point of engagement beyond which they could not get.

I saw the patient in consultation. Interestingly, Marion's complaint about the therapy was that she was finding it increasingly difficult to feel that she was being torn apart inside during the therapy sessions and then to be left on her own with the pain until her next session. Marion was finding that in the therapy session itself she would be unable to cry, but each night, after her session, she would cry herself to sleep. She was haunted by the thought that she would be unable to have an intimate relationship with a man because of her fears of closeness and of intercourse.

In her session with me, she spoke at length about her father, a man who had been emotionally abusive to her. He would tease her mercilessly until she was in tears, and then he would laugh at her for crying; Marion would feel deeply ashamed for having given way to her tears. She went on to tell me she sometimes wished that her therapist would force her to talk more about her fears of intimacy and of sex. Marion expressed concern that her therapist might be afraid of her, intimidated by her. With anger, Marion recalled the many times her mother had faulted her for being a cold fish, selfish, nasty, provocative. Marion explained that when her therapist did not press her to "open up," she was left with the feeling that perhaps she was all those bad things her mother had accused her of being. "I want my therapist to call me on how closed I am. I want her to be tough. I don't want her to be put off by me when I get mean. I keep thinking to myself, 'Please, don't let me do this. Please, don't give up on me.'" It was becoming increasingly painful for her to continue in treatment because of how awful it was making her feel about herself.

As she continued to talk, it became clear that Marion hated the person she became when she was with her therapist—it really was way too much like the person her mother had always accused her of being. Because her therapist was neither insisting that she become more fully engaged in the treatment nor holding her accountable for her often provocative behavior, Marion was left with the horrible feeling that the therapist agreed with her mother that Marion was a bad person and, therefore, not salvageable.

In the consultation, I initially held back a bit, in order to get a feel for her and to decide how best to position myself in relation to her. The danger, of course, was that were I to push too much, I would run the risk of being too much like her father, who would push and push until he had brought his daughter to her knees. And yet were I not to push enough, I knew that I would then run the risk of being too much like her mother, who had never really been able to find her daughter.

But as the session progressed, I found myself becoming more aggressive in my efforts to reach her. I was beginning to realize that in order to engage Marion deeply, I might have to risk becoming some version of her controlling, humiliating father.

Because of scheduling constraints, Marion and I had originally agreed that instead of doing a three-session consultation (over the course of a week or two), we would do first a double session and then a single session. The only time we could find for the double session was in the late evening.

As we were nearing the end of our double session, Marion protested that she was getting very tired and wanted to stop the session a little early; she said she knew that she would be coming back for a follow-up session at the end of the week and perhaps we could finish up then.

I found myself telling her that I was not yet ready to stop, that our work for the evening had not yet been completed. She told me that my saying that made her feel cornered, trapped. But I did not relent: I told her that she was stuck—because I was between her and the door. (As it happens, she is a fairly large woman and I am a fairly small woman.)

Marion actually laughed in response to that and then, just as suddenly, became very sad. Softly, she protested, "I don't have it in me anymore. I'm on my own, and I just can't do it any longer." As she spoke of her exhaustion and of her despair, she began to sob—deep, heartrending sobs. As I listened, I could feel myself choking up as well.

Marion had let me in. I had had to do it by way of being a bit of a bully, a bit of a controlling, intimidating bully—but she had let me in. And she, no longer the cold, unfeeling fish, was now showing me her vulnerable, soft underside.

As she continued to cry, she became so much more accessible, so much more reachable. Her whole demeanor changed; her body relaxed, and at one point, she actually smiled at me through her tears. I smiled back through my own tears. She said that she had always wanted her therapist to make her cry; she explained, "I guess that's how my father showed me that he cared." Marion went on to say, "I have always wanted to be called on my toughness; I am not really cold and invulnerable." Interestingly, although her father had been abusive to her at times, Marion and I came to realize that her connection with him had always been more profound than her connection with her mother, who was so caught up in her own anxious concerns that she could never really be available to her daughter.

In pushing Marion as I had, in being (for the moment) her bullying, controlling, intimidating father, I had been able at last to reach her. I had been willing to take a risk on her behalf—she could feel that and appreciated it. Admittedly, in doing what I did, I initially became her old bad object (her bad father); but both by letting her know that I was committed to doing whatever I needed to do in order to reach her and by letting her see my own vulnerability and softness in response to her having finally let me in, I was demonstrating that I was not ultimately as bad or as humiliating as her father had been. I was giving her the corrective relational experience of bad-become-good.

As I later reconstructed it, it seemed to me that one way to understand what had happened in the interactive dynamic between us was a projective identification. Marion was unconsciously trying to find me by pressuring me to become her bad, controlling, intimidating father—a role I initially refused but eventually allowed myself to be drawn into accepting. Simultaneously, even if paradoxically, Marion was indicating that it was for me to stay out of her face, to hold back, to respect her need to keep me at bay; in essence, there was a part of her that was needing me to be her distant, emotionally unavailable mother. Knowing in advance from Marion's therapist about the potential dangers of going down that road gave me the courage to be more bold in my pursuit of Marion, even though it meant becoming (at least for a while) like her intrusive father.

When I later spoke to her therapist, I suggested that I thought the therapist, motivated by her desire to avoid being like Marion's bullying father, had inadvertently slipped into a still less tenable role—namely, that of Marion's distant, emotionally unavailable mother. I went on to say that I thought she and Marion would be able to find each other only once she could allow herself to be aggressive in her pursuit of

Marion—even if that meant forcing herself on Marion. But I thought this route would be better than holding back—thereby recapitulating for Marion the early-on experience of not being found. I said I believed that Marion needed to have the corrective relational experience of being engaged in an intimate relationship by someone who was not afraid—and that this would go a long way toward freeing Marion up with respect to being able to tolerate sustained intimacy with a male partner.

I present the above example because it speaks to how important it is that the therapist allow herself to be drawn into participating in a certain way by a patient who is needing her to be that way in order to feel truly engaged. It will then be in the context of the here-and-now engagement between patient and therapist (engagement involving mutual enactment) that the patient's issues can be addressed, as both patient and therapist examine the part each has played in what has unfolded between them. Model 3 gives permission to patient and therapist to do what they must in order to find each other.

CHAPTER

9

The Therapist as Authentic Subject

On the one hand, when we say that the Model 2 therapist participates as an empathic selfobject (in self psychology) or a good object–good mother (in Model 2 object relations theories), the emphasis is on the therapist's ability to offer the patient the experience of being met and held.

As an empathic selfobject, the therapist provides empathic recognition of the patient's need; as a good object–good mother, the therapist may do a little more than simply recognize the patient's need—she may respond to the patient by offering, say, gratification of the patient's need, much as a good mother, having recognized her child's need, responds in a way that enables her child to feel truly met.

But whether she participates as empathic selfobject or as good object–good mother, the Model 2 therapist (having decentered from her own experience in order not to contaminate, with her own subjectivity, her availability to the patient) operates from a position of "selflessness"—offering the patient whatever form of corrective provision the patient would seem to need in order to grow.

On the other hand, when we say that the Model 3 therapist participates as an authentic subject, the emphasis is on the therapist's ability to stay centered within her experience of self (within her own subjectivity), using herself to offer the patient the experience of being contained (when her focus is on the patient's relational conflict) and of being found (when her focus is on the patient's relational deficit). Whereas the Model 2 therapist decenters from the self (and is therefore selfless), the Model 3 therapist always remains very much centered within herself.

And so it is that whereas the Model 3 therapist remains firmly grounded in (and ever true to) her own experience of self, the Model 2 therapist—in the interest of giving the patient what the therapist senses the patient needs—must sometimes be willing to sacrifice her own truth for the sake of "doing the right thing" for the patient. Just as a mother who has been awakened from a sound slumber by her infant's wails must put aside her own need for sleep in order to offer her infant solace, so, too, a Model 2 therapist must be willing to step away from her own need in order to offer her patient the corrective experience the patient needs in order to get better.

In essence, the therapist who embraces a deficiency-compensation model of therapeutic action conceives of her "role" as the offering of some form of corrective provision; she gives, and her patient takes.

INTERNAL VERSUS RELATIONAL DYNAMICS

Earlier I had referred to the patient's internal dynamics (the province of the Model 1 therapist) and the patient's relational dynamics (the province of the Model 3 therapist). I would like now to elaborate further upon the distinction between the two.

When we speak of the patient's internal dynamics, we are referring to the internal workings of the patient's mind—that is, to how the patient's internal world is structured or configured. When we speak of the patient's relational dynamics, however, we are referring to what the patient plays out (or enacts) in relationship—to what the patient actually delivers of herself (and her internal dynamics) into her relationships with others.

In other words, whereas the patient's internal dynamics are about what goes on within the patient, the patient's relational dynamics are about what goes on between the patient and the people with whom she interacts. The way in which the patient engages interactively with her therapist in the here-and-now creates opportunities for the two of them to experience, firsthand, what the patient delivers of herself into relationships.

Clinical Vignette—Enactment of Competitiveness

Let us consider the situation of a patient who struggles to overcome her competitive feelings toward other women.

If the therapist's focus is on the patient's (internal) conflict between the competitive impulses she experiences and her need to deny the existence of such impulses (because their presence makes her feel anxious or guilty), then we speak of the therapist as a Model 1 therapist and of her focus as on the patient's internal dynamics.

Once the patient delivers her competitiveness into the relationship with her therapist (as happened in the case of Janet described above—whose parting shot to her therapist was "Great tan, bitch!"), then what had once been an internal dynamic now becomes a relational dynamic—that is, something that the patient is playing out (or enacting) in the here-and-now engagement with her therapist. What had once been a story about the patient now becomes a story about the relationship between patient and therapist.

Janet's enactment had an impact on the therapist who, initially taken aback, was subsequently able to recover her balance and, thereby, her therapeutic effectiveness; the therapist was then able to recognize Janet's competitive provocativeness as an effort to communicate to the therapist something important about Janet's internal dynamics—something that the therapist, prior to that point, had not fully appreciated.

When the therapist's focus is on what the patient is playing out (or enacting) in the relationship with her therapist, then we speak of the therapist as a Model 3 therapist and of her focus as on the patient's relational dynamics.

Clinical Vignette—Perhaps I Should Come Less Often

Let us consider the situation of a patient who struggles to overcome her fear of dependency on the therapist.

When the patient is articulating her fear about becoming dependent on the therapist, she is revealing something about her internal dynamics. If she goes on to say that she has been thinking about coming every other week (instead of every week), she is delivering her fear into the relationship.

As long as the patient is simply talking about how concerned she is that she might come to need her therapist too much, the therapist can easily resonate empathically with the patient's expressed concern. In an effort to help the patient gain insight into the genetic underpinnings of that fear, the therapist might encourage the patient to think about whether or not her fear is a familiar feeling and, if so, in what context it originally arose.

But once the patient delivers her ambivalence into the room by suggesting that she might want to start coming every other week, the therapist may have more difficulty staying with the patient in her experience because the therapist, in response to the patient's enactment, may find herself feeling worried and, perhaps, somewhat annoyed. The therapist's response of discomfort and irritation suggests that the therapist has now been drawn into participating in the patient's enactment. But if the therapist is able to step back from her countertransferential participation in the patient's transferential enactment, then she may be able to use the feelings engendered in her by the patient's interpersonally provocative behavior to inform her understanding of just how frightened (and angry) the patient may really be—at her (the therapist), or perhaps at a parent.

When the patient is simply talking about her fear (which, although experienced in relation to the therapist, does not actually involve the therapist nor therefore have a particular impact on the therapist), this is an instance of an internal dynamic. Perhaps the patient's fear of dependency derives from traumatogenic experiences she had had with her father, who had shamed her for having desire in relation to him.

But once the patient does something in the therapy relationship because of her fear (which now does directly involve the therapist and therefore does have an impact on the therapist), this is an instance of a relational dynamic. Perhaps the patient's difficulty sitting with discomfort and fear prompts her to do things in relationships that alienate and distance others.

To repeat, once the patient delivers her internal dynamics into the here-and-now engagement with her therapist, then what had once been internal becomes relational and what had once belonged to Model 1 belongs now to Model 3. Where once the therapist was a detached (even if sympathetic) observer of the patient's internal process, now the therapist finds herself caught up in the patient's enactment—no longer just an observer but now a participant too.

CORRECTIVE EMOTIONAL EXPERIENCE VERSUS CORRECTIVE RELATIONAL EXPERIENCE

As we had earlier noted, the Model 2 therapist offers some form of corrective provision that enables the patient either to feel validated and understood (the emphasis in self psychology) or, more generally, to have a corrective—emotional—experience (the emphasis in Model 2 object relations theories).

I would like now to suggest that the Model 3 therapist who offers the patient the experience of being contained (when the emphasis is on the patient's relational conflict) or the experience of being found (when the emphasis is on the patient's relational deficit) is able to give the patient a corrective—relational—experience.

Whereas a corrective emotional experience relates to the patient's experience of being held by an empathic selfobject or a good object/good mother, a corrective relational experience relates to the patient's experience of engaging interactively with an authentic subject. In Model 2, the therapist is thought to "give" the patient a corrective emotional experience; in Model 3, patient and therapist are thought to participate in a relationship characterized by "give-and-take," mutuality, and reciprocity—the net result of which is a corrective relational experience for the patient.

KNOWLEDGE VERSUS EXPERIENCE

Whereas a drive-conflict model involves enhancement of the patient's knowledge of her internal dynamics and a deficiency-compensation model involves the therapist's provision of the patient with a corrective emotional experience, a relational (interactive) model involves both knowledge and experience—both enhancement of the patient's knowledge of her relational dynamics (to which I refer as relational insight [Susan Gottlieb 1997, personal communication]) and the provision of the patient with a corrective relational experience (either of being contained when relational conflict is in the spotlight or of being found when relational deficit assumes center stage).

In Model 3, therefore, both knowledge and experience are involved—but it is in the context of a relationship between two co-participating subjects, both of whom are thought to shape what goes on in the space between them.

In Model 1, the knowledge (that the patient gains) relates to her internal dynamics. In Model 2, the experience (that the patient has) is a consequence of being met by an empathic selfobject or of being held by a good object—what has been described in the literature as a corrective emotional experience. In Model 3, the knowledge (that the patient gains) relates to her relational dynamics; and the experience (that the patient has) is a consequence of the give-and-take in a relationship characterized by mutuality and reciprocity—to which I am referring as a corrective relational experience.

In other words, the relational therapist believes that sometimes it is simply the experience of being engaged itself that is healing for the patient. But sometimes what is healing is the knowledge the patient acquires about herself and her relational dynamics by way of being so engaged.

THE THERAPIST'S CAPACITY

When relational conflict is in the limelight, the therapist's capacity to be malleable is emphasized. The therapist must be receptive, or permeable, to the patient's projections; she must allow herself to be drawn into participating with the patient in her enactments, so that the patient can have the experience of delivering all of herself into the room and discovering that both she and her therapist survive. The therapist must allow herself to be responsive to the roles imposed on her by the patient, so that the patient can have the opportunity to master her internal demons.

The therapist must be neither impermeable to the patient's projections (because if she is simply an observer, she will never be available to the patient as a participant) nor too permeable to the patient's projections (because if she is too much a participant, she may never be available to the patient as an observer). The optimal stance is one that involves semipermeability—the therapist allowing herself to be impacted upon but not completely taken over.

Then, once the therapist has been drawn into participating countertransferentially with the patient in the latter's transferential enactments, it will be crucial that the therapist have the capacity to recognize the fact of such participation and then to relent, if need be. It will be as the therapist recovers her objectivity that she will come to appreciate just how involved she has been; by the same token, it will be as the therapist comes to appreciate just how involved she has been that she will begin to recover her objectivity.

In any event, in working with patients who demonstrate relational conflict, the therapist must have (1) the capacity to relinquish her objectivity (as she allows her countertransferential response to be shaped by the patient's transferential activity) and (2) the capacity to wend her way out of her participation in the patient's enactment (so that she can recover her objectivity and, thereby, her therapeutic effectiveness).

When relational deficit is in the limelight, the therapist's capacity to go out on a limb on the patient's behalf is emphasized. The Model 3 therapist must allow herself to be vulnerable to the patient, so that the patient will not be in the untenable position of being the only person in the room who is vulnerable. Ever respectful of the patient's fear of being found, the therapist must nonetheless be also responsive to the patient's need to be found. The therapist may even need to become relentless in her pursuit of the patient, if the patient is ever to be reached.

In working with patients who demonstrate relational deficit, the therapist must hold in her mind the delicate balance between respecting who the patient is in the moment and having a vision of who the patient could become in the future (were the patient to let herself be found). In the first instance, the therapist must simply be with the patient where she is; in the second instance, the therapist may need to direct the patient's attention elsewhere, if the patient is ever to realize her potential.

The patient's fear is that she will put herself out there and not be found. It may well be that the patient with relational deficit can bring herself into the room only when the therapist herself is willing to take that risk. In other words, if the therapist finds herself lamenting the fact that her patient is not fully present, it may behoove the therapist to consider seriously the ways in which she herself may not be fully present. If the therapist has the capacity to bring more of herself into the relationship, it may then be possible for the patient with relational deficit to come a little more into the room as well.

HERE-AND-NOW ENGAGEMENT

In any event, whether the patient demonstrates relational conflict, relational deficit, or, more generally, an impaired capacity for relatedness because of fear that she brings from her past, the Model 3 therapist believes that what the patient most needs in the here-and-now is an opportunity to work through her fear by way of engaging, and being engaged by, an authentic other in a real relationship.

Whether the therapist participates as an old bad object (responding to pressure exerted by a patient who has the need to be failed), or, more generally, whether the therapist participates as an authentic subject (bringing her "real" self into the room and allowing her experience to be shaped by what happens there), the emphasis in Model 3 is always on the importance of the therapist's availability for authentic participation with the patient in the therapeutic encounter. Whereas the empathic perspective emphasizes the importance of affective attunement, the relational perspective emphasizes the importance of authentic engagement—or, in Guntrip's (1969) words, "moments of real meeting" (p. 353).

As Mitchell (1988) has observed:

> Unless the analyst affectively enters the patient's relational matrix or, rather, discovers himself within it—unless the analyst is in some sense charmed by the patient's entreaties, shaped by the patient's projections, antagonized and frustrated by the patient's defenses—the treatment is never fully engaged, and a certain depth within the analytic experience is lost. [p. 293]

In other words, whereas the empathic therapist decenters from her own experience in order to be available to the patient, the relational therapist believes that she can only be truly available to the patient if she remains very much centered within herself as a real person, drawing upon what it feels like to be in relationship with the patient to inform her understanding of the patient and the way the patient engages with her.

Relational therapists believe in the curative power of the relationship itself—relationship that involves authenticity, spontaneity, mutuality, reciprocity, and collaboration. It is a relationship that involves two subjects, both of whom are thought to have their own subjectivity, their own personal universe, their own unique experience.

Whereas the interpretive stance emphasizes the importance of the therapist's objectivity and the empathic stance emphasizes the importance of the patient's subjectivity, the relational stance emphasizes the importance of the intersubjective field—the intersection of the patient's and the therapist's subjectivities.

The relational therapist believes that the therapeutic work involves working and playing within the context of the patient–therapist relationship, the relational matrix, the transference–countertransference entanglement, the intersubjective field—ever appreciating that both patient and therapist can have an impact on each other.

The relational perspective has it that what is curative for the patient is neither enhanced knowledge (of the patient's internal dynamics) nor corrective provision. Rather, what is curative is the experience of finding, and being found by, a therapist who is not afraid—a therapist who is not afraid to be used by the patient as a container for the patient's disavowed psychic gunk, a therapist who is not afraid to put herself out there on behalf of a patient who is keeping herself out of relationship—a therapist who is able to use her authentic self to engage, and to be engaged by, the patient.

I present the following vignette in order to demonstrate the therapist's use of self to locate and to be located by the patient. Sara has, over time, become very dear to me, although our journey has by no means been easy.

Clinical Vignette—A Moment of Real Meeting (My Tears and Hers)

I have been seeing Sara, an extraordinarily gifted 55-year-old physicist, three or four times a week for the past four years.

Four years ago, at the very beginning of our work together, I said something to Sara that made her feel I did not want to work with her. (I apologize for not being able to share the specifics of what I actually said—but Sara asked me not to. She did, however, give me permission to share the rest.)

In any event, Sara considers what I said to her in our third session those four years ago to have been a mistake for which she will never be able to forgive me—although she desperately wishes that she could.

At the time, I was horrified that Sara would have so "misunderstood" what I was saying; but given what I have since come to know about her, I can now appreciate why what I said was deeply hurtful to her.

Over the course of our years together, Sara has spent much time trying to decide whether or not she feels safe enough to continue our work. She fears she may never be able to trust me (and that she should therefore terminate) because she feels so hurt by the mistake I made—and so unable to forgive me.

Although periodically I have attempted to clarify (rather defensively I think) what I had thought I was trying to say in our third session those four years ago, Sara has understandably not been all that interested in listening and has held fast to her experience of me as untrustworthy and of the therapy as a place that is not safe—certainly not safe enough to bring her pain, her tears, her anger, her loneliness.

Over time, what Sara and I have come to understand about our dynamic is that we have unwittingly re-created, between us, the powerfully tormenting relationship that she and her toxic mother had when Sara was very young. At times, Sara is her toxic mother and I am the Sara who, as a little girl, was tormented by her double-binding mother. At other times, I am her toxic mother and Sara is tormented by me as she was once tormented by her mother.

In my work with Sara, it has been extremely important to her that I be able to confirm her experience of things—not just that I validate her perceptions as "plausible constructions" of reality (Hoffman 1983) but that I actually confirm them. In other words, Sara needs me to agree that her reality is "the truth." Otherwise, she begins to feel crazy.

Almost without fail I have been able to confirm Sara's perceptions, most of which have seemed to me to be uncannily on target. I will say things like: "From what you're saying, indeed it would seem that your husband behaved abominably." Sara has appreciated my willingness to confirm the reality of her experience.

Unfortunately, some of her uncannily accurate perceptions have been about me. Although it is more difficult when the focus is on me and my vulnerabilities, ultimately (with one exception) I have been able (and willing) to confirm these perceptions as well.

I offer the following as an example of how she will zero in on me: When recently she came to a session and asked to schedule a number of extra sessions, I was obviously very pleased (I actually said something to the effect of, "Yes! Yes! Yes!"). Indeed it meant a great deal to me that she would want the extra time, despite her experience of me as having failed her so unforgivably early on in our relationship.

We spent some time scheduling the extra sessions and then I said, gently: "You know I am so pleased to be scheduling additional appointments, but it occurs to me that I should be asking you how you feel about having these extra sessions."

Sara did not answer for a long time. After what seemed like an eternity to me, she said finally, sadly, that she was now not sure the extra sessions were such a good idea after all; she said that she was suddenly feeling that maybe I did not really want her to be coming for the additional appointments.

Although I was initially stunned at her response, in time she helped me to understand something about myself that I had not previously understood: By asking Sara to share with me how she felt about having the extra sessions, I was, in a way, humiliating her. Obviously she would not have asked for the extra time if a part of her had not wanted the additional contact with me. For me to be now asking of her that she admit to wanting more time with me was to shame her for having desire in relation to me. Had I, in advance, thought more about my somewhat formulaic question, then I would probably have known not to ask it.

What I now understood was that in asking her to tell me how she had felt about getting the extra time, I really was more going by the book than coming from my heart. I really was more going by what I had been taught (namely, to explore whatever underlying expectations, hopes, or fears the patient might have had about asking for something from her therapist) than by what I really did know—namely, that despite Sara's deep reservations about me, a part of her was beginning to trust me a little more and was wanting me to know this without her having to say it right out.

Indeed, I came to see that Sara's experience of me as having humiliated her was not just a story about her but also a story about me. I was able to understand that I really was shaming her by asking of her that she acknowledge wanting to have extra time with me.

Sara has been a wonderful teacher—she has devoted considerable time and energy to teaching me to be a better therapist to her and, in all honesty, a better therapist period. I am so much wiser for my time with her. I am increasingly coming to see how often I will unconsciously fall back on going by the book instead of coming from my heart—not always in big ways, but in little ways (some of the rituals, some of the routines that I will do without really thinking them through).

This we have accomplished.

But there has been between us an ongoing issue that we have not yet been able to resolve—and that is what to do with respect to the unforgivable mistake I made those several years ago about which I feel absolutely terrible and for which I have apologized many times over from the bottom of my soul.

Periodically Sara will turn to me and ask, point-blank, that I confirm her perception of me as having failed her unforgivably in that third session four years ago. And, over the years, she has made it very clear that were I to confirm that perception, she would have no choice but to terminate her treatment with me. On the other hand, when I do not confirm that perception, then she feels she has no choice but to continue to feel unsafe with me.

When Sara and I get into this place, as we have many times over the course of our years together, my mind almost snaps from the pressure of how crazy-making the whole thing is. In wishing, deep within me, that Sara would someday both trust me and forgive me, I know that I put Sara in an untenable position. But by the same token, Sara, in asking of me that I confirm her perception of me as untrustworthy and of my early-on mistake as unforgivable, puts me in an untenable position. I ask of Sara something that she cannot do; she asks of me something that I cannot do.

It is indeed agony for us both, yes. But I think we are doing the work that needs to be done—namely, attempting to negotiate our way through and out of an intensely powerful, mutually torturing, hopelessly enmeshed relationship that is a re-creation of the toxic relationship she had with her mother. It is a mutual enactment in we which both are participating.

But by way of the drama that has been reenacted between us, Sara is enabling me to experience, firsthand, what the experience must have been like for her in relation to her mother.

There has, as yet, been no resolution to our dilemma. The experience for both of us is excruciatingly painful, even as it is telling—telling us a great deal about the mutually tormenting, convoluted, double-binding, no-win situation she had with her mother. We need someday to find our way out of this Catch-22 situation, but, for now, we must both sit with the uncertainty of not knowing what will ultimately unfold.

The other day, however, something different did happen. Sara was once again begging me to admit that what I had said to her those numbers of years ago was unforgivable. As I listened, I found myself feeling so sad, so trapped, so anguished, and so tormented that I suddenly burst into tears. I rested my head in my hands and just sobbed. Sara sat there very still, barely breathing, watching, waiting. Eventually I stopped, and we continued our talking. This time I knew not to ask her the pat question: "How was it for you, my crying?"

But later in the session, I think she showed me what it must have been like for her. She herself began to cry—she put her head in her hands and wept. I sat there very still, barely breathing, watching, waiting. What made it particularly poignant for me was that I knew that as an adult she had never before cried in front of anyone.

Our work continues.

CHAPTER 10

The Therapist's Use of Self

I want now to focus more specifically on how the relational therapist uses her authentic self (that is, uses her countertransference) to find, and to be found by, the patient.

As noted earlier, Ehrenberg (1974) writes about working at the intimate edge between patient and therapist. She suggests that when the therapist has been either too bold or too cautious, patient and therapist will be unable to find each other. It will then be the process of focusing on, and making explicit, the "gulf" between them that will bridge that space and transform it into an intimate edge.

By way of example, Ehrenberg (1984) was seeing in treatment a mute child of 3 who was thought to be retarded. Over time, Ehrenberg found herself becoming increasingly frustrated in her efforts to make contact with the child. And so one day, in exasperation, Ehrenberg blurted out: "I feel at a total loss. I don't know how you feel but I feel so terrible I want to scream and I am going to." And Ehrenberg did.

The child, Ehrenberg reports, lost her glazed look—and, at that point, the real therapeutic engagement began. Ehrenberg had used herself to find her patient.

As we have said repeatedly, the Model 3 therapist believes that she can be truly available to the patient only if she remains centered within her own experience and allows herself to be impacted upon by the patient.

When the therapist allows herself to be shaped by the patient's need for her to participate in certain ways, the therapist is no longer simply observing but also participating, no longer just "understanding" but "enacting" as well. Irwin Hirsch (1987) has aptly described the relational therapist as an "observing-participant" (p. 209).

The therapist must eventually be able to work her way out of what has become a mutual enactment; she must be able to recover her objectivity and, thereby, her therapeutic effectiveness so that patient and therapist can go on to explore the interactive dynamic that had transpired in the space between them.

There is a paradox involved here. It is by means of recovering her objectivity that the therapist is able to wend her way out, although it is by means of wending her way out that the therapist is able to recover her objectivity—only to be drawn back in once again.

And so we might say of the Model 3 therapist that she shifts back and forth, back and forth, between participation and observation, involvement and detachment.

The successful handling of the therapist's countertransferential participation in the patient's transferential enactments is a matter of balance: the therapist must be sufficiently open that she can be drawn into participating with the patient in her enactments and yet secure enough within herself to preserve a perspective that enables her to have some understanding of what has been mutually enacted in the relationship.

The Model 3 therapist must be able to shift back and forth—to be sometimes a participant and sometimes an observer. Merton Gill (1987) speaks to this positioning of the therapist when he suggests that the relational therapist alternates between periods of "unwitting enactment" (in which the therapist falls into transference–countertransference patterns) and "witting interpretation" of such enactment (p. 259).

When the Model 3 therapist has the wisdom to recognize the part she has been playing in what has become a mutual enactment, the integrity to acknowledge it (certainly to herself and perhaps to the patient as well), and the ability to use her participation in a way that will be analytically useful to the patient, then both patient and therapist will be able to deepen their engagement as well as to advance the patient's understanding of what she brings of herself to her relationships.

Clinical Vignette—Reaching the Therapist's Hate

As an example of something the patient might deliver of herself into the transference and the therapist's response to it, Winnicott (1947) writes about the patient's need to be able to elicit "objective hate" from her therapist. Sometimes the patient can believe in being loved only after reaching being hated. He writes: "in certain stages of certain analyses the analyst's hate is actually sought by the patient, and what is then needed is hate that is objective. If the patient seeks objective or justified hate he must be able to reach it, else he cannot feel he can reach objective love" (p. 199).

I would like to present a piece of my work with Ann, a woman with whom (over the course of the years) I have been to hell and back many times over. Although she inevitably relents, there have been a number of occasions when she has been extremely difficult—and I have hated her. Ann and I have come to understand that when she doesn't always get her way, she will express her outrage by "acting like a big baby" or, even, "behaving like a fuckin' asshole."

Ann can indeed be tough. But she is also someone I love very deeply—and she knows this.

Every now and then, however, she forgets.

One day, when she was feeling particularly shaky, she asked me if I would be willing to write down in her journal that I loved her, so that she would have a permanent record, would have something to hold on to. At Ann's prompting, I therefore wrote, "I love you very, very much." And I signed it.

She studied it carefully and, very pleased, left the session.

But when she returned several days later, she said she had done a lot of thinking and had decided that what she really wanted to see in writing was that I loved her despite all the "bad" stuff, despite all the "ugly" stuff that I knew about her.

So I took her journal once again and wrote, "I love you very, very much, even though sometimes you act like a big baby and sometimes you behave like a fuckin' asshole." Again I signed it.

Ann was delighted with this and carries around with her, to this day, the little scrap of paper on which it is written.

In reaching my hate, Ann was able to reach, and to believe in, my love.

I present the following vignette in order to demonstrate the relational therapist's use of self to engage the patient and the opportunity this use of self then affords the therapist to hold the patient more accountable for her provocative behavior—accountability that also empowers the patient.

Clinical Vignette—Sadistic Enactment

At the end of an hour, a patient of mine, Jane, with whom I had been working once a week for two years, announced rather offhandedly and after the fact, that she had started to see a psychic healer who was also a hypnotherapist. I was surprised and somewhat taken aback. It was both the fact of it (namely, that she would have done something like this without first discussing it with me) and the very casual, almost flip way she mentioned it that got to me. Without much thought, I pressed her: "Had you thought about bringing it up in here first?"

Jane immediately, and angrily, remonstrated that she thought it was unprofessional for me to be having personal feelings about her desire to see another kind of therapist. She reminded me that her therapy was not supposed to be about me and my feelings, but about her. She went on to say that, as I obviously knew, she had been working on becoming more comfortable with being autonomous and so needed me to offer not disapproval, but support for decisions she was making independently of me.

We were now out of time. Whereas before I had felt taken aback, I now felt quite angry.

The next session I opened by saying that I wanted to pick up where we had left off the previous week. I said a number of things. Jane appeared to be listening intently to all that I said—although, at least initially, she said nothing whatsoever in response.

First of all, I told her that I was certainly willing to think about whether or not my response to her announcement the week before about her session with the other therapist had been inappropriate or out of line.

I granted that I knew my reaction had been rather dramatic and that if it had been inappropriately so, I did want to apologize.

But I went on to say: "It occurs to me that something important happened in here between us last week—something difficult for both of us, something in which both of us had a part, both of us participated. We both behaved somewhat uncharacteristically. You did something that seemed to me to be different from your usual behavior and it upset me—it caused me pain. I then did something that seemed to you to be different from my usual behavior and it upset you—it caused you pain."

Over the course of the first fifteen minutes or so, I also observed: "I can't shake the idea that last week, when you said what you did in the way that you did, you were trying to show me something, trying to communicate something important to me—something that you might have felt I did not yet fully understand about you." When I said this, I wasn't even quite sure what I meant, but it did seem to me that Jane was attempting to convey something important to me that she might have been at a loss to convey in any way other than by way of a provocative enactment.

Christopher Bollas (1987) has suggested that although the therapist may not know with certainty what is going on in the interaction between them, it may nonetheless be useful to the patient for the therapist to share with the patient some aspect of what is going on within the therapist (in reaction to the patient). The patient must, however, understand that such countertransferential disclosures are in the nature of "reports" from within the therapist and are done in the spirit of furthering the analytic endeavor—they are not intended to be taken as "the truth."

At one point, I also remarked to Jane, "It occurs to me that you did to me something that had been done at some time in your life to you." At another point, I suggested, "I wonder if the surprise and the hurt I felt in response to what you were saying—particularly in light of how open I had been feeling toward you—I wonder if those aren't feelings you've had in the past in relation to somebody you've cared about."

For a long time, Jane just listened as I struggled to make sense of things from my end. Finally, she remarked: "You know, when I was talking to you last time, I remember feeling that I was outside myself; I was watching myself and could see myself being sadistic to you in much the same way that my brother used to be sadistic to me."

I was blown away by the content of what she was saying and by her willingness to let me know this about her. I was also deeply touched that she would have been able to relent in the way that she was now doing.

I thanked Jane from the bottom of my heart for having allowed us to see this part of her that she must (on some level) always have known was there—without ever having thought it. I am here reminded of

Bollas's "unthought known"—the patient may know something about her early experience in relation to an important other but may not yet have organized it in the form of words. Says Bollas (1987) of the unthought known, "the patient knows something, but has as yet been unable to think it" (p. 235).

I also thanked Jane for her integrity and for her willingness to reflect upon her piece in what had transpired between us, thereby taking ownership of it.

We then did indeed begin to look at something we had never before really considered—namely, her own sadism. Yes, we had spoken often of Jane's masochism but never, specifically, of her sadism. We had explored in some detail the tortured relationship she had with her boyfriend (a narcissistic young man whom she was relentlessly pursuing because she was unwilling to take his no for an answer), but we had never examined her relentless outrage, and her subsequent abusiveness, in the face of his refusal to say yes to her.

With respect to what Jane and I were mutually enacting in our relationship: on the one hand, when I (in response to her casually rendered announcement that she had decided to pursue treatment with a psychic healer/hypnotherapist) demanded to know why Jane had not brought it up with me first, I was probably responding with an unnecessary degree of vehemence and counteraggression. On the other hand, what Jane and I came to understand was that by behaving so provocatively in the first place, she had set me up from the start to fail her; my feelings of upset and anger were therefore, in part, an understandable reaction to her "disrespecting" of me.

We further came to understand that when Jane had not gotten from me the approval she was seeking, she had then delivered her rageful disappointment into the therapy relationship, thereby exposing both of us to the sadism she had never before dared to acknowledge to anyone, not even herself.

In other words, Jane had set me up to fail her; and then, when I did indeed fail her by overreacting to her announcement about her decision to work with the psychic healer, she unleashed a torrent of abuse toward me.

In retrospect, it occurs to me that my earlier reluctance to recognize this aspect of Jane's character might have made it more difficult for her to address the issue of her sadism. It could have been my resistance to seeing her sadism that made it necessary for her to enact it in the transference with me.

Once this aspect of her psychology had been revealed, Jane felt both horrified and tremendously relieved. On the one hand, it dismayed her to recognize that she could be hurtful to others in the way that her brother had been hurtful to her; on the other hand, it was something Jane had always (deep within her) known about herself—and now that it was out in the open between us, Jane was able to be more real, to feel more integrated, and to be more present with me. Our connection became much deeper once we had come to know about her sadism and had demonstrated our ability to survive it.

Later still, Jane was to say to me: "I guess I also now understand, from your reaction, that you really do care about me and are deeply invested in our work—which means a lot to me." She then began to weep softly.

By putting myself out there in the way that I had, I was signaling my refusal to allow her to render me therapeutically useless to her; I was prepared and willing to fight to preserve our relationship. Equally importantly, I was showing Jane that I was up to the task of holding her accountable for her provocative behavior in relation to me, which was ultimately very reassuring to Jane because it enabled her to feel contained.

Near the end of the session, Jane remarked, with some surprise: "So it's like I put feelings into you that I have lived with and can't handle. In that way I get you to experience them firsthand. But you were then able to stand up for yourself—which is something I have never been able to do."

Interestingly, Jane then remembered that over the course of the previous week, she herself had been able to stand up to her landlord, thereby reclaiming some of her own power.

Indeed, it was a very powerful session for us both. Such sessions speak very poignantly to the transformative power of an interactive model in which the relationship itself (and the negotiation of its vicissitudes) is used as a vehicle for therapeutic change and for empowering the patient.

Subsequent to the session just cited, Jane has been much more easily able to recognize those situations in which either she is being abused or she herself is being abusive.

CHAPTER 11

Mutual Recognition

Wilfred Bion (1967) once made the succinct remark that when two people get together, they make a relationship whether they like it or not; this applies to all encounters, including of course what transpires in the therapy room.

Although most theories of development, such as Margaret Mahler's (1967) separation-individuation theory, have emphasized the goal of autonomy rather than relatedness to others, some theorists are becoming increasingly interested in the relatively unexplored territory of how it is that two subjects find each other and come to recognize each other as separate entities—something Benjamin (1988, 1992) describes as development of the capacity for mutual recognition.

Let us first address the subject's need to be recognized.

Benjamin (1988) speaks to how important it is for the subject to be able to know that she can elicit a response from the other—to which Benjamin refers as the baby's (or the patient's) need for recognition. Benjamin (1988) notes, "Increasingly, research reveals infants to be active participants who help shape the responses of their environment, and 'create' their own objects" (p. 16). It is crucial that a baby be able to know that she has had such an impact, because it will be experiences like this that will enable her to develop a sense of personal agency. As Benjamin (1992) observes, "Mother's recognition is the basis for the baby's sense of agency" (p. 48).

Elsewhere Benjamin (1988) writes, "The subject declares, 'I am, I do,' and then waits for the response, 'You are, you have done'" (p. 21).

Benjamin speaks not only to the subject's need to be recognized by the other but also to the subject's need to recognize the other. She believes that the capacity to recognize the existence of the other as a separate center of subjective experience is a developmental achievement.

The process by which the child develops the capacity to recognize the other as a subject in her own right is described by Benjamin (1988) as follows: "When I act upon the other it is vital that he be affected, so that I know that I exist—but not completely destroyed, so that I know he also exists" (p. 38).

Interestingly, many years earlier Winnicott (1969)—although in somewhat different terms—was speaking to this same issue when he wrote about development of the child's capacity for "ruth." The capacity for ruth derives, he suggested, from the capacity to recognize the other as a separate subject, a separate entity with its own inner world, its own experience, and its own center of initiative. Prior to development of the capacity for ruth is the state of ruthlessness, or pre-concern, when the other (mother) is not recognized as a person in her own right.

Winnicott hypothesizes that the child comes to experience mother as a person in her own right by way of discovering that mother survives the child's attempts to destroy her.

For example, the infant is presented with a noxious stimulus. The infant closes her eyes for a moment in order to be rid of it. Upon reopening her eyes, she discovers, with a mixture of horror and relief, that the object is still there. Repeated experiences of this kind force the child, over time, to abrogate some of her omnipotence and to recognize the externality of objects, the existence of things outside the sphere of her omnipotence. In essence, the object's survival of the child's attempts to destroy it establishes the object's separateness.

Winnicott goes on to propose that it is only once mother has been recognized as a separate other that the child can begin to "use" her—in the sense of internalizing various aspects of her. In other words, the object's survival of the child's attempts to destroy it enables it then to be used.

The Model 3 therapist believes that in order for the patient to develop a capacity for healthy, authentic relatedness, she must have developed the capacity for mutual recognition with respect to the therapist: It is as important that the patient recognize the therapist as an entity in her own right as it is that the patient have the experience of being recognized by the therapist as an entity in her own right. By the same token, it is as important that the patient find the therapist as it is that the patient be found by the therapist.

CHAPTER

12

Focus on the Here-and-Now

*I*f patient and therapist are to find each other as subjects, then both must let themselves be known.

The Model 3 therapist participates authentically in a real relationship with the patient—the intent being both to enhance the patient's understanding of her relational dynamics and to deepen the level of their engagement.

Accordingly, the relational therapist might choose to focus the patient's attention on (1) the patient's impact on the therapist, (2) the therapist's impact on the patient, or (3) the here-and-now engagement (or lack thereof) between them.

THE PATIENT'S IMPACT ON THE THERAPIST

With respect to the patient's impact on the therapist, the therapist might choose to focus either on her own countertransferential response to the patient's transferential activity or on the patient's transferential activity in relation to her.

The therapist's countertransferential response to the patient is an important source of data about the patient. In an effort to focus the patient's attention on what is transpiring at the intimate edge between them, the Model 3 therapist might share some aspect of her experience of being in the room with the patient. She is encouraged to be judicious in the disclosure of her countertransference and to offer only those aspects of her self-experience that she believes will advance the analytic endeavor (Bollas 1987, Ehrenberg 1984). When used responsibly, countertransference disclosure can be an extraordinarily effective therapeutic resource.

Parenthetically, it is important to keep in mind the distinction between the therapist's reporting on aspects of her subjective experience that are informed primarily by the here-and-now of the therapeutic engagement and those that are informed primarily by the there-and-then of the therapist's past. I would like to suggest that we use the term *self-disclosure* in the first instance and the term *self-revelation* in the second.

When the therapist is self-disclosing, she shares aspects of her experience informed by what it is like for her to be in relationship with the patient; these self-disclosures are thought to be primarily a story about the patient (and the patient's impact on the therapist). But when the therapist is self-revealing, she shares aspects of her experience informed by her developmental past; these self-revelations (even if stimulated by the patient's activity in relation to the therapist) are thought to be primarily a story about the therapist.

What I am here proposing is that I think the authentic therapist, in an effort to further the therapeutic process, should selectively "disclose" aspects of her experience of being in relationship with the patient. I think that it is generally a much less effective therapeutic tool for the therapist to indulge in "revealing" to the patient aspects of her own life—unless she deems it absolutely necessary.

The following interventions disclose to the patient some aspect of the therapist's countertransferential response to the patient.

"Sometimes it seems that when you're vulnerable and telling me something very important, after a little while you become very still and I lose track of you. I wonder if in this stillness, you are trying to show me how you, as a child, were sometimes abandoned after an intense connection."

Here the therapist (Carolyn Stack 1991, personal communication) understands her own experience of abandonment in relation to the patient as a reflection of the patient's experience of abandonment early on—abandonment after intense connection. As it happened not only did the therapist's intervention enable the two of them to engage more deeply but it also prompted the patient to remember the feelings of abandonment she had experienced as a little girl in relation to an older brother, a brother to whom she had felt deeply attached until he broke her heart by abusing her sexually.

Another example: "It occurs to me that I may now be able to understand something that I had never before entirely understood. I wonder if this feeling I am having that no matter what I do it will never be good enough is like the feeling you have spoken of having in relation to your father—for whom nothing was ever quite good enough."

When the relational therapist says things like, "It occurs to me that you may be trying to communicate something important to me about what is going on inside you," or "I think I am starting to understand something I had never before understood," the therapist is framing the patient's transferential activity in relation to the therapist as an enactment—that is, as activity specifically (even if unconsciously) designed either to elicit a particular countertransferential response from the therapist or to communicate something important to the therapist about the patient's internal state. The therapist's framing of the patient's activity in this way dignifies the patient's behavior and may make it a little easier for the patient when she is then held accountable for having behaved in the way that she did.

Alternatively, the therapist might choose to say things like, "I wonder if my difficulty appreciating just how suicidal you are made you feel that you had to do something dramatic in order to get my attention," or "It occurs to me that by way of your behavior in here, you may be trying to communicate something important to me that I was refusing to recognize." Here the therapist is suggesting that her inattentiveness to the patient's internal state (or even her resistance to hearing something the patient was trying to tell her) might have forced the patient to resort to an enactment in an effort to get herself "heard."

More generally, a lot of the patient's activity may be an unconscious attempt to get the therapist to understand. It is important, therefore, that the therapist be ever attuned to her internal responsiveness to the patient and that she have a highly refined and sophisticated capacity to "get it"—so that the patient need not expend time and energy in an effort to "make" the therapist understand.

In Model 3 it is postulated that in order for the therapist truly to appreciate just how despairing the patient is, the therapist might need to use her authentic (centered) self to take on the patient's despair—or at least some version of it—as her own. When the therapist has trouble sitting with the patient's despair and instead feels a need to make the patient feel better, then the patient may be placed in the untenable position of being left utterly alone in her pain. Furthermore, when the therapist does not have the capacity to tolerate the intensity of the patient's desperation and, instead, defends herself against it, then patient and therapist may never find each other, because a therapist who is defended will not be able to be deeply engaged with her patient.

If, on the other hand, the therapist truly understands how hopeless a patient is feeling and is able convincingly to convey that understanding to the patient, then it may relieve the patient of the burden of acting out her desperation in the form, say, of a suicide gesture. Paradoxically, such gestures are often made by a patient who is frantically trying to reach the therapist, desperately attempting to get the therapist to take her seriously. It may be that the patient does not want so much to die as that she wants the therapist to understand just how desperate she is—and to be with her in that.

Another example of a Model 3 intervention that involves countertransference disclosure is the following: "As you have been talking about how much you hate your father and how enraged you are at him for being so insensitive, I have been feeling strangely sad, as if my heart were going to break. I wonder if some of the sadness I am feeling belongs to you—sadness that you do not want to feel because it would mean having to admit that your father really does matter to you and that he really did break your heart by betraying you in the way that he did."

In each of the situations above, the therapist is understanding the dynamic that has taken place between herself and the patient as an instance of mutual enactment (initiated by the patient's transferential enactment—or projective identification). By way of the patient's transferential enactment, the patient compels the therapist to relive (with the patient) the patient's early life; in what then becomes a mutual enactment, both patient and therapist participate in the reliving of the patient's early history.

Expressed in somewhat different terms, the patient lives out (or enacts) her "unthought known" in the transference (Bollas 1987), which the therapist is able to recognize by way of remaining close to her own experience of being in relationship with the patient and selectively sharing aspects of that experience with the patient for mutual observation and understanding.

The unthought known is unconscious not because it is being defended against (Freud's dynamic unconscious), but because the patient has never had occasion to become aware of its existence. When the therapist is able to speak up on behalf of her own (the therapist's) subjective state, then patient and therapist can go on to explore what the patient is unwittingly delivering of her early life into the treatment situation—the patient sometimes placing her therapist in the role of the parent and sometimes placing her therapist in the role the patient once had as a child in relation to her parent.

Bollas (1987) once offered his patient the following poignant intervention: "You tell me something about yourself, I am just in the process of digesting it and storing it for further understanding of you, and then along you come—wham!—and tell me what I have digested and stored inside me did not come from you at all. The problem I find is how to live with this despair occasioned by your disappearances" (p. 224).

Bollas (1987) writes also about his work with a woman who, during the course of a session, would periodically disappear and reappear without announcement of either action. Over time, Bollas found himself becoming increasingly disconcerted. He writes: "After several months of analysis, when I thought the patient was ready to receive an indirect expression of my countertransference, I told her that I was aware of something taking place in me that I thought was of interest, and I wanted to put it to her for reflection and ultimately analysis" (p. 213). He continues, "I proceeded to tell her that her long pauses left me in a curious state, one in which I sometimes lost track of her, and it seemed to me that she was creating some kind of absence that I was meant to experience" (p. 213). Bollas reports that when he spoke up for his own subjective state, the patient was immediately relieved.

With another patient, Bollas (1987) found himself feeling disengaged. He decided, therefore, to share with the patient this aspect of his experience of her. And so he said, "You know, I want to put forth for mutual analysis a feeling I have, because I think it is essential to do so in order to find you. I have this sense that you are only partly here in this analysis and that you have resigned yourself to a failed therapy, even though it will have appeared on the surface to have been meaningful" (p. 220). The patient, Bollas observes, was eventually able to tell him that his refusal to allow her to give up on herself had "given her hope that perhaps she might [some day] be found after all" (p. 221).

The aim, says Bollas (1987), is always to reach the patient. He writes, "in order to find the patient, we must look for him within ourselves" (p. 202).

Disclosure of Internal Conflictedness

Hoffman (1992) has suggested that the therapist who is conflicted might want to say to the patient: "I'd like to say X, but I'm concerned about Y" (p. 299). The therapist expresses aloud the conflict with which she is struggling—a conflict that may well be reflective of the patient's internal dividedness.

As an example, "I am tempted to give you the advice for which you are looking, but my fear is that were I to do so, I would be robbing you of the opportunity to find your own answers."

As another example, "I find myself feeling angry at you for being late and wanting to tell you how it affects me, but it occurs to me that perhaps it would be more important for us to understand what you might be trying to communicate by way of your lateness."

To another patient, "I am tempted to respond to your request by saying that of course you can borrow one of the magazines in my waiting room, but I'm also realizing that were I simply to say yes, we might then lose an opportunity to understand something more about you and, perhaps, about us."

Or, to a patient who says she wants the therapist's approval regarding her decision to terminate—a termination that the therapist thinks is premature: "I am tempted simply to offer you the approval you seek—it is, after all, important that you do what feels right for you; but I am also aware of feeling, within myself, that the time is too soon and that were I to support your decision to leave, I might ultimately be doing you a disservice."

In essence, Hoffman encourages the therapist to disclose those aspects of her internal experience (her countertransference) that reflect the patient's impact on her. The therapist puts them forth for mutual observation and analytic understanding. By "coming clean" about the patient's impact on her, the therapist both (1) becomes more present and (2) forces the patient to take more responsibility for her interpersonal activity. The net result is a more authentic connection between patient and therapist and a holding of the patient accountable for what she is enacting in the therapy relationship—and perhaps enacts, more generally, in her other relationships as well.

The Patient's Enactments

Instead of sharing with the patient selected aspects of her countertransferential response to the patient, the Model 3 therapist might choose to draw the patient's attention more specifically to what the patient is contributing to the interaction—that is, to what the patient is playing out, or enacting, in the room.

To that end, the relational therapist might put forth the following: "I find myself feeling annoyed and impatient and am wondering if some part of you is pulling for that response," or "I am aware of feeling stirred up inside. I wonder if your intent was to provoke such a reaction," or "I wonder if by way of your lateness, you are trying to communicate something to me about how difficult it is for you to be here," or "You have been speaking increasingly about how helpless you feel and how depressed you are. I wonder if you are concerned that I might be missing something important about how desperate you are feeling."

In each of the above situations, the therapist is framing the patient's activity in relation to her as an enactment, the intent of which is to have a particular impact on her.

Alternatively, whenever the patient does something that the therapist experiences as interpersonally provocative, the Model 3 therapist has the option of asking the patient any of the following:

1. "How are you hoping that I'll react?"—which addresses the patient's id;
2. "How do you fear that I'll react?"—which addresses the patient's superego; or
3. "How do you imagine that I'll react?"—which addresses the patient's ego.

As we had noted earlier, when the patient's activity is seen as an enactment, it is thought to be the way the patient is attempting to engage the therapist, either by way of provoking some kind of response from the therapist or by way of transmitting something important to the therapist about the patient's internal world.

The three interventions above are efforts to encourage the patient to put into words what she might be trying to convey by way of her enactment; all three ask of the patient that she take some responsibility for her interpersonally provocative activity in relation to the therapist.

Acting Out versus Enactment

What is the distinction between acting out and enactment?

Classical psychoanalytic theorists have long believed that whenever the patient "acts out," she is violating the unspoken rule that requires the patient to put into words (not actions) whatever she might be experiencing. The patient who acts out is thought to be a bad patient who needs containment.

Contemporary psychoanalytic theorists conceive of things a little differently. For them, the patient's activity is seen as an enactment, the intent of which is to communicate something for which the patient may not yet have found words.

Perhaps the patient is communicating her need for containment; but, more probably, the patient may be attempting to communicate something about her internal experience that, at this point, is outside the realm of words. The patient's activity is therefore seen as offering patient and therapist the opportunity to understand something they might not otherwise have been able to understand.

So when the patient's activity is seen simply as acting out, then it becomes an obstacle to treatment; but when the patient's activity is seen as an enactment (with intentionality), it becomes a powerful therapeutic tool that conveys important information to both patient and therapist about the patient's internal state.

Clinical Vignette—Desperately Trying to Be Heard

The following vignette demonstrates the power of conceptualizing the patient's activity as an enactment, the intent of which is unconscious communication of something the patient cannot (in the moment) acknowledge consciously.

The patient, Carol, is engaged to be married. She is delighted that she has finally found a man, Tom, who would seem to be a perfect match for her—appropriate, available, a fine man, and very much in love with her. All her friends are excited; her family is proud; her therapist is pleased. Indeed, Tom, a successful lawyer who works long hours, appears to enjoy her, to delight in spending whatever time he can with her, and to love her; he is clearly eager to share the rest of his life with her.

But as the wedding date approaches, Carol finds herself becoming more and more jealous—even the slightest attention Tom pays another woman drives her wild. When he is watching a movie and a woman appears on the screen, unless he averts his gaze, she throws a fit and, at such times, can become quite verbally abusive.

Carol is not entirely sure why she reacts as she does—but she does know that if Tom even looks at another woman it devastates her and makes her feel completely out of control. One time, in the midst of her outrage, she threw a potted plant at him; another time, she broke a vase by throwing it at the TV; she has also, on occasion, struck him with her fists—in exasperation and in anger.

The therapist, alarmed, attempts discreetly to remind Carol, in as nonjudgmental a fashion as possible, that Carol may end up losing Tom unless she can learn to contain herself. The therapist encourages Carol to try to put into words just how painful it is for her when Tom shows interest in another woman.

Intent upon unearthing the genetic underpinnings of what would appear to be Carol's inappropriately intense jealousy, the therapist also encourages Carol to talk about what it was like for her to have to bear witness to her father's constant flirting with other women. Carol speaks with some affect about how outraged she was that her father would ogle other women and attempt to engage them in conversation; she also talks about how much it pained her to see how passively ineffectual her mother was in the face of her husband's repeated betrayals of her—mother simply endured the constant humiliation of having a husband who was obviously more interested in other women than he was in his wife. Carol recognizes that she may be identifying herself with her long-suffering mother and may be identifying Tom with her betraying father.

She also acknowledges how deeply it had hurt that her father was so often away.

But despite the therapist's cautionary words and Carol's willingness to talk in a heartfelt manner about her father's dalliances, Carol continues to abuse Tom—her periodic meltdowns increasing in frequency and intensity.

It is only when the therapist, with the help of her supervisor, begins to recognize Carol's obsessive jealousy (and consequent abusiveness) as an enactment, as an unconscious effort to convey something about her internal state that she might not otherwise have realized, that patient and therapist come to understand Carol's jealous tantrums as an attempt to communicate something important—namely, that Carol is not entirely sure she wants to marry Tom after all! Even though he would seem to be a perfect mate for her, it may well be that Tom is not, in fact, the man with whom Carol wants to spend the rest of her life.

With this permission given to talk about the negative side of her ambivalence about Tom, Carol talks first about how much of a workaholic he is and how driven he is to find success, power, and money. Although she recognizes that he spends as much time with her as he can, she acknowledges that she had hoped he would want to spend much more of his time with her.

But as Carol continues to explore her angry disappointment in him, it also becomes clear that she is equally afraid that he will be disappointed in her, that he will eventually find her lacking, not a suitable partner for him. She talks about her fear that she will not be able to hold his attention, that she will lose him. As she admits to how frightened she is, she begins to cry.

But as she continues crying, she begins to recognize how much Tom really does matter to her and how devastated she would be were she to lose him.

Interestingly, as Carol gets in touch with the positive side of her ambivalence toward Tom, her jealous rages ease considerably and the abusiveness stops entirely. As she acknowledges to herself how grateful she is to have him in her life, she begins to let herself appreciate and enjoy him. As Carol gets back in touch with how much she loves Tom, she finds herself wanting very much to marry him—and feeling ready to take that step.

THE THERAPIST'S IMPACT ON THE PATIENT

I would like to move now from a consideration of the patient's impact on the therapist to the therapist's impact on the patient: I had earlier made reference to Winnicott's extraordinarily useful distinction between the subjective countertransference (as primarily a story about the therapist) and the objective countertransference (as primarily a story about the patient and the patient's impact on the therapist).

I had gone on to suggest that we retain this distinction between what the therapist brings to the interaction and what the patient brings to the interaction in order to inform our understanding of the patient's transference—that is, the patient's experience of the therapist.

I had proposed, therefore, that not only is the countertransference co-created but so, too, the transference. The patient's transference has contributions from both patient and therapist; I refer to the patient's contribution as the *subjective transference* (what the patient brings from her there-and-then) and the therapist's contribution as the *objective transference* (what the therapist brings in the here-and-now).

In fact, the Model 3 therapist conceives of the transference as always both subjective (a story about the way the patient makes meaning of the therapist's participation) and objective (a story about the way the therapist actually participates in the therapeutic encounter). Meanwhile, how the therapist actually participates is thought to involve both what the therapist brings to the interaction from her there-and-then and how the therapist responds to the patient in the here-and-now.

Expressed in somewhat different terms, the patient's experience of the therapist is both part old (a story about the patient) and part new (a story about the therapist); it is both part imagined (deriving, as it does, from experiences the patient had in her past) and part real (deriving, as it does, from how the therapist actually participates in the present).

Although a Model 1 therapist conceives of the patient's experience of the therapist as primarily a story about the patient, the Model 3 therapist conceives of it as a story about both patient and therapist.

Plausible Constructions

In order to understand the therapist's impact on the patient, the Model 3 therapist might choose to encourage the patient to explore the "realistic aspects" of the therapist's contribution to the transference—that is, the objective transference.

To that end, the relational therapist might ask: "Is there something I have done or said that has led you to believe that I don't care?" or "Have you noticed something in me that would seem to suggest my discomfort with your decision to terminate?" or "Have you observed anything in me that would lead you to feel that I may be having trouble with your success?"

Or let us imagine a situation in which the patient is afraid that no man could possibly sustain feelings of sexual attraction for her. In time, she delivers both her desire and her fear into the therapy relationship; she finds herself experiencing both an intense yearning for her therapist to find her sexually attractive and an equally intense fear that he won't. She recognizes that her anxiety about being able to arouse her therapist's interest in her derives from the unrequited love relationship she had had with her father, a dashingly handsome, charismatic man who had lavished his attention not on her but on her older sister.

George Fishman (1998) has suggested that the relational therapist, intent upon opening up for exploration whatever his own contribution might be to the patient's experience of anguished yearning in relation to him, might ask such a patient the following: "If you are continually feeling that I am not and could not be attracted to you, what might I be doing or not doing that is getting translated into this conviction?"

In each of the examples above, the patient is being invited to observe the therapist and to speculate about him or her. The relational therapist, by way of such questions, is hoping to encourage exploration of the objective transference—that is, those aspects of the patient's experience that are thought to be primarily a story about the therapist and the therapist's participation in the analytic encounter.

Although both Model 1 and Model 3 therapists might ask the patient to say more about her experience of the therapist as, say, angry, what distinguishes a Model 1 from a Model 3 therapist is the therapist's intent.

(1) If the therapist's intent is to focus the patient's attention inward (to her internal process) and backward (to her there-and-then) so that the patient can understand more about how her past informs her experience in the moment, then we would say of such a therapist that she is operating as a Model 1 therapist, because her interest is in the subjective transference.

(2) But if the therapist's intent is to focus the patient's attention outward (to the here-and-now) so that the patient can understand more about how the present informs her experience in the moment, then we would say of such a therapist that she is operating as a Model 3 therapist, because her interest is in the objective transference as well.

The Model 3 therapist takes the patient's perceptions seriously. But the respect accorded the patient's plausible interpretations (Hoffman 1983) of the therapist's experience does not imply that the therapist should accede to the patient's perspective (as happens, for example, in self psychology, where the patient's subjective experience is thought to be what matters most).

But when the therapist is struck by how "accurate" the patient's construction is, Greenberg (1986a) recommends that the therapist not too readily "confirm" the reality of it but, rather, that the therapist pursue the often more difficult path of holding open (for further investigation) the possibility that the patient's construction is at least a plausible one. Paradoxically, confirming the patient's reality by disclosing aspects of one's self-experience can foreclose a more thoroughgoing exploration of the patient's experience (as happens, for example, when the therapist acknowledges that perhaps she is somewhat tired or perhaps there was an edge to her voice when she offered her response to the patient).

Interestingly, although Freud's primary interest was in the subjective transference (that is, the patient's experience of the therapist as a story primarily about the patient), in actual practice he was not altogether oblivious to the impact of the therapist on the patient's experience.

As early as 1905, in a postscript to the ill-fated Dora case, Freud (1905) notes that—in retrospect—he believes he should have said to Dora, "It is from Herr K. that you have made a transference on to me. Have you noticed anything that leads you to suspect me of evil intentions? . . . Or have you been struck by anything about me or got to know anything about me which has caught your fancy, as happened previously with Herr K.?" (p. 118).

Freud goes on to suggest that had he realized, at the time, the importance of focusing Dora's attention on him, then

> Her attention would . . . have been turned to some detail in our relations, or in my person or circumstances. . . . But I was deaf to this first note of warning. . . . In this way the transference took me unawares, and, because of the unknown quantity in me which reminded Dora of Herr K., she took her revenge on me as she wanted to take her revenge on him, and deserted me as she believed herself to have been deceived and deserted by him. [pp. 118–119]

Even if it was after the fact, Freud clearly recognized the importance of giving patients the opportunity to elaborate upon their experience of the therapist's contribution to the transference—that is, the objective transference.

IMPINGEMENT

The ever-present danger, of course, is that if the therapist focuses too much on the here-and-now engagement (or lack thereof) between the two of them, the patient may experience the therapist as being "in her face." There are times when the patient needs to have the experience of being "left alone" in the presence of the therapist—so that the patient can have the experience of an uninterrupted continuity of being without impingement by the therapist (Winnicott 1965).

Furthermore, active focusing on the relationship in the here-and-now may interfere with the curative aspects of regression that can only occur when the patient feels safe enough to become disorganized and less intact. If the therapist is forever busy focusing on the interactive dynamic in the room, there may not be space enough for the patient to settle into a therapeutic regression.

In other words, the patient must be able to "play" in the analytic space, without being always forced to take into account the presence of the therapist. Aron (1992) speaks to this issue when he cautions that the therapist should beware of imposing object usage (which requires recognition of the object as a separate entity in its own right) on a patient who is only capable of object relating (which involves experiencing the object as within one's sphere of influence).

FOCUS ON THE INTERACTIVE DYNAMIC

Instead of focusing on the patient's impact on the therapist or the therapist's impact on the patient, the Model 3 therapist might choose to focus the patient's attention on the interactive dynamic between them: "There seems to be a lot of tension between us today," or "We are both disappointed that things did not turn out as we had hoped they would," or "Isn't it interesting that neither one of us remembers what happened last time?"

To a patient who rebuffs every attempt the therapist makes to give her something, the therapist might say: "It seems to me that every time I try to offer you something, you push me away," or "I don't seem to be getting anything right in here today, do I?"

The therapist might simply call the patient's attention to the here-and-now engagement (or lack thereof) between them, or might offer the patient her own understanding of what she thinks is going on at the intimate edge between them.

LOCATING THE PATIENT

I would like now to develop two more examples that demonstrate how the therapist can use herself to find her patient. The first is the situation of a female patient and a male therapist. In the vignette that follows, please consider the two different positions the therapist assumes in relation to his patient's relentless hopelessness.

Clinical Vignette—Taking on the Patient's Despair

The patient, Jennifer, has long struggled with feelings of despair; she speaks repeatedly of her anguish, her desperation, and her outrage that the therapy has done so little to ease her pain.

The therapist hypothesizes to himself that, for whatever the reason, the patient (aware only of her hopelessness) would seem to need him to carry, on her behalf, the hope that she cannot access.

And so it is that even in the face of the patient's unremitting despair and constant threats to terminate, the therapist refuses to be daunted. He is able to resonate empathically with Jennifer's experience of despair but on a deeper level maintains his faith in the patient, his confidence in his own ability to persevere, and his belief in the healing power of their connection; he holds fast to his conviction that if Jennifer stays in the treatment, she will ultimately get better.

In essence, the therapist carries the hope, whereas the patient carries none. The therapist cares very deeply about his patient, thinks of her as one of his favorite patients, and would like to believe that she will someday be able to find her own hope.

Every now and then, there will be a session in which the therapist begins to feel that he and Jennifer are actually making some progress; inevitably, however, Jennifer will come to the next session and will say that she thinks the treatment is going nowhere—that perhaps she really should terminate this time.

Then one day, after several years, the therapist, listening to the patient's anguished cry that no one will ever be able to understand, no one will ever be able to help, becomes aware of feeling (this time) a profound weariness and a heaviness in his heart that he cannot shake as the patient continues to express her angry dissatisfaction with him, with the treatment, with her life, with everything, with everybody.

No longer able to keep the patient's despair at bay, the therapist shakes his head slowly, sighs deeply, and, resigned, says finally, "I don't think I can keep doing this."

Initially startled, Jennifer looks at her therapist intently. This is something familiar, something deeply familiar. The therapist is expressing feelings of resignation and hopelessness with which the patient has lived her entire life.

At first very still, after a little while, Jennifer visibly relaxes, chuckles to herself, and says quietly, "Now you know what I've been feeling all these years!"

The rest of the session is spent in silence—an easy, comfortable silence.

To the next session Jennifer comes with a different energy about her; she appears to be a little lighter, a little more spontaneous. At one point, she remarks, almost casually, "You know, sometimes I begin to think that maybe things aren't so bad after all."

Neither patient nor therapist says anything for a while—both exquisitely aware that this is the first time Jennifer has ever admitted to having any hope whatsoever.

How do we understand this sequence of events?

For a number of years, the therapist (despite pressure from Jennifer) had steadfastly refused to be drawn into taking on her weariness and despair as his own. Unflinchingly he had clung to his hope, refusing to relinquish his faith in her and in the healing power of their relationship.

But then one day that all changed. Something rather dramatically shifted in the dynamic between the two of them, and the therapist finally allowed himself to be drawn into experiencing Jennifer's resignation and despair firsthand, which he signaled by giving voice to his own frustration and sense of futility.

Where once the therapist had been relentlessly hopeful and the patient relentlessly hopeless, now the therapist was able to join Jennifer in her despair. Where once the therapist had been only empathically attuned to Jennifer's despair (having taken it on only "as if" it were his own), now the therapist was authentically engaged with Jennifer in her despair (having taken it on "as" his own).

By the same token, where before the patient could not have known that her therapist was truly with her, now Jennifer was able to know that her therapist deeply understood. She could feel that her therapist was no longer fighting her, because he had finally opened himself up to her frustration and despair—and she was no longer alone.

Interestingly, once the therapist relinquished his investment in carrying the hope (on Jennifer's behalf), Jennifer became able to access and to articulate some of her own hope, which then allowed the two of them to share the responsibility for the treatment and for carrying the hope.

So we have a way to understand how it came to pass that the therapist would find himself able to engage authentically with Jennifer in her despair (that is, he finally let himself be drawn into taking on her despair as his own). But how do we understand the therapist's relentless hope during the early years of their work prior to his acceptance of Jennifer's despair? Why did he maintain so steadfastly his hope for Jennifer's ultimate recovery?

On the one hand, the therapist's refusal to be daunted could be understood as related perhaps to his inability to tolerate Jennifer's despair, perhaps to his need to believe in the healing power of the therapy relationship, or perhaps to his theoretical conviction that it was his responsibility (as the therapist) to carry the hope that his patient was unable to access within herself. On the other hand, the therapist's relentless hopefulness could also be understood as related (in part) to his responsiveness to the patient's need (at least during the initial years of their treatment) for him to carry that hope on her behalf.

We might then say of the therapist's relentless hopefulness during the initial stages of the treatment that it was co-created, codetermined—that aspects of it were a story about the therapist (and his need) and aspects of it a story about the patient (and her need).

We might then understand the sudden shift between patient and therapist as related perhaps to an internal shift within the therapist (such that he was now more receptive to the patient's despair) or perhaps to an internal shift within the patient (such that she was now needing him to position himself differently in relation to her despair).

In any event, once both patient and therapist were on the same side (of guarded optimism), they were no longer in opposing camps. The work that followed was difficult, demanding, and exhausting for both patient and therapist; but neither participant was alone. The work was done jointly, collaboratively.

What patient and therapist came to appreciate, over time, was that the early years of their relationship had been a replay of the relationship Jennifer had had with her father, who had loved his daughter but had never been fully available to her because he had always been distracted, preoccupied with his own concerns. This interactive dynamic had been re-created in the patient's relationship with her therapist—until something shifted in the intersubjective field and the therapist, finally allowing himself to be found by the patient, opened himself up to her despair and in so doing became at last truly available to her.

The grieving that Jennifer was able to do could only have been done against the backdrop of her having experienced the therapist as now understanding something fundamental and profoundly important about her experience of being in the world, understanding that turned out to be deeply healing for a patient who had never before had the experience of finding someone willing to go with her into her darkest places. In finding the therapist, she herself became found.

Clinical Vignette—I Want My Mommy

I would like now to present my work with Susan, a 30-year-old woman with whom I have been working very intensively for six years now. This too is a story about a patient's despair—but, as you will see, the dynamic between us unfolded in a way that was different from the way it evolved in the example just cited.

Over the course of the past several years, Susan has made some rather remarkable changes in her life. Once a poorly paid secretary with few friends and a deep fear of men, she is now a therapist with a number of friends and occasional dates.

But as our work has deepened, Susan has become increasingly aware of a profound loneliness, a deep despair. We have also come to understand just how much she hates herself, denies herself, and punishes herself. She is relentless in terms of what she demands of herself. There is little pleasure in her life, no real joy. She has created for herself an existence in which each day, in essence, is a test of courage that must be lived through and, somehow, survived.

With time, Susan and I have developed a very deep connection. I mean the world to her; and, for that matter, she means the world to me.

Periodically, however, she will come into the session and be on a tear, lashing out at everything and everybody around her. She will beat up on herself, rail against the world, lash out against me and the therapy—screaming out her pain and her outrage. When she is like this, it feels as if there is nothing I can do to contain her relentlessness.

Over time, I have tried a number of approaches. Most of them are not particularly effective; although eventually, somehow, she does become less tortured and less torturing—and we do get to a more settled place. Sometimes it takes hours, sometimes it takes days, sometimes weeks, and several times it took months for her to relent.

But one day I did something a little differently, something that I think enabled her to relent much sooner than she would have otherwise.

She had come to the session in a rage at herself, her parents, me, and the world. I had done my usual, saying things like: "I think you are wanting me to feel what you used to feel in relation to your mother," "You want me to know just how desperate you are," "I wonder if you are wanting me to feel as helpless and as inadequate as you feel," and "I think you're showing me what it was like to be at the receiving end of your mother's relentlessness." And so on and so forth. Even I was tired of these interventions, as I'm sure she was too.

But then as I sat there, feeling with her the pain, the despair, the rage, feeling my own pain (some of it a sympathetic response to her pain, some of it my own pain—from way back and stirred up in me now in response to her pain), I suddenly felt an incredible yearning to be held by somebody, to be soothed and comforted—because the world seemed so bleak, so barren, so desolate.

And so I blurted out, "I want my Mommy." At that moment, I did want my Mommy.

That stopped her dead in her tracks. Some of it might have been the shock value. But I think that most of it had to do with my having put into words something that in the moment, she too would have wanted, if she could but have let herself have such yearnings.

I cannot say that she then did a complete about-face; but I can say that by the end of the session, Susan had relented and was at last facing, head-on, some of the anguish and some of the outrage she felt about just how unavailable, just how ungiving, and just how relentlessly critical her narcissistic mother had always been. She could now grieve in a way that she had never, prior to this point, been able to.

In retrospect, I think that what was transformative was my ability to be with Susan in her loneliness and her despair and then (in the midst of that bleak desolation) to remember a way out, to remember the possibility of connection and engagement. I think that it was my capacity to recover hope that enabled Susan ultimately to wend her way out of the quagmire of relentlessness and unrelatedness in which she had thought she was destined to spend the rest of her days.

As I try to conceptualize the interactive dynamic that was played out between us, I reconstruct it as follows. Initially I took on despair that the patient found impossible to bear—that is, I accepted her projection. Then I "metabolized" the patient's intolerable despair by lending some of my own capacity to a "psychological processing" of it: I "used" my "self" to summon up the memory of a comforting other. What I was then able to return to the patient for re-internalization was a more tolerable version of the original unmanageable despair.

But what enabled me to access my own desire for a comforting other in the face of such bleakness and desolation? A truly relational perspective (that is, a perspective that believes all experience is co-created, codetermined) would have it that my ability to access my desire was not just a story about me but also a story about my patient and her desire—a desire (for connection) that had perhaps been silenced early on by a mother who did not know how to satisfy that desire.

With respect to Susan and me, there had earlier, and have since, been other powerful moments in which the two of us were connected in a very profound manner, both of us extremely open and vulnerable to the other—but it is the interaction just recounted that stands out for us both as having been a turning point for the recovery of her hope and the re-finding of her desire.

THE TRANSFORMATIVE POWER OF AUTHENTIC ENGAGEMENT

The Model 3 therapist brings herself, as an authentic subject, to the interaction, which enables her both to find the patient and to be found by the patient. The relational theorist believes that it is by means of such mutual discovery that the patient will ultimately be healed.

Aron (1996) recently wrote:

> Unless patients can feel that they have reached their analysts, moved them, changed them, discomforted them, angered them, hurt them, healed them, known them in some profound way, they themselves may not be able to benefit from their analyses. From this perspective, psychoanalysis is a profound emotional encounter, an interpersonal engagement, an intersubjective dialogue, a relational integration, a meeting of minds. [p. 136]

Patient and therapist engage in a collaborative process of discovery. Each helps to find the other; the process of *we* becomes the recognition of two individual *I*s. There is a paradox involved here: it is only by means of staying grounded in one's own reality that one can locate another; but it is only by means of locating another that one can become more grounded in one's own reality.

The therapist's capacity to use her authentic self is the way she makes meaningful contact with the patient and accesses what is most genuine, most personal, and most alive in the patient.

If the therapist does not bring her authentic self into the room, then the patient may end up analyzed—but never reached. If the therapist does not allow herself to become a participant in what unfolds between them, then the patient may end up much wiser than when she started—but still not found. By using herself, the therapist is able to find, and to be found by, the patient.

CHAPTER

13

The Repertoire of the Contemporary Therapist

I am proposing that the repertoire of the contemporary therapist includes formulating interpretations, offering some form of corrective provision, and engaging interactively in a relationship that is reciprocally mutual.

I think that the most therapeutically effective stance is one in which the therapist is able to achieve an optimal balance between (1) positioning herself outside the therapeutic field (in order to formulate interpretations about the patient and her internal process so as to resolve the patient's structural conflict), (2) decentering from her own experience (in order to offer the patient some form of corrective provision so as to fill in the patient's structural deficit), and (3) remaining very much centered within her own experience (in order to engage authentically with the patient in a real relationship so as to resolve the patient's relational difficulties).

Patrick Casement (1985), in speaking to how the therapist positions himself optimally in relation to the patient, suggests that the therapist must "learn how to remain close enough to what the patient is experiencing" to be able to be affected by the patient—"while preserving a sufficient distance" to function as therapist. "But that professional distance should not leave him beyond the reach of what the patient may need him to feel. A therapist has to discover how to be psychologically intimate with a patient and yet separate, separate and still intimate" (p. 30).

In the language we have been using here, the therapist must empathically join the patient where she is even as the therapist preserves her distance so that she can still function interpretively. But the therapist should never be so far away that the patient cannot find her and engage her authentically. Intimate without losing the self, separate without losing the other.

It will be a challenge for any therapist to attempt to hold in mind, simultaneously, the three different perspectives without pulling for premature closure—closure that may ease the therapist's anxiety but will probably limit the realm of therapeutic possibilities. The most effective therapists will be those who (1) manage somehow to tolerate—perhaps even for extended periods of time—the experience of not knowing or, in Bollas's (1987) words, the experience of necessary uncertainty; (2) are open to being shaped by the patient's need and by whatever else might arise within the context of their intersubjective relationship; and, more generally, (3) are willing to bring the best of themselves, the worst of themselves, and the most of themselves into the room with the patient—so that each will have an opportunity to find the other.

A wonderful anecdote comes to mind for me as a way of capturing the quintessential struggle in which all of us as therapists must engage as we attempt to master our art. It is about the composer Stravinsky (first recounted by Powers [1984], later by Mitchell [1988]).

> [Stravinsky] had written a new piece with a difficult violin passage. After it had been in rehearsal for several weeks, the solo violinist came to Stravinsky and said he was sorry, he had tried his best, [but] the passage was too difficult; no violinist could play it. Stravinsky said, 'I understand that. What I am after is the sound of someone *trying* to play it.'" [Powers 1984, p. 54]

As therapists, our work is exquisitely difficult and finely tuned—and often we will not be able to get it just right. Perhaps, however, we can console ourselves with the thought that it is the effort we make to get it just right that ultimately counts.

PART II

Clinical Applications

CHAPTER

14

The Therapist's Stance

In Part II, we will fine tune our understanding of how the therapist positions herself, from moment to moment, in relation to the patient. Each moment is replete with possibility; at any given point in time, there are an infinite number of directions in which it could go.

Each moment in time is of course unique; there will never again be such a moment—never again this particular configuration of opportunities. The moment is constituted by both its history and its potential; that is, each moment is determined by both what has been and by what could be.

As we saw in Part I, the position the therapist assumes moment by moment relates to how she comes to know the patient and to how she then intervenes.

AFFERENCE AND EFFERENCE

At a meeting of the American Psychoanalytic Association in December of 1995, Dale Boesky made an off-the-cuff remark about the relationship between nerve conduction and the analyst's neutrality. A nerve impulse is said to be afferent when its direction is toward a nerve center and efferent when its direction is away from the nerve center. Boesky made the extraordinarily useful distinction between afferent neutrality as speaking to how the analyst listens and efferent neutrality as speaking to how she intervenes.

I think that such a distinction applies to a number of psychoanalytic concepts.

As an example, let us think about the way contemporary psychoanalytic theory employs a concept like "use of the countertransference."

Use of the countertransference refers to a particular way that the therapist uses her experience of self—that is, uses her experience of being in the room with the patient. But it refers sometimes to how the therapist listens and sometimes to how the therapist intervenes.

In other words, there are times when use of the countertransference describes how the therapist gathers information about the patient's internal experience (namely, by way of the therapist's remaining very much centered within her own experience) and there are times when it describes how the therapist responds to the patient (namely, by way of the therapist's disclosing to the patient selected aspects of this experience).

In the first instance, the therapist is using her experience of self in order to facilitate her understanding of the patient; and, in the second instance, the therapist is sharing with the patient selected aspects of this experience in order to facilitate the patient's understanding (both of herself and of her impact on others).

And so it is that *afferent countertransference* relates to how the therapist arrives at understanding and *efferent countertransference* relates to what the therapist then says or does.

More generally, afference has to do with how the therapist listens and efference has to do with how the therapist then intervenes.

I think the distinction is a useful one, inasmuch as it speaks to the therapist's different roles: she is both someone who receives input from the patient and someone who offers output to the patient.

THE THERAPIST'S LISTENING STANCE

In Part I, I had suggested that the optimal listening stance involves a dialectical tension between the therapist as an object watching the patient, as a selfobject joining alongside the patient, and as a subject using her self to react to the patient.

(1) As a neutral object, the Model 1 therapist remains very much centered within her objectivity. She positions herself outside the therapeutic field, all the better to be an objective observer of the patient and the patient's internal dynamics. In order to preserve her objectivity, the Model 1 therapist strives as best she can to maintain her position as an observer and to avoid being drawn in as a participant.

(2) As an empathic selfobject (or good object–good mother), the Model 2 therapist decenters from her subjectivity. She positions herself alongside the patient, a stance that enables her to immerse herself empathically in the patient's internal experience. In order to understand the patient's experience, the Model 2 therapist strives as best she can to attend to what the patient is experiencing and to pay much less attention to what she is herself experiencing. The Model 2 therapist attempts to arrive at understanding of the patient from a position within the patient's subjectivity—uncontaminated by her own (the therapist's) subjectivity.

When the Model 1 therapist is described as an object, the word is used to suggest the therapist's objectivity—the therapist not involved but detached, not participating but observing.

When the Model 2 therapist is described as an object, the word is being used in a different context. Now the word "object" connotes a good object (or good mother) and suggests a certain capacity for empathic attunement on the therapist's part—a certain capacity to decenter from her own needs in order to attend to her patient's needs.

As we know, the Model 2 therapist empathically resonates with the patient's experience, taking it on "as if" it were her own. (In contradistinction to this is the Model 3 therapist, who takes on the patient's experience "as" her own.) Of note is that the Model 2 therapist, in order to achieve deep understanding of the patient's experience, may need to summon up memories from her own past involving similar (even if not identical) situations—to which Kohut (1982) refers as "vicarious introspection."

To take an extreme example: If the patient is upset because he has just been denied membership in the Ku Klux Klan, then the therapist may be able to resonate with the patient's experience of upset only if she is able to call upon memories from her own past of a time when she was excluded from membership in an organization that had been important to her. In other words, the therapist may be able to understand the patient's experience of upset at being excluded only by way of remembering something from her own past that relates to this theme.

The above example also speaks to the following: to be empathic with another's perspective is to understand it, even if it is at odds with one's own.

(3) As an authentic subject, the Model 3 therapist remains very much centered within her subjectivity. She brings herself as a subject to the interaction, recognizing that she is always a participant in the relation-

ship that is continuously unfolding. The Model 3 therapist arrives at an understanding of the patient and the patient's relational dynamics by way of focusing on what it feels like to be in relationship with the patient—by way of focusing on what it feels like to interact with the patient (whether such interaction involves engagement, disengagement, or something in between).

The Model 3 therapist strives neither to maintain her objectivity (as she does in Model 1) nor to maintain her "decenteredness" or her "selflessness" (as she does in Model 2); rather, she strives to maintain her "centeredness" so that she can use her subjectivity—her experience of self—to inform her knowledge of the patient and of how the patient participates in relationship. The Model 3 therapist arrives at understanding as a fellow participant (and enactor) in the therapeutic encounter.

Whereas Model 2 emphasizes the therapist's affective attunement to the patient as a way of arriving at understanding, Model 3 emphasizes the authentic engagement between patient and therapist as a way of coming to know.

And so it is that in Model 1, the focus is on the patient's internal dynamics; in Model 2, the focus is on the patient's affective experience; and in Model 3, the focus is on the patient's relational dynamics and the interactive dynamic between patient and therapist.

In sum, as object, as selfobject, and as subject, the therapist arrives at understanding of the patient.

Even though each stance involves a different use of the therapist's self, the therapist will be able to optimize what she comes to understand moment by moment if she is able to oscillate rapidly from one stance to another—listening almost simultaneously as object, as selfobject, and as subject. The picture of the patient that emerges as a result of the therapist's positioning of herself in these three stances will be a composite that is greater than the sum of its parts.

Empathic Selfobject versus Authentic Subject

Let us imagine a situation in which the patient is talking about how sad she is feeling.

(1) The Model 2 therapist, decentering from her own experience, takes on the patient's sadness as if it were her own, although it never

really becomes her own. The therapist's sadness is a story about the patient, not a story about the therapist.

But the therapist, both by listening very attentively to what the patient is saying about how sad she feels and by drawing upon her own knowledge of what it is like to be so sad, will then be able to respond to the patient in a way that enables the patient to know that her experience of sadness is being deeply understood.

The Model 2 therapist's empathic understanding of just how sad the patient is may also enable the patient to delve more deeply into her actual experience of sadness.

(2) In contradistinction to the Model 2 therapist is the Model 3 therapist who, remaining very much centered within her own experience, may find herself taking on the patient's sadness as her own. In fact, the therapist may find her own eyes welling with tears—tears that belong, in part, to the patient and, in part, to her. The patient's sadness has now become a story about both the patient and, through the therapist's countertransferential response, the therapist as well.

The Model 3 therapist's heartfelt reactivity to the patient's sadness enables the patient to know that her experience is being shared and that she is not alone, which may enable the patient to delve more deeply into her actual experience of sadness.

It is when the therapist comes to experience the patient's sadness as her own that we are dealing with a situation in which the therapist has truly allowed herself to be shaped by the patient. Now the sadness she is feeling is very real—it is co-created, co-constructed, a story about both the patient's sadness and her own (perhaps sadness deriving from her own past). When the Model 3 therapist brings her self and her own vulnerability into the room in this fashion, we speak of authentic engagement (as opposed to the emotional—or affective—attunement of the Model 2 therapist).

In actual practice, the sadness the therapist comes to feel by way of entering into the patient's sadness (as happens in Model 2) may not seem to the therapist to be all that different from the sadness she feels when she allows the patient's sadness to enter into her (as happens in Model 3). But, in theory, there is a very real difference between the Model 2 therapist's experience of the patient's sadness and the Model 3 therapist's experience of it. More importantly, the theoretical distinction has important clinical ramifications.

In the first instance, the therapist is very respectful of the patient's experience of sadness and stays out of the patient's way—simply offering understanding and validation. In the second instance, the therapist is much more present in the room and engaged in relationship with the patient—a relationship to which she brings her own vulnerability.

In the first instance, the therapist strives to keep her own reactivity out of the room; in the second instance, the therapist stays very much centered in her reactivity, using that as a way to find the patient.

So, too, in the first instance, the therapist strives to keep her countertransference out of the room; in the second instance, the therapist uses her countertransferential response to the patient to deepen the level of her understanding of the patient's internal experience.

There is no right or wrong way to be; I am simply making the distinction between a deficiency-compensation model, in which the therapeutic action is thought to involve the therapist's availability as an empathic selfobject (availability that provides the patient with the experience of affective attunement) and a relational model, in which the therapeutic action is thought to involve the therapist's availability as an authentic subject (availability that provides the patient with the experience of authentic engagement).

Both listening stances are important ways the therapist comes to know the patient, but each has certain advantages and certain disadvantages. On the one hand, the Model 2 therapist is less likely to contaminate her understanding of the patient's experience with her own subjectivity; but the Model 2 therapist, by keeping herself out of the room, may never really be able to know the patient's experience deeply. On the other hand, although the Model 3 therapist (by bringing her self into the room in the way that she does) may come to know the patient's experience deeply, her understanding of the patient will always be contaminated by her own subjectivity.

THE THERAPIST'S INTERVENTIVE STANCE

Earlier I had suggested that the optimal interventive stance involves a dialectical tension between the therapist as someone who formulates interpretations, who offers some form of corrective provision, and who engages interactively in relationship.

How the therapist chooses to intervene will depend, in large part, on how the therapist conceives of the therapeutic action—that is, whether it involves knowledge, experience, or relationship.

As we have said, this focus will shift moment by moment.

(1) When the therapist's focus is on the patient's structural conflicts, then the therapist's intent will be to strengthen the patient's ego by way of formulating interpretations that will enhance the patient's knowledge of her internal dynamics. Enhanced knowledge will result, ultimately, in resolution of the patient's structural conflicts.

(2) When the therapist's focus is on the patient's structural deficits, then the therapist's intent will be to "meet" the patient where she is by way of offering corrective provision—be it in the form of recognizing the patient's need (as happens with self psychology) or actually responding to it (as happens with those object relations theories that emphasize "absence of good"). This experience of being recognized and/or responded to will result, ultimately, in repair of the patient's structural deficits.

(3) And when the therapist's focus is on the patient's impaired capacity to enter healthily and authentically into relationship with others, then the therapist's intent will be to engage the patient in a real relationship by using her authentic self to find, and to be found by, the patient. The therapist's interventions will direct the patient's attention to the here-and-now engagement between them; her particular interest will be in what each brings to the relationship and its impact on the other. The ultimate goal will be a deepening of the connection between them and, more generally, development of the patient's capacity for relatedness.

NONLINEARITY

I might seem to be suggesting that it is (1) only by way of watching that the therapist (as object) is then able to formulate interpretations that enhance the patient's knowledge, (2) only by way of joining that the therapist (as selfobject) is then able to offer the patient some form of corrective experience, and (3) only by way of using the self that the therapist (as subject) is then able to engage the patient in relationship.

In fact, I do not mean to be suggesting such a linear relationship between how the therapist positions herself to listen and how she positions herself to intervene. The therapist comes to know the patient on all three levels because she is always listening from all three vantage points. Based on the understanding she acquires by way of assuming these various listening postures, she is then able to offer the patient insight, a corrective experience, and/or engagement in relationship—depending on what she senses will be most therapeutically useful to the patient in the moment.

Clinical Vignette—Sexual Titillation

I offer the following vignette to demonstrate a clinical situation in which the therapist comes to understand something deeply important about the patient by way of using one model and then makes a choice to intervene using another model. More specifically, the example speaks to a situation in which the therapist uses Model 3 to inform her understanding of the patient—understanding that the therapist then offers the patient in the form of a Model 1 interpretation.

The patient is speaking of the sexual abuse she had suffered at the hands of her father. Clearly the patient is in a rage at him and feels devastated by his betrayal of her.

But as the patient recounts the details of that abuse, the therapist (much to her horror) finds herself feeling strangely titillated. Strongly tempted to dismiss the feeling, the therapist nonetheless forces herself to take note of it and to reflect upon its possible significance. In other words, instead of assuming that her state of arousal is simply a story about her own psychology (or psychopathology), the therapist recognizes that it may also speak to something that is going on within the patient—something of which the patient is not consciously aware. Perhaps the patient, defending herself against acknowledging whatever excitement she might also have been feeling, is aware only of her outrage; she protects herself from having to know that there was something exciting for her about all the attention she was getting from her father by disavowing that pleasure and placing it in her therapist instead. It is then the therapist who, by way of this projective identification, ends up experiencing the patient's disavowed excitement as her own.

Although the therapist may well never disclose to the patient her internal experience of titillation, she is nonetheless able to use her (countertransferential) experience to frame the following interpretation: "Your father's sexual abuse of you fills you with rage and breaks your heart. I wonder if part of what makes it more difficult still is your knowing that despite how devastated you were by what he did to you, it did also sometimes feel good to be the center of his attention."

The above is a Model 1 intervention, inasmuch as it addresses itself to something inside the patient of which she is not yet aware; its aim is to make the patient conscious of something she had not previously been able to let herself know. But the therapist, in order to formulate such an interpretation, must pay close attention to information she has gained by way of having assumed a Model 3 listening stance. She then uses her experience of self (her objective countertransference) to heighten her awareness of what might be going on within the patient. The above, then, is an example of a Model 1 intervention (efference) that is inspired by a Model 3 listening stance (afference); in essence, it is a countertransference-inspired Model 1 interpretation.

In other words, although the therapist may ultimately offer the patient a Model 1 interpretation, how the therapist gathers the data necessary to formulate such an intervention need not be simply by way of positioning herself outside the therapeutic field as a Model 1 neutral observer watching the patient and reflecting upon what she sees. In the above vignette, for example, the therapist formulates a Model 1 interpretation on the basis of information she has acquired by way of assuming a Model 3 position in which she pays close attention to her countertransferential response to the patient.

OPTIMIZATION OF EFFECTIVENESS

My belief is that the most effective listening stance is one in which the therapist achieves an optimal balance between positioning herself as object, as selfobject, and as subject—that is, as a neutral object watching and reflecting upon what she observes about the patient and the patient's internal dynamics, as an empathic selfobject joining alongside (and immersing herself in the affective experience of) the patient, and as an authentic subject using her experience of self to inform her understanding of the patient and the patient's relational dynamics.

My belief is that the most effective interventive stance is one in which the therapist achieves an optimal balance between formulating interpretations (with an eye to advancing the patient's knowledge of her internal dynamics); offering some form of corrective provision (with an eye either to validating the patient's experience or, more generally, to providing the patient with a corrective emotional experience); and engaging the patient interactively in relationship (with an eye to advancing the patient's knowledge of her relational dynamics and/or to deepening the connection between patient and therapist).

Advancing the patient's knowledge of her internal dynamics leads ultimately to resolving her structural conflicts; providing the patient with a corrective emotional experience leads ultimately to filling in her structural deficits; and engaging the patient interactively in relationship leads ultimately to resolving her relational difficulties (whether relational conflict, relational deficit, or, more generally, problems with relatedness).

It will be the therapist's intent that determines whether her intervention is in the province of Model 1, Model 2, or Model 3. In other words, if her intent is to offer the patient an opportunity to achieve insight into her internal dynamics, then it is a Model 1 response; if her intent is to offer the patient an opportunity to feel recognized and responded to, then it is a Model 2 response; and if her intent is to engage the patient more deeply in relationship, then it is a Model 3 response.

The patient's response will determine how effective the therapist's intervention has been. In Model 1, for example, the therapist's intent may have been to advance the patient's understanding of her internal process, but if it misses the mark or makes the patient more defensive, then the therapist's interpretation (although still a Model 1 intervention) will have been ineffective. So, too, the Model 2 therapist may have intended a particular response to be empathic, but if the patient feels misunderstood, then the therapist's intervention (although still a Model 2 intervention) will have been an instance of inaccurate empathy. Finally, the Model 3 therapist may have intended a particular intervention either to advance the patient's understanding of her relational dynamics and/or to deepen the level of their engagement, but if it misses the mark or makes the patient more defensive, then the therapist's intervention (although still a Model 3 intervention) will have been ineffective.

If the therapist tries a particular kind of intervention and it fails to advance the analytic endeavor, then she may want to try another kind of intervention, understanding that, because of her earlier intervention (and the patient's response to it), the intersubjective field has now shifted slightly. The therapist will never have an opportunity to revisit the original situation; although with each passing moment, all sorts of new possibilities arise. The field itself is continuously being shaped and reshaped by both the therapist's interventions and the patient's responses, such that no two moments in time are ever exactly the same.

CLASSIFICATION OF THE PATIENT

What makes a patient a Model 1, a Model 2, or a Model 3 patient?

In other words, at any given point in time, is the patient inherently a Model 1 patient (that is, a patient ridden with structural conflicts) or is it that the patient becomes a Model 1 patient by virtue of the fact that the therapist is focusing on the patient's internal dynamics? Is the patient inherently a Model 2 patient (that is, a patient ridden with structural deficits) or is it that the patient becomes a Model 2 patient by virtue of the fact that the therapist is focusing on the patient's impaired capacity to be a good mother to herself? And is the patient inherently a Model 3 patient or is it that she becomes a Model 3 patient by virtue of the fact that the therapist is focusing on the patient's relational dynamics and/or the interactive dynamic between them?

Admittedly, there are certain kinds of patients who would seem to have psychopathology that makes them ideal candidates for Model 1, Model 2, or Model 3 interventions: (1) neurotic patients (who, by definition, have structural or neurotic conflicts) are particularly suited to Model 1 interventions; (2) narcissistic patients (who, by definition, have structural deficits) respond well to Model 2 interventions; and (3) character disordered patients (who, by definition, externalize their conflicts because they lack the capacity to tolerate internal conflicts) are good candidates for Model 3 interventions.

In other words, there are certain kinds of patients who would seem to be prototypical Model 1, Model 2, and Model 3 patients.

But my experience suggests that it is more clinically useful to think of all patients as manifesting, at some point or another, structural conflict, structural deficit, and relational difficulties (including relational conflict and relational deficit). If a patient is pigeonholed as neurotic or as narcissistic or as character disordered, then a certain depth may be lost in the therapeutic endeavor.

A related question has to do with the issue of timing. Is it possible that early on in the treatment the patient requires a particular kind of intervention—whereas, with time, the patient becomes amenable to other kinds?

Nearer the beginning of the treatment, it may well be that the patient will respond especially well to empathic interventions that validate the patient's experience and enable her to feel understood. In fact, the patient may not be receptive to interpretations that highlight recurring themes, patterns, and repetitions in her life until she becomes more comfortable in the therapy. Or she may not be receptive to interpretations that challenge her to recognize what she is playing out (or enacting) in her relationships until she becomes more trusting of the therapist.

But here, too, my experience suggests that it is more clinically useful to think of all patients as requiring sometimes interpretation of their structural conflict (so that they can gain insight into their internal dynamics), sometimes validation of their experience (so that they can feel provided for in the way that a good mother provides for her young child), and sometimes engagement in relationship (so that they can have the experience of being found).

If the therapist is adept at positioning herself simultaneously—and paradoxically—as a neutral object, as an empathic selfobject, and as an authentic subject and has a broad repertoire of interventions within her armamentarium, then she will have access to many levels of understanding about the patient and will be able to respond in a variety of ways that will enable her to meet the patient wherever the patient is. The more versatile the therapist, the more effective she can be.

I believe that every patient, whatever her underlying psychodynamics and relational patterns, will display, alternately, structural conflict, structural deficit, and relational difficulties—and sometimes all three simultaneously. In other words, every patient will, at some point or another, be able to profit from enhancement of knowledge, validation of experience, and engagement in relationship.

And so it is that although the Freudian patient would seem to need insight, the Kohutian patient would seem to need a new good object, the Fairbairnian patient would seem to need the old bad object, and the Guntripian patient would seem to need to avoid the object altogether, the Freudian patient, the Kohutian patient, the Fairbairnian patient, and the Guntripian patient may well be the very same patient—but at different points in time.

CLASSIFICATION OF THE THERAPIST

As I have suggested, my intent is to offer a model of therapeutic action that integrates all three perspectives—enhancement of knowledge, provision of experience, and engagement in relationship. I believe that each perspective offers something unique to our understanding of the therapeutic process.

All this notwithstanding, there would seem to be some therapists who, for whatever reason, appear to embrace one particular model in preference to the other two. Perhaps because of their training, their orientation, their cognitive style, certain blind spots, or their personal preference, these therapists may find themselves (1) more interested in advancing the patient's understanding of her internal process than in anything else, (2) more interested in offering the patient the experience of being recognized and responded to than in anything else, or (3) more interested in focusing on the here-and-now analytic engagement between patient and therapist than in anything else.

Sometimes therapists do not themselves recognize that they are partial to a particular stance; it may be that their colleagues recognize this about them, where they do not.

In any event, theorists who are considered Model 1 therapists include Freud (1912, 1914, 1923), Brenner (1955), Gray (1973, 1994), and Davison (1984). Theorists who are considered Model 2 therapists include Kohut (1966, 1968, 1971), Balint (1968), Schwaber (1979, 1983), Anna Ornstein (1974), Paul Ornstein (1974), and Rogers (1961). Theorists who are considered Model 3 therapists include Ehrenberg (1974), Davies (1994), Hoffman (1983, 1992), Aron (1996), Renik (1993), Levenson (1991), Bollas (1987), Casement (1985), and Ogden (1979, 1983).

Winnicott straddles Models 2 and 3. Sometimes his interest would seem to be in the "give" that characterizes the patient–therapist relationship and sometimes his interest would seem to be in its "give-and-take."

(1) On the one hand, Winnicott (1958, 1965) speaks to the importance of the facilitating (or holding) environment—the mother's (the

therapist's) provision of a protective envelope within which the inherited potential of her young child (her patient) can become actualized. To the extent that Winnicott's emphasis is on this form of corrective provision by the maternal object, his is a Model 2 theory.

(2) On the other hand, Winnicott (1963b) also speaks to the issue of the patient's impact on the therapist; he believes that patients get their therapists to fail them in old, familiar ways. Winnicott writes,

> Corrective provision is never enough. . . . In the end the patient uses the analyst's failures, often quite small ones, perhaps manoeuvred by the patient. . . . The operative factor is that the patient now hates the analyst for the failure that originally came as an environmental factor, outside the infant's area of omnipotent control, but that is *now* staged in the transference. So in the end we succeed by failing—failing the patient's way. This is a long distance from the simple theory of cure by corrective experience. [p. 258]

To the extent that Winnicott's emphasis is on negotiation at the intimate edge between patient and therapist (an edge to which both patient and therapist contribute), then his is a Model 3 theory.

Guntrip positions himself sometimes as a Model 2 theorist and sometimes as a Model 3 theorist. When Guntrip (1973) writes about the therapeutic action as involving the therapist's participation "in loco parentis"—the therapist operating in the place of a parent upon whom the patient becomes, as Guntrip (1961) suggests, "therapeutically dependent," he is very much in the tradition of a Model 2 theorist. But when he (1969) describes the schizoid personality as someone who has retreated from all relationships (both external and internal) because it hurts too much to be in relationship, he is poignantly capturing the essence of the stance assumed by the patient with relational deficit—which places him squarely in the tradition of a Model 3 theorist.

In Stolorow's (Stolorow 1978, Stolorow and Lachmann 1980) earlier writings, he appeared to be a Model 2 therapist—because of his emphasis on (1) the therapist's need to decenter from her own subjectivity so that she could immerse herself empathically in the patient's experience and (2) the re-activation of the patient's arrested developmental needs in the therapy relationship. In recent years, it would seem that Stolorow (1987) has shifted into the relational realm of Model 3, as he has come to emphasize the importance of focusing on the intersubjective field between patient and therapist (seen as the intersection of two differently organized subjectivities).

But there are aspects of Stolorow's theory that are more in keeping with a Model 1 theory of therapeutic action, which posits enhancement of the patient's self-knowledge as its goal. For example, Stolorow (1988, Stolorow and colleagues 1987) appears to conceive of the therapeutic action as involving advancement of the patient's insight into her internal process through developing her reflective self-awareness of the organizing principles that structure her experience of the world. Although Stolorow's goal is not resolution of structural (neurotic) conflict, as it is in classical psychoanalysis, his goal is still insight and the rendering conscious of what had once been unconscious—which is very much in keeping with a Model 1 perspective.

Admittedly, the analyst's interpretations derive their mutative power from the intersubjective matrix in which they take form—but Stolorow contends that it is the insight achieved by way of such interpretations that is the primary therapeutic agent in the intersubjective perspective. And so it is that the intersubjective relationship (Model 3) is a means to an end—the end being "attainment of psychoanalytic understanding" (Model 1).

Interestingly, some Model 2 theorists believe that it is the experience of being met (or the experience of working through disappointment at not being met) that facilitates structural growth, consolidation of the self, and the filling in of deficit. Other Model 2 theorists contend that the experience of being met is a means to an end, with the ultimate end being the acquisition of insight into the internal workings of one's mind (Model 1). Schwaber (1981), for example, suggests that the experience of being failed in the transference revived, for one of her patients, early-on memories of having been failed by his parent and offered the patient an opportunity to understand his current experience in light of that earlier experience. It was this that was transformative.

Because (upon closer examination) no therapist can rightfully be considered exclusively interpretive, empathic, or relational (whether in theory or in practice), I am less concerned with typecasting different therapists as Model 1, 2, or 3. My interest is in highlighting the options all psychodynamic therapists have, from moment to moment, with respect to how they position themselves in relation to the patient.

A final note: when I make reference to the therapist as, say, a Model 1 therapist, I mean to be suggesting that in the moment, she is positioned outside the field as an objective observer of the patient, teasing out recurring themes, patterns, and repetitions, and formulating hypotheses about the internal workings of the patient's mind. In the next moment, if her position shifts to, say, a focus on her own experience of being in the room with the patient and on what that experience tells her about the patient's presence in the room, then she will become a Model 3 therapist. Or if she abandons both her objectivity and her subjectivity to immerse herself empathically in the patient's internal experience, then in that moment she will have become a Model 2 therapist. In other words, as the therapist's perspective shifts from moment to moment, so too the model of therapeutic action that she is embracing shifts.

THE DIRECTION OF FOCUS

I find it a useful distinction to think in terms of the direction in which the therapist focuses the patient's attention. In Part I, I spoke of the therapist as sometimes joining the patient where she is and as sometimes directing the patient's attention elsewhere. I said that the therapist joins the patient where she is when the therapist responds empathically to the patient (in an effort to help the patient feel understood—Model 2); I said that the therapist directs the patient's attention elsewhere when the therapist formulates interpretations about either the patient's internal dynamics or her relational dynamics (in an effort to help the patient understand—Models 1 and 3).

But now I would like to suggest that we think, more specifically, about where the therapist encourages the patient "to look."

The Patient's Internal Process

With a Model 1 intervention, the therapist directs the patient's attention to her internal process—that is, to what is going on inside her. Perhaps the therapist encourages her to take note of the fact that she appears to become angry when she feels thwarted, perhaps that she has trouble sustaining good feelings about herself in the face of being disappointed by her therapist, perhaps that she tends to experience others (including her therapist) as critical when she does not get much feedback, perhaps that she fears intimacy because she is afraid she will be engulfed, or perhaps that she thinks others (including her therapist) do not like her.

In any event, a Model 1 intervention directs the patient's attention to her internal process. Even though the intervention may relate indirectly to how the patient feels in relationship to others (including her therapist), the focus is more upon what is going on intrapsychically than upon what is going on interpersonally; it is more upon the patient's internal dynamics than it is upon her relational dynamics.

The Patient's Affective Experience

With a Model 2 intervention, the therapist directs the patient's attention to her affect—more specifically, to what the patient is actually feeling in the moment (the "points of emotional urgency" [Strachey 1934]). As we have noted, with a Model 2 intervention, the emphasis is on affect of which the patient is aware (or dimly aware) and not on affect against which the patient is defending herself (and of which she is therefore unaware). Perhaps the therapist resonates with the patient's experience of upset that she does not feel understood by the therapist, perhaps with the patient's anger that the therapist was late, perhaps with the patient's relief that the therapist has finally understood just how desperate the patient is, or perhaps with the patient's confusion about how she is really feeling.

By encouraging the patient to take note of her affective experience in the moment, the therapist is also hoping to give the patient space to delve more deeply into her affect, so that patient and therapist can come to understand more about it.

In any event, a Model 2 intervention directs the patient's attention to her affective experience in the moment—to what is emotionally immediate for her.

The Here-and-Now Engagement

With a Model 3 intervention, the therapist directs the patient's attention to what is going on in the room between patient and therapist. The therapist may do this by way of

1. Disclosing some aspect of her experience of being in the room with the patient (in order to highlight the patient's impact on the therapist);
2. Focusing the patient's attention more specifically on the patient's relational dynamics (in order to highlight the ways in which the patient is contributing to what is going on in the room);
3. Focusing the patient's attention on some aspect of the therapist's participation (in order to highlight the therapist's impact on the patient); or
4. Focusing the patient's attention more specifically on the interactive dynamic in the room (in order to emphasize mutuality of impact between patient and therapist).

In any event, the Model 3 therapist directs the patient's attention to their here-and-now engagement, a two-way relationship thought to involve give-and-take, mutuality of impact, and reciprocity.

THE INSIDE, THE OUTSIDE, AND THE IN-BETWEEN

With respect to the therapist's focus, we might say of the Model 1 therapist that she works from an outside position, of the Model 2 therapist that she works from an inside position, and of the Model 3 therapist that she works with the in-between—that is, at the interface between the inside and the outside. In other words, in Model 1 the therapist, as a neutral observer, positions herself outside the therapeutic field; in Model 2 the therapist, as an empathic selfobject, positions herself alongside the patient (all the better to enter into the patient's internal experience); and in Model 3 the therapist, as an authentic subject, positions herself at the intimate edge between them.

CHAPTER

15

A Pure Definition of Empathy

I have been suggesting all along that whereas Model 3 involves the therapist's authentic engagement with the patient, Model 2 involves the therapist's empathic attunement to the patient.

I would like now to highlight some distinctions within Model 2 between the self psychologists and those Model 2 object relations theorists who focus on the internal recording of traumatic parental failure in the form of deficit. As we know, both groups embrace a deficiency-compensation model of therapeutic action, but the focus of each is a little different:

1. Whereas self psychologists focus on empathic recognition of need, Model 2 object relations theorists focus not only on recognizing but also on responding to such need;
2. Whereas self psychologists speak to the importance of the therapist's providing validation of experience, Model 2 object relations theorists speak to the importance of the therapist's providing a corrective emotional experience (that is, the therapist's holding provision);
3. Whereas the self psychologist is thought to participate as an empathic selfobject, the Model 2 object relations theorist is thought to participate as a good object/good mother; and
4. Whereas self psychologists focus on the patient's experience of the therapist as a new good object, Model 2 object relations theorists focus on the therapist's actual participation as that new good object.

But though there are some differences (at least in theory) between the two groups in terms of emphasis, in actual practice there is much that is the same, particularly with respect to the central role played by the patient's affective experience.

I would like now to explore some fine points about what is required of the Model 2 therapist who is attempting to remain affectively attuned, moment by moment, to the patient's emotional experience.

THE EMPATHIC LISTENING STANCE

Schwaber (1979, 1981, 1983) writes eloquently about the empathic listening stance—a stance that characterizes the listening style of self psychologists and, though less rigorously, many Model 2 object relations theorists.

Schwaber writes that empathy requires a certain capacity: the therapist must be able (1) to enter into the patient's internal world and (2) to experience it as if it were her own.

The empathic therapist takes on the patient's experience only "as if" it were her own—and not "as" her own. In order for the therapist to be truly empathic, Schwaber notes, her sense of self must not be altered. Once the therapist's sense of self is altered (as happens in Model 3, where the therapist is ever busy responding to the patient's impact), then the therapist is no longer being empathic.

Schwaber's position is a bold one, but I think she captures the essence of the empathic listening stance in its purest form.

Schwaber cites the situation of a mother who becomes anxious when her child is anxious. Such a mother, Schwaber contends, is having difficulty being empathic, because the mother is responding as much to her own anxiety as to the child's. The mother will be truly empathic only if she (1) can sense the child's anxiety without herself being made unduly anxious (afferent empathy) and (2) can then do whatever she must in order to ease the child's anxiety (efferent empathy). But when she herself is made anxious, then (says Schwaber) her sense of self becomes altered in a way that makes her less available to her child as an empathic object.

Schwaber (1981) would say of such a mother that her countertransference is interfering with her ability to be empathic with her child.

As another example, Schwaber cites the situation of a mother who, in rocking her baby to sleep, so merges with its rhythm that she herself falls asleep. Her claim here, too, is that such a mother is no longer being empathic—because her sense of self has been altered.

Schwaber notes that an empathic listening stance requires of the therapist that the integrity of her own separate self remain intact. If the mother allows her child to have an impact on her and allows herself to be changed as a result of that impact, then she is no longer being empathic.

Once we begin to talk about the child's impact on the mother or the patient's impact on the therapist, we must shift our focus to Model 3, which deals specifically with the subject's impact on the other.

When the mother's self is altered by virtue of her child's impact on her, we are talking about the mother's participation not as an empathic selfobject but as an authentic subject—an equally effective but nonetheless quite different way of relating to her child.

Again, for empathy to remain, the integrity of the therapist's own separate self must stay intact—it cannot be altered by the patient's impact.

And so it is that in Schwaber's theorizing about empathic listening, there is little place for the impact of the patient on the therapist. In fact, listening empathically does not involve the therapist's "use of self." Listening empathically requires of the therapist that she decenter from her experience of self in order to immerse herself in the patient's experience, so that she can come to understand deeply the patient's perspective, uncontaminated by her own.

A 1992 article written by Schwaber entitled "Countertransference: The Analyst's Retreat from the Patient's Vantage Point," speaks to this very issue of the analyst's countertransferential response to the patient as interfering with her ability to immerse herself empathically in the patient's experience and to appreciate fully the patient's perspective.

Responsiveness to the Patient's Desire

Before I go on to highlight differences between involvement of the therapist's self in self psychology and involvement of the therapist's self in Model 3, I would like to address the participation of Model 2 object relations theories—a gray zone in the literature.

With respect to Model 2 objects relations theories, it is not clear (1) to what extent the patient is thought to have an impact on the therapist; (2) to what extent the therapist's reality is thought to be shaped by the patient's reality; and (3) to what extent the therapist's self is thought to be affected by the patient's need.

Let me therefore pose the following two questions with respect to Model 2 object relations theories (questions that I later revisit from a slightly different perspective): To what extent does the therapist participate as a new good object by virtue of her responsiveness to pressure from the patient to participate in that way? And to what extent does the therapist participate as a new good object because she believes that what deficit-ridden patients most need is the opportunity to experience a good mother?

As noted above, because self psychology emphasizes that the therapist must decenter from her own experience of self in order to enter into the patient's experience of self, it does not (in self psychology) make sense to think in terms of the therapist's self as being altered by the patient.

But Model 2 object relations theorists are less committed to the idea that the therapist must decenter from her own experience in order to immerse herself in the patient's experience. These theorists focus more on the therapist's participation as a good mother, participation that would seem to be a story about both the therapist's responsiveness to the patient's need and the therapist's theoretical belief that what deficit-ridden patients most need in order to get better is a corrective experience provided by a good mother.

And so the answers to the two questions posed above are complicated. Although self psychology does not allow for the therapist to respond actively to the patient's need (empathically recognize, yes; actively respond, no), Model 2 object relations theories are less clear as to whether or not they believe that the therapist allows herself to be shaped by the patient's desire (which I will later be describing as displacive identification).

When in what follows I suggest that the focus in Model 2 is on empathic attunement and the focus in Model 3 is on authentic engagement, I will therefore be excluding from consideration Model 2 object relations theories and focusing more on self psychology.

Involvement of the Therapist's Self

Let us return now to the issue of what happens when the therapist's self is altered as a result of the patient's impact.

As we have just seen, although there is no place in Model 2 (self psychology) for the patient's impact on the therapist, in Model 3 the therapist invites the patient's impact.

And once we begin to address the patient's impact on the therapist, we find ourselves thinking about the concept of the patient's need either to elicit a particular response from the therapist or to convey something important to the therapist about the patient's internal experience—described as an enactment by many Model 3 theorists. We have now moved beyond Model 2, which deals only with the therapist's shaping of the patient's reality and not with the patient's shaping of the therapist's reality.

It is therefore to Model 3 that we must turn in order to understand the relationship between the patient's need to communicate her internal experience to the therapist and the therapist's capacity to respond. This latter situation, however, is not thought to involve empathy—at least not as purists (Geist 1995, Schwaber 1979) conceive of it.

In fact, when the therapist, by way of her responsiveness to a patient's enactment, is drawn into experiencing the patient's affect as her own (and her sense of self is thereby altered), then we no longer use the word empathy—in its strictest sense—to describe what has happened. We are now in the realm not of empathic attunement to the patient but of authentic engagement with the patient—the therapist no longer decentered from her self (so as to be empathically attuned) but very much centered within her self (so as to be available to the patient for authentic engagement).

In Model 2, if the therapist allows the patient to have an impact on her, then the therapist's subjective countertransference is implicated and the therapist is encouraged to seek either consultation, supervision, or therapy.

In Model 3, however, the therapist's countertransferential participation in the patient's transferential enactments is believed to be not only unavoidable but a crucial aspect of what ultimately heals the patient.

Because (in a relational model) it is thought that part of how the patient engages her therapist is by way of drawing her into experiencing all kinds of feelings, the therapist's willingness and ability to be so engaged facilitates the therapeutic process. Now our focus is less on the therapist's subjective countertransference and more on her objective countertransference—a wonderfully rich source of data about the patient's internal world.

Schwaber's (1979, 1981, 1983) stance is what I will be calling empathy in its narrower sense—the province of Model 2 theorists (or, at least, most self psychologists). Then there are those (Tansey and Burke 1989) who suggest adopting a broader definition of empathy, one that includes those situations in which the therapist's sense of self is altered as a result of taking on the patient's internal experience. By way of example, Tansey and Burke believe that the therapist is responding empathically when she accepts the patient's projections (projective identifications)—projections that, once accepted, shape the therapist's experience and deepen her understanding of the patient.

I believe, however, that these latter situations (involving alteration of the therapist's self) should be included in Model 3—because this perspective conceives of the patient–therapist relationship as involving mutuality of impact, the therapist ever responsive to the patient's need to communicate aspects of her internal experience by way of placing them in her therapist.

I find it both theoretically and clinically useful to preserve the distinction between empathy (in its narrower sense) as speaking to the therapist's decentering from her own experience in order to arrive at understanding of the patient and empathy (used more broadly) as speaking to the therapist's remaining centered within her own experience in order to arrive at understanding of the patient. This latter I prefer to classify as the therapist's "use of self" (that is, the therapist's use of her objective countertransference) to inform her understanding of the patient.

In Model 2, then, at the point when the therapist is changed by the patient, the therapist is thought to be no longer empathic. In Model 3, however, the therapist is always being changed by the patient. In fact, for the relational therapist, to be in relationship is to have one's experience continuously shaped by the other, even as one is also continuously shaping that other's experience.

And so it is that when the therapist—in response to the patient's heartrending sobs—finds her own eyes tearing, the therapist is no longer responding empathically. She is responding authentically, but not empathically—because her sense of self has been altered. To describe it as an empathic response would be to eclipse the important distinction between the therapist's entering into the patient's experience (Model 2) and the therapist's allowing the patient's experience to enter into her (Model 3).

Model 2 involves the therapist's more-or-less selfless attunement to the patient's affective experience, uncontaminated by her own experience; Model 3, however, involves interactive engagement between two subjects—both of whom bring their authentic selves into the intersubjective field, both of whom affect (and are affected by) the other.

THE NEED TO BE EMPATHICALLY FAILED

We have spoken repeatedly about the patient's need to be failed in ways specifically determined by her history—a need prompted, in part, by her desire to achieve mastery of her internalized traumas.

How would we describe the behavior of a therapist who allows herself to be drawn into participating as the old bad (familial and, therefore, familiar) object?

Again, some (Tansey and Burke 1989) would say that such a therapist is simply responding empathically to the patient's need.

But if we were to describe such a response as empathic, then we would find ourselves in the untenable position of suggesting that the therapist is being empathic when she is (empathically) failing the patient.

Admittedly, there are those who believe that empathy involves giving the patient what she needs in order to get better—even if that means failing her (so that she can rework her internalized traumas). But conceptualizing empathy in this way obscures the crucial distinction between the therapist's ability to respond to something inside the patient's awareness (something that is experience-near) and the therapist's ability to respond to something outside the patient's awareness (something experience-distant that the patient may be unconsciously needing in order to be healed).

I think that it makes more sense to reserve the term "therapeutic" for these latter situations in which the therapist is giving the patient what she needs in order to get better. But just because the therapist is advancing the therapeutic endeavor does not necessarily mean that she is being empathic.

Taking my lead from Kohut (1982), Schwaber (1979), and other purists (Geist 1995), I am going to reserve the term empathy for those situations in which the therapist resonates with something emotionally immediate and real for the patient—not for those situations in which the therapist responds to something (say, the need to be failed) of which the patient is unaware.

The Need for Containment

How would we describe the behavior of a therapist who "meets" the borderline patient's need for containment?

Elsewhere (Stark 1994a), I suggest that the hallmark of a borderline patient is her impaired ability to sit with internal conflict and intense affect (particularly rageful disappointment) and her tendency instead to act out her feelings in impulsive, destructive ways. In essence, she has an impaired capacity to be self-containing. The patient's deficit creates a need—that is, the patient's inability to provide internal containment creates a need for external containment.

Would we say of the therapist who provides such containment that she is being empathic? Admittedly, containment is what the borderline patient most needs—but it is not, specifically, what she is aware of wanting. The therapist's provision of containment may well be therapeutic but it will not be empathic—because it will not be a response to something that is experience-near for the patient.

More specifically, the therapist's provision of containment (that is, her responsiveness to the borderline patient's need to be contained) will be an instance of "meeting" the patient, which, as we will later explore in greater depth, is what object relations theorists are thought to provide in their role as the good parent the deficit-ridden patient never had—again, this is what I call displacive identification.

Therapeutic versus Empathic Responses

In other words, if a patient needs castor oil in order to get better, does giving her a spoonful of it constitute an empathic response?

I am here suggesting that it does not. The therapist may in fact choose to give the patient a spoonful of castor oil and the patient may indeed be better off because of it; but the therapist's response (no matter how therapeutic) will still not be described as empathic by those purists who insist that for a response to be considered empathic, it must resonate with what the patient is experiencing in the moment.

In sum, if the patient is not aware that she "needs" a particular something to get better, then it will not be empathic when the therapist provides that particular something, whether it is acceptance of the patient's projection (when, say, relational conflict is involved), empathic failure (when, say, structural deficit is involved), or containment (when, say, the patient is a borderline). Even if the therapist is absolutely correct and the patient does indeed need that particular something, unless the patient is herself aware (or, at least, partially aware) of her need and of her wish to have it responded to, then the therapist's provision will not be considered empathic.

The therapist's empathic responsiveness involves recognizing and responding to something that the patient is actually feeling; thus it involves only that which is experience-near for the patient.

AFFERENT VERSUS EFFERENT EMPATHY

Schwaber (1979) describes empathy as a mode of observation (or perception); an empathic response, she suggests, is a derivative of empathy—it is what one does with what one has come to know by way of an empathic immersion in the patient's experience. In the first instance, empathy is a mode of observation (afferent empathy); in the second instance, empathy is a mode of intervention (efferent empathy).

In the psychodynamic literature, empathy is sometimes used to suggest how the therapist listens to the patient, and is sometimes used to suggest how the therapist responds to the patient; the former is about how the therapist arrives at understanding of the patient and the latter is about how the therapist intervenes—an intervention that will be based, amongst other things, on what the therapist has come to understand about the patient by way of her empathic immersion in the patient's internal experience.

In other words, empathy sometimes is used to indicate a way of listening to the patient and is sometimes used to indicate a way of responding to the patient; it is therefore thought to serve simply an epistemological function (what I am describing as afferent empathy) at some times, and a therapeutic function (what I am describing as efferent empathy) at others.

Near the end of his life, Kohut (1982) himself recognized the importance of distinguishing between empathy as a mode of observation and empathy as a mode of responding. In a paper published posthumously and entitled "Introspection, Empathy, and the Semi-Circle of

Mental Health," Kohut (1982) speaks to this distinction when he suggests that empathy itself is simply an "information-collecting, data-gathering activity." He goes on to suggest that it is not the mother's empathy per se that satisfies her child's need; rather, her actions and her responses to her child will do that. Kohut notes: "Empathy is thus a precondition for a mother's appropriate functioning as the child's selfobject; it informs parental selfobject function vis à vis the child, but it is not, by itself, the selfobject function that is needed by the child" (p. 397).

In other words, empathy enables the therapist to arrive at understanding of the patient; the understanding so acquired can then be used by the therapist to inform a response that the patient will experience as supportive (or therapeutic). The former is afferent empathy; the latter is efferent empathy.

Several years later, Mark Blechner (1988) also made this same distinction between empathy as a mode of observation and empathy as a mode of response. In a paper entitled "Differentiating Empathy from Therapeutic Action," Blechner advances his idea that there is less confusion when a distinction is made between empathy as serving an epistemological function and empathy as serving a therapeutic function. In that paper, he writes that empathy is "an epistemological process that can be used in the service of therapy, but not as a therapeutic process per se" (p. 307). Here Blechner is suggesting that empathy makes possible an empathic response—but that it is not, in and of itself, where the therapeutic action lies.

I too am using empathy to speak both to how the therapist listens (afference) and to how the therapist responds (efference). In Model 2, the empathic therapist listens by way of a decentering from her own experience so that she can come to know the patient's experience from a position within. So, too, the empathic therapist, ever attuned to what the patient is experiencing in the moment, responds in a way that she hopes will convey to the patient that the therapist does indeed understand the patient's experience.

It will usually be clear from the context the way in which the term empathy is being used.

So what will I be meaning when I say of the therapist that she is being empathic? A purist would have it that the therapist is being empathic when, by way of immersing herself in the patient's internal experience, she is able (1) to resonate with what the patient is feeling in the moment (without herself being changed as a result), and (2) to offer some kind of response in the way of validation, recognition, or affirmation of that experience. As discussed earlier, the first is an instance of afferent empathy; the second an instance of efferent empathy—in both instances, it could be said of the therapist that she is "being empathic."

EMPATHY AS UNDERSTANDING

Empathy is about understanding; it is about entering into the patient's experience in such a way that the therapist can come to understand it from the patient's perspective.

Easy Empathy

Easy empathy, as I have mentioned elsewhere (Stark 1994b), involves understanding aspects of the patient's experience that are not too dissimilar from the therapist's own—or that would not be too dissimilar from the therapist's own were the therapist to be in the patient's shoes.

For example, it may be quite easy for the therapist to empathize with a patient who is upset because she feels she is being exploited by her boss; the therapist would herself be upset were she to be in such a position. It may be quite easy for the therapist to empathize with a patient who has just lost his girlfriend and is devastated; here too, the patient's reaction is probably not all that different from what the therapist would feel were the therapist to be in a similar position.

Difficult Empathy

Difficult empathy, however, involves understanding aspects of the patient's experience that are at variance with the therapist's worldview, aspects that are discrepant from the therapist's experience.

For example, it may be difficult for the therapist to empathize with a patient who continues to pine for a man who has done nothing but use and abuse her. If the patient's experience is very different from what the therapist imagines her experience would be were she to be in such a situation, the therapist may have to work hard to put aside her own prejudice in order to enter into the patient's experience of intense yearning for this man.

As another example, it may be difficult for the therapist to empathize with a patient who, at the age of 38, still lives at home and is terrified that his father will tell him to find his own place. If the patient's reaction is very different from what the therapist's reaction would be under similar circumstances, the therapist may have to struggle to let go of some of her own convictions about the way things should be.

As yet another example, it may be difficult for the therapist to empathize with a patient who wants, more than anything else in the world, to have an affair with her boss; as different as the patient's reaction might be from the therapist's reaction, empathy involves the therapist's capacity to set aside her own biases about what is right in order to understand the patient's investment in having such an affair.

Finally, it may be difficult for the therapist to empathize with a patient who is needing to keep important parts of herself and her experience out of the therapy relationship. If the therapist is deeply convinced that the patient will get better only if she commits to the work and allows herself to be vulnerable, then the therapist may have a hard time understanding why the patient refuses to engage in the treatment.

In fact, there are patients (whom I describe as having relational deficit) who cannot deliver themselves into the treatment. For whatever the reason, they do not let the therapist become all that important to them—although they may stay in treatment because they feel it is their last hope. They continue to come, but their hearts are not in it. They may be physically present, but they are not really there. The therapist, because of her own need to see the patient as invested in the treatment, may not always fully appreciate just how disengaged the patient actually is.

EMPATHY AS STRUGGLE

Schwaber (1992) and Friedman (1985) have written about the therapist's struggle to embrace the patient's point of view; both observe that the therapist must often work hard to maintain an empathic stance. Implicit in what they are saying, I believe, is the idea that there is something in the therapist that impedes her ability to immerse herself wholeheartedly in the patient's internal experience.

From a Model 2 vantage point, whenever the therapist finds herself unable to enter into the patient's experience, then it is thought to be a situation in which the therapist's countertransference is interfering with her ability to be fully available to the patient as an empathic selfobject. When the therapist has difficulty being empathic, then something must be going on inside the therapist that is prompting her retreat from the patient's vantage point—and this something is the therapist's (subjective) countertransference. The something going on relates ultimately to the therapist's involvement in her own experience in such a way that her capacity to be totally present for the patient is disrupted.

From the point of view of Model 2, the therapist's impaired capacity is thought to be a reflection of the therapist's subjectivity (her preconceptions, her biases, her prejudices); but from the point of view of Model 3, it is thought to have other aspects that reflect the therapist's reactivity to something the patient is enacting in their here-and-now engagement.

Whatever the case, however, it is the therapist's difficulty decentering from her own experience (fueled, as it is, by her countertransference) that interferes with her ability to enter into and sustain her interest in the patient's internal experience.

Dumb Spots, Hard Spots, Blind Spots

James McLaughlin (1991) has captured well the essence of the therapist's struggle to be fully present for the patient with the following:

> When at work we bumble, stumble, and get lost, we know we are into mixes of not yet knowing (our dumb spots), not being free to know because of acquired biases and preference for theory and technique (our hard spots), or having lost, for reasons of intrapsychic conflict, our hold on what we know or thought we knew (our blind spots). [p. 600]

Empathy requires of the therapist that she recognize her dumb spots, put aside her hard spots, and work through her blind spots. It involves the therapist's willingness and ability to relinquish her investment in what she thinks is "right," what she thinks is "wrong." It requires of her that she move beyond her own prejudices, her own theoretical biases, her own preconceptions. Empathy involves the capacity to step out of one's own shoes and into the patient's. It is about neither the therapist nor what the therapist thinks, feels, or knows—it is about the patient and the patient's experience, the patient's reality.

Empathy, then, is about neither agreeing nor disagreeing with the patient. It is not about sitting in judgment or trying to decide if the patient's reality is accurate or not. It is not about telling the patient that what she did was not so bad; it is not about reassuring her that anyone in such a position would have done the same thing. It is not about telling her that what she did was good. It is not about offering the patient advice. It is not about reminding the patient of all the gains she has made over the course of the treatment.

The therapist may choose to do any of these things—but we do not then say of her that she is being empathic (in its purest sense). To be empathic, the therapist must decenter from her own reality; for the therapist to agree, to disagree, or to reassure (with any genuineness or conviction), the therapist must be centered within her own reality. But as soon as she centers herself within her own reality, she automatically steps out of her empathic stance.

The therapist may choose to do any of these things—but giving reassurance to a patient who is doubting, offering hope to a patient who is despairing, offering advice to a patient who is floundering, is not being empathic, because the intent of her activity is not to validate the patient's experience but to give the patient support.

Empathy is about understanding, and an empathic response is one that conveys to the patient that understanding. To be empathic, the therapist must step away from her own experience and into the patient's experience. An empathic response has, as its intent, the goal of recognition—empathic recognition of the patient's experience, thereby enabling the patient to feel understood.

When the therapist formulates an interpretation, her intent is to enhance the patient's knowledge, and when the therapist uses her self to engage the patient, her intent is to deepen their relationship. When the therapist responds empathically to the patient, her intent is to validate the patient's experience.

Clinical Vignette—Are You Disgusted by Me?

Now let us imagine a situation in which the patient says that she feels she is a bad person because she once touched her daughter's genitals when her daughter was 8 months old; she says that she is haunted by the memory of what she did and that she feels she is a loathsome, despicable human being because of it.

What would constitute an empathic response? As we have seen, empathy is about the therapist's willingness—and ability—to set aside her own subjectivity (including her own judgment as to how "bad" the patient's behavior really was) in order to enter into the patient's experience of herself as a bad person. If the therapist is willing and able to immerse herself in the patient's internal world, the patient will have an opportunity to elaborate upon how haunted she is by what she did and how loathsome she therefore experiences herself as being.

The therapist must be able to bear the intensity of the patient's self-denigration. The therapist knows that the patient's unrelenting self-hatred predates the patient's touching of her daughter's genitals. The therapist's hope is that within the context of safety provided by a relationship with someone the patient knows does care, does understand, and can tolerate the intensity of the her self-loathing and her despair, the patient will be able (1) to expound upon just how awful she feels about herself; (2) to explore some of the genetic underpinnings of this self-hatred; (3) to have the experience of being listened to without judgment; and (4) to discover that both she and her therapist not only survive the experience but have a deeper connection because of what they have shared between them.

Let us imagine, however, that the patient now turns to the therapist and asks (either directly or indirectly) what the therapist thinks about the patient's touching of her daughter's genitals. The therapist may be tempted to reassure the patient that, in the grand scheme of things, what the patient did was not that bad. The therapist could do this, although it would not be considered an empathic response, intended to resonate with the patient's internal experience (of confusion, uncertainty, and anguish).

In order to offer the patient reassurance, the therapist needs to think of herself as being "in the know," as having an inside track on the truth, as being an arbiter of reality, as being an expert on such matters as child abuse. The therapist may indeed conceive of herself in these terms and may therefore feel comfortable offering the patient the reassurance she seeks—but, again, such a response will not be about empathy.

Actually, reassuring the patient will be neither specifically empathic nor specifically unempathic. What such a response will be is an attempt to offer the patient a corrective experience by way of gratifying her need for reassurance.

In other words, there may be times when the therapist will choose not only to resonate empathically with the patient's need but also to offer something she feels will more directly address the need. Gratification of the patient's need may well serve (at least temporarily) to reassure the patient and it may even be therapeutic—but that still does not make it an empathic response.

There are also some potential problems with an approach that involves gratification of need.

1. When the therapist reassures the patient that what she did was not all that bad, the patient may not actually feel all that much better—because what such a patient may need is not reassurance but an opportunity to confess all her sins and to know that her badness has been seen and can be tolerated.
2. If the therapist offers the patient reassurance but is not entirely convinced within herself of the truth in what she is saying, then the patient may well pick up on the therapist's lack of sincerity and experience the therapist as untrustworthy.
3. The therapist's willingness to position herself as "in the know" may give rise to the expectation that the therapist has more answers where that one came from.
4. The therapist's reassurance may be offered to a patient who, deep within her heart, knows that what she did was really not okay—in which case she may come to experience the therapist as not really getting it and/or as needing not to know something important about the patient (and the patient's badness).
5. And, finally, the therapist's reassurance may foreclose further discussion of the patient's lifelong sense of herself as bad, despicable, and loathsome, such that she will never have a chance to examine in greater depth, and to arrive at a more thoroughgoing understanding of, the source of her internal demons.

As we will later explore, when the therapist finds herself providing more and more in the way of actual gratification of need (and not simply empathic recognition of it), then we may be dealing with a situation of *displacive identification*—in which the therapist allows herself to be drawn into participating as the good mother the patient never had, participation that involves the making of exceptions, the flexing of boundaries, the breaking of rules, the giving of special consideration.

As we will later see, when displacive identification is involved, the therapist's self is changed as a result of being impacted upon by the patient's need.

But in response to the patient's more or less directly expressed wish or need to be reassured that what she did was not so bad, the empathic therapist puts aside whatever judgments she might be tempted to make and instead resonates with (1) the patient's confusion about whether what she did was terribly bad or not, (2) the patient's anxiety about what the therapist might now think of her for having done it, and (3) the patient's wish to be reassured that she is really not so bad after all.

To that end, the empathic therapist might offer the patient any of the following: "You are feeling terribly confused and are not sure whether what you did was terribly bad or not," "You are filled with uncertainty and would wish that somebody could tell you what the truth really is," "You are not sure what it really means that you did what you did and are wishing there could be some clarity," "You are afraid that what you did to your daughter makes you a really bad person and so are hoping that I can reassure you that you are not," "You become frightened that I might think ill of you," or "You want to be reassured that I'm still with you in all of this."

Although there may be times when the therapist resorts to reassurance, for the most part what is more to the point is the empathic therapist's willingness and capacity to sit with the patient and to bear witness to her struggle as she dares to explore why she is so convinced of her inherent badness—so that its genetic underpinnings can be unearthed. The patient will then be able, over time, to have the experience of delivering the worst parts of herself into the relationship and discovering that both she and her therapist survive.

VALIDATION OF EXPERIENCE

Empathy, then, is about the therapist's capacity to enter so completely into the patient's experience that the therapist is able to come to know, in the very deepest of ways, what the patient is experiencing. An empathic response involves not gratification of the patient's need but validation of her experience.

Kohut (1984) once observed that in the clinical practice of psychoanalytic self psychology

> the analyst truly grasps the patient's perception of his psychic reality and accepts it as valid. This is tantamount to saying that the self psychologist does not confront the patient with an "objective" reality that is supposedly more "real" than his inner reality, but rather confirms the validity and legitimacy of the patient's own perception of reality, however contrary it might be to the accepted view of reality held by most adults and by society at large. [p. 173]

THE ROLE OF PARADOX

The therapist, by way of immersing herself empathically in the patient's experience, comes to understand and to appreciate many things about the patient's internal reality, including the latter's investment in her defenses—her investment in being who she is and doing what she does, even when it works to her disadvantage to be so invested.

The therapist can now do one of two things.

Because the therapist has acquired an empathic understanding of how invested the patient is in defending herself in the ways that she does, the therapist can offer the patient an empathic intervention that will demonstrate understanding acceptance and will enable the patient to feel supported and validated.

Alternatively, the therapist, armed with the understanding she has acquired by way of immersing herself empathically in the patient's internal experience, may decide to do something else instead. The therapist may decide to offer the patient not an empathic intervention but a paradoxical intervention—in which she suggests that she knows the patient may well be so invested in maintaining the status quo of things (so invested in her defenses) that she may ultimately choose not to change.

By way of examples, to a patient who is desperate for love but who refuses to put herself out there, the therapist—in an effort to paradox her patient—might offer something to the effect of: "I think I am beginning to appreciate a little more clearly why you are convinced that you will never find a boyfriend. Over the years your heart has been broken so many times that, at this point, you are simply not interested in continuing your pursuit—particularly because it feels to you as if doing so would just be setting yourself up for further disappointment and heartache."

Or, "I think I am beginning to see why you feel that you cannot afford to trust anyone. Based on what you're telling me about the number of times your trust has been betrayed in the past, I can now understand why you feel that it is safer just not to put yourself out there. Even if it does mean being lonely, at least you'll know that no one will ever be able to hurt you again."

The clear message from the therapist to the patient is that obviously there can be no change unless the patient is motivated to change; if the patient is clearly signaling that she does not experience herself as being in a position to change, then the therapist takes her at her word, accepts it, does not fight it.

Or, to a patient who complains endlessly about how much he hates his job but never does anything to change his situation: "Although you dread going to work each day because you hate your job so much, it does provide financial and emotional security. And so, at this point in your life, you are feeling that it may simply not be in the cards for you to change jobs. Maybe it was just meant to be that you continue in your current job for the rest of your working days."

If the patient is made angry by the therapist's paradoxical intervention, then the patient's anger may well empower the patient, may well provide the necessary motivation (or impetus) for her to change—if only to prove the therapist wrong!

It is crucial that the therapist who offers her patient a paradox not be simultaneously expressing disappointment in, or disapproval of, the patient; rather, the therapist must be offering the patient a dispassionate statement of "fact"—based upon what the patient has been saying.

The therapist gets it, understands it, has no problem with it, is willing to make her peace with it. It's no skin off her back.

In other words, for a paradoxical intervention to be effective—that is, for a paradox to force the patient to take ownership, on some level, of her choice not to do things differently—the therapist must not need the patient to change.

Finally: "You hate it that your husband abuses you in the ways that he does, but then you begin to think about how old and tired you feel and decide that perhaps it is too late, the time to have divorced may already have come and gone."

Note that even as the therapist is letting the patient off the hook, the therapist is also highlighting the fact that it is the patient who has chosen not to do what she (the patient) knows she would need to do in order to feel better. In other words, even though the patient is not being held accountable for moving forward in her life, the patient is being indirectly held accountable for choosing to fail. In essence, by being confronted with the reality that what "happens to her" is actually her responsibility and her choice, the patient is being empowered.

In sum, empathic understanding of where the patient is in the moment enables the therapist to offer the patient either an empathic response that will enable the patient to feel understood or a paradoxical response that will force the patient to take ownership of the choices she is continuously making about how she lives her life.

Upon the invitation of a colleague of mine with whom I was sharing these ideas, we discussed the issue of her weight. When (after listening intently to all that she was saying about how she felt about food and her weight) I offered her a paradoxical intervention, she and I discovered something very interesting. Our conversation proceeded as follows:

She had talked first about how desperately she wanted to lose her excess pounds, and the price she felt she was paying for having the extra weight on.

Then we had gone on to explore what was getting in the way of her taking her weight problem more seriously; she had talked about all the reasons she was reluctant to commit, at this particular juncture in her life, to a rigorous diet and a strict exercise regime.

As I listened, I began to understand that because her life is so stressful these days, it may well not be the time for her to be starting a diet that will deprive her of food—one of her few sources of pleasure right now.

I recognized that my colleague is distressed about the price she pays for keeping the weight on; but I was also understanding more deeply some of the reasons she has been reluctant to make a commitment to restricting her food intake.

I therefore said something like: "These past several years have been very stressful for you. And food has been one of the only real pleasures you've had. Admittedly, you would wish that you could take the weight off, but I do also hear you saying that, at this point in your life, it may not be worth the sacrifice you would have to make were you to go on a serious diet. Maybe you need to give yourself a break and recognize that, right now, it really may be more important simply to allow yourself the freedom to eat as you have been eating. You will want to make sure that you don't allow yourself to gain any further weight; but maybe you should just cut yourself some slack and let things be, for now. You'll get serious about the weight when you're ready to."

Once we got this named (and I paradoxed her by encouraging her to maintain the status quo of things for now), my colleague began to relax and reported feeling a little freer, a little more comfortable within herself.

In essence, I think she was empowered by our recognition that, indeed, it is a "choice" she is making—a choice to be "not dieting" right now.

As we made explicit her decision not to diet, it eased things for her. By way of a paradox, my colleague got to the point where she could admit to herself that right now she is choosing not to change—although implicit in this awareness is also the recognition that, at some point in the future, she may become ready to change.

CHAPTER

16

The Therapist as New Good Object

As we have suggested, a deficiency-compensation model of therapeutic action is thought to involve the therapist's compensation of the patient in the here-and-now for deprivation the patient sustained early-on at the hands of the infantile object. In such a model, the patient is seen as an innocent and passive victim of maternal (or environmental) failure; the Model 2 therapist provides belatedly that which was denied the patient as a child.

The therapeutic action in a deficiency-compensation model is thought to involve the patient's experience of the therapist as a new good object—that is, as the good mother she never had. It is ultimately this new relationship that will compensate the patient for childhood deprivation and neglect by providing the opportunity for a filling in of the patient's deficits and a consolidation of the patient's self.

As we observed in Part I, it would seem that the deficiency-compensation literature sometimes emphasizes the role played by the patient's need to experience the therapist as a new good object and sometimes emphasizes the therapist's actual participation as that new good object. Self psychology, as we have seen, is more interested in the patient's contribution to the transference (in the form of her need for a new good mother) than in the therapist's contribution; Model 2 object relations theories, however, are more interested in the therapist's contribution to the transference (in the form of her actual participation as that new good mother) than in the patient's contribution.

THE PATIENT'S NEED FOR RESTITUTION

The self psychologists focus on the patient's need to believe that, in the form of her therapist, she has at last found a good mother. Their contention is that it is crucial for the therapist to be able to offer the patient such an experience, in order that she have the opportunity to believe that she will be compensated for the damage she suffered early-on at the hands of the mother—even though such belief is based, in part, on illusion.

But most self psychologists believe that this experience, though necessary, is not sufficient, because it is simply backdrop for what then occurs. The real therapeutic action is thought to revolve around the patient's mastery—through grieving—of the inevitable disillusionment she experiences when it turns out that her therapist is not all that she had hoped the therapist would be.

In self psychology, of more interest to the therapist than objective reality is the patient's subjective reality. More specifically, the patient's internal experience of the therapist is thought to be more important than the "reality" of who the therapist is or how the therapist actually participates. And so it is that, in self psychology, the patient's experience of the therapist as a new good object is more a story about the patient's need for a new good object than a story about the therapist's actual participation as that new good object.

By the same token, the patient's experience of having been failed empathically is more a story about the patient's perception of having been failed (the so-called "perceived empathic failure" [Schwaber 1979]) than a story about the therapist's actual failure of the patient.

In other words, just as there is no such thing as objective reality, so too there is no such thing as an objective empathic failure.

Let us imagine that a patient angrily remarks to her therapist, "You don't understand!" The therapist could have sworn that she did understand. Who is right? The therapist or the patient?

Another patient asserts, "You're being critical"—when the therapist could have sworn that she was not being critical. Again, who is right? The therapist or the patient?

The self psychologist would protest that these questions are not to be asked because they make no sense. Such questions would be asked by a therapist who is experiencing herself as the object (or the target)—and not the subject—of the patient's accusations (Schwaber 1981) and who mistakenly believes there is a truth that can be known.

A truly empathic perspective concerns itself always with subjective reality and not objective reality—it is never an issue of who is right, who is wrong. Rather, what matters is the patient's perception—the patient's perception of having been failed. In the above examples, what counts is the patient's perception of her therapist as not understanding (in the first instance) and as being critical (in the second instance).

In self psychology, the therapist's perception is not relevant.

Conceptual Difficulties in Self Psychology

There are numbers of unanswered questions in self psychology—problem areas that I think some of the Model 2 object relations theories indirectly address when they give the therapist more permission to participate, in actual fact, as a new good object.

But let us now explore some of the conceptual difficulties with which self psychology struggles by virtue of its insistence—at least in theory—that:

1. The therapist offers empathic recognition of need (not its actual gratification);
2. The empathic stance involves the therapist's decentering from her own experience in order to enter into the patient's experience (which then makes it difficult for the therapist to respond to the patient "authentically"—that is, from a centered place);
3. What matters is the patient's subjective reality (not objective reality);
4. Empathic failures are in the eyes of the beholder (which lets the therapist off the hook); and
5. The therapeutic action lies in the patient's experience of the therapist as a new good object (not the therapist's actual participation as that new good object).

Selfobject Functions

Reference is often made in the self psychological literature to how important it is that the therapist be able to perform (on the patient's behalf) the psychological functions the structurally impaired patient assigns her. These functions are assigned her by a patient who lacks the capacity to perform such functions on her own.

The patient with structural deficit therefore uses the therapist as a selfobject to fill in for her missing psychic structure; in essence, the deficit creates a need—the need is for the therapist to perform those psychological functions assigned her.

But what exactly does it mean when the self psychologist suggests that the therapist is to perform the function assigned her? Is it enough that the therapist simply resonate empathically with the patient's need to have the therapist perform such a function? Or does the therapist actually have to offer something in the way of fulfilling the function assigned her?

Expressed in somewhat different terms, does a selfobject simply resonate empathically with the patient's need or does it actually provide some form of gratification for that need?

Most self psychologists would protest that they believe the emphasis should be on the therapist's empathic recognition of need, not on its actual gratification. In fact, they bend over backward to emphasize that their psychoanalytic self psychology is not a theory about gratifying the patient; therapy is not supposed to be simply a "feel good" experience for the patient. Rather, what is important is the therapist's ability to recognize the patient's need and to respond to it in such a fashion that (in time) both patient and therapist will come to understand, more deeply, its significance—including its childhood origins.

What then does it mean when reference is made in self psychology to a loving selfobject? Does a loving selfobject provide empathic recognition of the patient's need to be loved or does it provide actual gratification of that need? And what does it mean to say that the therapist functions as an approving selfobject? Does an approving selfobject resonate affectively with the patient's need to be approved or does it offer actual approval?

Self psychology, as originally conceived (Kohut and Wolf 1978), emphasized empathic recognition of need—not its gratification. Were the patient to look to the therapist for reassurance, then the therapist (in her capacity as a reassuring selfobject) was expected to resonate empathically with the patient's need for such reassurance. "It's important to you that I approve of what you're doing," or "In order for you to feel okay about what you're doing, you would want to hear from me that I too am okay with it." It was not expected of the selfobject therapist that she actually offer the patient the reassurance for which the patient was looking, but that she recognize it and work (with the patient) to understand the latter's need for it.

Even so, it would seem that when self psychologists make reference to the therapist as a selfobject assigned a particular function, sometimes their focus (in the clinical situation) is on the therapist's provision of the actual function. Here their interest is not so much in the therapist's ability to recognize the patient's need as in the therapist's ability to respond to it.

By way of another example, let us think about the situation of a patient who has an impaired capacity to admire herself and therefore looks to the therapist to provide such admiration. There will certainly be times when the therapist's understanding of the patient's need to be admired will enable the patient to feel met. There may also be times, however, when the therapist finds herself actually providing some of the admiration the patient so desperately seeks—as might happen, for instance, when the therapist responds with heartfelt appreciation to a beautiful poem the patient has written and now shares with her therapist.

In other words, sometimes empathic recognition of need may further the therapeutic endeavor; at other times, however, it would seem that it is the therapist's (perhaps unwitting, perhaps more considered) responsiveness to the patient's need that facilitates the therapeutic process.

And although (in theory) self psychology emphasizes the therapist's empathic recognition of the patient's need, in actual practice it would seem that the therapeutic action is thought sometimes to involve the therapist's compliance with the patient's need.

The Empathic Therapist as Decentered

Another area of confusion in the literature involves the extent to which the self psychologically informed therapist is expected to remain decentered from both her subjectivity (what she feels) and her objectivity (what she thinks).

With respect to how the selfobject therapist listens, it is expected of her that she decenter from her subjectivity (as well as her objectivity) so that she can enter into the patient's experience. Afferent empathy involves this decentering.

But with respect to efferent empathy it becomes more complicated. If all that is expected of the selfobject therapist is that she offer an empathic response in which she conveys to the patient her deep appreciation for where the patient is (affectively) in the moment, then there is no need for her to recover her "self" so that she can be available to the patient in a more authentic way.

But if the selfobject therapist is to offer anything more than simply empathic recognition, then it would seem that the therapist must be allowed to step out of the patient's experience and back into her own, so that she can re-find her own center of initiative (her own reality) and can then respond to the patient from a more centered, authentic place. Were efferent empathy to involve the therapist's actual responsiveness to the patient's need, then she would need to be given permission to become once again centered within her own subjectivity, so that she would be able to offer the patient something real, something genuine, something from within herself.

In other words, if the selfobject therapist decenters and leaves herself behind, then what is left of her that is authentic and that can, in a heartfelt manner, be offered to a patient who is so in need of narcissistic supplies? Does not the selfobject therapist have to preserve something of herself in order to perform in a meaningful way the psychological functions assigned her?

To the extent that self psychology expects the therapist to offer the patient something more than mere empathic recognition, then to that extent must self psychology recognize how necessary it is that the therapist recover her self, so that she can truly be available to the patient in a way that is credible and authentic.

Perceived Empathic Failures

With respect to the therapist's empathic failures of the patient, and as mentioned earlier, in self psychology the focus would seem to be more on the patient's experience of having been failed by the therapist than on the therapist's "actual" failure of her patient—more on the patient's subjective reality than on the objective reality of what is transpiring in the patient–therapist relationship. In other words, with respect to the patient's disillusionment, the emphasis would appear to be more on the patient's than on the therapist's contribution to the disrupted positive transference.

Self psychologists warn us that in the aftermath of the patient's experience of having been failed, the therapist must not experience herself as the object of the patient's angry disappointment (Schwaber

1979); rather, the therapist must remain decentered from her own experience, so that she can immerse herself empathically in the patient's experience of outrage and devastation.

On the one hand, I think it is more important that the therapist direct her efforts toward understanding the patient's experience (of having been failed) than that the therapist focus on what she thinks "really" happened. It is unfortunately all too easy for the untutored therapist to feel defensive when she becomes the target of the patient's disillusionment. But the self psychologist believes that the therapist, instead of focusing on the legitimacy of the patient's upset, would fare far better were she to be able to put aside her own concerns about the "reality" of the situation in favor of a more directed focus on the patient's affective experience of disillusionment.

On the other hand, when the emphasis is entirely on the patient's experience of disillusionment, then the therapist may never really be held accountable for whatever part she might have played in the creation of that distress—because the focus is more on the patient's devastation and outrage in response to being failed than on the failure itself and on why the therapist might have done what she did. But, by the same token, neither is the patient ever really held accountable—because the focus (in self psychology) is more on the patient's vulnerability to feeling that she has been failed than on that part of her that might have needed (perhaps unconsciously) to be failed and that might therefore have pulled for the therapist to participate as the old bad object.

Interestingly, because self psychology focuses so exclusively on the patient's experience of having been failed, neither therapist nor patient is required to take responsibility for understanding what her own motivation might have been and what impact her own behavior might have had on the other.

Instead, the focus is always on encouraging the patient's elaboration of her feelings of upset and outrage at having been failed in the way that she was—in both the here-and-now (with respect to the selfobject therapist) and, if the patient associates to it, her there-and-then (with respect to the infantile object).

Transmuting Internalizations

Another confusing issue involves the concept of transmuting internalization—that is, the building of self structure (Kohut and Wolf 1978). What is it that is actually taken in from the selfobject therapist in order to accrete internal psychic structure? According to self psychology, in the treatment situation a major impetus for structural growth (the adding of new good) is thought to be the working through of optimal disillusionment experienced by the patient at the hands of the selfobject therapist. The patient is thought to master her experience of disenchantment by way of grieving—a process that involves defensive and adaptive internalizations (Stark 1994a,b).

More specifically, in order to come to terms with her disappointment that the therapist is not all that the patient had hoped the therapist would be, the patient is thought to take in the good that had been there prior to the introduction of the bad. In this way, she preserves internally a piece of the original experience of external goodness.

If, however, the patient's original experience of the therapist as a new good object has been determined in large part by the patient's illusory need for new good (and not so much by the therapist's actual participation), then it does not make sense to think in terms of the therapeutic action as involving the patient's internalization of that which was primarily illusory to begin with, that which was more a story about the patient (and her need) than a story about the therapist (and her actual provision). In other words, it would seem that only something deriving from the outside and therefore external to the self can be internalized.

Winnicott (1963a,b) speaks to this very issue when he posits the existence of three maturational stages, culminating in the child's development of an awareness of the externality and the otherness of her mother: (1) absolute dependence; (2) relative dependence; and (3) toward autonomy. Winnicott describes the stage of absolute dependence, in which the mother is related to as a "subjective object" indistinguishable from the self, as a stage of object relating. The infant cannot yet use mother, in the sense of internalizing various aspects of her, because mother has not yet come to be experienced as outside the infant's sphere of omnipotence. Winnicott asserts that when an object is not recognized as separate from the self, there is no impetus for internalizing it.

It is only with achievement of the third and final stage of development (when the infant abrogates her omnipotence, accepts the limits of her power, and recognizes the independent existence of others) that she can begin to use the mother. It is only when mother becomes an "objectively perceived object" that various aspects of her can be taken in. According to Winnicott (1969), therefore, the capacity to use (or to internalize) an object is a developmental achievement made possible by the infant's recognition of mother's externality or otherness.

In any event, perhaps it would make more sense were the therapeutic action in self psychology—at least to the extent that it involves taking in something from the outside—thought to encompass not just the patient's need for a new good object but also the therapist's actual participation as that new good object. Of course, the patient's ability to profit from the therapist's actual participation would have to be predicated on the patient's capacity to recognize the therapist as separate from the self.

In other words, in order to avoid the absurdity of suggesting that the therapeutic action involves the patient's taking in of something that was hers to begin with, let us conclude that the patient's experience of the therapist must be not just a story about the patient and the patient's need (subjective transference) but also—at least to some extent—a story about the therapist and the therapist's actual participation (objective transference).

It will then make sense to think in terms of transmuting internalization as involving the taking in of the actual good that had been there prior to the therapist's failure of the patient, and it will be in this way that healthy psychic structure actually develops.

In sum, the self psychological literature would seem to emphasize the role played by the patient's need for a new good object in the establishment of a positive selfobject transference, as opposed to the role played by the therapist's actual participation as that new good object. Similarly, the emphasis would seem to be on the role played by the patient's experience of having been failed, as opposed to the role played by the therapist's actual failure of her patient.

I believe, however, that the positive transference must be a story as much about the therapist as it is about the patient; so, too, empathic failures (which disrupt such transferences) must be a story as much about the therapist as they are about the patient. In other words, the patient's perceptions of her therapist are determined as much by the reality of the therapist's actual participation in the present as by the impact of the patient's developmental past on the meaning she makes of her therapist's activity.

Furthermore, although this is generally not made explicit in the self psychological literature, I believe that—within any selfobject therapist—there is always a dialectical tension between the decentering she must do in order to lose herself in the patient's experience and the recentering she must do in order to give of her authentic self to the patient. In fact, my contention is that it is this very tension that will enable the therapist to be maximally effective.

THE THERAPIST'S PARTICIPATION AS A NEW GOOD OBJECT

Unlike self psychologists, Model 2 object relations theorists speak more directly to the therapist's participation as a new good object—in fact, and not just in the patient's fantasy. They conceive of the patient as the hapless victim of maternal deprivation or neglect and therefore encourage the therapist to provide the holding the patient never received in a consistent, reliable fashion early on. They believe it is important that the patient have a chance to revisit the scene of the original crime so that she can start anew.

As we have said throughout, whereas self psychology is more about the therapist's recognizing the patient's need, object relations theory is more about the therapist's recognizing and responding to that need.

Whereas self psychologists tend to conceptualize the therapeutic action as involving the patient's experience (and mastery) of optimal frustration, Model 2 object relations theorists tend to conceive of the therapeutic action as involving the patient's experience of gratification.

In Model 2 object relations theories, the therapist is thought to participate in loco parentis (Guntrip 1973)—that is, as a good-enough mother who provides a holding environment (Winnicott 1958, 1965) and the opportunity for a new beginning (Balint 1968).

Let's look, more specifically, at what Balint and Guntrip have to say about the therapist's participation as this good mother.

Harmonious, Interpenetrating Mix-Up

Like many Model 2 object relations theorists, Balint (1949, 1950, 1952, 1968) believes that the therapist participates in actual fact as the good mother the patient never had—although Balint never loses sight of how important it is that the therapist not force herself on the patient, that she not demand, impinge, intrude, or interfere, that she be unobtrusive.

Both Winnicott and Balint emphasize that the patient (within the context of safety provided by her therapist) needs to be given the opportunity to regress to the point where the original disruption occurred. Whereas Winnicott (1958) refers to it as a "starting place" or "being born again," Balint (1968) writes about the importance of giving the patient an opportunity to have a "new beginning"—an experience accompanied by the hope that she will someday get better.

Just as there must be a "harmonious, interpenetrating mix-up" between infant and caregiver, so too there must be a harmonious fitting together of patient and therapist for healing to occur. Balint offers the eloquent idea that the therapist must be to the patient as amniotic fluid is to the fetus, the sea is to fish, and air is to the lungs. For Balint, what is healing for the patient is not simply her experience of being understood—but rather her experience of being "as one" with the therapist.

Balint (1952, 1968) believes that the infant is born into a state of intense relatedness to her mother and that her subsequent growth is absolutely dependent upon the continuation of such relatedness. If there is a failure of fit between infant and mother, then the infant develops a basic fault.

In the treatment situation, over time the patient with a basic fault will come to a point where she experiences something as missing inside her, a "defect" that must be "put right" by way of some form of external provision from the therapist. Her demand is that this time she should not, indeed must not, be failed.

Balint conceives of regression as benign and potentially beneficial when the therapist is able to provide an accepting atmosphere in which the patient can feel safe enough to open up. More specifically, in order to facilitate a benign regression, the therapist must provide a form of empathic recognition that enables the patient (1) to return to the area of the basic fault and (2) to bear—with at least manageable anxiety—the unstructured experience of primitive terror surrounding that area. The therapist must be able herself to bear this experience of unspeakable dread, so that she and her patient can tolerate the regression as a mutual experience.

But not all patients will be able to regress—because not all patients will have the capacity to overcome, in Masud Khan's (1969) words, their "dread of surrender to resourceless dependence" (p. 240). Nor will all patients have the opportunity to regress if the therapist does not consent to be used in the way that the patient needs to be able to make use of her.

The therapist must accept and carry the patient in the way that water accepts and carries a person who entrusts her weight to it. In describing the therapist's stance, Balint (1968) writes: The therapist "must not resist, . . . must not give rise to too much friction, . . . must prove more or less indestructible, must not insist on maintaining harsh boundaries, but must allow the development of a kind of mix-up between the patient and himself" (p. 145). Balint continues: "All this means consent, participation, and involvement, but not necessarily action, only understanding and tolerance; what really matters is the creation and maintenance of conditions in which events can take place internally, in the patient's mind" (p. 145).

Balint sums up as follows: "The aim is that the patient should be able to find himself, to accept himself, and to get on with himself, knowing all the time that there is a scar in himself, his basic fault, which cannot be 'analysed' out of existence" (p. 180).

Sleeping Beauty and the Prince

In Part I, our emphasis had been on Guntrip's (1969) depiction of the schizoidally withdrawn patient as someone who is so fearful of being retraumatized by yet another interpersonal disappointment that she keeps her authentic self out of relationship. For her, no object at all is preferable to running the risk of encountering a bad object. I had suggested that Guntrip's schizoid personality is a prototype for patients with relational deficit, that is, patients who require—in order to be found and engaged—that their therapists be more vigorously personal in their pursuit.

But we will now focus less on the patient's fear (which fuels her resistance to being found and engaged) and more on the patient's need to be brought back to life by some form of corrective provision from her therapist. Guntrip (1973) is squarely in the tradition of those other deficiency-compensation theorists who advocate for the therapist to abandon her neutral, more passive stance in favor of a more actively gratifying one.

Guntrip conceives of the patient's psychopathology as arising from failure in the early-on environmental provision—failure in the early-on relationship between infant and mother. He conceives of the cure, therefore, as involving a corrective experience in the here-and-now, that is, the provision now (by way of the actual relationship between patient and therapist) of that which was not provided by the mother early-on.

In fact, Greenberg and Mitchell (1983) have observed that Guntrip's account of psychopathology and the analytic process resembles the story of "Sleeping Beauty." They write:

> A terrible trauma has occurred in early childhood, inflicted on the passive and innocent child from the outside (a disgruntled fairy). The terror and helplessness of this traumatic event remain imbedded in the heart of the personality, awaiting a call back to life by a more hospitable environment. The self of the patient is ultimately passive; lack of good mothering produces a retreat to a lifeless withdrawal, until the analyst (the prince) awakens it from its slumber. [p. 218]

Guntrip both absolves the child (the patient) and holds the mother (the therapist) accountable. Psychotherapy must therefore be a process whereby the patient is helped, through the largely maternal relationship with her therapist, to re-enter the world. By way of the therapist's participation as a new good (ideal) mother, the patient's weak and helpless infantile ego is transformed, over time, into a strong mature ego that no longer fears life. In other words, it is in the context of the patient's relationship with her therapist that her ego is strengthened, its underlying ego-weakness healed, and the world of objects once again discovered.

What is at stake in the therapy, then, is the "saving of the ego." Guntrip believes that the therapist rescues the patient from the terror and paralysis generated by maternal deprivation. The therapist gratifies in whatever ways she can, providing now what was not provided consistently and reliably by the infantile object. Most importantly, the therapist offers the patient the experience of being seen and accepted for who she is.

The regressed patient wants to be treated like a baby; Guntrip (1969) believes that the patient must be allowed to be that baby. In fact, the therapist must be prepared to offer the patient whatever degree of "therapeutic regression" proves necessary.

The demanding patient, like the demanding child, is demanding a love she feels is being refused. Guntrip believes that she is entitled to this love. The patient says: "If I could feel loved, I'm sure I'd grow." Guntrip believes that, indeed, such is the case. The patient says: "Can

I be sure you genuinely care for the baby in me?" Guntrip believes that the therapist must totally accept and care for the baby in the patient.

If the patient senses that her therapist is made anxious by, and needs to defend herself against, the patient's deepest, most primitive needs, the patient may be driven to become ever more demanding and entitled in relation to the therapist whom she now experiences as rejecting. Frustrating the patient, Guntrip contends, accomplishes nothing; what it does do is to force the patient either to clamor all the more vehemently to have her infantile needs met or to take flight once again because it hurts too much to be in a state of desire in relation to someone who can so completely devastate her.

What the patient is seeking is a relationship that is sufficiently reliable and understanding that the results of the early-on environmental failure can be corrected. Only that can rescue the patient from succumbing to the terror of her aloneness. The patient is in urgent need of a relationship so that she can come back to life.

Guntrip envisions the ultimate goal to be achievement of the capacity (1) to be alone without feeling isolated (that is, without losing the other) and (2) to engage healthily in relationship without losing one's individuality (that is, without losing the self).

In sum, whereas self psychologists speak to the importance of the patient's need to experience the therapist as a new good object, Model 2 object relations theorists (like Balint and Guntrip) speak to the importance of the therapist's actual participation as that new good object. And whereas self psychologists emphasize the importance of recognizing the patient's need, Model 2 object relations theorists emphasize the importance of recognizing and responding to that need.

But whether the emphasis is on recognition of need (as in self psychology) or responsiveness to need (as in Model 2 object relations theories), a deficiency-compensation model of therapeutic action posits the importance of "meeting" the patient where she is affectively so that she can have the experience either of being understood and validated or, more generally, of being held in the way that a good mother holds her young child.

It is for this reason that I have chosen to suggest that the therapeutic action in a deficiency-compensation model involves the therapist's offering the patient some form of corrective provision—be it in the form of recognition of the patient's need or responsiveness to that need.

CHAPTER

17

New Good Object versus Old Bad One

In Part II, our focus to this point has been on the therapist as a new good object—the province of a deficiency-compensation model of therapeutic action, in which the therapist (as an empathic selfobject or a good object–good mother) offers the patient some form of restitution.

We will now shift our focus to the therapist as the old bad object—the province of a relational model of therapeutic action, in which the therapist (as an authentic subject) allows herself to be engaged by the patient as the old bad object.

When the therapist focuses her attention on the patient's structural deficits (deficits that speak to the internal absence of good), Model 2 is the most clinically useful model. Here the spotlight is on the patient's need to find a new good object so that restitution can be made. What is then required of the Model 2 therapist is that she be willing and able to offer the patient some form of corrective provision, which will enable the patient to have the experience of being met and, over the long haul, the opportunity to have her deficits filled in and her self consolidated.

When, however, the therapist focuses her attention on the patient's relational conflicts (conflicts that speak to the internal presence of bad), Model 3 provides the most clinically useful approach. Here the spotlight is on the patient's conflict about being in relationship with a new good object (because of her attachment to the now-internalized old bad object). What such a patient most needs is an opportunity (1) to deliver herself (and her bad object(s)) into the relationship with her therapist and (2) to rework, in the context of the here-and-now engagement between patient and therapist, her now-externalized badness.

In these latter instances, it is not only the patient who brings her authentic self into the relationship; so, too, the Model 3 therapist brings her availability as someone who can be affected by what transpires at the intimate edge between them. This takes the form, first, of the therapist's vulnerability to being acted upon and, thereby, drawn into participating with the patient in what becomes a mutual enactment. Then, it takes the form of the therapist's ability to step back from such participation in order to make available to the patient (for re-internalization) aspects of her own, healthier capacity—such that what the patient now takes in will be slightly modified, that is, less bad.

In essence, when the relational-conflict therapist brings her authentic self into the relationship (both her vulnerability to being impacted upon and her capacity to use her self to metabolize this impact), she will be able to serve as a container for the patient's disavowed psychic contents. By making herself available to the patient in this way, the therapist will then be able to facilitate detoxification of the patient's internal bad objects and separation of the patient from her infantile objects, such that the patient will no longer have either the same investment in the old ways or the same compulsive need to re-create her past in the present.

For the patient who has had difficulty tolerating new good objects because of her attachment to the old bad ones, the net result will therefore be containment, resolution of relational conflict, and development of the capacity to engage more healthily in relationship.

BEING MET VERSUS BEING CONTAINED

Note the distinction I am making between being met and being contained: When the therapist participates as a new good object, the patient will have the experience of being met. But when the therapist, after first allowing herself to be used as a receptacle for the patient's disavowed psychic gunk, is then able to lend her own capacity to a detoxification of the extruded psychic contents, the patient will have the experience of containment.

More specifically, the patient with structural deficit (and, therefore, a need for new good) must have the experience of being met by someone who is able to recognize and respond to her need—be it in the form of empathic recognition, optimal frustration, or actual gratification. When the Model 2 therapist provides the patient with a corrective emotional experience, she is offering the patient the experience of being met.

On the other hand, the patient with relational conflict (and, therefore, a need for old bad) must have the experience of being contained by someone who—after initially accepting the patient's assignments—is eventually able to step back from participating as the old bad object so as to recover both her objectivity and her therapeutic effectiveness. When the Model 3 therapist provides the patient with a corrective relational experience, she is offering the patient the experience of being contained.

Let us now look at what Greenberg has to say about the therapist's participation as both new good object and old bad one.

A RELATIONAL DEFINITION OF NEUTRALITY

Squarely in the tradition of a relational theorist, Greenberg (1986a,b) reminds us that it is never a question of whether the therapist participates or not; rather, the question is how she participates. In fact, Greenberg's technical recommendation is that the therapist adopt a posture of analytic neutrality in order to optimize her effectiveness.

The traditional model of neutrality encourages the therapist to position herself at an equal distance ("equidistant") from id, ego, and superego. But Greenberg redefines neutrality from a relational perspective. For him, neutrality is not so much about the therapist's impartiality; rather, in his view, the therapist must strive to position herself in such a way as to provide the patient with the experience of both new good (so there can be structural growth) and old bad (so there can be structural change).

After all, the patient has a healthy need both to find a new good object (so that there can be restitution) and to re-find the old bad object (so that there can be a reworking of internalized traumas).

If the therapist pays close attention to how open or closed the patient is to new experience, then she will be able to adjust the level of her activity accordingly, so that the patient will be able to develop both positive and negative transference. By continuously monitoring the level of her activity, the neutral therapist will be able to create an optimal tension within the patient between the latter's experience of new good in the therapy relationship and her experience of old bad.

Greenberg's belief is that the appropriate degree of activity on the therapist's part will depend largely on the intensity of the patient's attachment to her internal bad objects.

If the patient is tenaciously attached to the old bad (now-internalized) infantile object and therefore has difficulty experiencing current objects as anything other than old and bad, then the therapist may need to assert her "newness" more affirmatively if the patient is ever to relinquish her attachment to the old bad object in favor of a new good object. That is, when the patient's tendency is to develop negative transference, then—if a positive transference is ever to emerge—the therapist may need to be more actively present.

If the patient, however, is looking to her current objects to complete her and is therefore hungry for new experience, then the therapist's affirming presence may make it hard for the patient to experience her as anything but new and good, which will rob the patient of the opportunity to find containment of her internal demons. That is, when the patient's tendency is to develop positive transference, then—if a negative transference is ever to emerge—the therapist may need to be less active, less affirming, less present.

In general, the more active and self-revealing the therapist, the more a patient will be inclined to experience her therapist as a new good object; and the more silent and anonymous the therapist, the more a patient will be inclined to experience her as the old bad object.

It is therefore crucial that (with each patient) the therapist be able to achieve, by way of a careful monitoring of her own activity, a balance between being active and participatory on the one hand and being less involved and less responsive on the other, so that she can provide the patient with the salutary experiences the patient must have in order both to add new good (structural growth) and to modify existent bad (structural change).

For example, if the patient was repeatedly traumatized by an abusive parent, it will be extraordinarily difficult for her to experience her therapist as anything but abusive, because the patient will be experiencing her therapist through the distorted lenses of the abuse she sustained early on, internally recorded and structuralized in the form of abuser–abusee pathogenic introjects. If such a patient is ever to have a chance to experience her therapist as a new good object (and an opportunity to develop healthy psychic structure), then her therapist may have to be more actively present. By so doing, she overrides the patient's distorted perception of others as invariably abusive.

By the same token, if as a child the patient experienced more privation and deprivation than insult or injury and now, therefore, suffers more from deficit than from conflict, it may be much easier for her to embrace her therapist as a new good object. In fact, as we noted in Part I, the patient with structural deficit is ever in search of the good mother she never had early on; she is relatively unconflicted in her quest for a new good object and, unless actively thwarted, will deliver that need into the transference. But if such a patient is ever to have a chance to experience her therapist as the old bad object (and an opportunity to rework whatever pathogenic psychic structures she does have), then her therapist may have to be less actively present. By so doing, she creates an empty space into which the patient can deliver whatever internal demons she might harbor.

Thus, Greenberg (1986a,b) suggests that (1) the more closed a patient, the more active the therapist must be if the patient is ever to be reached and that (2) the more open a patient, the more silent the therapist must be if the patient is ever to be able to re-enact, in the transference, her early-on traumatic experiences so that they can be mastered and transformed.

Along similar lines, Aron (1991) addresses this issue of whether the therapist participates as a new good object or an old bad one when he suggests that "a dynamic tension needs to be preserved between responsiveness and participation on the one hand and nonintrusiveness and space on the other, intermediate between the analyst's presence and absence" (p. 43).

CHAPTER

18

Experience as Co-created

As we have seen, in a relational model of therapeutic action, all experience is thought to be co-created, with contributions from both participants. So, too, the countertransference (which is the therapist's experience of the patient) is never just a story about the therapist; nor is the transference (which is the patient's experience of the therapist) ever just a story about the patient. Rather, both experiences involve the here-and-now of the therapeutic interaction.

A RELATIONAL DEFINITION OF TRANSFERENCE

As I suggested in Part I, my proposal is that we think in terms of the patient's experience of the therapist—that is, the transference—as consisting of both more-or-less unrealistic perception (deriving from who the patient is and what she brings to the interaction) and more-or-less realistic perception (deriving from who the therapist is and what she brings to the interaction).

The patient's unrealistic/inaccurate/distorted perceptions of the therapist are nothing other than what is generally meant when reference is made to the patient's transference—in both the classical psychoanalytic literature and even some contemporary circles. As we saw in Part I, I refer to this as subjective transference.

In some of the contemporary psychoanalytic literature, however, we are advised to keep in mind the patient's more-or-less realistic and accurate perceptions of the therapist (described by Hoffman [1983] as the patient's plausible interpretations, or constructions, of the therapist's experience and by Aron [1991] as the patient's interpretation of the therapist's subjectivity).

Some of these contemporary theorists remind us that the patient's experience of the therapist always has elements of both realistic and unrealistic perception; they suggest that therapists would do well to remember that the patient's transference is always a story about both the reality of who the therapist is and the meaning the patient makes of that reality (that is, how the patient interprets it).

Of note is that this two-person conceptualization of the transference certainly holds the therapist more accountable than does the more classical approach.

In other words, the transference as originally conceived was thought to be not an interpersonal event occurring between two people; rather it was understood to be a process occurring within the mind of the patient—and therefore not something for which the therapist was at all responsible. The transference was seen as endogenously determined, as a story about the patient's developmental history. More specifically, the transference was thought to arise independently of the therapist's contribution.

It was believed that if the therapy were going well and the therapist were able to stay out of the patient's way, then the transference would spontaneously unfold, uncontaminated by contributions from the therapist. The person of the therapist was considered to be irrelevant or, at most, a hook on which to hang the contents of the patient's intrapsychic projections.

Contemporary psychoanalytic theory, however, conceives of the therapist's participation in the therapeutic process as an inevitability. It is, therefore, a description of what invariably happens; it is not a prescription for what should happen (Greenberg 1981). The therapist participates in response to the patient's relational demands; participation is done inadvertently—as a response to the patient, not as a deliberate provocation. Thus it is very different from the role-playing associated with Franz Alexander's (1946, 1948) corrective emotional experience.

A relational definition of transference, therefore, conceives of it as a joint creation of patient and therapist. The transference never emerges solely from within the patient; it is always and ever responsive to the analytic interaction.

Wachtel (1982) has suggested that the language of emerging and unfolding (as it applies to the transference) is a verbal sleight of hand that eclipses the recognition that psychological events are never just a function of internal imperatives but are always derived from interactions with others.

From the perspective of contemporary psychoanalytic theory, however, the impact of the therapist needs to be examined systematically as an intrinsic part of the transference.

In other words, whereas the classical literature would have it that the therapist is a blank screen onto which the patient casts shadows that are then interpreted by the therapist as figments of the patient's imagination, contemporary theory has it that the therapist is never a blank screen but is always contributing to what goes on inside the patient. The patient's response, therefore, is thought to contain elements that are both (1) a story about the therapist and the impact such a therapist would have on any patient (objective transference) and (2) a story about the patient and the particular way the patient interprets the therapist's subjectivity (subjective transference).

Let us now look more closely at how the three models of therapeutic action conceive of the transference.

As we have seen, the Model 1 therapist (whose particular interest is in the patient's internal dynamics) conceives of the transference as primarily a story about the patient.

Interestingly, the Model 2 therapist (whose particular interest is in the patient's internal experience of the therapist) sometimes uses the term transference in the more classical sense (as a story about the patient) and sometimes uses the term in the more contemporary sense (as a story about both patient and therapist).

In other words, some Model 2 therapists (most notably, self psychologists) focus on the patient's experience of the therapist as the good parent she never had. Other Model 2 therapists (most notably, those object relations theorists who emphasize the patient's internal absence of good) focus on the therapist's actual participation as that good parent.

In both situations, the therapist conceives of the therapeutic action as involving the making good of a deficiency; but whereas self psychology emphasizes the patient's perception of the therapist as a new good object (subjective transference), Model 2 object relations theories speak also to the therapist's actual participation as that new good object (subjective and objective transference).

From this it follows that self psychologists conceive of disruptions of the patient's positive transference as occasioned by the patient's perception of having been empathically failed; Model 2 object relations theorists, on the other hand, conceive of such disruptions as occasioned by the therapist's actual failure of the patient.

In other words, self psychologists tend to conceptualize the therapist's failures as more a story about the patient's narcissistic vulnerability to injury than a story about the therapist's failure to come through for the patient, whereas Model 2 object relations theorists tend to conceptualize the therapist's failures as more a story about the therapist's "actual" failure of the patient than simply the patient's perception of having been failed.

In the aftermath of the therapist's failure of the patient, the therapist (ever attuned to her impact on the patient) may ask the patient either "How do you feel I have disappointed you?" or "How have I disappointed you?"

In the first intervention, the therapist is clearly implying that the patient's experience of disappointment is probably more a story about the patient (and the patient's vulnerability to injury) than a story about the therapist (and the therapist's actual failure of the patient); in other words, the therapist would appear to be addressing herself to the "perceived" empathic failure.

In the second intervention, the therapist would seem to be suggesting that she thinks it is possible that she (the therapist) did, in fact, let the patient down—an "objective" empathic failure; the therapist is here giving the patient permission to elaborate upon her experience of the therapist as having actually failed her.

But whether the therapist's empathic failure of the patient is subjective (perceived) or objective (actual), it is the working through of such disruptions that most Model 2 therapists consider to be the primary means by which structural deficits are filled in and the self is consolidated.

Thus, in both self psychology and those object relations theories that emphasize the patient's internal absence of good, the focus is on the patient's experience of the therapist as the good parent she never had (whether that experience is only in her mind's eye or it actually happened) and, in the aftermath of an empathic rupture, the patient's experience of the therapist as having failed her (whether that experience is only in her mind's eye or it actually happened).

But whether the Model 2 therapist considers the transference to be simply subjective or is open to considering its objective aspects as well, she considers the countertransference to be simply a story about the therapist and about what aspect of the therapist's subjectivity is interfering with her ability to be fully present for her patient. In other words, the countertransference (in Model 2) is not thought to be a story about the patient's impact on the therapist; it is not thought to be a story about the patient's force field and her efforts (whether conscious or unconscious) to draw the therapist into participating in the ways that she needs the therapist to participate, whether as a new good or as the old bad object. The countertransference is thought by the Model 2 therapist to be, simply, a story about the therapist.

As we had earlier noted, in Model 2, the patient is thought to be unambivalent in her search for missing positive experiences. Her longing is find a new good object; she is not thought to have a need to re-find the old bad object or to be now failed in the transference as she was once failed in the relationship with her parent.

By way of example, if the therapist (whether subjectively or objectively) fails the patient by being critical, little attention is paid by the Model 2 therapist to whatever might have been the patient's need to be so failed. Rather, the failure is thought to be a story about the therapist.

Let us now move to a consideration of how the Model 3 therapist conceives of the transference. As we have repeatedly emphasized, the relational therapist (whose particular interest is always in both what the patient brings to the interaction and what the therapist brings) conceives of the transference as a story about both patient and therapist.

In a relational model, the therapist is never thought to be a blank screen; she is always seen as a participant—with her own subjectivity, her own prejudices, her own perspective, her own needs, her own interests, her own vulnerabilities, and so on. As such, she is always shaping the patient's reality. The Model 3 therapist is therefore ever mindful of both the subjective and the objective aspects of the patient's experience of her.

Model 3 therapists believe that who the therapist is, her very character, makes a real difference to the patient and to the interaction between patient and therapist. They contend that it is not possible to conceive of the patient's experience of the therapist (that is, the transference) as independent of the ongoing interaction between patient and therapist.

A relational definition of the transference, then, has it that the patient's experience of the therapist is always a story, at least in part, about the therapist (in the form of both what the therapist proactively brings to the relationship and what she reactively brings because of her responsiveness to the patient), as it is also a story about the patient—and the meaning the patient makes of the therapist's participation. The patient is always responding to the therapist.

Just as Greenberg's (1986a,b) relational definition of neutrality reframes neutrality as speaking not simply to something about the therapist but rather to the therapist's responsiveness to something going on in the patient, so too the relational definition of transference espoused by many contemporary theorists reframes transference as speaking not simply to something about the patient but rather to the patient's responsiveness to something going on in the therapist.

Plausible Interpretations

In his landmark 1983 article entitled "The Patient as Interpreter of the Analyst's Experience," Hoffman captures the essence of this contemporary relational perspective when he asserts that the therapist, far from being a blank screen, is actually very much a participant. The classical perspective has it that the therapist is a blank screen and that the patient's perceptions of the therapist are distortions of reality. Hoffman's social-constructivist perspective has it that (1) the therapist is not outside the interactive field but very much a participant in it and that (2) the patient's perceptions of the therapist are plausible interpretations of the therapist and of her behavior.

Hoffman offers a critique of the blank-screen concept, suggesting that there are two categories: one, a conservative critique and the other, a radical critique.

The conservative critique of the blank-screen concept retains the dichotomy between realistic perception and transference (as distortion) but argues that more attention should be paid to the ways in which the therapist's actual behavior either promotes the analytic process (when the therapist offers herself as a new good object) or interferes with the analytic process (when the therapist acts out countertransferentially).

Included in this category of conservative critics are (1) those theorists who emphasize the role of the therapist as a new good object (Kohut

1968, 1971, Loewald 1960, Stone 1954, Strachey 1934); (2) those theorists who emphasize the role of the analyst's countertransference (Langs 1979, 1988); and (3) those theorists for whom the real relationship encompasses the patient's experience both of the working alliance and of the countertransference (Greenson 1967).

The radical critique of the blank-screen concept contends that reality is neither absolute nor a pre-established given; reality is always ambiguous, multifaceted, and amenable to a variety of interpretations. More specifically, the patient is ever busy formulating plausible interpretations of the therapist's experience. Such interpretations are credible—not necessarily accurate, but at least credible. Furthermore, the experience of both patient and therapist is continuously shaped by the participation of the other.

From this perspective, transference is seen as a "selective attention to certain facets of the analyst's highly ambiguous response to the patient," that is, as a selective attention to particular aspects of the analyst's subjectivity.

Expressed in somewhat different terms, some contemporary theorists suggest that the patient's experience of the therapist is both part old (a story about the patient) and part new (a story about the therapist); it is both part imagined (informed, as it is, by the patient's subjectivity) and part real (informed, as it is, by the therapist's subjectivity).

Along these same lines, Merton Gill (1982) writes that he considers the transference to be "always an amalgam of past and present" (pp. 177–178).

By way of summary: I am here advancing the idea that just as the countertransference can be seen as having both subjective and objective elements, so too the transference can be seen as having both subjective and objective aspects.

I am suggesting, further, that (1) the Model 1 therapist conceives of the transference as subjective (a story about the patient); (2) some Model 2 therapists similarly conceive of the transference as subjective (a story about the patient and her need to find a new good object), but some Model 2 therapists conceive of the transference as having elements of both the subjective and the objective (a story about the patient's experience of the therapist as a new good object and a story about the therapist's actual participation as that new good object); and

(3) the Model 3 therapist conceives of the transference as always both subjective (a story about the way the patient makes meaning of the therapist's participation) and objective (a story about the way the therapist actually participates in the therapeutic encounter).

Although the term transference is used in these different ways (sometimes in the more classical sense and sometimes in the more contemporary sense), the way in which it is being used will usually be clear from its context.

CHAPTER 19

Interplay between Objectivity and Subjectivity

In a slightly different vein, I would like now to explore the issue of the therapist's objectivity and her subjectivity. Let us look more specifically at the role each plays in the three different models of therapeutic action.

As we will see, there are times when it is important that the therapist preserve her objectivity (as she does in Model 1), times when it is best that she put aside both her subjectivity and her objectivity (as she does in Model 2), and times when it is best that she remain very much centered within her own subjectivity (as she does in Model 3).

Again, it will be the therapist's ability to assume at different times (and sometimes simultaneously) all three modes that will enable her to optimize the effectiveness of her interventions.

THE THERAPIST'S OBJECTIVITY

As we have seen, Model 1 would seem to be about the therapist's objectivity. The therapist is thought to be objective—in the sense that she strives as best she can to be an observer (stationed outside the therapeutic field) and not a participant (entangled in transference–countertransference enactments). As such, the therapist is thought to have an inside track on the truth; in other words, she is thought to be the arbiter of reality—a reality that is both objective and knowable.

In essence, in Model 1 the bottom-line assumption is that there is such a thing as objective reality—and that it is knowable. More specifically, it is for the therapist to come to know the truth and, over time, to communicate that knowledge to the patient (by way of interpretation) so that the patient, too, will come to know. The province of the patient's ego expands as she gains insight into the internal workings of her mind.

The Model 1 therapist believes that observers preserve their objectivity by virtue of their detachment and that participants lose their objectivity by virtue of their involvement. When the therapist loses her objectivity and allows herself to be drawn into the patient's transferential enactments, countertransference is implicated. Such countertransference is thought (by the Model 1 therapist) to obstruct the therapeutic progress, because it is thought to be a story not about the here-and-now of the therapeutic situation but about the there-and-then of the therapist's developmental past. It is the therapist's responsibility to do whatever she must (on her own time) to resolve her countertransferential difficulties, so that she can recover her objectivity and the analytic work can proceed unimpeded.

In describing this classical stance, McLaughlin (1991) writes,

> I had come to expect that I was to accomplish my best analytic work through an objectifying and assessing stance that allowed me to see and convey to my patient my surer grasp of the reality of his situation. This latter I was to articulate with an interventive precision that could be expected to promote mutative growth in my patients. [p. 601]

THE PATIENT'S SUBJECTIVITY

Model 2 would seem to be about the patient's subjectivity. The patient is thought to have the inside track on the truth; what matters is her perception, her internal experience, her subjective reality.

In order to enter into the patient's subjective experience, the Model 2 therapist must strive as best she can to leave herself behind, both her subjectivity and her objectivity. The therapist positions herself alongside the patient, the better to be affectively attuned to what the patient is experiencing in the moment. The therapist is then able to provide empathic recognition (or validation) of the patient's subjective reality or, as a good object–good mother, to meet (that is, to recognize and respond to) the patient's developmental needs.

The Model 2 therapist believes that when the therapist is unable to decenter from her own experience, countertransference is implicated—countertransference that is thought to obstruct the therapeutic progress. It is thought to be a story not so much about the here-and-now of the therapeutic situation as about the therapist's difficulty stepping outside her own experience in order to immerse herself empathically in the patient's experience. It is the therapist's responsibility to do whatever she must (on her own time) to resolve her countertransference, so that she can recover her ability to decenter from her own subjectivity and thereby recover her therapeutic effectiveness as an empathic selfobject or a good object–good mother.

THE INTERSUBJECTIVE FIELD

Whereas the Model 2 therapist attempts to decenter from her own experience in order better to be available to the patient, the Model 3 therapist believes that she can only be truly available to the patient if she remains very much centered within her self as a real person, drawing upon what it feels like to be in relationship with the patient to inform both her understanding of the patient and how she then intervenes.

What is the role of objectivity and subjectivity in Model 3? As we know, Model 3 embraces an interactive or relational perspective; it embraces an intersubjective perspective, in the sense that there are thought to be always two subjects in the room, both of whom have their own subjectivities, both of whom contribute continuously to the ongoing psychoanalytic engagement.

No longer is the therapist thought to have the inside track on the truth, as happens in Model 1. No longer is the patient thought to have the inside track on the truth, as happens in Model 2. Rather, the truth is thought to be something that is created in the transitional space between patient and therapist. Like a transitional object, it is part found and part created; it is part real and part imagined, as Winnicott (1963a,b) observed, reality is both objectively perceived and subjectively conceived. More generally, as we have already seen, Model 3 theorists believe that the truth is always co-constructed and co-determined by the two participants in the therapeutic encounter.

In Model 3, then, reality (whether described as truth, meaning, or experience) is thought to be relative, not absolute; by the same token, it is thought to be subjective, not objective. The emphasis is always on the construction of meaning. Reality is not a given; it is created by patient and therapist in the context of their interactive engagement.

In other words, there is no inside track on the truth—because there is no truth. But even if there were an inside track, however, the therapist would not have exclusive rights to it, because the Model 3 therapist is thought to be always a participant in the therapeutic process, never simply an observer.

Renik (1993) has captured the essence of the Model 3 perspective with the following:

> Instead of saying that it is *difficult* for an analyst to *maintain* a position in which his or her analytic activity objectively focuses on a patient's inner reality, I would say that it is *impossible* for an analyst to be in that position *even for an instant*; since we are constantly acting in the analytic situation on the basis of personal motivations of which we cannot be aware until after the fact, our technique, listening included, is *inescapably* subjective. [p. 560]

In the spirit of recognizing that the therapist does not always "know the truth," Bollas (1987) has suggested that when he offers the patient an interpretation, he will often acknowledge the subjective factor in what he is saying with qualifiers like: "What occurs to me . . . ," or "I am thinking that . . . ," or "I have an idea . . ." Bollas, like Winnicott (1965) and Aron (1992), believes the therapist's interpretations are to be played with by the patient—"kicked around, mulled over, torn to pieces—rather than regarded as the official version of the truth" (1987, p. 206).

In Model 3, therefore, the bottom-line assumption is that the therapist is not an authority; her interpretations of the patient's subjectivity are simply plausible constructions (Hoffman 1983). So, too, the patient is able to formulate plausible interpretations of the therapist's subjectivity. And thus it is that simultaneously the therapist interprets the patient's subjectivity and the patient interprets the therapist's subjectivity. Whether the interpretation is formulated by the therapist or by the patient, all interpretations should be taken seriously but with a grain of salt—because there is no such thing as absolute truth.

The respect accorded the patient's plausible interpretations of the therapist's experience, however, does not imply that the Model 3 therapist accedes to the patient's perspective—as happens, say, in Model 2 where, if the patient's perception is that she has been failed by her therapist, then she is thought to have been failed.

In fact, in Model 2, reference is often made to the perceived empathic failure (Schwaber 1983), not to the reality of the therapist as having objectively failed the patient. When the therapist, despite her best efforts, inadvertently fails the patient, a disruption (of the positive transference) occurs. The therapist directs her efforts toward identifying the offending failure. The work involves a focus not on the legitimacy of the patient's upset but rather on an understanding of the precipitating event(s) that led to the patient's outrage, devastation, and retreat.

In other words, it is not the regressive position itself but the need for it that is the focus of the Model 2 therapist's attention. A correct identification by the therapist of the exact nature of the offending failure, no matter how minor, is necessary if the relationship is to survive, the disappointment to be mastered, and the positive transference to be recovered.

As we noted earlier, in order to pinpoint the exact nature of the offending failure, the therapist might choose to ask the question: "How have I let you down?" or "How have I failed you?" Note that the emphasis is not on the patient's pathology. The question is not "How do you feel that I have disappointed you?" but, rather, "How have I disappointed you?" The reality is that the therapist (by being less than perfect) has indeed disappointed the patient.

In order to highlight the distinction between the way Model 2 therapists deal with the therapist's failure of her patient and the way Model 3 therapists deal with it, I offer the following guidelines.

In Model 2, if the patient is upset because she feels that her therapist has failed her, then, as we have seen, it is not for the Model 2 therapist (at least not the self psychologist) to focus on whether she really has or has not failed the patient. Model 2 is not so much about the therapist's "actual" behavior; it is much more about the patient's experience of it. If the patient's perception is of having been failed, then the Model 2 therapist (positioning herself as subject and not as object or target [Schwaber 1981]) tries as best she can to take the patient's subjective experience as a starting point and to proceed from there.

In Model 3, if the patient is upset because she feels that her therapist has failed her, then it is important that the interactive dynamic between patient and therapist be explored, in order to understand both the patient's contribution and the therapist's contribution to the patient's perception of having been failed. In other words, because a relational model conceives of all experience as co-constructed, it is important that patient and therapist come to understand what part of the patient's experience is primarily a story about the patient and what part primarily a story about the therapist—as long as it is clearly understood that both patient and therapist are so intertwined, so continuously acting/reacting in relation to each other, that nothing can ever be purely a story about either one.

Clinical Vignette—I Feel Criticized

Let us now consider in greater detail the situation of a patient who is upset because she feels that her therapist is being critical of her.

(1) The Model 1 therapist will see this as an instance of negative transference (distortion) and will want to explore its genetic underpinnings (so that the patient can gain insight into why she tends to experience new good objects as old bad—critical—ones). The therapist, in an effort to tease out unconscious connections between the patient's past and her present, may offer the patient interpretations that encourage her to look inward and backward, so that she can observe her compulsive tendency to misinterpret her present in terms of her unresolved past. The Model 1 therapist's goal will be to advance the patient's understanding of her unconscious motivation.

(2) The Model 2 therapist will want to give the patient the experience of being understood. To that end, the therapist will resonate empathically with the patient's experience of upset in the here-and-now, striving to create a safe space within which the patient can elaborate upon this experience—perhaps, in the process, recovering memories of early-on experiences of upset at the hands of a critical parent.

Within the context of safety provided by the relationship with her therapist, the patient may dare to re-experience some of the original hurt, the original pain, the original outrage. The patient may be able to do now what she could not possibly do as a child—namely, confront the pain of her heartache about her parent (and the parent's limitations). The patient will have the opportunity to grieve both the parent's early-on failure of her and the therapist's current failure of her; in the process, the patient will be able, by way of transmuting internalization, to take in whatever "good" the object had offered prior to failing the patient.

Internalizing the good is the process by which energy is transformed into structure, need is transformed into capacity (Stark 1994a,b). More specifically, the functions the selfobject parent–therapist had been performing prior to her failure of the child–patient are internalized and can then be performed internally. Taking in the good that had been is part of the grieving process and is the way the child–patient masters her experience of the parent's/therapist's failure of her.

Internalized selfobject functions become structures—structures that perform those functions the patient had originally needed the selfobject to perform. In essence, internalized functions become psychic structures that enable the patient to have capacity—where before she had need.

The Model 2 therapist's goal will be to offer the patient a corrective experience that will transform the patient's need for a good parent into the capacity to be a good parent unto herself.

(3) The Model 3 therapist will want to explore with the patient the interactive dynamic between them, in order to understand the contribution of each to the patient's experience of upset.

The Model 3 therapist may ask the patient to elaborate more specifically on what the patient had observed about the therapist that had led the patient to believe that the therapist was being critical. The Model 3 therapist considers the patient's response to be a story about not just the patient's there-and-then but also the here-and-now of the therapeutic situation. The patient's observations are thought to be plausible constructions of the therapist's participation and, as such, are taken seriously by the therapist. The therapist may not have (consciously) intended her intervention to be critical; the Model 3 therapist recognizes, however, that if the patient's experience was that the therapist's intervention was critical, then it may well be that the patient was picking up on something of which the therapist was not aware.

Just as the therapist interprets the patient's unconscious, so too the patient can interpret the therapist's unconscious. And just as the therapist's interpretation may enable the patient to become aware of something within her that she had not previously recognized, so too the patient's interpretation may enable the therapist to become aware of something within her that she had not previously recognized.

Once the therapist's contribution to the patient's experience of her as critical has been recognized, patient and therapist go on to explore the patient's contribution—perhaps hypersensitivity on the patient's part that makes her experience others as critical, perhaps provocative behavior on the patient's part that elicits the very reaction (of criticism) she most fears. Please note that even if patient and therapist are able to identify something in the patient's activity that was experienced by the therapist as provocative and to which the therapist was probably reacting, this by no means gets the therapist "off the hook" with respect to accountability for her critical response to the patient.

The net result of working at the intimate edge between patient and therapist will be enhancement of the patient's understanding of what she plays out in her relationships and a deepening of the connection between patient and therapist. (In the process, the therapist may well also achieve increased self-awareness.) The Model 3 therapist's goal is to facilitate development of the patient's capacity to enter healthily and authentically into relationship with others.

OBJECTIVITY LOST AND THEN REFOUND

In contradistinction to the Model 3 therapist who works more generally with an interactive model in which nothing is absolute but is instead thought to be continuously shaped by both participants, the Model 3 therapist who works more specifically with a relational-conflict model does not focus (in the same way) on the therapist's ever-present participation in the therapeutic encounter. Rather, the relational-conflict model focuses on the therapist's ability to shift back and forth—to be sometimes subjective and sometimes objective, to be sometimes a participant and sometimes an observer, to be sometimes involved and sometimes detached.

We are not now using the term subjective to suggest that the therapist is always a participant and, therefore, always biased, never objective. Rather, we are using it to suggest that the therapist is no longer objective—by virtue of having allowed herself to respond to pressure from the patient to relinquish her more neutral stance in order to participate as the patient's old bad object.

In other words, when the therapist accepts the patient's projections, we say that she loses her objectivity inasmuch as she is no longer observing but participating, no longer understanding but enacting. The therapist loses her objectivity when she relinquishes her more detached observer stance and allows her moves to be choreographed by the patient.

Interestingly, when the patient's relational conflict assumes center stage, the focus is not so much on the therapist's subjectivity as on her permeability and her malleability—the therapist's ability to be receptive to the patient's projections and her willingness to allow herself to be drawn into participating countertransferentially with the patient in the latter's transferential enactments.

In fact, in the relational-conflict model, the therapist is thought to be an objective, detached observer who is nonetheless open to being acted upon by the patient. When the therapist allows herself to be shaped by the patient's need for her to participate in certain ways—that is, when the therapist allows herself to respond to interpersonal pressure the patient exerts on her, the therapist is said to lose her objectivity. At that point, the therapist becomes involved—a participant, a subject.

But the relational-conflict therapist must also be able, eventually, to wend her way out of what has become a mutual enactment; the therapist must be able to recover her objectivity and, thereby, her therapeutic effectiveness—which enables the patient to have the corrective relational experience of bad-become-good. The therapist recovers her objectivity when she recovers her ability to understand and is no longer enacting. The therapist may (or may not) then choose to share her newfound understanding with the patient—perhaps in the form of an intervention that highlights the interactive nature of their engagement.

There is a paradox involved here: although it is only by way of recovering her objectivity that the therapist is able to work her way out, it is only by way of working her way out that the therapist is able to recover her objectivity—only to be drawn back in once again. And so we might say of the relational-conflict therapist that she is alternately involved and detached, alternately participant and observer. By the same token, her interventive stance is alternately subjective and objective.

If, because of her own unresolved issues, the therapist comes to experience herself unconsciously as she is portrayed in the patient's projective fantasy, and cannot therefore find her way out, then she will be unable effectively to contain the patient's projection (or projective identification). It is when the therapist loses her objectivity entirely that she loses her ability to be therapeutically useful to the patient.

It will be only as the therapist recovers both her objectivity and her ability to understand that she will be able to function as a container for the patient. Where before she was simply participating with the patient in a mutual enactment, now she will be able to step back in order to observe what has been played out between them.

The successful handling of the therapist's participation in the patient's enactments, then, is a matter of balance: The therapist must be sufficiently open that she can be drawn into participating with the patient and yet secure enough within herself that she can maintain enough psychological distance to have some understanding of what has been mutually enacted in the relationship.

THE THERAPIST AS A REAL PERSON

Let me highlight here what is meant when it is said that the Model 3 therapist participates as a real person (or as an authentic subject).

In Model 2 theory, reference is often made to the corrective experience provided by the real relationship between patient and therapist. What this means is that the patient is being offered some form of corrective provision by a therapist who allows herself to be a little warmer, a little more emotionally accessible, than she would be were she to be adhering to a more regimented classical stance. But what is irrelevant is the therapist's subjectivity (that is, who the therapist *really* is)—warts and all.

Indeed, the Model 2 therapist who participates as a new good object may be more warmly present than the Model 1 therapist who strives to preserve her objectivity, her neutrality, and her anonymity—but she is still not being real in the way that a Model 3 therapist, participating as an authentic subject, is being real.

Model 2 does not speak to the importance of the therapist as a real person with blind spots, sensitivities, biases, likes and dislikes, and idiosyncrasies. Model 2 does not speak to the importance of the therapist as a subject in her own right, with her own inner world, her own experience, and her own center of initiative.

Whereas the corrective-provision perspective of Model 2 appreciates the therapist's willingness to be involved as a good object, the relational perspective of Model 3 appreciates that the therapist is a unique individual with her own idiosyncratic, particularistic features—some of which are good, some of which are bad, and some of which are just aspects of her subjectivity. Whereas Model 2 values the therapist as a good object, Model 3 values the therapist as an authentic subject.

In essence, the distinction to which I am here referring is the one that exists between a therapist's bringing *the best* of who she is (as happens in Model 2) and a therapist's bringing *all* of who she is (as happens in Model 3) into the therapy relationship.

OBSERVER VERSUS PARTICIPANT

With respect to the therapist as observer or participant, whereas the Model 1 therapist is thought to be primarily an observer, Model 2 and Model 3 therapists believe that an important part of what makes the therapist an effective transference object is her ability (and her willingness) to become a participant in the therapeutic encounter.

A Neutral Observer

The Model 1 therapist conceives of herself as a blank screen onto which the patient displaces (thereby creating positive transference) and projects (thereby creating negative transference). These transferences the therapist then interprets as a story about the patient and the patient's internal dynamics. Although the patient may experience the therapist as either a new good object or the old bad one, the Model 1 therapist is secure in her knowledge that the patient's experience of her as the good parent the patient never had is but illusion (positive transference) and that the patient's experience of her as the bad parent the patient did have is but distortion (negative transference).

The Model 1 therapist works with the patient's transference; but the patient's experience of her is thought to be a figment of the patient's imagination.

A Good Object

The Model 2 therapist conceives of herself as the good parent the patient never had in a reliable and consistent fashion early on.

In self psychology, even though the therapist conceives of herself as a new good object, the emphasis in the self psychological literature is more on the patient's experience of the therapist as a new good object than on the therapist's actual participation as that new good object. Just as the emphasis is more on the therapist's empathic recognition of the patient's need than on her actual responsiveness to it (in the form, say, of gratification) and just as the emphasis is more on the patient's perception of having been failed by her therapist than on the "reality" of having been so failed, in self psychology the focus is always on the patient's subjective experience—not "objective reality."

On the other hand, in those Model 2 object relations theories that speak to the internal registering of traumatic parental failure in the form of absence of good, the emphasis is on the therapist's actual participation as a new good object. In such theories the belief is that it does not suffice for the therapist simply to recognize the patient's need; the therapist must also in some way respond to that need. Nor does it suffice for the therapist simply to understand that the patient's experience was of having been failed; the therapist must also be able to recognize how she might in actual fact have failed her patient.

And so it is that although self psychology speaks to the importance of empathic recognition of need, Model 2 object relations theories speak to the importance of meeting the patient's need (in the sense of both recognizing and responding to it).

But whether the emphasis is on the patient's experience of the therapist as a new good object (in self psychology) or on the therapist's actual participation as that new good object (in object relations theories that emphasize deficit), in Model 2 the therapist conceives of her role as that of the good parent the patient never had early on.

An Authentic Subject

With respect to Model 3, let us consider first the situation that accrues when relational conflict is in the limelight, then when relational deficit assumes center stage; and then when, more generally, the patient's relational difficulties come to the fore.

Relational Conflict

As we have seen, patients with relational conflict enter ambivalently into new good relationships. The concept of relational conflict is embraced by (1) those object relations theorists who think in terms of the internal recording of traumatic parental failure in the form of internal bad objects and (2) those contemporary psychoanalytic theorists who think more generally (and without specific reference to internal bad objects) in terms of the patient's conflictedness about being in new good relationships.

Relational-conflict theory advances the idea that inevitably the therapist will get drawn into participating as the bad parent the patient did have because the therapist will not be able to avoid responding to pressure from the patient to participate in that way. Whereas Model 1 speaks to the patient's experience of the therapist as the old bad object (an instance of projection or negative transference), Model 3 speaks to the patient's exerting of pressure on the therapist to draw the therapist into participating as that old bad object (an instance of projective identification or actualization of the negative transference).

The unhealthy aspect of the patient's compulsion to repeat has to do with maintaining her attachment to the infantile object. The unhealthy aspect of the patient's transferential enactments has to do, then, with her need for more of same (because it is this with which she is most familiar, and, therefore, most comfortable). But the healthy aspect of the patient's transferential enactments involves her desire to achieve belated mastery of her now-internalized traumas.

The relational-conflict therapist must be able to receive the patient's projection and then to use aspects of her own, more mature capacity to process the projection—such that what the therapist returns to the patient will be psychologically processed and slightly detoxified. The patient with relational conflict will have the corrective relational experience of bad-become-good, offered by a therapist who has been able to allow herself first to participate as the old bad object (so that there can be authentic engagement) and then to recover herself (so that there can be containment). The therapist who is able to lend aspects of her healthy self to a psychological processing of the patient's disavowed psychic contents will be able to return to the patient something different from, something better than, the original projection.

Fairbairn's Contribution

It is to Fairbairn (1958) that we owe much of our understanding about the patient's need to find the old bad object so that she can achieve belated mastery of her internal demons. After all, it was Fairbairn who wrote about the mother as a seductive object, as someone who first offers her child the enticing promise of relatedness and then fails to deliver. The child, when brought face-to-face with the excruciatingly painful reality of just how unavailable her mother really is, cannot possibly confront the pain of her grief about the mother's limitations.

In order to preserve the illusion of her mother as good and as ultimately forthcoming, if she (the child) could but get it right, the child takes the burden of her mother's badness upon herself, in the form of internal bad objects to which she is both libidinally and aggressively attached. In other words, the child's attachment to her internal bad objects is ambivalent—her internal objects are both loved (because they excite) and hated (because they betray).

The patient, unconscious of her compulsion to repeat the early-on situation of seduction and betrayal in subsequent relationships, is ever in search of love objects with whom she can reenact her internal drama, love objects whom she can make into exciting/rejecting objects, promising but never fulfilling. Her hope is that perhaps this time it will be different, perhaps this time she will find the gratification for which she has been searching a lifetime.

But, interestingly, Fairbairn (1958) insists that when the patient delivers her need to be failed into the therapy, the therapist must resist being made into a bad (seductive) object—that is, an exciting but ultimately rejecting object. And, says Fairbairn, to the extent that the therapist is able successfully to resist being drawn into participating countertransferentially as a bad object, to that extent will the treatment be successful.

Fairbairn's stance, therefore, is somewhat paradoxical. Like the relational-conflict theorist who believes that the patient is (1) deeply conflicted about finding a new good object and (2) therefore ever busy exerting pressure on the therapist to participate as the old bad one, Fairbairn believes that the patient's attachments to her internal bad objects are so intense that she is always seeking love objects with whom she can replay her internal dramas. But unlike the relational-conflict theorist who believes that the therapist must allow herself to be drawn into participating with the patient in her dramatic re-enactments, Fairbairn believes that the therapist must remain steadfast in her refusal to participate in this way.

And so it is that Fairbairn helps us to understand the patient's need for the therapist to participate as the old bad object (because of the patient's intensely ambivalent attachment to her internal bad objects). But Fairbairn—because of his insistence that the therapist must always strive to participate, even so, as a new good object—is more a proponent of Model 2 than he is of Model 3. Despite interpersonal pressure from the patient, Fairbairn's contention is that the therapist must resist the temptation to respond to the patient's (unconscious) need to be failed.

Relational Deficit

When relational deficit is in the spotlight, the therapist must be exceptionally attuned to whether the patient wants to remain hidden or is waiting (and desperately wishing) to be found.

(1) When the patient would seem to be invested in remaining not known, not found, then the therapist must accept with grace the patient's need for distance and must be able to tolerate being in the position of being neither needed nor used. The therapist must be able to bear it that, for the time being, the patient's need is to be disengaged.

(2) When the patient would seem to be wanting to be found, then the therapist (in order to access the patient) may need to bring herself into the room in a "vigorously personal" way. She must be willing to make herself vulnerable and to put herself out there on behalf of a patient who truly does not know how to engage with others. The relational-deficit therapist believes that it is not fair to expect a patient—desperate to be found but terrified of being shattered by an unempathic response—to be vulnerable when the therapist is not herself willing to be vulnerable.

For instance, there are some patients who cannot bear to acknowledge an affect (like shame, outrage, envy, love, hatred) until they have managed to induce that affect in the therapist. Such patients cannot tolerate the experience of feeling an affect in the presence of another unless the other is willing to take on the affect as her own. In other words, before such patients dare to deliver themselves into the treatment, they may need to know that the therapist is able to tolerate their affect as a shared experience.

A patient of mine (with relational deficit) was terrified of exposing genuine affect to others. As a result, I had much difficulty locating her. Nor did she feel that she could find me. What I came in time to understand was that she could not tolerate the experience of being alone with her feelings and that the only way she could let herself experience them in my presence was if I too were experiencing them.

For example, before my patient could dare to let me witness her shame, she would need to know that I too was feeling shame. To elicit that feeling in me, she would behave in all kinds of provocative, shaming ways. It was only after she had succeeded in eliciting the feeling in me that she could feel truly connected to me and our work could proceed.

In other words, if the patient cannot get her therapist to make herself vulnerable in this way (that is, by taking on the patient's affect as her own), then the patient with relational deficit may refuse to deliver herself into the treatment—and there will be no real engagement.

In sum, with a patient who has relational deficit, the therapist (if she is to engage the patient) must participate as an authentic subject—ever responsive to the patient's need for the therapist either (1) to be unobtrusively present (until the patient signals her desire for more) or (2) to bring herself into the room in a more personal fashion.

Relational Difficulties

Our understanding of the patient's relational conflict and her relational deficit is informed by object relations theories that emphasize the internal presence of bad; as we saw in Part 1, the patient's internal bad objects prompt her either to re-create with the therapist the old bad traumatic failure situation (relational conflict) or to keep herself out of authentic engagement altogether (relational deficit).

More generally, contemporary psychoanalytic theory has as its focus the patient's relational (or interpersonal) difficulties, which are thought (1) to arise in the context of early-on traumatogenic parent–child interactions and (2) to be played out (or enacted) in subsequent relationships.

Whatever the nature of the patient's relational difficulties (that is, whatever trouble the patient might have engaging healthily and authentically with others because of what she brings to the present from her past), the therapeutic action in Model 3 is thought to involve the relational therapist's participation as an authentic subject, as someone who brings her real self into the room—ever aware that her subjectivity has an impact on the patient and that the patient's subjectivity has an impact on her.

The Model 3 therapist is thought to be both proactive (that is, an initiator) and reactive (that is, a responder); she is thought both to contribute to the patient's experience and to respond to the patient's contribution. It is this mutuality of impact that establishes both participants as subjects in the therapeutic encounter.

Please note that when we speak of the therapist's authenticity or realness in the therapeutic encounter, it is generally understood that reference is being made to what we might want to call "analytic authenticity" or "analytic realness"—similar to the concept of "analytic love" (Hoffer 1985) used by some to describe the love experienced between patient and therapist.

In other words, the authentic therapist who brings her real self into the relationship will be judicious in the disclosure of her countertransference, selective in the sharing of aspects of her self-experience, and considered in her use of self to further the therapeutic endeavor.

But describing the therapist's participation as authentic or as real is not intended, in any way whatsoever, to give the therapist license to do whatever she wants because she feels like doing it. It is always crucial that the Model 3 therapist, even as she dares to bring more of herself into the room, should maintain her integrity and her professional demeanor. Ongoing supervision and consultation is always important; but for the therapist who works with a relational model, it is crucial—so that the therapist can have an opportunity to understand the ways in which her activity and her reactivity might be hindering, rather than promoting, the therapeutic process.

With respect to the therapist's participation as an authentic subject, Russell (1995) speaks to the "almost-but-not-quite" realness of the therapist. In the treatment relationship, Russell writes, "I am myself, *almost*" (p. 4).

Of his work with patients, Russell goes on to say, "What *is* real is the therapy. The therapy depends upon us both being in a place where we can discover who we both really are in a way that is less costly than it would be anywhere else" (p. 4). And with respect to reciprocity in the therapy relationship, Russell remarks, "Probably, in the long run there is no such thing as a reciprocal relationship. [And] it may be that therapy takes place only while that fiction is in place. But, even if it is a fiction, I need it to do the work" (p. 4).

By way of review, in Model 3, the therapist participates as an authentic subject.

1. Sometimes the emphasis is on the therapist's participation as the old bad object (when the patient's relational conflict comes to the fore);
2. Sometimes the emphasis is on the therapist's willingness to make herself vulnerable in her pursuit of a patient who wants desperately to be found but is afraid of being hurt or disappointed (when the patient's relational deficit takes the spotlight);
3. Sometimes the emphasis is on the therapist's participation simply as a real person engaged with the patient in a real relationship characterized by reciprocity, mutuality, and give-and-take (when the patient's relational difficulties assume center stage).

CHAPTER

20

Interface between Theory and Practice

My particular interest has long been the interface between theory and practice. How do theoretical constructs translate into the clinical situation? More specifically, how do the three different models of therapeutic action inform the choices therapists are continuously making with respect both to how they listen to the patient and to how they then intervene?

My intent throughout this book is not to suggest that there is a right way or a wrong way for therapists to behave. Rather, my intent is to provide therapists with a theoretical framework—a way to conceptualize (on a moment-to-moment basis) the choices they are continuously making about how to position themselves in relation to their patients.

To some extent, I am simply offering a description of what therapists already do; but my hope is that by presenting the three different models of therapeutic action (each of which focuses on a different aspect of the patient–therapist interface), I will be stimulating therapists to think more conceptually about what they are actually doing—and why.

To review what I have been saying to this point, in order to gather as much information about the patient as she can, the therapist listens from three different vantage points. The therapist attempts to achieve a balance between positioning herself as (1) a neutral object outside the therapeutic field (observing the patient and the internal workings of her mind); (2) an empathic selfobject joining alongside the patient (immersing herself in the patient's affective experience); and (3) an authentic subject interacting with the patient (using her own experience of being so engaged to inform her understanding of the patient). Earlier I had described this as afference—the direction of flow toward the therapist.

Armed with what she has come to know about the patient by way of listening to her, the therapist will intervene in a manner that involves either (1) enhancement of knowledge, (2) provision of experience, or (3) engagement in relationship as the primary therapeutic modality.

In other words, how the therapist conceptualizes what she thinks will be most therapeutically useful to the patient in the moment will determine her choice of intervention. If her intent is to advance the patient's understanding of her internal dynamics, then the therapist will formulate an interpretation. If her intent is to give the patient the experience of being met, then the therapist will offer some form of corrective provision. And if her intent is to advance the patient's understanding of her relational dynamics and/or to deepen the level of their connection, then the therapist will focus on some aspect of their here-and-now engagement. Earlier I had described this as efference—the direction of flow away from the therapist.

It is always the therapist's intent that places her intervention in either Model 1 (knowledge), Model 2 (experience), or Model 3 (relationship). Of course, there may be times when the therapist's intent is to focus on more than one of these modalities, in which case we would say that she is making use of more than one model of therapeutic action.

Sometimes the therapist, despite her intent, is not able to accomplish what she had hoped to accomplish—that is, a Model 1 intervention may not advance the patient's knowledge of herself, a Model 2 intervention may not be experienced as affirming, or a Model 3 intervention may confuse rather than clarify the interactive dynamic between patient and therapist. But even though the intervention may prove to be ineffective, or even counterproductive, it is still the therapist's intent that makes of it a Model 1, 2, or 3 intervention.

There may also be times when an intervention, designed to target one particular dimension, ends up having an impact on another instead. For example, an intervention intended to resonate with the patient's affective experience may not be felt by the patient to be validating but may ironically end up advancing the patient's understanding of herself. Again, it is the therapist's intent that makes of it a Model 1, 2, or 3 intervention—although, in this case, we would say of the therapist's statement that it was an instance of inaccurate empathy.

Or there may be times when an intervention, designed to target one specific dimension, ends up having an impact on another one as well. For example, an interpretation addressing the patient's internal dynamics may also either make the patient feel understood and validated and/or deepen the level of engagement between patient and therapist. Here, too, it is the therapist's intent that makes of it a Model 1, 2, or 3 intervention—although it may turn out to be doubly or even triply effective because it has had an impact on several different levels.

Remember also that although the immediate goal in Model 1 is advancing the patient's knowledge of her internal dynamics, the longer-term goal is resolving the patient's structural conflicts by way of strengthening her ego through the acquisition of insight. The net result will be less internal tension and more energy available to be directed toward the realization of the patient's personal and professional dreams.

Although the immediate goal in Model 2 is validating the patient's experience and/or providing a corrective experience for the patient, the longer-term goal is filling in the patient's structural deficits and consolidating the patient's self by way of the therapist's corrective provision. The net result will be enhanced self-esteem for the patient, a more secure sense of self, a stronger feeling of well-being, a firmer sense of self-reliance, and greater emotional resilience.

And although the immediate goal in Model 3 is advancing the patient's knowledge of her relational dynamics and/or deepening the level of engagement between patient and therapist, the longer term goal is resolving the patient's relational difficulties by way of focusing on the here-and-now engagement between patient and therapist and on what the patient plays out (or enacts) in that relationship. The net result will be development of the patient's capacity for healthy, authentic relatedness with others—as the patient with relational conflict transforms her need to be failed into a capacity to tolerate new good relationships and the patient with relational deficit transforms her need to avoid engagement altogether into a capacity to deliver her real self into relationship.

With that said, I would like now to demonstrate, through the use of clinical vignettes (some of them hypothetical), application of the three models of therapeutic action to the clinical situation.

Some of the vignettes elaborate upon theoretical points I made earlier in this book, and some of them develop in greater depth clinical situations to which I made passing reference in Part I.

In each vignette, however, the hypothetical responses I propose are but a sampling of the different kinds of interventions the therapist might have chosen to offer the patient. In no way whatsoever do I intend to be suggesting that these interventions constitute an exhaustive inventory of every possible response. They are offered simply in the hope that readers will be stimulated to craft some of their own.

In the vignettes that follow, I have chosen not to develop the clinical material but instead to highlight what goes into the making of Model 1, Model 2, and Model 3 interventions.

Clinical Vignette—Accessing the Sadness

Let us imagine a situation in which the patient is recounting a very sad story, but with little affect. In fact, the patient has always had much difficulty expressing intense affect; in her family, feelings were not well tolerated, particularly because of her mother's discomfort with intense affect. In fact, the patient's mother would call her a "sissy," whenever she expressed deep affect.

As we know, the therapist arrives at understanding of the patient in three ways—as object observing, as selfobject joining, and as subject reacting.

The Model 1 therapist watches the patient and reflects upon what she observes. She can see that the patient is sad and hypothesizes (to herself) that the patient's need to defend herself against feeling that sadness derives from experiences the patient had early on in relation to her mother, who could not tolerate the expression of genuine affect.

The Model 2 therapist decenters from her own experience in order to join alongside the patient. She can feel both the patient's sadness and, more poignantly still, the patient's struggle not to experience it.

The Model 3 therapist stays closely attuned to what it feels like to be in the room with the patient. As she listens, she finds herself feeling deeply touched and becoming, suddenly, very sad.

The therapist must now decide how she wants to intervene.

If her goal is to enhance the patient's understanding of her internal conflict and its genetic underpinnings, then the therapist might choose to interpret the patient's need to defend herself against her sadness as deriving from her mother's denigration of her whenever she would express her feelings. To that end, the therapist might offer the patient the following: "You appear to be as intolerant of your sadness as your mother used to be."

It both startles and horrifies the patient to think that she might have become like her mother in this way. She bristles as she remembers all the times her mother would tell her how important it was to remain strong, to keep a stiff upper lip, never to cry. The patient recollects a time when she had lost her favorite doll (a little girl doll she had named Tinkerbell) and her mother had told her that she should not give way to her tears because that was what crybabies did; the patient finds herself feeling first angry and then, suddenly, very sad. Belatedly, she weeps for the little girl whose heart had been broken when she lost her Tinkerbell.

Alternatively, if the therapist is more intent upon providing the patient with the experience of being understood, then the therapist might resonate empathically with where she senses the patient is affectively in the moment. The Model 2 therapist can feel how hard it is for the patient to let herself be in her sadness. To that end, she offers the patient the following: "It is difficult for you to let yourself feel the pain of your sadness," or "You are fighting hard to hold back your tears," or, simply, "It's important to you to be able to stay in control."

The patient, visibly relaxing, goes on to elaborate upon how difficult it has always been for her to let herself feel intense affect. She talks about how frustrating it is not to be able to cry, not to be able to access her tears. Because she is always holding back, she often has the experience of simply skimming the surface of things—unable to delve more deeply into the moment, unable to immerse herself in what is heartfelt and real.

The patient becomes upset and angry as she thinks about the price she has paid for having had to live a lie, for having had to pretend that everything was okay when it really wasn't. She says she is exhausted from the effort of trying to hold everything together for her mother's sake.

Within the context of safety provided by her therapist who, unlike the patient's mother, appears to be comfortable with whatever affect she (the patient) might have, the patient begins to cry—because she is sad, she is tired, and it breaks her heart to think about how strong she has always had to pretend to be.

Whereas a Model 2 therapist strives to remain ever attuned to the patient's internal experience as she recounts her story, the Model 3 therapist strives to remain ever attuned to her own experience of being in the room with the patient. Deeply moved by the patient's story, the therapist finds herself feeling tears in her own eyes and, as she listens, giving voice to such sympathetic utterances as: "How sad!" or "Oh, that's terrible."

As the session progresses, the patient herself begins to get more and more in touch with the sadness—the content of which relates both to the specific story she has been recounting and, more generally, to disappointment about her mother that she has carried inside her for a long, long time. No longer unconsciously "pressuring" the therapist to carry the sadness for her, no longer unconsciously needing the therapist to feel something she herself cannot, the patient now becomes able to acknowledge her own sadness, which enables her to engage more affectively and more authentically in the therapy relationship. The connection she is able to establish with her therapist is much deeper by virtue of the patient's ability to be more present with her own feelings.

Whether the therapist is responding as a Model 1, a Model 2, or a Model 3 therapist, the therapist is dealing with the patient's sadness and her need not to feel it, which makes the patient less available both to herself and to the therapist. Although the focus is a little different from one model to the next, with each of the above interventions the patient is enabled to gain access to her underlying sadness.

In Model 1, the therapist offers the patient an interpretation about her need to stay in control of her sadness; as the patient gains insight into the relationship between her mother's intolerance of affect and her own difficulty tolerating it, she becomes better able to sit with the sadness against which she has spent a lifetime defending herself.

In Model 2, the therapist resonates empathically with the patient's need to stay in control of her sadness; with the therapist's recognition of how important it is to the patient that she be able to stay defended, the patient is freed up to access the other side of her conflict—namely, her sadness, including her sadness about how tired she is from having always had to pretend that things were fine when really they were not.

In Model 3, the therapist uses her self to take on the patient's disavowed sadness as her own, processes it with her own higher level of functioning, and returns a modified version of it to the patient; as the patient internalizes the now slightly modified bolus of sadness, she becomes better able to integrate it into her own experience and it becomes part of her own psychic structure.

In each of the models of therapeutic action, the therapist ultimately facilitates the patient's gaining of access to her underlying pain (and its integration into the rest of her psyche), but the route by which the patient gets there varies from one model to the next. As we will see, it is not always the case that all three approaches are viable options—but in the example just cited, all three are not only viable but also effective. As we will also see, it does not always happen that all three approaches produce the same result, even though they did in the example just cited.

Clinical Vignette—Misunderstood

Let us imagine a situation in which the therapist says to her patient: "You're angry with me because I do not seem to understand."

If the therapist's intent is to resonate empathically with the patient's experience of anger (anger with which the patient is in touch), then it is a Model 2 intervention.

If, however, the therapist's intent is to make the patient conscious of anger with which the patient would seem to be out of touch, then it is a Model 1 intervention.

Now let us imagine that the therapist goes on to suggest: "Say more."

Whereas both Model 1 and Model 2 therapists conceive of the patient's experience of the therapist as primarily a story about the patient (subjective transference), Model 3 therapists conceive of the patient's experience of the therapist as always both subjective (a story about the way the patient makes meaning of the therapist's participation) and objective (a story about the way the therapist actually participates in the therapeutic encounter).

When the therapist encourages the patient to say more, if the therapist's intent is now to focus the patient's attention on what the therapist is or is not actually doing that would lead the patient to experience the therapist as "not understanding," then it is a Model 3 intervention, inasmuch as the therapist's intent is to address the objective transference. In fact, in order to highlight that her interest is in exploring what the patient might have observed about her (the therapist's) participation, the therapist might make this explicit by saying something like: "Perhaps there is something in what I have said that has led you to believe that I do not understand?"

But when the therapist encourages the patient to say more, if the therapist's intent is simply to focus the patient's attention on what might be going on within the patient to "distort" her perception of the therapist, then it is a Model 1 intervention, inasmuch as the therapist's intent is to advance the patient's understanding of her internal process.

By the same token, if the therapist's intent is simply to signal her interest in understanding more deeply the patient's actual experience of being misunderstood, then it is a Model 2 intervention, inasmuch as the therapist's intent is to resonate empathically with the point of emotional urgency within the patient.

In both of these latter situations, the therapist is much more interested in the patient's subjective transference than she is in the patient's objective transference. In other words, the therapist is much more focused on either the patient's internal dynamics (Model 1) or the patient's affective experience (Model 2) than she is on the nature of the here-and-now engagement between patient and therapist.

Clinical Vignette—Can I Trust You?

The patient says anxiously to her therapist, "I'm so scared. I don't know if I can trust you!" The patient is someone who has always had an intensely conflicted relationship with her father.

The following would be a Model 1 intervention: "Because your father was so untrustworthy, it's very frightening to think about ever trusting again." Here the therapist's intent is to enhance the patient's knowledge of her internal dynamics, namely, the connection between her current fear and the early-on relationship with her untrustworthy father. If the therapist's intent is also to resonate with the patient's experience of fear in order to give the patient the experience of being understood, then it would also be a Model 2 intervention.

The following would be a Model 3 intervention: "When you speak of your fear, it helps me to understand better why you hold back in here." The therapist is now focusing on the relationship between the patient's fear and her actual behavior in the room, with an eye to enhancing the patient's understanding of her relational dynamics—that is, how her internal dynamics influence the way she engages in relationship. In an attempt to deepen the level of their engagement, the therapist is also bringing herself a little more into the room by making reference to her own increased understanding.

Clinical Vignette—On Having the Right to a Life

The patient is a young woman who, by dint of much hard work in her therapy, has done well in her life. She has developed herself professionally, and she has found a good man whom she plans to marry. But in the therapy she speaks often (and anxiously) about how overwhelmingly depressed she continues to feel. Well known to both patient and therapist is the fact that during the patient's childhood, mother—disabled by a profound depression—had spent years in bed.

When the therapist assumes a Model 1 listening stance, she finds herself thinking about the possible connection between the patient's depression and her mother's depression. She hypothesizes to herself that the patient's negative identification with her mother may relate to unconscious guilt the patient experiences about having otherwise separated from her mother—the depression serving as the last link to her mother.

When the therapist assumes a Model 2 listening stance, she finds herself resonating empathically with the patient's experience of depression. As the therapist imagines herself in her patient's shoes, she can feel the weightiness of the depression, how constricting it is, how immobilizing—and how frightening it is for the patient to be finding herself feeling still so depressed.

When the therapist assumes a Model 3 listening stance, she finds herself feeling deeply moved by the patient and by her plight. She becomes aware of feeling pain in her own heart—what she suspects is a countertransferential response to the patient's desperate plea that the therapist understand just how anxiously depressed the patient still feels (despite the rather remarkable gains she has otherwise made in her life).

Armed with what the therapist has come to know by way of listening from these three vantage points, she is then in a position to do one of three things.

(1) As a Model 1 therapist, she may choose to offer the patient an interpretive response: "I wonder if your depression is an unconscious effort on your part to remain loyal to your mother—even after all these years," or "Perhaps it is easier for you simply to be in the depression than to deal with the guilt you might feel were you to let yourself know just how desperately you wish to be free of both the depression and your mother." The intent of such interventions is to make the patient aware of what the therapist senses may be the patient's unconscious

identification with her mother—an identification motivated perhaps by separation guilt (Modell 1965).

(2) Alternatively, as a Model 2 therapist, she may choose to offer the patient an empathic response, the intent of which is to resonate with what the therapist senses the patient is feeling. To that end, the therapist might say something like: "Your depression makes it hard for you to get through your day," or "Perhaps you sometimes feel so depressed that you wonder how you will be able to keep going." If, in the moment, the therapist intuits that the patient is more in her fear about being like her mother than in the depression itself, she may opt to pick up on that by offering the patient the following: "It scares you to death to think that your depression might become immobilizing in the way that your mother's depression was." (Here the therapist, in addition to resonating with the patient's experience of fear, is also indirectly speaking to the patient's unconscious attachment to, and negative identification with, her mother.)

(3) Finally, as a Model 3 therapist, she may decide to focus the patient's attention on their here-and-now engagement as follows: "It's important to you that I understand just how scared you are about how overwhelming the depression still is," or "You want me to know that you are scared to death about how immobilizingly depressed you are feeling." The intent of such interventions is to highlight the relational aspect of their work, in the form of the patient's need to know that she is being heard by the therapist and is therefore not alone.

Clinical Vignette—Is It Time to Go Yet?

Suppose the patient says that she is ready to terminate and wants very much to have her therapist's approval. The patient says that she needs to know both that her therapist supports her in her desire to be autonomous and that the therapist thinks the time is right for her to be going out on her own.

The Model 1 therapist finds herself thinking that the patient's decision to leave the treatment is coming just as she is at last getting to some very important, intensely painful material about her controlling mother—material that the therapist thinks the patient needs to deal with before she will really be ready to go.

The Model 2 therapist can feel how desperately the patient wants her therapist both to appreciate her desire to be independent and to recognize that it is the right time for her to be ending the treatment.

The Model 3 therapist is aware of feeling conflicted about what to do in response to the patient's desperate plea to have her therapist's approval.

How might the therapist intervene?

A Model 1 therapist might choose to highlight the relationship between the patient's desire to stop treatment and her reluctance to delve more deeply into the feelings she has about her mother. To that end, the therapist might offer the following response: "I notice that you began to talk about termination just as you started to get in touch with some of the grief you have about how controlling your mother has always been. I wonder if there is any connection?"

A Model 2 therapist might pick up on the patient's obvious concern that her therapist will not offer her the needed approval for her decision to terminate. To that end, the therapist might say: "You are wanting very much to be free, and you want me to assure you that you have my support."

Suppose the therapist were to say something like the following: "You would so want to have my approval, and it saddens you to think that I might not be feeling the time is quite right for you to go." Here the therapist is intimating that, indeed, it may not be quite yet the right time.

To the extent that the therapist is also intending to highlight the discrepancy between the patient's desire for the therapist's approval and the sadness the patient would feel were the patient to let herself know the truth about how the therapist really feels, to that extent is the therapist's intervention both a Model 2 and a Model 1 response; the patient will feel understood even as it is also being named that she may not in fact have her therapist's support for her decision to terminate—the truth of which the patient is protecting herself from knowing.

The above is a disillusionment statement (Stark 1994a) because it first acknowledges the patient's desire (her illusion) and then indirectly reminds the patient of the reality that she may end up thwarted in her desire (which names the fact of her disillusionment). Even though the therapist, in the second half of the statement, is resonating with the sadness she knows the patient would feel were the patient to relinquish her defense against letting herself know the truth about where her therapist really stands, the therapist's primary intent is to get named the reality that the patient may not find the support she is wanting and feels she must have. Disillusionment statements are efforts to facilitate the patient's grieving by making explicit the relationship between what the patient would have wanted (illusion) and the reality of what she will get (disillusionment).

A Model 3 therapist might choose to focus the patient's attention on their here-and-now engagement with the following: "How would you want me to respond?" Here the therapist is attempting to hold the patient more accountable for her actions—that is, the therapist is wanting the patient to look at what she might be attempting to elicit from the therapist.

Alternatively, the Model 3 therapist might choose to share with the patient her dilemma about how best to respond to the patient: "I am tempted simply to give you the approval you seek—it is, after all, important that you do what feels right for you; but I am also aware of feeling, within myself, that the time is too soon and that were I to support your decision to leave, I might ultimately be doing you a disservice." Here the therapist is using her experience of self (namely, her confusion) to inform an intervention that she is hoping will enable the patient to recognize both sides of her own ambivalence about her decision to terminate.

The following response has aspects of Model 1, Model 2, and Model 3 in it: "We both know that there is further work to be done about your mother; but maybe what you're saying is that, at this point, you've done what you feel you can do (or, perhaps, you've done what you feel you want to do) and are now ready to go. I understand that it's important to you that I appreciate this and not ask you to stay." Here the therapist is able (1) to get named something the patient is conflicted about acknowledging (namely, that there is additional work to be done), (2) to recognize how important it is to the patient that she be able to feel her therapist's support, and (3) to get named her own presence in the room as someone with her own perspective. The therapist is able to offer the above without compromising her integrity.

Clinical Vignette—It's Hard to Remember

Let us imagine a situation in which the therapist says: "When you're feeling this upset with me, it's hard for you to remember that you once felt good about me and our work," or "It's hard for you to hold in mind simultaneously both good and bad feelings about me—particularly when you're this angry with me," or "When you're hurting as you are now, it's difficult for you to summon up good feelings about me and our work."

What kind of interventions are these? On the one hand, they would seem to be attempts to validate the patient's experience; on the other hand, they would seem to be attempts to enhance the patient's knowledge.

They are Model 2 interventions if the therapist's intent is to let the patient know that the therapist understands just how difficult it is for the patient to be holding on to her good feelings in the fact of her current distress.

Let us imagine, however, that the patient is not in the moment struggling to recover her good feelings; the interventions will then be more in the realm of Model 1 interpretations than Model 2 empathic responses. They will be more interpretive than empathic because they will be more an attempt to make the patient conscious of something the therapist deems worthy of the patient's consideration than an effort to resonate with what is emotionally immediate for the patient. Admittedly, the therapist is resonating with an affect, but it is not an affect that the patient is aware of experiencing—and so the interventions are described more aptly as Model 1 interpretations than as Model 2 empathic responses.

Clinical Vignette—Masochistic Surrender

Let us imagine the situation of a 47-year-old patient who has sacrificed several years of his life in order to be available to his demanding, entitled, and emotionally abusive mother (a woman who has been dying in a nursing home for the past several years). The patient's self-sacrifice is, of course, the story of his life with respect to his mother (and, for that matter, with respect to many of his contemporary objects as well). Patient and therapist have worked together for almost a year; both patient and therapist know that the patient is more willing to sacrifice his own needs for the sake of his mother's needs than to acknowledge (even to himself) how enraged he is that his mother is so selfish and has always been such an emotional drain. What the patient is able to remember, from time to time, is how much regret he feels about all the time he has wasted in his life.

The therapist finds herself feeling confused about how best to deal with her patient's situation. On the one hand, the therapist wants to be sensitive to her patient's need to be there for his mother; on the other hand, the therapist is aware that, by validating the patient's need, the therapist runs the risk of supporting the patient's masochistic surrender to his mother—that is, the therapist runs the risk of enabling the patient's dysfunctional attachment to his mother.

Were the therapist to offer the patient empathic understanding, the therapist would be participating as a new good object, inasmuch as she would be doing what mother was rarely able to do. But were the therapist to resonate empathically with the patient's need to be there for his mother, the therapist would also be participating as the old bad object, inasmuch as she would be indirectly supporting the patient's masochistic self-sacrifice.

In order both to advance the therapeutic effort and to bring herself more into the room, the therapist might therefore decide to disclose to the patient some version of the dilemma with which she is struggling (Hoffman 1992): "A part of me recognizes that I should give you the support for which you are, quite understandably, looking; but another part of me hesitates, fearing that were I to do so, I would be encouraging you to continue your masochistic surrender to your mother—which, as we both know, has been the story of your life and now fills you with much regret." In addition to sharing with the patient the fact of her own conflict, the therapist is also reminding the patient of the price they both know he has paid for having been willing, all these years, to sacrifice his own needs for the sake of his mother's needs.

What does the Model 3 therapist accomplish by sharing with the patient her conflictedness? The therapist knows that she is uncertain about what to say, unsure about how to position herself in relation to the patient, uncertain about how to proceed at this juncture. By sharing with the patient her dilemma, the therapist is demonstrating that it is possible to experience, simultaneously, both a desire to do something and a reluctance to do that something. The therapist is also indirectly communicating her interest in understanding before she takes action.

In other words, the therapist, by bringing together both sides of her own conflict, is offering herself as a container for the patient's disavowed conflictedness. Although, in the moment, the patient would seem to have lost sight of the part of him that knows how self-destructive it is to be ever sacrificing himself for the sake of his mother, the therapist is able to remember and to carry it on the patient's behalf.

The therapist has capacity where the patient has need—the therapist has the capacity to sit with and to hold in mind simultaneously both sides of the conflict, whereas the patient, for now, is wanting not to remember the price he pays for his self-sacrifice.

When the therapist names her own conflict (about how best to respond to the patient), the patient is being encouraged to get in touch with his own conflict (about how best to respond to his mother).

Ultimately, it will be for the patient to acknowledge and to understand both sides of his conflictedness about his mother. In other words, it will be for him both to understand his investment in remaining so attached to his mother (perhaps because he refuses to confront the reality that his mother is not, and will never be, the kind of mother he would have wished her to be) and to appreciate deeply just how costly it is for him to maintain such an attachment (because it means that he has no life of his own).

Only once the patient has understood both the "gain" and the "pain" will he be able to relinquish his intense attachment to his mother and, in the process, his infantile hope that perhaps someday, somehow, someway, he may yet be able to get his mother to love him as he so desperately wants to be loved. He will then have to confront, at last, the devastation and the outrage he feels about just how damaging and neglectful his mother has always been.

Then, armed with the knowledge he now has about what fuels both sides of his conflict about how involved to be with his mother, the patient will be able to make a more informed, more deliberate decision about how best to position himself in relation to his mother. Important throughout this whole process will have been the therapist's ability to hold thoughtfully in mind both sides of her own conflict about how best to position herself in relation to her patient—her own ability in this regard translating ultimately into a strengthening of the patient's own capacity to acknowledge both sides of his conflict about his lifelong surrender to the needs of others.

Clinical Vignette—Resonating with the Patient's Conflictedness

Let us now think about the situation that accrues when the patient is feeling conflicted about something (and is aware of both sides of her conflict). What does the Model 2 therapist do in order to resonate with the patient's affective experience in the moment? In other words, if the patient is feeling two things at the same time, then with which affect does the Model 2 therapist resonate in order to give the patient the experience of being understood?

By way of illustration, suppose that the patient is conflicted about coming each week—she both wants very much to come each week and is afraid that making that kind of commitment to the treatment will make her too dependent upon the therapist.

What does the Model 2 therapist do? By way of decentering from her own experience, the empathic therapist is able to recognize that the patient is deeply conflicted about what she should do with respect to the frequency of her sessions. The therapist might choose, therefore, to resonate with the patient's experience of confusion, conflictedness, and uncertainty.

To that end, the Model 2 therapist might offer the patient any of the following: "It is so hard not to be knowing what you should do," or "It feels awful to be so confused," or "You are just not sure whether it is or is not a good idea to be coming each week." Perhaps the therapist goes on to say something like: "You want very much to be doing the right thing, but you're confused about what that might be." This latter intervention frames the patient's uncertainty in positive terms—as an effort to do right by herself.

Alternatively, the therapist might choose to spell out both sides of what she senses is the patient's conflict: "As you think about it, you recognize that there is both something very appealing about the idea of coming more often and something very frightening about making that kind of commitment."

It is hoped that the patient, in response to such empathic interventions, will go on to explore in greater depth the uncertainty she has about how willing she is to commit to more regular sessions—to delve more deeply into both her experience of desire and her experience of fear.

The Model 2 therapist must not have too much expectation with respect to where the patient will go as she drops down into her feelings. But when patients are given the space to get in touch with the depth of their feelings, they are often then able to understand such feelings in light of experiences they had early on in relation to the parental objects. In other words, when given the opportunity to be nondefensively in their feelings, patients often become curious about how it would have come to pass that they have become who they are.

CHAPTER

21

Transference, Countertransference, and Enactment

An interactive (Model 3) perspective has it that (1) both patient and therapist contribute to the patient's transferential response to the therapist, and (2) both therapist and patient contribute to the therapist's countertransferential response to the patient. In other words, because the patient's experience is always being shaped by the therapist (and the therapist's activity/reactivity) and because the therapist's experience is always being shaped by the patient (and the patient's activity/reactivity), there is a continuous interplay of proactivity and reactivity at the intimate edge between patient and therapist.

But, even so, when Model 3 makes reference to the patient's transference, the emphasis is more on the patient's internal response to the therapist than on what the patient then does or enacts as a result of that response. When, however, attention is directed more specifically to what the patient is actually doing or enacting in the therapy relationship, we speak of transference enactment—or, sometimes, transference re-enactment (if the emphasis is on the patient's re-creation of the old bad traumatic failure situation).

By the same token, when Model 3 makes reference to the therapist's countertransference, the emphasis is more on the therapist's internal response to the patient than on what the therapist then does or enacts as a result of that response. When, however, attention is directed more specifically to what the therapist is actually doing or enacting in the therapy relationship, we speak of countertransference enactment—or, sometimes, countertransferential acting out.

When attention is focused on what both patient and therapist are enacting in the therapy relationship, then we speak of mutual enactment.

As we noted in Part I, *enactment* is here being defined as activity aimed at either eliciting a particular response from the other or communicating something important to the other about one's internal reality. By its very nature, an enactment involves intentionality (even if unconscious) and requires an object; the intent of an enactment is to have some kind of impact on the other. In the absence of others, there can be no enactment.

Whereas the patient's transference is a story about the patient's internal dynamics (even as it is also a story about the meaning the patient makes of the therapist's actual participation in the relationship), the patient's transference enactments are a story about her relational dynamics—that is, what she actually delivers of herself into the therapy relationship.

By the same token, whereas the therapist's countertransference is a story about the therapist's internal dynamics (even as it is also a story about what gets stirred up in her in response to the patient), the therapist's countertransference enactments are a story about the therapist's relational dynamics—that is, what she actually delivers of herself into the therapy relationship.

Clinical Vignette—A Power Struggle

Let us consider the situation of a patient and a therapist who are quietly (and unwittingly) engaged in a power struggle. Over the course of the previous year, the patient has done some good work in the therapy and, every now and then, brings up the issue of termination. The therapist agrees that the patient has done good work but thinks (at least to herself) that it is not yet time for the patient to go.

The patient's presenting complaint had centered around her lack of fulfillment both professionally and personally. The therapist is certainly aware that the patient is now in a much better place with respect to her career, but the therapist is concerned that the patient's personal relationships still lack a certain depth and richness. The therapist believes that the patient could get much more out of the treatment were she to stay a while longer.

In order to demonstrate her point, the patient periodically cites the number of gains she has made over the course of the previous year (with particular reference to how much better she does in her job); she talks about how busy she has become with the number of new commitments she has taken on at work; and she expresses frequently her gratitude to the therapist for having helped her get to where she is professionally.

The patient is indeed proud of the gains she has made in the treatment, but part of why she boasts about the progress she has made is because she is attempting to elicit a particular response from her therapist—namely, acknowledgment that the patient is ready to go.

The therapist, at her end, periodically offers the patient interpretations that speak directly to issues that the patient has not yet resolved. In their content, these interpretations are certainly accurate enough; but the therapist's intent is to highlight those areas that remain problematic for the patient in her life. The therapist is attempting to elicit a particular response from the patient—namely, recognition that the patient is not yet ready to go.

In each participant's enactment is intentionality. The patient is wanting the therapist to see things her way; and the therapist is wanting the patient to see things her way.

Ultimately, the way in which patient and therapist are engaging each other in the relationship needs to be addressed and made explicit, so that what is being played out between them can be processed and worked through. Until the mutual enactment is recognized and the therapeutic impasse resolved, patient and therapist will remain deadlocked for an indefinite period of time in their power struggle—and no real progress will be possible.

Clinical Vignette—Refusal to Be Held Accountable

Let us now consider the situation of a patient—a woman in her early sixties with multiple complaints about her husband, her children, and her job—who comes to therapy week after week and expresses her angry dissatisfaction with everything and everybody. Interestingly, she exempts her therapist from such criticism. In fact, the patient appears to enjoy coming to therapy and, on occasion, has said that she sees the therapist as her lifeline.

The therapist has come to care deeply about the patient and is very concerned about the patient's life circumstances—a loveless marriage, children who take advantage of her, and a job in which she is demeaned and exploited. The therapist would like the patient both to recognize the part she plays in perpetuating some of the difficult situations in which she finds herself and to take some responsibility for doing things differently.

In other words, the therapist would like to be able to help the patient improve the quality of her life by holding her a little more accountable. Even though the patient has repeatedly stated that she likes coming to therapy because it provides her with much-needed support, the therapist wants the patient to get more than just support—the therapist wants the patient to "get better."

In an effort to facilitate the patient's taking on more responsibility for her life, the therapist tries to pique the patient's curiosity by gently drawing her attention to some of the recurring themes and patterns in her life. The therapist highlights first this, then that.

But the more the therapist attempts to engage the patient in this way, the more stuck the patient becomes; the more the therapist "acts out" her countertransferential need to "get the patient better," the more entrenched the patient becomes—and the more miserable.

The therapist's enactment of her need to do something useful for the patient (to which she is hoping the patient will respond by taking a more active interest in her own behavior) creates a stalemated situation. Ultimately, the therapist must recognize the part her countertransferential acting out is playing in perpetuating the therapeutic impasse: it is interfering with her ability to be there for the patient in the way that the patient, at least for now, would seem to need her to be.

MUTUAL ENACTMENTS

More generally, when either patient or therapist is doing something in the relationship that is intended to elicit a particular response from the other, it is important that the enactment be recognized and mutually understood. The patient's enactments are very telling about her internal and relational dynamics; what she does with the therapist may be a reaction to the therapist and/or a reflection of what she does, more generally, in many of her important relationships. By the same token, the therapist's enactments are very telling about her own internal and relational dynamics; what she finds herself doing with the patient may be a reaction to the patient and/or a reflection of what she tends to do in her intimate relationships.

In any event, transference and countertransference enactments are a rich source of material about internal and relational dynamics and must ultimately be addressed in order for patient and therapist to engage more deeply. When enactment is involved, it needs to be processed and worked through before patient and therapist can let go of their need to get a reaction from the other, the need to elicit a particular response.

A point of interest: in contemporary circles, there is controversy as to whether the therapist's countertransference can ever be a private matter (known only to her) or whether it is always picked up on in some fashion by the patient—even if unconsciously. Although some therapists protest that it is possible to keep hidden from a patient the therapist's countertransferential response to her, most relational therapists believe that the therapist's countertransference can never be a private matter because it is always recognized (on some level) by the patient, whether the therapist acts it out or keeps it more contained.

INTERNAL VERSUS RELATIONAL DYNAMICS

Let us now revisit the distinction between the patient's internal dynamics (the province of Model 1) and the patient's relational dynamics (the province of Model 3).

Internal Dynamics

Model 1 interventions address the internal workings of the patient's mind—her internal dynamics. They focus on the patient's psychic structures, like id impulses, derivative affects, ego defenses, pathogenic introjects, and internal conflict (whether it is the conflict that exists between the patient's drives and her defenses or the conflict that exists within the introjective pairs that populate the patient's internal world [Stark 1994a,b]).

Admittedly, such structures and forces may well derive from interactions with the infantile object, but as long as they now reside within the patient, we will refer to them as the patient's internal dynamics. Furthermore, such structures and forces may well have an impact on how the patient experiences external objects (whether the infantile object, the transference object, or contemporary objects). But, again, as long as they remain a story about what is taking place within the patient, then here, too, we will refer to them as the patient's internal dynamics.

Let us imagine that a patient expresses her fear that she will become dependent on her therapist—perhaps she goes on to explain that she is afraid she will discover intense feelings of longing for her therapist if she lets down her guard. She is here talking about her internal dynamics.

Although such dynamics may well (1) derive from early-on traumatogenic interactions between the patient and her parent, (2) relate now to the therapist, and (3) affect ultimately what the patient delivers into the therapy relationship, at this point the focus is upon what is going on within the patient (in relation to the therapist)—the focus is not upon what the patient is enacting or playing out in the therapy relationship. Thus, they are internal dynamics.

And as long as the therapist addresses the patient's fear of dependency and not what the patient might actually be enacting in the therapy relationship because of such fear, then it will be a Model 1 intervention.

Relational Dynamics

Model 3 interventions, however, address the patient's relational dynamics, in that their focus is upon on how the patient interacts with her surrounding. They are not about what goes on within the patient but about what goes on between the patient and her objects. The patient's relational dynamics (that is, what the patient actually does in her relationships) derive in large part from her internal dynamics (that is, how the patient's internal world is structured or configured).

As we will see, the patient's relational dynamics bear the same relationship to her internal dynamics as the patient's relational conflict bears to her internal conflict. The one is an external manifestation of the other.

Continuing with the example from above, let us imagine that the patient, motivated by her fear of dependency, suggests that she is thinking about coming every other week instead of every week. Now she is enacting her fear in the therapy relationship; she is behaving in a manner that will have an impact on the therapist—an interpersonal consequence.

If the therapist now addresses this aspect of the here-and-now engagement between herself and her patient, then it will be a Model 3 intervention.

As long as the focus is upon what is going on inside the patient (even if in relation to her objects), we are speaking to the patient's internal dynamics—the province of Model 1. Once the focus becomes what the patient is enacting in the therapy relationship, then we are speaking to the patient's relational dynamics—the province of Model 3.

In other words, it is when the patient translates what is going on inside her head into something she is actually doing (or enacting) in the relationship with her therapist that we move into the realm of Model 3, in which the here-and-now engagement between patient and therapist assumes center stage. Now the spotlight is on what the patient plays out in her relationships (especially in the relationship with her therapist).

Of note is the fact that the therapist has an opportunity to explore the patient's relational dynamics only once the patient's internal dynamics are delivered into the room and played out in the interpersonal arena.

INTERNAL VERSUS RELATIONAL CONFLICT

I would now like to move from a consideration of the distinction between the patient's internal dynamics and her relational dynamics to a consideration of the distinction between the patient's internal conflict (the province of Model 1) and the patient's relational conflict (the province of Model 3).

Internal Conflict

In drive theory, the patient's internal world is thought to be populated by id, ego, and superego. Here internal conflict refers to conflict within the patient between any two of these structures—conflict, for example, between id impulse (or derivative affect) and ego defense. To name a few, such conflict might be between (1) an aggressive drive and the need to keep it hidden, (2) a longing to be held and the need to deny such longing, or (3) sadness and the need to protest that things are all right.

In object relations theory, the patient's internal world is thought to be populated by internal bad objects or pathogenic introjects. These internal presences are the way bad experiences at the hands of the infantile object are recorded and structuralized; they derive developmentally from internalization of the child's negative interactions with her parent.

The child does not simply internalize the bad parent; rather, she takes in the negative interactive dynamic that had existed between herself and her parent. In other words, the child internalizes the relationship in the form of pairs of introjects—introjective configurations (Meissner 1974, 1980). One pole represents the characteristic position of the powerful parent; the other pole is complementary and represents the characteristic position of the vulnerable child. What had once been external conflict (between parent and child) is replaced by internal conflict.

In object relations theory, then, internal conflict refers to conflict within the patient between the poles of her introjective configurations—conflict, for example, between inferior and superior introjects (experienced as shame on the one hand and self-contempt on the other) or between victim and victimizer introjects (experienced as guilt on the one hand and self-punitiveness on the other).

In any event, whether the frame of reference is drive theory or object relations theory, internal conflict refers to conflict in the patient between psychic structures or within introjective configurations. And whatever the nature of this conflict, it gets played out internally.

Relational Conflict

What, then, is relational conflict? And what is the relationship between internal conflict and relational conflict?

Mitchell (1988), who introduced the term relational conflict, never clearly defines it; but, in his writings, Mitchell appears to use the term to refer to the patient's conflict about being in relationship with new good objects because of her attachment to the old bad (familial and, therefore, familiar) objects. Although he does not spell this out, implicit in his conceptualization of relational conflict is the idea that such conflict will inevitably get played out in the interpersonal arena. It will get played out, for example, in the form of the patient's need to be failed by her current objects in the old familiar ways and her consequent pressuring of these objects to conform to her expectations.

It has long been known that the patient is conflicted about being in relationship with new good objects, which is why the patient develops both positive transference (thereby expressing the positive side of her ambivalence about finding good objects) and negative transference (thereby expressing the negative side of that ambivalence). The patient longs to find the good parent she never had even as she fears/expects/needs to find the bad parent she did have (Stark 1994a,b).

Mitchell's magnificent contribution is in his insistence that we think in terms of how such ambivalence, how such conflict, gets played out in the actual relationship between patient and therapist.

(1) What had once been a story about what was going on inside the patient's head now becomes a story about what is going on in the room between patient and therapist.

(2) What had once been a story about projection now becomes a story about projective identification—the translation of expectation into reality.

(3) Finally, what had once been a story about negative transference now becomes a story about actualization of the negative transference.

I would like to propose, however, that we think in terms of relational conflict as involving not just how the patient's internal conflict about being in relationship is externally enacted but, more generally, how all the patient's internal conflicts (whatever their nature) are externally enacted.

This broader definition of relational conflict speaks not only to the conflict about which Mitchell writes but also to the internal conflicts of drive theory (between id, ego, and superego) and to the internal conflicts of object relations theory (within the introjective configurations).

My proposal, therefore, is that we use the term *relational conflict* in either its narrower sense (which speaks to how the patient's conflict about being in relationship translates into what she enacts interpersonally) or its broader sense (which speaks to how the patient's internal conflicts—whatever their nature—translate into what she enacts interpersonally). The sense in which the term relational conflict is being used will usually be clear from its context.

Relational conflict thus has to do with how the patient's internal conflict manifests itself externally. Examples include the following:

1. A patient who is conflicted about her aggressive impulses may, in her interactions with the therapist, present in a rather bland fashion—on some level fearing that her aggression will get out of

control and, therefore, needing to avoid engagement with her therapist.

2. A patient with superior/inferior introjects, who is ever fearful of being shamed, may hold back, lest exposure of what is going on inside her provoke the therapist's contempt.
3. Or such a patient may unconsciously pull for the very thing she most fears (namely, the therapist's contempt) by presenting herself as woefully pathetic, as worthy of nothing but the therapist's utter contempt.
4. Finally, a patient who both longs to be understood and fears being misunderstood may say very little in the therapy sessions and then find herself angrily disappointed when the therapist does not always "get it."

Each of the above is an instance of the patient's internal conflict being played out, or enacted, in the therapy relationship—with interpersonal consequences. As with all enactments, the patient's intent is to engage (or to disengage) the therapist in some particular fashion.

Countertransferential Enactment

The hallmark of a patient with relational conflict, then, is the way in which she attempts to engage her objects. In the therapy relationship, the patient is ever busy exerting pressure on the therapist to accept her projections (disavowed psychic contents) and to participate countertransferentially in her transferential enactments.

The therapist who is the recipient of such pressure may find herself experiencing feelings she would not ordinarily have, behaving in ways she would not ordinarily behave, perhaps even becoming someone she would not ordinarily be. Although the patient will unwittingly have succeeded in recreating something very familiar, the therapist may find herself having an eerily "not-entirely-me" feeling about the role into which she has been inducted.

When only projection is involved, the patient simply assigns the therapist a role. At this point, we are dealing with a situation of negative transference that does not involve the person of the therapist. Projection is an intrapsychic mechanism.

Once the therapist, responding to pressure from the patient, takes on the patient's projection as her own, we speak of projective identification. No longer are we dealing with something that is taking place intrapsychically; now we are dealing with something that is being played out interpersonally in the here-and-now engagement between patient and therapist. No longer are we talking about something the patient is simply experiencing; now we are talking about something that is actually happening.

At this point, we are dealing with a situation of actualized negative transference that does indeed involve the person of the therapist. Projective identification is an interpersonal phenomenon.

With respect, then, to the patient's conflict about being in relationship with new good objects—conflict that is fueled by the presence of internal bad objects:

1. Projection refers to what the patient does intrapsychically with her pathogenic introjects; these negative internal presences become filters through which the internally conflicted patient experiences her world of objects, thereby distorting her perceptions of them.
2. Projective identification, however, refers to the way in which the patient's internal conflict is delivered into the interpersonal arena and becomes actualized; this latter situation, which involves the therapist's actual participation as the old bad object, involves both patient and therapist.

In both situations, the patient is conflicted about finding new good objects. When the patient (by way of projection) simply experiences the therapist through distorted lenses, the situation is one of negative transference, in the classical sense of the word. But when the patient (by way of projective identification) exerts pressure on the therapist to participate with her in a re-enactment of the early-on traumatic failure situation, the situation becomes more complicated.

Now we are dealing with a situation of relational conflict, in which the patient's need to be failed has been enacted in the treatment situation and the therapist has been enlisted by the patient to participate in the latter's dramatic re-enactment.

When only projection (and internal conflict) is involved, the negative transference that develops is a one-person phenomenon (a story simply about the patient); when projective identification (and relational conflict) is involved, the negative transference that develops is a two-person phenomenon (a story about both patient and therapist).

Once the therapist accepts the role assigned her, we speak of mutual enactment.

The following situations speak to the patient's relational conflict.

Clinical Vignette—Pulling for Disapproval

Let us imagine that the patient, unable to tolerate having critical feelings, defends against them by projecting them onto the therapist. In an effort to get the therapist to accept the critical feelings, the patient may tell the therapist things of which the patient knows the therapist disapproves. Here the patient is attempting to draw the therapist into participating as the critical parent. And now the patient's experience of the therapist as critical will be a co-constructed and co-determined event—that is, a story about both patient and therapist.

Clinical Vignette—Helpless

Consider the situation of a patient who is struggling with the issue of her own power. By presenting herself as powerless, as helpless, and as therefore incapable of taking responsibility for her life, the patient exerts pressure on the therapist to intervene on her behalf. In such a situation, the therapist may find herself feeling overly responsible for the patient and working much harder in the therapy than she ought to be working.

The good news for the patient is that such behavior on the therapist's part enables the patient to feel taken care of; the bad news for the patient is that the situation perpetuates the patient's feelings of impotence, ineptitude, and incapacity.

This is another instance of relational conflict, in which the patient has pulled for a particular form of participation by the therapist and the therapist has unwittingly obliged by allowing herself to be drawn into participating in that way. The therapist's overly responsible behavior will be both a response to the patient's call for help and a demonstration of her own readiness to be called upon for such help.

Clinical Vignette—Denigration of the Therapist

Let us imagine a situation in which the patient is constantly devaluing and belittling the therapist's interventions. In time, the therapist comes to feel frustrated, ineffectual, and incompetent. Perhaps this marks success for the patient, who has now succeeded in putting the therapist in the vulnerable position the patient (as a child) once had in relation to her powerfully discounting parent. The therapist's experience of ineptitude and disempowerment may well be both a story about the patient's need to provoke those feelings in the therapist and the therapist's tendency to feel that way when challenged.

All three examples speak to how the patient with relational conflict gets the therapist, by way of projective identification, to participate in a certain way—a way that re-creates for the patient the early-on negative dynamic that had existed between her and her parent.

As the above examples demonstrate, the therapist may be induced to assume either a concordant or a complementary position in relation to the patient. For example, the patient who experiences herself as inferior and defective may engender feelings within the therapist either of superiority (by way of the therapist's complementary identification) or of inferiority (by way of the therapist's concordant identification with the patient). The therapist is made to feel either what the belittling parent must have felt in relation to the child or what the belittled patient must have felt as a child in relation to the parent.

Elsewhere I have suggested the term direct negative transference for those situations in which the therapist is assigned the role the parent had in relation to the patient as a child and the term inverted negative transference for those situations in which the therapist is assigned the role the patient had as a child in relation to the parent (Stark 1994a,b). The former is an instance of the therapist's complementary identification; the latter is an instance of the therapist's concordant identification.

In any event, the unconscious wish on the patient's part is to engage the therapist in a re-enactment of the patient's internal dramas, with the therapist assigned, at times, the position of the powerful parent and, at other times, the position the patient once had as a vulnerable child in relation to her powerful parent.

And so it is that whenever the therapist finds herself drawn into participating with the patient as someone she (the therapist) is not ordinarily, whenever the therapist finds her moves choreographed by a patient who is needing her to be a certain way in order to conform to certain (often unconscious) expectations the patient has about how her objects should be, then we are dealing with a situation of projective identification—fueled by the patient's relational conflict.

CHAPTER

22

Projective Identification

I would like now to focus more specifically on projective identification as a two-person phenomenon involving proactivity and reactivity, mutuality of impact, and reciprocity. Because it involves give-and-take in the here-and-now engagement between patient and therapist, it falls squarely within the relational model of therapeutic action.

The term projective identification has fallen into ill repute in certain contemporary circles, however, because its emphasis is on the patient as proactive, not reactive—that is, its focus is on the patient as initiating the "spiral of reciprocal impact" (Ehrenberg 1974), not as responsive to the therapist's impact. Those who take issue with using the term encourage us to remember that although it might seem that the patient is "starting" the spiral of reciprocal impact (by way of initiating the projective identification), the patient's activity may be in part a reaction to the therapist's—earlier—impact.

PROJECTIVE IDENTIFICATION AS TRANSFORMATIVE

In the context of the patient–therapist relationship, projective identification can be a very powerful vehicle for psychological integration and structural growth. There are many, including Bion (1967), who consider projective identification to be the single most important form of interaction between patient and therapist.

The therapist who is able to accept the patient's projections, the therapist who is able to let the patient have an impact on her and even change her, has access to a very rich source of data about the patient's internal world.

The feelings that the patient induces within the therapist, by way of projective identification, are at once alive and immediate. They are also extremely elusive and difficult for the therapist to verbalize because the information is in the form of nonverbal enactments in which the therapist is a participant and not in the form of words upon which the therapist can reflect.

The concept of projective identification offers the therapist a way to understand her own internal experience as a reflection of the patient's internal experience.

Unfortunately, psychoanalytic theory suffers from a paucity of concepts that describe the interplay between a one-person psychology and a two-person psychology. Projective identification is one of the few concepts that provide such a bridge between the intrapsychic and the interpersonal.

Projection is an intrapsychic mechanism and, as such, requires the presence of only the projector; the therapist is not a participant in the patient's internal drama. Projective identification, on the other hand, cannot exist in a vacuum and requires the presence of both the projector and the recipient; the therapist is now very much involved as an actual participant.

Furthermore, in order to interpret a projection, the therapist need not bring herself into the picture. On the other hand, in order to interpret a projective identification, the therapist may well need to bring some aspect of her internal experience of the patient into the picture—to which we had earlier referred as the therapist's judicious disclosure of selective aspects of her countertransferential experience.

In order to highlight the distinction between how the therapist works with a projection and how she works with a projective identification, I offer the following:

"Although your experience is that I am the one who is disappointed in you, it may well be that it is you who are disappointed in me."

In this Model 1 interpretation, the therapist is giving voice to her hypothesis—formulated on the basis of what she suspects is going on in the patient's unconscious—that the patient, unable to acknowledge her own disappointment, instead attributes it (by way of the unconscious defense of projection) to the therapist.

"Because you were so often criticized by your father, it is not difficult to understand your fear that I too will be critical of you."

In this Model 1 interpretation, the therapist is appreciating that the patient's anxious concern about being criticized may be fueled in large part by painful experiences she had had in relation to her critical father as she was growing up. The therapist is attempting to make the patient more aware of the unconscious connection between her past and her present, between her early-on experience of her father and her current perception of her therapist.

"It upsets you terribly when you experience me as holding back. I wonder if part of what makes it so painful is that it reminds you of just how unwilling your mother was to put herself out there on your behalf."

Here the therapist is offering her recognition of how upsetting it must be for the patient to be experiencing in the transference the very same dynamic that had characterized her earlier relationship with her withholding mother. Although the therapist's focus is on the patient's vulnerability in the present, the therapist is also calling to the patient's attention the possible impact of her previous experience in relation to her mother on her current experience in relation to her therapist. The therapist's intervention is therefore both a Model 2 intervention (inasmuch as its aim is to resonate empathically with the patient's experience of current distress) and a Model 1 intervention (inasmuch as its aim is to highlight a recurring theme or pattern in the patient's life).

On the other hand, the therapist might offer the following:

"I am aware of feeling frustrated and sad when you don't let me in and don't respond to my efforts to reach you. I wonder if that is your way of letting me know what it was like for you when you tried to get your father's attention—and couldn't."

"I realize that I have been feeling powerless in here. It occurs to me that this may be your way of getting me to understand something important about your internal experience—namely, just how powerless you have always felt in relation to your parents."

"I find myself feeling critical of you and wonder if those feelings reflect a need on your part to get me to fail you in the very way that most of the others in your life eventually fail you. It occurs to me that some part of you may be wanting to re-create that dynamic in here with me so that we can explore, firsthand, this aspect of your life."

In these Model 3 interpretations, the therapist has made use of what it feels like for her to be in the room with the patient—namely, that she feels frustrated and sad in the first instance, powerless in the second, and critical in the third. The therapist goes on to suggest that she senses this may be the way the patient has chosen to communicate to the therapist something very important about the patient's experience—namely, that these are feelings (or that this is an interactive dynamic) with which the patient has struggled her entire life. It is by way of enacting her internal dramas in the therapy relationship that the patient is able to convey to the therapist aspects of her internal world that might otherwise have gone unrecognized.

In sum, if the situation is one in which simple projection is involved, the therapist does not "use her self" but instead makes an interpretation in which she calls the patient's attention to her internal experience of the therapist. She directs the patient's attention inward and backward, encouraging the patient to observe what is taking place within her. It is a Model 1 interpretation because it is being offered in an attempt to advance the patient's understanding of her internal dynamics.

If the situation is one in which projective identification is involved, the therapist may choose to "use her self" to make an interpretation in which she shares with the patient something about her own experience (thought to be a story, at least in part, about the impact on her of the patient's activity in the transference). She directs the patient's attention outward, encouraging the patient to take note of the impact her behavior has had on the therapist; she is, of course, speaking to the issue of the patient's accountability. It is a Model 3 interpretation because it is being offered in an attempt to advance the patient's understanding of her relational dynamics—that is, what she plays out in her relationships.

PROJECTIVE IDENTIFICATION AS ENACTMENT

I would like now to elaborate upon the sequence of steps involved in a successful projective identification: (1) the patient's extrusion of disavowed aspects of her psyche; (2) the patient's exerting of pressure on the therapist to accept them; (3) the therapist's psychological processing of them; (4) the therapist's returning to the patient for re-internalization a modified version of them; and (5) the patient's assimilation of them into her psychic structure. The net result is the patient's development of capacity (to tolerate previously unmanageable aspects of herself), where before she had need (to deny their existence by disowning them).

The Patient's Activity

First, the patient has the unconscious fantasy of projecting into the therapist a part of herself and of having that part take over the therapist from within.

The patient's wish is to rid herself of some part of the self, either because she fears that it will destroy the self from within or because she fears that it is itself in danger of attack by other parts of the self and must therefore be safeguarded by being held inside someone else.

What kinds of parts are extruded? We are here talking about anything that is anxiety-, guilt-, or shame-provoking, anything that causes pain, is uncomfortable, or cannot be integrated—more specifically, primitive impulses, unacceptable thoughts, unmodulated affects, uncontrollable urges, infantile longings, neurotic fears, overwhelming anxiety, intensely negative affects, intensely positive affects, internal objects, irreconcilable conflicts, and so on. Anything that the ego finds unacceptable and, therefore, "toxic" may be disowned and projected.

Second, by way of the interpersonal interaction, the patient exerts pressure on the therapist to accept the projection, that is, to comply with the projection by feeling, thinking, or behaving in a manner congruent with the projection.

This is not imaginary pressure but real pressure, exerted by way of a variety of interactions between patient and therapist.

As an example of such interpersonal pressure: Consider the patient who talks incessantly about a deeply unfulfilling relationship that he has with his distant and emotionally unavailable girlfriend. The patient says that he desperately wants the relationship to work out, but meanwhile he talks about the relationship in such a way that the therapist cannot help but find herself thinking horrid things about the girlfriend. In essence, the therapist finds herself experiencing the negative side of the patient's unacknowledged ambivalence about staying in the relationship with his girlfriend.

Instead of owning both sides of his ambivalence, the patient has managed to get the therapist to carry that (healthy) part of him that knows he needs to end the relationship. It is as if the patient finds intolerable the tension created by the internal conflict between his healthy wish to get better and his unhealthy need to preserve the status quo of things; and so he externalizes one of the poles, thereby relieving himself of his anxiety and the responsibility for resolving his conflict.

In other words, he defends himself against the experience of anxiety by externalizing his conflict—that is, by projecting one pole onto the therapist.

In essence, the patient is unwilling/unable to tolerate internal conflict. In somewhat different terms, we would say that the patient is unwilling/unable to carry, simultaneously, both sides of his ambivalence.

Those patients who do not have the capacity to experience internal conflict will be in the position of forever externalizing either one or the other pole—and the battle is then waged with the outside instead of experienced internally and eventually resolved. Those patients who do not have the capacity to sit with internal conflict will be in the position of forever giving important parts of themselves away, leaving themselves feeling internally impoverished and excessively dependent upon others.

If such a patient is ever to recover himself and, in the process, to become more integrated, then he will need help owning both sides of his conflict, which (as we will see) involves the therapist's psychological processing of the patient's projection and making it available to the patient in a form that the patient will be better able to assimilate.

In fact, part of the reason people become pathologically dependent upon others may have to do with their inability to hold within themselves both sides of their conflict—their tendency, by way of projective identification, to draw others into holding important (but unacknowledged) aspects of themselves.

More generally, the presence within the self of an unwanted part creates anxiety and, once it is extruded and placed in someone else, the experience is one of relief.

For example, the patient places intolerable feelings of hopelessness and despair in her therapist, which relieves the patient of the burden of their presence within herself. If the therapist then shows signs, say, of tension or frustration, the patient unconsciously experiences a sense of relief, since there is now proof that noxious but familiar aspects of herself have been extruded and preserved.

By the same token, a relentlessly despairing patient may place unacknowledged hope in the therapist because the patient is not yet prepared to own it, but then neither is she willing to lose touch with it entirely. Here, too, the patient experiences relief when the therapist demonstrates that she has received and accepted the patient's projection.

Projective identification, then, offers a compromise solution whereby the patient can, in fantasy, rid herself of some noxious aspect of herself at the same time that she can keep that part of herself alive in someone else.

When reference is made to what the patient delivers into the therapist, it could mean either of two things. Sometimes it refers to something inside the patient that the patient experiences as intolerable (like an anxiety-provoking affect) and that must therefore be extruded. But sometimes it refers to a negative interactive dynamic that had once characterized the patient's relationship with her traumatogenic parent and that is now being enacted by the patient in the transference.

By the same token, when reference is made to what the therapist is being pressured to accept, it could mean either of two things. Sometimes the emphasis is on the therapist's acceptance of something the patient experiences as intolerable. But sometimes the emphasis is on the therapist's acceptance of a particular role assigned her by a patient whose unconscious need is to re-create the early-on traumatic failure situation in the transference.

It will usually be clear from the context whether what the patient is delivering into the here-and-now engagement with her therapist (and needs the therapist to accept) is some aspect of the patient's self or some aspect of the patient's self in relation to another.

Not only do projective identifications take place within the patient–therapist relationship, but also they take place all the time within families and within couples.

The literature (Dicks 1967) is replete with examples of ways in which one member of a family may manipulate reality in an effort to coerce another member to "verify" a projection. The prudish mother who cannot own her sexuality, for example, outfits her daughter in sexy clothes and then accuses her daughter of being sexually provocative, a whore.

Also well known are the pressures the mother exerts on her baby to become what she most fears or wishes; the mother puts pressure on the infant to behave in a manner congruent with her own pathology. For example, because of unresolved issues around her own appetite, the mother may worry that her baby will become fat and may therefore feed her baby with so much anxiety that her child develops an eating disorder.

Or, consider the situation of a husband who, uncomfortable acknowledging his softer, more vulnerable side, puts that into his wife for safekeeping. She, meanwhile, has difficulty taking ownership of her more assertive, more competent side, which she then places in her husband.

As many couples do, this couple has worked out a system whereby neither has to take full ownership of his or her capacity.

In any event, whether we are talking about the patient–therapist, a parent–child, or a husband–wife relationship, projective identification involves activity on the part of one member of a dyad and acceptance on the part of the other.

The Therapist's Activity

We have seen that when a projective identification is played out in the arena of the therapy, it involves the patient's extruding unwanted parts of herself and, by way of exerting pressure interactively, drawing the therapist into accepting those parts.

But the therapist must do more than simply carry the patient's projection. As we will see, the therapist (with her higher level of ego functioning and greater capacity) is expected to do something with what gets placed within her: the therapist must be able to process the projection and to make a less toxic version of it available to the patient for re-internalization.

As we know, it is important that the therapist, at least initially, accept the patient's projection. The therapist allows herself to be affected by the patient; she allows herself to be acted upon and made over into something else. No longer is the patient simply experiencing her as the old bad object; the therapist has become that old bad object. The therapist, once just an observer of the patient, is now an actual participant in the unfolding of the patient's internal drama.

When the therapist is drawn into participating in the patient's dramatic re-enactment, the therapist is thought to lose her objectivity. But she must be careful not to allow the patient's experience to enter so deeply into her that she loses her objectivity entirely.

It is such a fine line that the therapist must tread. On the one hand, the therapist must have the capacity to respond to the patient's need to be failed, the patient's need to have the therapist be the old bad object. On the other hand, the therapist must also have the capacity to step back from her participation in the patient's re-enactment in order, ultimately, to provide containment.

Relational-conflict therapists believe that the patient will draw the therapist into her dramatic re-enactments as she has drawn everyone else in. The therapist is not expected to avoid this unwitting participation. But what is expected of the therapist is that she be able to recognize such participation once it is in process (or has already happened), and that she have the capacity to do something about it.

If the therapist is to be an effective container for the patient's projections (projective identifications), the therapist must be able to tolerate being made to feel and to be all kinds of things that are not at all congruent with the way the therapist would like to conceive of herself. For example, the therapist must be able to sit with feelings like shame, contempt, vindictiveness, and competitiveness—to name a few. Similarly, she must be able to tolerate it that the patient may need her to become, at least for a while, inept, condescending, impatient, harsh, or judgmental—again, to name a few.

Ultimately, of course, the therapist must be able to metabolize the noxious feelings induced in her so that they can be detoxified. The therapist does this by way of lending aspects of her own capacity to a psychological processing of such feelings, so that a modified version of them will be available to the patient for re-internalization and assimilation.

But before the therapist can do something with the charged toxic feelings, she must be able to acknowledge to herself and, where appropriate, to the patient herself (about which I will later say more) what she is experiencing. The therapist must be able to accept the fact that such feelings are not only a story about the patient and the patient's need to engage the therapist in certain negative ways, but also a story about the therapist and the therapist's capacity to be so engaged.

In other words, what is required of the therapist is that she be able to access within herself her own potential to be all that the patient is needing her to be—like hateful, contemptuous, filled with shame, despairing, helpless, competitive, hostile, critical, annoyed, sadistic, or abusive. What is required of the therapist is that she be able to access her own potential to be all that the patient is herself.

The feelings the patient engenders within the therapist are always both a story about the patient (and the patient's impact on the therapist) and a story about the therapist (and the therapist's capacity to be affected in this way).

Along these lines, Lawrence Epstein (1979) has written about the damaging effects of "meeting" the patient's aggression with benign understanding and forbearance. Epstein observes that if the therapist presents herself as unflinchingly kind, loving, compassionate, and accepting, then a patient who experiences herself as morally despicable will be faced with the "hideous prospect of a long-term relationship with a person who is defined as, and might actually turn out to be, something like a paragon of moral excellence" (p. 222). In such situations, "The contrast between [the patient's] badness and the therapist's goodness is too great, and [the patient's] feelings of inferiority and envy may become [unbearable]" (p. 222).

More specifically, a therapist who meets the patient's provocativeness with benign understanding and forbearance is not responding at all to where the patient is and to what the patient is needing. Such a therapist is responding more to her own need to see herself as benign, understanding, and tolerant than to the patient's need to find the therapist. Such a therapist cannot therefore be an effective container for the patient's projections (projective identifications); in fact, the therapist's benign understanding and forbearance may well serve to reinforce the patient's feelings of isolation, unworthiness, inadequacy, and badness.

And so it is that if the patient's (usually unconscious) need is to engage the therapist sadomasochistically so that the patient can have an opportunity to transform her masochism and her sadism into healthy capacity, then the therapist must have the ability to be so engaged—by virtue of her capacity to recognize her own potential to be masochistic and sadistic. Otherwise, the patient will be robbed of the opportunity to rework her sadomasochism within the context of the here-and-now engagement with her therapist.

As we will later see, when the sadomasochistic patient dons her masochistic hat, she becomes relentless in her pursuit of her objects, hoping against hope that perhaps, this time. . . . When she dons her sadistic hat, she becomes relentless in her outrage at being thwarted in her desire. If the patient is ever to transform her masochism into a capacity to harness her libidinal energy in the interest of pursuing realistic dreams and if she is ever to transform her sadism into a capacity to harness her aggressive energy in the interest of protecting herself from being violated, then the therapist must be comfortable with the idea that she herself might have some unresolved sadomasochistic issues—or, at least, the capacity to be relentless.

In other words, the therapist must recognize that it is not just the patient who can be unrelenting. It is only when the therapist can relinquish her investment in being always good and can tolerate being sometimes bad, that she will become for the patient an effective transference object—that is, someone who can provide containment and can facilitate, ultimately, transformation of the patient's relentless desire.

Where the patient has need, the therapist must have capacity. In other words, where the patient has the need to defend herself against all sorts of unacceptable feelings, the therapist must be able to tolerate the presence of such feelings within herself—or, at the very least, her own potential to have such feelings. The therapist must be able to do (for the patient) what the patient cannot yet do (for herself)—that is, the therapist must have the capacity to sit with bad feelings without needing to disavow them.

If the patient is to have a chance to rework some of her internalized traumas (internally recorded and structuralized in the form of internal bad objects), then she must be able to deliver herself and her pathogenic structures into the here-and-now engagement with her therapist. It is the task of the therapist to contain the patient's disowned psychic contents, which means being able both to live with them inside her and, in time, to integrate them into her own healthier structure, so that she can return a modified version of them to the patient for re-internalization.

Let us imagine a situation in which a patient needs her therapist to know, firsthand, the kind of guilt with which she has lived her entire life. If the therapist is to be truly useful to the patient, the therapist must have the capacity to tolerate the experience of being made to feel guilty. In other words, the therapist must be able to respond to the patient's need to elicit the therapist's guilt—because it may be only by way of inducing that feeling in the therapist that the patient will be able to acknowledge her own guilt.

But then, as we mentioned earlier, it is crucial that the therapist, after sitting with the guilt for a while, be able to step back from her participation in the patient's enactment in order to recover her objectivity. As we will later discuss, the therapist's ability to find her way out may involve either a subtle (and often unconscious) shift or a more dramatic (and sometimes more conscious) shift in her position.

Or perhaps the patient needs the therapist to know, firsthand, what it is like to experience feelings of helplessness and inadequacy. If the therapist is to be an effective container for the patient in such a situation, the therapist must be able, at least for a while, to tolerate the patient's (and her own) feelings of helplessness and inadequacy without immediately hastening to suggest courses of action for the patient in an attempt to empower her.

In other words, the therapist must be able to sit with the feelings engendered within her by the patient without denying them or discharging them impulsively through action. She must be able to live with the feelings without pretending they are not there or trying in some other way to rid herself of them. That is what the patient does and that is why the patient has relational difficulties.

If the patient is never able to engage the therapist in the dysfunctional ways that the patient is needing to engage her, then the therapist will never be able to facilitate transformation of the patient's need to engage in those ways into a capacity to engage (with others) both more healthily and more authentically.

I am here suggesting that projective identification is powerfully mutative by virtue of the fact that the therapist is ultimately able to contain the patient's disavowed psychic contents—before returning a somewhat modified, less toxic version of them to the patient.

Actually, it has been proposed (Carpy 1989, Pick 1985) that, paradoxically, part of what makes projective identification so effective is the fact that the therapist can never completely contain what the patient projects into her and, in fact, may well have to struggle to contain it at all.

In other words, the therapist will often partially act out her countertransference, which, as Irma Brenman Pick (1985) has hypothesized, allows the patient to see that the therapist (1) is affected by what the patient has projected into her; (2) must struggle to tolerate it; but (3) ultimately manages to contain it without grossly acting it out. Denis Carpy (1989) hypothesizes that it is through this process that the patient is able gradually to re-internalize previously unmanageable aspects of herself. Particularly transformative is the patient's recognition of the therapist's capacity—despite her struggle—to tolerate the patient's toxic parts.

Carpy (1989) goes on to suggest that so too,

> the normal infant needs to be able to sense that her mother is struggling to tolerate her projected distress without major disruption of her maternal function. [The mother] will be unable to avoid giving the infant slight indications of the way she is affected by [her infant], and it is these indications which allow the infant to see that the projected aspects of herself can indeed be tolerated. [p. 293]

The infant is then able to re-introject these now somewhat modified aspects of herself and, in addition, to take in the capacity to tolerate them (a capacity that she has observed in her mother).

Bion (1959) writes about the mother who, in response to her screaming hungry baby, becomes gripped by a panic that her infant is going to die and that she will be unable to feed her quickly enough. If, however, the mother is eventually able to master her panic, she will be able to feed her baby. Carpy (1989), in discussing this situation, contends that "what is 'containing' about this is that the baby will have an experience of being fed by a mother in whom she can sense panic, but who is nevertheless able to give her milk" (p. 293). It is this that makes the experience transformative—what I have been referring to as a corrective relational experience.

What is crucial is the degree to which the therapist acts out. Some acting out, as we have just seen, is thought to be inevitable and, even, desirable. If there is too much acting out, however, the patient may experience the "badness" of the therapist's panic as more powerful than the "goodness" of the therapist's milk—with subsequent retraumatization of the patient.

It is important, therefore, that the therapist attempt to refrain from doing something until she has lived with the evoked feelings for some time. Otherwise, the therapist's interventions may be motivated by conscious and unconscious efforts to get the patient to stop doing whatever it is she is doing, so that the therapist will not have to sit with the uncomfortable feelings engendered in her by the patient.

The therapist's handling of the feelings the patient projects requires considerable effort, skill, and strain on the therapist's part, because the feelings with which the patient struggles are highly charged, painful areas of human experience that are probably as conflictual for the therapist as they are for the patient. But it is hoped that because of the therapist's greater psychological integration resulting from both her own developmental experience and the work she has done in her own treatment, the therapist (in contradistinction to the patient) will be less frightened of, and less prone to run from, these feelings.

McLaughlin (1991) suggests, in addition, that part of what makes the experience so transformative is the fact that a projective identification may go unnoticed for some time before it is recognized, processed, and eventually repaired. He notes,

> In such instances I have the strong impression that the period of tension and impasse and then the phase of discovery, reworking, and resolution [combine] to make for levels of affective intensity and an immediacy of actual experience that [add] appreciably to the clinical value of the experience for patient and analyst. [p. 613]

Clinical Vignette—Tolerating the Intolerable

By way of demonstrating how transformative it can be for the patient when the therapist is able to tolerate something about the patient (and himself) that the patient cannot yet tolerate, I offer the following example presented by Thomas Ogden (1979).

The patient had been in analysis for about a year, and the treatment seemed to both patient and analyst to have reached some kind of impasse. The patient repeatedly questioned whether he was getting anything out of the treatment and stated frequently that he thought the treatment was a waste of time and that it all seemed so pointless.

The patient had always paid his bills grudgingly but had begun to pay them progressively later and later, to the point where the analyst began to wonder if the patient would discontinue treatment leaving one or two months' bills unpaid. Also, as the sessions dragged on, the analyst began to think enviously about colleagues who charged the same fee as he did but whose sessions were not fifty but forty-five minutes.

The analyst found himself shortening several sessions by making the patient wait several minutes before being let into the office. Then the analyst found himself having trouble ending the sessions on time because of intense guilt that he was not giving the patient his money's worth.

When this difficulty with time had occurred repeatedly over several months, the analyst gradually began to understand that the trouble he was having maintaining the ground rules of the analysis related to the guilt he was feeling about his "greedy" expectation that he be paid for "worthless" work.

With this newfound understanding of the feelings that were being engendered in him by the patient, the analyst was able to take a fresh look at the patient's material. The patient's father had deserted his wife and his son when the patient was 15 months old. Without ever actually saying so, the patient's mother had clearly felt that her son was to blame for her husband's abandonment of them. The unspoken shared feeling was that the patient's greediness for his mother's time, energy, and affection had resulted in the father's desertion.

Over time, the patient had developed an intense need to deny and to disavow all feelings of greed. He was unable to tell his analyst that he wished to meet more frequently because he experienced this wish as greediness that would result in abandonment by the (transference) father. The patient insisted instead that both the analysis and the analyst were worthless.

How the analyst dealt with the intense feelings of greed and of guilt engendered in him by the patient were what ultimately enabled the analyst to serve as an effective container for the patient's disavowed greed and guilt.

The analyst initially found the feelings engendered in him by the patient so unacceptable that he too tried to deny and to disown them. But once he recognized that he was indeed feeling greedy and then guilty because of his greed, he was able to mobilize an aspect of himself that was interested in understanding his greedy and guilty feelings, rather than in trying to deny, disguise, displace, or project them. Essential for this aspect of the work was the analyst's knowing that he could have greedy and guilty feelings without being damaged by them.

In fact, it had not been the analyst's greedy feelings that were interfering with the therapeutic work; rather, it had been his need to disavow such feelings by denying their existence that was disruptive to the work.

As the analyst became aware of, and was able to live with, this aspect of himself and of his patient, he became better able to handle first the time and then the financial boundaries of the analysis. He no longer felt that he had to hide the fact that he was glad to receive money given in payment for services rendered.

After some time, the patient commented as he handed the analyst a check (on time) that the analyst seemed happy to be getting such "a big, fat check" and that that wasn't very becoming to a psychiatrist. The analyst chuckled and said simply that it was nice to receive money.

During this interchange, the analyst was conveying to the patient both his ability to accept his hungry, greedy, devouring feelings and his ability to integrate these feelings with other feelings of healthy self-interest and self-worth. It was in this way that the analyst was able to return to the patient an amalgam—something bearing both the patient's and now the analyst's stamp. What had been unacceptable to the patient (hungry greed destroys) became, by way of the therapist's detoxification, much more acceptable and even pleasurable (it feels good to have one's hunger gratified).

The patient was then able to integrate this detoxified version of the original projection into his own psychic substance.

The analyst chose not to interpret the patient's fear of his own greed, something that would have been more in the way of a Model 1 intervention had he chosen to do so. Instead, the analyst, donning his Model 3 hat, conceived of the therapeutic action as lying in the here-and-now engagement between the two of them—as lying in his own ability initially to accept the patient's projection, then psychologically to process the projection in order to detoxify it, and finally to make available to the patient (for re-internalization) a modified version of it.

Therapy can progress only to the extent that therapists can do this, can allow themselves to feel (although usually with diminished intensity) what patients are feeling, can process it with their own higher level of ego functioning and greater capacity, and can return to patients a more digestible version of what they had previously been unable to assimilate into the rest of their psyche. It is this that makes it possible for there to be genuine psychological growth and integration on a higher level.

The Therapist's Reactivity

As we have seen, in order for a projective identification to be successfully processed, the therapist must first allow herself to be drawn into participating with the patient in her enactment (which happens when the therapist accepts the projection) and must then be able to step back from such participation (which happens when the therapist challenges the projection).

Subtle Acceptance, Subtle Challenge

Sometimes the therapist's involvement is so subtle that neither patient nor therapist will be aware that it is happening.

By way of example, in Part I, I presented the case of a patient who, unable to tolerate the sadness he is feeling about his grandmother's recent death, compels his therapist to take the sadness on as her own by recounting in a monotone the details of his grandmother's death. The therapist's heartfelt "Oh, no!" and "That's awful!" enable the patient, by the end of the hour, to become more comfortable with his own sadness; the therapist's ability to sit with the patient's grief makes it less toxic for the patient to feel it as his own.

Both the therapist's quiet acceptance of the patient's disowned sadness and the therapist's subtle challenging of its toxicity by way of her capacity to bear it are done so effortlessly that it is barely perceptible to either participant in the interaction.

Whereas sometimes the therapist's involvement in the processing of the patient's disavowed psychic contents is so subtle that it is hardly noticed by either participant, sometimes there is a more dramatic jolt, signaling some shift in the relationship between patient and therapist.

Such a jolt may be occasioned either by the therapist's sudden and involuntary acceptance of the patient's projection (as the therapist is drawn into participating in the patient's enactment) and/or by the therapist's forceful ejection of the patient's projection (once she is able to step back from her participation in the patient's enactment).

By way of illustration, I offer several scenarios.

Dramatic Acceptance, Subtle Challenge

Let us imagine the situation of a patient who tends to feel that others are always being critical of her. The patient can cite numerous instances of times when she has been criticized by her husband, her children, her boss, her colleagues.

The patient, the victim of a serious car accident years earlier, has been repeatedly advised by her physical therapist that she must do exercises on a regular basis or her medical condition will continue to deteriorate.

There comes a session in which the patient, reporting to her psychotherapist about her most recent visit to her physical therapist, acknowledges that she rarely does her exercises anymore because she just does not have the time and there is no guarantee that such exercises will really make a difference anyway.

The therapist finds herself feeling concerned about how irresponsibly the patient is behaving with respect to her health. Although it is something she considers, the therapist resists her temptation to share her concern with the patient because she does not think it would be analytically useful to the patient at this point. It occurs to the therapist that her desire to caution the patient about the importance of continuing with her exercises may be more a story about her own need than the patient's need—and so she shares nothing of her concern.

The therapist does decide, however, to pursue the patient's resistance and her seeming investment in not doing what she knows she should do in order to take care of herself. To that end, the therapist offers the patient the following Model 2 response: "Perhaps it just doesn't seem worth it to do difficult exercises when you're not convinced that they will do any good anyway." The therapist's hope is that the patient will feel that her despair has been validated and will respond by elaborating upon her feelings of frustration, helplessness, and hopelessness—feelings that the therapist senses are probably the story of the patient's life and that are now interfering with the patient's ability to do what she knows she should do.

The patient responds in the affirmative with, "Exactly! Why should I waste my time doing something I don't want to do?" and then goes on to talk about how busy she has been anyway—so búsy that she has neither the time nor the energy to add something to her already insane schedule. The therapist decides, for now, to continue to wait and not, by way of a somewhat confrontational Model 1 interpretation, to direct the patient's attention to her obvious self-sabotage.

But when later in the session, the patient makes reference to an exam the next day for which she has barely studied at all (an important exam that will determine whether she advances to the next level in her studies), the therapist finds herself feeling, once again, concerned about (and critical of) the patient's irresponsible behavior—and, this time, also annoyed.

Without much thought, the therapist finds herself blurting out, "How can you expect to have things work out for you when you refuse to take responsibility for your life!" to which the patient responds sharply with "You shouldn't be critical of me! I need your understanding and your support—not your judgment!"

Fortunately, the therapist has the integrity to acknowledge to herself and then to the patient, her countertransferential participation in the patient's enactment, which she does with a sincere apology. But patient and therapist are then able to go on to look at the drama that has just been played out in their interactive engagement. They come to understand how the patient gets others (including, even, her therapist) to fail her in ways specifically determined by her past.

In other words, by presenting herself in such a way that others cannot help but feel critical of her, the patient manages to re-create the old, familiar (but comfortable) dynamic that had characterized her relationship with her critically demanding mother. The patient comes to recognize how she is ever busy hoping against hope that, perhaps this time, she will find the nondemanding acceptance she never found as a child—even as she is repeatedly setting it up (by behaving so provocatively) to be failed. Ultimately, the patient understands something deeply important about her relational dynamics—she comes to recognize that what she enacts in her relationships elicits the very response she is most needing–expecting–fearing to encounter.

Even as the patient comes to appreciate the "gain" in her compulsive repetitions (that is, they enable her to hold fast to her hope), so, too, the patient comes to see the "pain" (that is, the price she pays for refusing to relent).

Before the patient can let go of her old behaviors, she must confront the reality of just how heartbreakingly cold and unaccepting her mother really was; the patient must confront that intolerably painful reality, grieve it, and master it—so that she will not always feel such a compulsion to repeat that drama in her contemporary relationships. As part of her grieving, the patient must confront the pain of her disappointment that her mother was as she was and could not support her in the ways that the patient would so have wanted.

As the patient begins to relinquish her compulsive repetitions, as she begins to let go of her irresponsible behaviors, she starts to feel much better about herself and becomes able to engage much more healthily (and much less conflictedly) in relationship.

Where once there was need (the need to make others, by way of her irresponsible behavior, into her critical mother), now there is capacity (the capacity to behave more responsibly and self-respectingly). No longer does the patient need to re-create the old traumatic failure situation; now she is able to accept things as they are.

This is a situation in which the therapist, initially able to avoid being drawn into the patient's transferential enactments, is finally drawn in when the patient makes reference to how unprepared she is for an exam that the therapist knows is very important to her. No longer able to resist the pull, the therapist, rather dramatically, accepts the role assigned her (that of the critical mother) when she blurts out her accusatory statement "How can you expect to have things work out for you when you refuse to take responsibility for your life!"

But in response to the patient's protest that the therapist is being critical, the therapist is able to respond nondefensively (and apologetically) and, recovering her objectivity, is then able to examine, with the patient, the details of what had transpired between them, the details of what had been mutually enacted.

In essence, patient and therapist collaboratively process their interactive engagement. By so doing, the therapist is subtly challenging the patient's tendency to experience her objects as unjustifiably critical. In other words, by encouraging the patient to see the ways in which her provocative behavior affects the object's response to her, by highlighting the patient's participation in (and contribution to) what befalls her, the therapist is gently challenging the patient's conviction that she will inevitably and unfairly be criticized.

Subtle Acceptance, Dramatic Challenge

Let us now imagine a situation in which the patient struggles with issues of worth, alternately experiencing herself as inferior (the other as superior) and herself as superior (the other as inferior).

The therapist has just offered the patient an interpretation. The patient contemptuously dismisses the interpretation, says she thinks that she (the patient) does a much better job with her own patients than the therapist does with hers. The patient goes on to tell the therapist about an intervention that she (the patient) had made the previous day with one of her own patients—an intervention that had turned out to be profoundly transformative for the patient.

The therapist is aware of feeling angry that the patient is so disdainful and dismissive; she also finds herself feeling strangely inadequate, even pathetic.

Once the therapist is able to step back from her participation in the patient's enactment and to recover her objectivity, several things become clear to her. This, she realizes, is not the first time an intervention of hers has been summarily dismissed by the patient. Nor is this the first time the patient has made her feel sorely lacking.

The therapist is also able to recognize that the patient is now doing to her (the therapist) the very thing the patient has all along reported that her father would do to her as a child; the therapist is now able to see that the patient's disdainfully dismissive behavior toward the therapist may be motivated, in part, by her need to have the therapist understand, firsthand, what it is like to be at the receiving end of someone's contemptuous dismissal.

The therapist therefore offers the patient the following: "When you dismiss what I say to you, I think I begin to understand a little better how painful it must have been for you when your father would dismiss what you had to say." Here the therapist is resonating with how hard it must have been for the patient to have had the difficult father she had.

The therapist might instead choose to share, more explicitly, some of her own experience: "When you dismiss what I say, I am aware of feeling annoyed. But I am also aware of feeling strangely inadequate—as if I weren't good enough somehow. I am wondering if this is how you felt as a child, when your father would offhandedly dismiss what you had to say."

Alternatively, the therapist could decide to focus the patient's attention a little more directly on how difficult the patient herself can be—particularly when she is identified with her "aggressive" father. "It occurs to me that when you dismiss what I say, you are letting me know how your father used to treat you."

Once the therapist is able to step back from her countertransferential participation in the patient's transferential enactment, the therapist is in a position to challenge the patient's projection (or, perhaps more accurately, projective identification). When the therapist recovers her stance as an observer, she is then able to offer the patient a Model 3 interpretation—the aim of which is to hold the patient accountable for her provocative behavior. No longer a participant, the therapist now focuses the patient's attention on what she has been playing out in their relationship—namely, her relational dynamics.

By focusing the patient's attention on either the patient's experience of being dismissed or the patient's dismissive behavior, the therapist is calling the patient's attention to the interactive dynamic (of dismissal) that has characterized her relationships. In the form of a somewhat dramatic challenging of the patient's projection (that is, by way of the therapist's rather bold refusal to let herself be dismissed), the therapist insists that the patient take responsibility for her dismissive behavior.

Let us imagine that in response to such a challenge, the patient (although initially defensive) is eventually able to recognize that indeed she does often do to others the very thing she most complains about her father's having done to her. Together, patient and therapist go on to explore the many arenas in the patient's life that have been affected by this (negative) identification with her father. The patient also confronts the pain she has about how hurt she was by her father's contemptuous dismissal of her. She grieves for the little girl who tried so hard to get her father to be proud of her; she grieves for the little girl whose heart was broken again and again by a father who could never see how hard his daughter was trying to please him.

Now that both patient and therapist understand what the patient had been enacting (namely, her need to re-create with her therapist the negative interactive dynamic that had characterized her relationship with her father), much of the tension that had existed between patient and therapist eases and the two develop a much deeper level of commitment and connection. Over time, their collaborative effort to understand what the patient does (more generally) in her relationships deepens their engagement even further. It is with some relief that the patient comes, ultimately, to recognize and to own just how provocative she can be in her relationships.

In sum, as a result of processing the interaction that had transpired between them, the patient comes to understand something deeply important about how she interacts with others in relationship (that is, she comes to understand something important about her relational dynamics)—understanding that empowers her and enables her to engage more healthily and more authentically in the relationship with her therapist and in subsequent relationships.

Where once there was need (the need to be dismissive), now there is capacity (the capacity to be more accepting and more appreciative).

The above is an example of a situation in which the therapist had been very subtly drawn into participating with the patient in her enactment. Then, once the therapist had recovered her objectivity, she somewhat dramatically confronted the patient with her provocative behavior—subtle acceptance of a projection and subsequent dramatic challenge of it.

Dramatic Acceptance, Dramatic Shift

Finally, let us revisit the situation mentioned in Part I in which the patient, Jennifer, is unrelentingly hopeless and despairing. Her therapist, initially steadfast in his refusal to be drawn into taking on Jennifer's despair as his own, one day blurts out, "I don't think I can keep doing this."

Here the therapist signals that he has at last allowed himself to be drawn into participating countertransferentially with the patient in her transferential enactment. In other words, he has allowed himself to experience her weariness and her despair as his own (clearly an instance of concordant identification [Racker 1953]).

The therapist, initially the mouthpiece for hope, is rather dramatically drawn into voicing frustration and despair. Where once the therapist was the hopeful one and the patient the hopeless one, now the therapist joins the patient in her despair.

With relief, the patient responds: "Now you know what I've been feeling all these years!"

Once the therapist allows himself to relinquish his investment in carrying the patient's hope, the patient is then freed up to access some of her own hope. She responds, "You know, sometimes I begin to think that maybe things aren't so bad after all."

How might we understand this sequence of events?

For a long time, the therapist steadfastly maintains his faith in the patient and his investment in her treatment. Perhaps we could say that his unflinching commitment to Jennifer is motivated both by something in him and by something in her—that is, the therapist may have his own need to be hopeful and Jennifer may have her own need for him to be hopeful on her behalf. In other words, the therapist's hopefulness has elements of both his own need (subjective countertransference) and the patient's need (objective countertransference).

Perhaps the therapist's need to be hopeful is related to difficulty he has tolerating despair; or perhaps to how hard it would be for him to tolerate the inadequacy and the impotence he would feel were he to give in to the patient's despair. Perhaps the patient's need for him to be hopeful on her behalf speaks to her refusal to own her own hope.

In any event, when the therapist finally relinquishes his investment in being such a good guy and opens himself up to experiencing the patient's despair, there is a rather dramatic shift in the dynamic between them.

Where once the patient had needed her therapist to be the hopeful one and, in subtle ways, had urged him to be hopeful on her behalf (a need that as we have just said, might have dovetailed with his own need to be hopeful), that dynamic now changes. Something shifts (perhaps in the patient, perhaps in the therapist, perhaps in the interactive engagement between them) such that (1) the patient no longer needs the therapist to be relentlessly hopeful on her behalf and (2) the therapist himself no longer needs to relentlessly hopeful.

When the therapist, somewhat dramatically, protests, "I don't think I can keep doing this," he is signaling his acceptance of the patient's projection (of hopelessness). He has, at last, allowed himself to be drawn into participating in her internal drama, his role now the one she has played her entire life—namely, the role of the despairing one. Now the patient knows, where before she could not have known, that her therapist understands deeply what it is like to feel hopeless, despairing, and resigned.

Expressed in somewhat different terms, the therapist's rather dramatic relinquishing of his relentless hope makes it necessary for the patient to reposition herself in relation both to her own hope and to the treatment. A shift in the therapist's participation prompts a shift in the patient's participation.

And when the therapist relinquishes his position as the spokesperson for the patient's hope, the patient, rather dramatically, finds herself left with the responsibility for accessing (and, then, for articulating) her own hopefulness—which enables the two of them to share the responsibility for the treatment and for carrying the hope.

In each of the above scenarios, the therapist's participation in the patient's enactment involves the therapist's initial and unwitting acceptance of the role assigned her and the therapist's subsequent transformation of it, either by way of processing the patient's projection internally and returning to the patient a modified version of it or by way of stepping out of her participation to encourage an interactive, collaborative effort by both patient and therapist of what had been (mutually) enacted between them. Sometimes the therapist's involvement in the patient's relational process is subtle and understated; sometimes it is more dramatic and noisily ostentatious.

But whether the therapist processes the projection internally or interactively (in collaboration with the patient) and whether the therapist's participation is quiet or more dramatic, the therapist and her capacity are very much involved in the successful processing of the patient's projective identifications. An important result of a successful projective identification is development of the patient's own capacity both to tolerate what had once been intolerable and to engage in healthier, more authentic relationships.

PROJECTIVE IDENTIFICATION AS COMMUNICATION

Projective identification is one of the most important ways the patient gets the therapist to understand. So, too, the countertransferential feelings evoked in the therapist by the patient's transferential enactments are an important part of how the therapist comes to understand the patient.

As we mentioned earlier, there are times when the patient wants desperately for the therapist to feel exactly what she is feeling and may use projective identification to induce within the therapist the very same feelings she is having. In this way, the patient is able to feel understood by, and to be at one with, the therapist.

James Grotstein (1985) speaks to this with the following: "Powerful feelings are more often than not expressed by giving another person the experience of how one feels. . . . How else can a beleaguered patient know that her analyst understands than if he [the analyst] suffers that experience which the patient lacks the words to describe?" (p. 132). Grotstein continues, "We each . . . ultimately wish the other to know the experience we cannot communicate or unburden ourselves of until we have been convinced that the other understands. We cannot be convinced that they understand until we are convinced that they now contain the experience" (p. 133).

Along these same lines, Casement (1985) writes about the communication achieved by way of "interactive responsiveness" between patient and therapist. Casement's particular interest is in projective identification as a form of affective (or interactive) communication. Every therapist has to learn to be open to the otherness of the other; every therapist must be ready to feel whatever feelings result from being in touch with another person, however different that person is from oneself. Projective identification is particularly effective when the patient is wanting to communicate something to the therapist that is beyond words. Patients, says Casement, therefore use communication by impact (or projective identification) as a means whereby the unspeakable can be conveyed to the therapist.

Casement (1985) suggests that when projective identification is used as a form of affective communication, the patient has a need (usually unconscious) to convey some aspect of her internal experience to the therapist—and to know that she is being responded to. There is interactive pressure, the unconscious aim of which is to make the other person have the feelings the patient must disown.

What is then needed (for a therapeutic response to be possible) is for the therapist to be able to carry the feelings that the patient finds intolerable. When the therapist is able to demonstrate that she is able to do so, the previously unmanageable feelings become more manageable for the patient. They become less terrifying than before, by virtue of the fact that another person has actually felt them and been able to tolerate the experience of them.

Interestingly, the literature on projective identification usually emphasizes the patient's placing of feelings she cannot tolerate into the therapist (thereby ridding herself of them); in the clinical situation, however, it would seem that sometimes the patient places feelings she does recognize as her own into the therapist (so that she can know the therapist truly understands). Here the emphasis is less on the patient's defensive disavowal of feelings and more on the patient's adaptive efforts to communicate such feelings to the therapist in the form of a projective identification.

What comes to mind for me here is a patient of mine (with whom I have worked analytically for many years now), who cannot deliver her real self into authentic engagement with me unless she knows that I, too, have experienced the feelings she is experiencing. What I have come to understand over the years of our time together is that she cannot let herself feel something in my presence unless she has first managed to evoke that feeling in me.

For example, she was able to acknowledge just how much shame she felt in relation to me only after she had been able to elicit that feeling in me by shaming me. She was able to express her sadness only after she had been able to make me cry. She was able to acknowledge just how angry she was only after she had made me so annoyed with her that, at one point, I impulsively blurted out something that I regretted as soon as I had said it.

It is only when she is able to stir up in me the feelings with which she is struggling that she is able to feel safe enough with me to experience her feelings in my presence. It is only when she is able to know that she is not alone that she dares to deliver her authentic self into the relationship.

More generally, I believe that there are some patients who need to know that their therapist can be drawn into participating in this way before they are willing to risk delivering themselves into the relationship.

Furthermore, if the patient feels that her efforts to reach the therapist have not been successful, then she may become relentless in her efforts to get the therapist to understand. She may resort to drastic measures, refusing to stop, refusing to relent, until she can be assured that the therapist knows, truly, just what her internal experience really is.

CHAPTER

23

Interpersonal Pressure

I would like now to focus more specifically on the issue of the patient as proactive, as an agent, as an enactor, as someone whose need is to draw her therapist into participating in a certain way in the therapy relationship.

Let us begin by reviewing the Model 2 theorist's conception of the patient's participation in the therapeutic encounter.

As we know, in a deficiency-compensation model the emphasis is on the healing power of the patient's experience of the therapist as a new good object—whether that experience is informed more by the patient's need for a new good object (as it is in self psychology) or by the therapist's actual participation as that new good object (as it is in Model 2 object relations theories). Again, it is thought to be the patient's experience of the therapist as a new good object that provides the patient with a corrective (emotional) experience.

As noted before, in the self psychology literature, the emphasis is much more on the therapist's empathic recognition of the patient's need than on its actual gratification—much more on the therapist's participation as an empathic selfobject (who provides generic validation of the patient's experience) than on the therapist's participation as a new good object (who brings her authentic self into relationship with the patient).

But for those Model 2 object relations theorists who believe that the therapist does sometimes participate as a new good object, what is their understanding of how such participation comes to pass?

(1) Is it because therapists who are drawn to a deficiency-compensation model tend to be generally warmer, more emotionally accessible, and more inclined to offer gratification of the patient's need than therapists who are drawn to the other models of therapeutic action?

(2) Is it because therapists who embrace a deficiency-compensation model are so convinced that the structurally impaired, deficit-ridden patient should have the corrective experience of a new good object that they are pleased to make themselves available to the patient as a new good object in response to even the slightest indication of need on the patient's part?

(3) Or is some part of the therapist's participation as a new good object the result of the therapist's unwitting responsiveness to pressure exerted on her by a patient who is hungry for new good experience in the here-and-now to correct for the early-on parental deficiencies?

Whereas the first is primarily a story about the therapist and her character style and the second is primarily a story about the therapist and her theoretical orientation, the third is more clearly a story about the patient and her proactive efforts to elicit from her therapist what she senses she most needs in order to heal.

Most Model 2 object relations theorists would probably suggest that the answer is some combination of the above. This may well be what happens in actual clinical practice. But, at least in the literature (of Model 2 object relations theorists), little attention is paid to the patient's activity with respect to eliciting the therapist's participation as a new good object.

I would like, therefore, to focus more specifically on the relationship between the patient's need for new good and the therapist's responsiveness to that need. As noted above, it is an area that has received relatively little attention in the literature, perhaps, in part, because Model 2 tends to focus upon the therapist's impact on the patient and not upon the patient's impact on the therapist. Model 2, after all, is a theory about give and not a theory about give-and-take.

Before I explore the relationship between the patient's need for new good and the therapist's responsiveness to that need, I would like first to explore the relationship between the patient's need for old bad and the therapist's responsiveness to that need—to which we refer, of course, as projective identification.

THE PATIENT'S NEED

Need for Old Bad

Let us think about the patient's need for old bad (that is, the patient's need to find the bad parent she did have)—so that we can then compare it to the patient's need for new good (that is, the patient's need to find the good parent she never had).

In the treatment situation, the patient—with internal presence of bad—delivers (by way of projection) her internal bad objects into the relationship with her therapist. The patient has a compulsive need (aspects of which are unhealthy, aspects of which are healthy) to re-find the old bad parent. The unhealthy aspect of this repetition compulsion relates to the patient's desire to re-create that with which she is familiar and therefore most comfortable, as pathological as that might be; the healthy aspect relates to the patient's desire to achieve belated mastery of her internalized traumas by way of the relationship with her therapist.

And so it is that under the sway of the repetition compulsion and motivated by her need to re-find the old bad object, the patient projects the internal bad parent onto the therapist, thereby creating a distorted perception of the therapist as the old bad parent (an instance, clearly, of negative transference).

At this point, the therapist herself is not actually involved. Projection is an intrapsychic mechanism; it is a story about what is going on inside the patient—not about what is going on in the interactive dynamic between patient and therapist.

Sometimes, however, it would seem that the patient is so intensely attached to the internal bad parent that she does more than simply experience the therapist (by way of projection) as the old bad parent. Sometimes it would seem that the patient has a need to get the therapist to become the old bad parent, in fact and not just in fantasy.

In these situations, the patient behaves in such a way as to induce the therapist to accept the patient's projections—and then what had once been a case of mistaken identity becomes now a reality, as the therapist herself becomes a participant in the externalization of the patient's internal drama.

At this point, the therapist has become involved.

Projective identification is an interpersonal mechanism; it is a story not just about what is going on inside the patient but about what is going on in the interactive dynamic between patient and therapist. It is not just about what the patient imagines the therapist to be (because of the patient's internal dynamics); it is also about what the patient enacts in the relationship with her therapist (because of the patient's relational dynamics)—enactments that involve the patient's exerting of pressure on the therapist to conform to the patient's need to re-create the old traumatic failure situation.

Whereas the patient's internal dynamics involve only the patient, the patient's relational dynamics have an impact on the therapist. Whereas projection involves only the patient, projective identification involves both patient and therapist.

Need for New Good

Let us now think about the patient's need for new good (the patient's need to find the good parent she never had).

In the treatment situation, the patient—with internal absence of good—delivers into the relationship with her therapist (this time, by way of displacement) her infantile need to find a new good parent. The patient has a compulsive need (aspects of which are unhealthy, aspects of which are healthy) to get now what she never got reliably and consistently early-on. The unhealthy aspect of this repetition compulsion relates to the patient's infantile need to make her objects into good mothers; the healthy aspect relates to the patient's recognition that she needs an opportunity to begin anew.

And so it is that under the sway of the repetition compulsion and motivated by her need to find some form of corrective provision in the therapy relationship, the patient displaces her need to find a new good parent onto the therapist, thereby creating the illusion of the therapist as a new good parent (an instance, clearly, of positive—or idealizing—transference).

At this point, the therapist herself is not actually involved. Displacement is an intrapsychic mechanism; it is a story about what is going on inside the patient—not about what is going on in the interactive dynamic between patient and therapist.

Sometimes, however, it would seem that the patient is so intent upon finding a new good parent that she does more than simply experience the therapist (by way of displacement) as a new good parent. Sometimes it would seem that the patient has a need to get the therapist to become a new good parent, in fact and not just in fantasy.

In these situations, the patient behaves in such a way as to induce the therapist to accept the role of "ideal parent"—and what had once been a case of mistaken identity becomes now a reality, as the therapist herself becomes a participant in the externalization of the patient's internal drama.

At this point, the therapist has become involved.

Whereas the patient's exerting of interpersonal pressure on the therapist to become the old bad object is clearly an instance of projective identification, it is not clear what term we would want to use to describe those situations in which the patient exerts interpersonal pressure on the therapist to participate as a new good object.

In other words, if we use the term projective identification to describe what happens when the patient enacts her need for the old bad object, then what term should we use to describe what happens when the patient enacts her need for a new good object?

In fact, I do not think that the psychodynamic literature addresses itself to this particular form of interpersonal behavior. The relationship between the patient's need to be failed and what the patient then enacts in her relationships is certainly addressed—projective identification. But the relationship between the patient's need to find the good parent she never had and what she then enacts in her relationships is seldom addressed.

Whereas projective identification is the term used to describe the patient's active soliciting of the therapist's participation as the old bad parent, there is no analogous term used to describe the patient's active soliciting of the therapist's participation as a new good parent.

As Steven Stern (1994) has astutely observed, "there has been no systematic effort to define a . . . counterpart to projective identification, that is, the patient's unconscious efforts to evoke in the therapist specific responses that are different from those of the traumatizing figures of the past" (p. 320).

And yet I think most therapists have experienced in their work with patients pressure to be both the bad mother the patient had and the good mother the patient never had.

In other words, I am suggesting that it would be clinically useful were we to have a way to conceptualize the patient's proactive efforts in relation to the therapist—not just with respect to the patient's need to re-create the old bad object (so that the patient can achieve belated mastery of it) but also with respect to the patient's need to create a new good object (so that the patient can have the opportunity to start over).

Projection versus Displacement

In order to find a term that captures the essence of what is involved when the therapist is enrolled by the patient as a new good object, I would like first to highlight the distinction between projection and displacement as intrapsychic mechanisms used by patients who have suffered at the hands of their infantile objects.

Please note that whereas negative transference involves projection of something bad, positive transference involves displacement of the need for something good. But how does it come to pass that one kind of transference involves projection (of introject) and the other kind involves displacement (of need)?

As described elsewhere (Stark 1994a,b), in the beginning is the young child's need for a good parent. When such a need is thwarted by a traumatically frustrating parent, two things happen intrapsychically for the child:

(1) The traumatically frustrated need becomes intensified (because there is no opportunity for its transformation into healthy capacity by way of nontraumatic frustration and transmuting internalization).

(2) The traumatically frustrating parent is internalized (because the child, in an effort to master the experience of being failed, takes the burden of the parent's badness upon herself in order not to have to face the pain of her grief about just how limited the parent really is).

In other words, a child who has suffered at the hands of her parent will have two internal records of that failure: she will have both the need to find the good parent she never had and the need to re-find the bad parent she did have.

In the treatment situation, such an individual will experience two things in the transference. If the "need for good" is experienced in relation to the therapist, the intrapsychic mechanism involved will have been "displacement"; and we will here be talking about a situation of positive transference. If the "need for bad" is experienced in relation to the therapist, the intrapsychic mechanism involved will have been "projection"; and we will here be talking about a situation of negative transference.

The Therapist's Role

Before we return to a consideration of the patient's need to find the good parent she never had (and how that affects what she actually does—or enacts—in the therapy relationship), let us review how the therapist's role is conceptualized in a deficiency-compensation model of therapeutic action.

Although the Model 2 literature clearly speaks to how important it is that the patient be able to have a corrective experience at the hands of the therapist, almost nowhere is the nature of the therapist's actual participation clearly spelled out. To summarize some of the major points I made earlier:

1. When reference is made to the patient's experience of the therapist as the good mother she never had, is that thought to be a story primarily about the patient (and her need to imagine that she has at last found the good mother for whom she has been searching her entire life) or primarily about the therapist (and her willingness actually to participate as that new good object)?
2. When reference is made to the therapist's validation of the patient's experience, does that mean that the therapist simply offers empathic recognition of the patient's experience or that the therapist offers a more direct response—in the form, say, of confirming the reality of that experience?
3. To what extent does the therapeutic action in Model 2 involve empathic recognition? To what extent does it involve actual gratification? To what extent does it involve working through optimal frustration (or optimal disillusionment)? To what extent does the therapeutic action involve the therapist's provision of containment—by way of, say, loving restraint?
4. To what extent does the therapist's corrective provision for the patient involve internalization? And to what extent does it involve, more generally, a corrective experience that is not necessarily mediated by way of internalization?
5. What does it mean when the therapist who embraces a deficiency-compensation model of therapeutic action is said to meet the patient's need or to recognize and respond to it?
6. For that matter, what does it even mean to be a good object–good mother or to operate in loco parentis?

7. To what extent does the Model 2 therapist strive to decenter from her own subjectivity so that it does not contaminate her understanding of the patient's experience? But to what extent does the Model 2 therapist strive to remain centered within her own subjectivity so that what she gives the patient will bear the mark of her own subjectivity?
8. Or, expressed in somewhat different terms, to what extent does the Model 2 therapist's corrective provision involve her participation as a generic good object and what extent does it involve her participation as a more unique subject?
9. What makes a transference positive? Is it thought to be positive when the patient delivers her need for good into the therapy relationship? Or is it considered positive only when the therapist actually participates as a new good object?
10. What creates disruption of the positive transference? Is it the patient's subjective experience of having been failed, or is it that the therapist objectively fails the patient?
11. When we say that the Model 2 therapist offers the patient a holding (or facilitating) environment, does it mean that the therapist makes herself available to the patient for internalization of her holding functions or does it mean that the therapist provides a protective envelope within which the patient's inherited potential can become realized when allowed an uninterrupted continuity of being (Winnicott 1955)?
12. Finally, is an empathic response itself healing (that is, an end in itself)—or is it simply the means to another end (like enhanced knowledge of one's internal process)?

There is so much confusion in the literature surrounding the role of the Model 2 therapist. There is so much confusion about what even constitutes a corrective experience.

I believe that little attention has been paid in the literature to the impact on the therapist of the patient's need for good because of this confusion.

The Corrective Emotional Experience

I believe the confusion has to do, in large part, with the controversy surrounding Alexander's (1946) introduction of the concept of a corrective emotional experience—which, he suggested, was to involve manipulative gratification of the patient by way of the therapist's intentionally assuming a stance diametrically opposed to the traumatogenic parental stance. The entire concept has fallen into such ill repute over the years that most psychodynamic writers today either altogether avoid use of the term or place it in quotation marks. As a result, many therapists are reluctant to acknowledge publicly that they conceive of their role as one that sometimes involves gratification of the patient's infantile needs.

In other words, because the whole concept of a corrective experience has been so controversial, misunderstood, and abused, there has been a lack of clarity about what actually constitutes the therapeutic action in Model 2.

Clinical Vignette—Demandingly Insistent

The following example demonstrates some of the confusion surrounding the Model 2 therapist's provision of a corrective experience for the patient. More particularly, it speaks to the often fuzzy distinction between the therapist's providing gratification of the patient's need and the therapist's empathically resonating with the patient's affective experience in the moment.

Let us imagine that a patient says to her therapist with heartfelt urgency, "Please, tell me that I will get better!" Is it ever appropriate for the Model 2 therapist to oblige the patient—that is, to accommodate to the patient's insistent request by responding, presumably, in the affirmative? Or is it more appropriate for the therapist to respond empathically to the urgency with which the patient is seeking reassurance?

In fact, many Model 2 therapists (particularly self psychologists) speak to the importance of the patient's subjective reality, which the therapist is ever striving to understand by way of empathic immersion in that experience—leaving behind both that which she feels (her subjectivity) and that which she thinks (her objectivity). For such therapists, it is more important to resonate empathically with the patient's need, more important to provide validation of the patient's subjective experience, more important to understand eventually its genetic underpinnings, than to presume that there is some "objective truth" that can be "known" and offered to the patient.

A self psychologist might offer the patient something like, "It is important to you to be able to know that you will eventually get better," "You are wanting me to reassure you that I think you will get better," "You are feeling that you must hear from me a reassurance that I think you will get better," or, finally, "You are not sure that you can keep going unless I can reassure you that you will indeed get better in time."

In the first two empathic interventions, the therapist resonates with the patient's wish to be reassured; in the second two, the therapist resonates with the patient's entitled sense that this reassurance is her due.

Although such statements may satisfy the patient, they may instead fuel the patient's insistence that she be reassured—in which case the therapist (in an effort to facilitate the patient's mastery of her upset and her disappointment) might say something like, "And it bothers you that I appreciate your anxiety but don't then offer you reassurance," or, perhaps, "And it upsets and angers you that I don't simply tell you that you will get better."

With these last statements, the therapist is attempting to resonate empathically with the patient's experience of angry disappointment—that she has been thwarted in her wish or her need to find a good parent who will offer reassurance when she (the patient) is in doubt.

Would it ever be appropriate to offer the patient gratification of her need for reassurance? Possibly, although to do so requires of the therapist that she become once again more centered within her own experience, that she reflect upon what she really thinks and feels about the patient's prospects for improvement, and that she offer the patient her considered opinion—all of which requires that she relinquish her empathic, nonjudgmental stance. Furthermore, were the therapist simply to oblige the patient by offering her the reassurance she seeks (whether offered in a considered fashion or, perhaps, more by rote), then patient and therapist might be robbed of the opportunity to understand "why" the patient's need for reassurance (and perhaps even "why now").

The Patient's Impact on the Therapist

Although Model 3 therapists have long been interested in the impact on the therapist of the patient's need for the old bad object, Model 2 therapists have appeared to be relatively uninterested in the impact on the therapist of the patient's need for new good.

As we suggested above, one reason for this apparent lack of interest may be that there is already so much confusion about the Model 2 therapist's contribution to the therapeutic action that it would be even more confusing still were attention to be directed to the patient's contribution to the therapeutic action—in the form, say, of the patient's transferential enactment of her need for new good.

In other words, I believe that little attention has been paid by Model 2 theorists to the patient's enactment in the transference of her need for a new good object in part because there is such a lack of clarity regarding the nature of the therapist's participation to begin with.

To pose the question in three different ways:

(1) Is the therapist to be a more-or-less blank screen onto which the patient displaces her need for a new good object or does the therapist actually participate as that new good object?

(2) To what extent does the therapeutic action involve subjective transference (a story about the patient) and to what extent does it involve objective transference (a story about the therapist)?

(3) Finally, to what extent is the patient's experience of the therapist a figment of the patient's imagination (illusion) and to what extent is it the result of what is actually going on in the room (reality)?

Another reason for the lack of interest in the impact on the therapist of the patient's need for a new good object is that, in the Model 2 literature, the patient is presented as fairly disempowered. In fact, there is a pervasive sense of the structurally impaired and deficit-ridden patient as somehow less accountable, more a passive, helpless, innocent victim of maternal deficiency, deprivation, and pathology. The patient is not seen as an agent, as proactive, as responsible for what happened (or happens) to her. She is not seen, therefore, as someone who exerts interpersonal pressure (albeit unconsciously) on the therapist to bring about that which she most needs in order to heal.

Rather, it is for the Model 2 therapist to use her own intuition to determine how best to compensate the patient for what she suffered early on. The Model 2 therapist, therefore, takes the responsibility for providing now that which was not provided consistently and reliably by the mother early on—so that the difference can be made up to the patient, her deficiencies made good.

Finally, the deficiency-compensation models of therapeutic action do not clearly spell out the degree to which the therapist is to remain centered within her own subjectivity; they do not make explicit the degree to which the therapist is expected to maintain her own center of initiative. As a result, there is an abiding confusion about the extent to which the therapist should allow herself to be personally affected by the patient.

And, because the degree of the therapist's personal involvement in the therapeutic process is such a gray area to begin with, it becomes confusing then to think in terms of the impact on the therapist of the patient's transferential activity. In essence, for those Model 2 therapists (particularly self psychologists) who believe that it is for the therapist to decenter from her own subjectivity so that she can maintain an empathic perspective, it becomes a contradiction in terms then to posit that the Model 2 patient is ever busy striving to shape the therapist's response to her, striving to have an impact on the therapist's subjectivity.

In sharp contrast to this Model 2 perspective is, of course, the Model 3 perspective, in which the therapist is encouraged to remain close to her own experience, to be centered within her own subjectivity, and to be present as an authentic subject—so that the patient can have the empowering experience of knowing that she can have an impact on what unfolds in the therapeutic process.

But, whereas Model 3 involves give-and-take, Model 2 involves only give (the therapist's give). Whereas Model 3 speaks to the bidirectionality of impact, Model 2 speaks only to the therapist's impact on the patient.

In Model 2, then, the therapist is seen as someone whose responsibility it is to provide the patient with a corrective experience. The therapist is able to fulfill her duty because—by way of her empathic immersion in the patient's experience—the therapist is able (1) to sense when the patient is in need and (2) to respond in some fashion to that need.

But, again, in Model 2 the emphasis is rarely on the patient's activity with respect to the therapist—that is, behavior on the patient's part intended to elicit a positive response from the therapist. The emphasis instead is on the therapist's empathic attunement to the patient's state of need.

Nor is the role played by the patient's enactment of her need for new good addressed by Model 3 (relational) therapists:

(1) Contemporary relational theorists focus their attention on the therapist's participation as an authentic subject who remains ever true to herself; they would seem to be less interested in the therapist's participation as a new good object who, responsive to pressure exerted on her by the patient's need for new good, offers the deficit-ridden patient some form of corrective provision.

(2) And Model 3 object relations theorists focus on the therapist's participation as the old bad object (by virtue of her responsiveness to pressure exerted on her by the patient's need to be failed); their interest is not in the patient's enactment of need for new good, but in her enactment of need for old bad.

And so it is that neither Model 2 nor Model 3 deals with the issue of the deficit-ridden patient as proactive, as an agent, as actively soliciting the therapist's participation as the good mother the patient never had.

Because neither Model 2 nor Model 3 theorists have been interested in this aspect of the patient's transferential activity, no term has been coined to capture its essence. So whereas projective identification is the term devised by theorists to describe the patient's exerting of pressure on the therapist to participate as the old bad object, there is no equivalent term to describe the patient's exerting of pressure on the therapist to participate as a new good object.

I would like, therefore, to propose that since we use the term projective identification to describe those situations in which the therapist accepts the patient's projections, perhaps we could use the (unfortunately somewhat unwieldy) term "displacive identification" to describe those situations in which the therapist accepts the patient's displacements.

Just as projective identification is the term used when the therapist is drawn into participating countertransferentially as the old bad object, *displacive identification* will then be the term used when the therapist is drawn into participating countertransferentially as a new good object. And whereas projective identification speaks to actualization of the patient's negative transference, displacive identification will speak to actualization of the patient's positive transference.

Countertransference and Role-Responsiveness

Sandler is one of only a handful of psychoanalytic theorists to have addressed the issue of the therapist's responsiveness to both the patient's need for old bad and the patient's need for new good.

In his 1976 paper (now a classic in the field) entitled "Countertransference and Role-Responsiveness," Sandler speaks to the therapist's unwitting repetition with the patient of the latter's significant early relationships—a repetition that is both inevitable and necessary. In fact, Sandler contends that such role-responsiveness is at the heart of what enables the therapist to be maximally effective.

Sandler recognizes that the patient does not always "keep to the rules" of reporting rather than enacting; instead, the patient unconsciously attempts to "impose" internal "role-relationships" on the therapist. Sandler writes, "In the transference, in many subtle ways, the patient attempts to prod the analyst into behaving in a particular way . . ." (p. 44).

More specifically, the patient has intrapsychic representations of self and object in interaction; within the context of the relationship with her therapist, the patient attempts to "actualize" (in the sense of to make actual, to convert into an actual fact, or to realize in action) her internal representations of self in relation to object.

Parallel to the "free-floating attention" of the therapist is something to which Sandler refers as the therapist's "free-floating responsiveness" (or role-responsiveness), which enables the therapist to respond to the patient's need to re-create her past (both its negative and its positive aspects) in the transference. The therapist's role-responsiveness enables her to be unconsciously available to the patient for this purpose; it enables her to accept the role the patient is forcing on her, to accept the role into which the therapist is being "manoeuvred" by the patient.

Sandler is here speaking to the therapist's receptivity to both the patient's need for old bad and her need for new good.

But Sandler did not further develop his ideas about the therapist's role-responsiveness—nor was there ever a specific name given to the therapist's enrollment as a new good object by the patient.

It is unfortunate that so little attention has been paid to actualization of the patient's need to find the good mother she never had. The omission is one that has seriously hampered exploration of the interactive dynamic that goes on all the time in the patient–therapist relationship—a dynamic that is an important aspect of the therapeutic action (namely, the patient's enactment of her need to find now (in the context of the relationship with her therapist) what she was never able to find early on, and the therapist's (conscious and unconscious) responsiveness to that need. To deny the patient such an impact on her therapist disempowers her and robs her of the opportunity to be an active participant in her healing.

CHAPTER

24

The Patient as Proactive

*I*n an attempt to re-empower the patient, let us now think more specifically about the patient as proactive, as an agent, as someone intent upon bringing about that which she needs in other to get better, whether it be recreating old bad or creating new good.

With respect to the first situation, when the patient enacts in the transference her need to re-find the old bad parent, I would like to suggest that we describe the patient's behavior as *provocative*—the provocative behavior an attempt to elicit in the here-and-now the same negative (but comfortable because so familiar) response that the patient had experienced in the relationship with her bad parent. Whatever the nature of the negative interactive dynamic that had existed early on, the patient (by way of behaving provocatively) exerts pressure on the therapist to participate in a re-enactment of the patient's internal dramas.

With respect to the second situation, when the patient enacts in the transference her need to find a new good parent, I would like to suggest that we describe the patient's behavior as either *inviting* (when she attempts to draw the therapist into participating as the good mother she never had) or *entitled* (when, refusing to take the therapist's no for an answer, she persists—even so—in her efforts to draw the therapist into participating as the good mother she never had).

There is often a fine line between the patient's inviting behavior and her entitled behavior, but the distinction is an important one because of its clinical ramifications.

(1) When I describe a patient as inviting (about which I will have more to say momentarily), I mean to be speaking to the patient's active efforts to enlist the therapist as the good parent she never had.

(2) When I describe a patient as entitled, I mean to be speaking more specifically to the patient's active efforts to extract from the therapist something the therapist has already indicated she is not in a position to offer. Unable to tolerate the pain of her disappointment, the entitled patient pursues her therapist with a vengeance, outraged that she has been thwarted in her desire.

In other words, we describe the patient's behavior as inviting when she enacts her need for new good and the therapist's response is a yes. By the same token, we describe the patient's behavior as entitled when she enacts her need for new good and the therapist's response is a no—but the patient refuses to relent.

Now when do we speak of projective identification and when of displacive identification? When the patient's transferential activity is provocative and the therapist finds herself responding to it by becoming the old bad object, we are talking about projective identification. When the patient's transferential activity is inviting and the therapist finds herself responding to it by becoming a new good object, we are talking about displacive identification.

When the patient's transferential activity is entitled, we are talking about a situation of relentless hope. Here the patient refuses to confront the reality that the therapist is not available to participate in the way that the patient would have wanted her to participate. As we saw in Part I, the patient's relentless hope speaks to her refusal to grieve.

In other words, I am using the term provocative to describe the patient's behavior when she is seeking to re-create the old bad object situation, inviting to describe her behavior when she is seeking to create a new good object situation, and entitled to describe her behavior when, confronted with a reality that she finds intolerable, she persists nonetheless—unrelenting in her entitled sense that it is her right to have her infantile needs met.

I choose these fairly dramatic terms because I want to highlight the element of choice that the patient has. My aim is to hold the patient accountable for her transferential behavior; but in so doing, my goal is to acknowledge the very real power the patient has. The patient can behave in a provocative, in an inviting, or in an entitled manner—and the interpersonal consequences of each will be dramatically different.

As with all enactments, in the treatment situation the patient's intent is to elicit a particular response from the therapist or to communicate to the therapist something important about the patient's internal experience. The patient is thought to enact whatever she must in order to draw the therapist into participating with her in the way that the patient needs the therapist to participate. As with all compulsive repetitions, there is both an unhealthy aspect (the desire for more of the same because it is so familiar, even if pathological) and a healthy aspect (the desire to bring about what is needed in the interpersonal arena in order ultimately to get better).

If the patient has internal bad objects and therefore a need to find now the bad parent she did have early on, she may well need to deliver her need to be failed into the therapy relationship so that it can be reworked in the context of the here-and-now engagement with her therapist. The patient may well behave provocatively in order to draw her therapist into failing her in the ways that the patient needs to be failed so that she can eventually achieve belated mastery of her internalized traumas.

By the same token, if the patient has a reinforced need to find now the good parent she never had early on, she may well need to deliver her infantile strivings into the therapy relationship so that they can be reworked in the context of the here-and-now engagement with her therapist. The patient may well behave invitingly in order to draw her therapist into treating her in the ways that the patient needs to be treated so that she can eventually obtain the gratification of need that she has spent a lifetime trying to secure.

Finally, when the patient is relentlessly entitled (and the therapist, perhaps, relentlessly withholding), a therapeutic impasse may develop that cannot be resolved until either one of them relents or until they both can come to understand the nature of the interactive dynamic that is being played out between them. (We will later have much more to say about this form of engagement between patient and therapist.) In any event, it will be the process of patient and therapist wending their way out of the therapeutic impasse that will advance the patient's understanding of her relational dynamics and facilitate development of her capacity for healthy, authentic relatedness.

Admittedly, when the patient is enacting her need to find either the old bad parent or a new good parent and the therapist is participating countertransferentially with the patient in her transferential enactment, there is much room for error. But when there is this level of engagement, there is also the greatest potential for deep, lasting therapeutic change—if patient and therapist have the wherewithal to negotiate their way out of their mutual enactment.

Furthermore, it may even be that the patient must have the opportunity to be, at different times, provocative, inviting, and entitled if she is ever to be authentically engaged in the treatment.

Some would say that if the patient has never been loved by her therapist, then she has been cheated. I would like now to suggest that if the patient has never been both hated and loved by her therapist, if she has never had the opportunity first to actualize both her need for old bad and her need for new good and then to work that through with someone who is able eventually to offer containment, then the patient will have been denied all sorts of possibilities for healing.

To review, when the patient enacts in the transference her need for the old bad object, we speak of projective identification. This dynamic involves the patient's exerting of pressure on the therapist to become the old bad object and the therapist's ability to be responsive to such pressure. I have been suggesting that in such situations the patient's enactment takes the form of provocativeness.

When the patient enacts in the transference her need for a new good object, we speak of displacive identification. This dynamic involves the patient's exerting of pressure on the therapist to become a new good object and the therapist's ability to be responsive to such pressure. I have been suggesting that in such situations the patient's enactment takes the form of an invitation.

Finally, if the patient persists in pressuring her therapist to participate as a new good object even in the face of the therapist's inability or unwillingness to comply with the patient's need, then we speak of the patient's transferential activity as entitled.

ACTUALIZATION OF THE TRANSFERENCE

When the therapist accepts the patient's projections, the negative transference is actualized. This, of course, happens when the patient (by way of her provocative behavior) enacts her need for old bad and the therapist accommodates—projective identification.

By the same token, when the therapist accepts the patient's displacements, the positive transference is actualized. This happens when the patient (by way of her inviting behavior) enacts her need for new good and the therapist accommodates—displacive identification.

Actualization of the transference, then, always involves the therapist's acceptance of the patient's assignments, such that the therapist becomes in fact (and not just in the patient's fantasy) the embodiment of that which the patient, in the moment, is needing her to be. In this regard, it is important to remember that although the patient consciously fears being failed, on a deeper level she has a need to be failed (so that she can achieve belated mastery of her internalized traumas).

In any event, when the therapist allows her behavior to be shaped by the patient's transferential enactments, the transference (whether negative or positive) is said to have become actualized.

CHAPTER

25

The Patient's Relentless Hope

Before we look at the dynamic that unfolds when the patient (by way of her inviting behavior) succeeds in drawing her therapist into participating as a new good object, I would like first to discuss the situation that accrues when the patient attempts to draw her therapist into participating as a new good object, is thwarted in her efforts, but—even so—persists in her relentless quest.

Elsewhere (Stark 1994a) I have written about this as the defense of relentless hope (or relentless entitlement), a defense that speaks ultimately to the patient's refusal to grieve.

I would like to describe such a defense in some detail, because I believe that the concept may help us to understand what sometimes happens when the patient enacts her need for good in the transference.

There are many patients who, never having had the experience of a good-enough mother, find themselves hoping against hope that their love objects will be able to offer them in the here-and-now the good mothering they were denied early on.

A young child needs the experience of being cherished, in a nondemanding, lovingly accepting fashion, by a mother who is emotionally present and empathically attuned. At least for a while, the child needs the experience of being the center of someone else's world, of having her every need, her every gesture, recognized and responded to.

If the child is denied such an experience, the need for a good mother becomes reinforced and intensifies over time. Unable to confront the truth about just how unavailable her mother really is, the child defends herself against the pain of her disappointment by taking the burden of the mother's badness upon herself. By so doing, she creates a distorted sense of herself as bad; but it does also enable her to hold on to her illusion of the mother as good and as ultimately forthcoming—if she, the child, could but get it right.

The child defends herself against facing her pain; it hurts too much to acknowledge the truth about her mother and her mother's limitations. She protects herself against the pain of such knowing by deciding that it must be she who is bad, her mother who is good. In order to go on living, the child must deny the reality of what she really does, on some level, know to be the truth.

Meanwhile, the defensively reinforced need for a good mother persists. Even as an adult, the patient brings to her relationships a desperate need to be known, understood, and loved—in the ways that a perfect mother would love her young child. Ever hopeful, she looks to each new love object to offer her the kind of empathic attunement, emotional availability, and unconditional love that her mother should have been able to provide, but did not.

In essence, to subsequent love relationships, the patient brings her illusions about what could be. She brings her infantile need for her objects to be other than who they are; she does not accept them as they are but, instead, asks of them that they be who they are not—namely, perfect mothers.

These unrelentingly hopeful patients have never really mourned the mother's failure of them; instead, they have spent a lifetime defending themselves against the pain of their grief by clinging to the hope that perhaps someday, somehow, someway, if they were but good enough and tried hard enough, they might yet be able to extract from a current object (a stand-in for the mother) the love they were denied early on.

And so it is that the patient pursues her objects relentlessly, hoping against hope that perhaps this time . . . Her relentless hope is the way she defends herself against the pain of her grief.

The patient's refrain is that she herself "cannot" (distortion), the object "can" (illusion), and the object "should" (entitlement).

Relentlessly, she pursues her objects, unwilling/unable to confront the reality of their limitations. The patient neither accepts that things were then as they were (in relation to the infantile object) nor accepts that things are now as they are (in relation to the transference object and to her contemporary objects); she wants desperately for things to have been different then and to be different now. Her hoping against hope is a desperate attempt to deny the reality of what was and is.

I refer to such a defense as relentless entitlement (or relentless hope) because such a designation emphasizes the patient's unwillingness, perhaps inability, to bear the disappointment experienced in the face of the object's failure of her. It arises in the context of the patient's refusal to grieve.

The patient is deeply convinced that her love objects could be her good mother if they were but willing. She is sure that they have "it" to give but are choosing to withhold it, that they have the capacity to offer it but are refusing to do so.

When such a need is delivered into the treatment situation, an idealizing transference emerges in which the patient comes to expect that her therapist will be the perfect mother she never had as a child. On some level, it is not unreasonable that the patient would find herself looking to her therapist to be sensitive, understanding, empathic, and responsive. In fact, that may not be too different from what the therapist herself would want to be.

So, too, it is not unreasonable that the patient would find herself wanting unconditional love and total acceptance, that she would find herself wanting to be special, wanting exceptions made, wanting her therapist to know without being told, wanting magic, answers, and guarantees. It is easy enough to understand the patient's desire for these things.

The situation is made more difficult, however, by virtue of the fact that what the patient is wanting may well be something that on the surface of things is not all that unreasonable for her to be wanting but, as it happens, is not something the therapist feels prepared to offer. The relentlessly entitled patient comes to know this—but persists even so.

Were the patient to be searching for something that her therapist could not possibly provide, then it would be so much easier for the therapist to be in the position of saying no. But, inevitably, what the patient wants is something that the therapist could conceivably offer—under other circumstances, or if the therapist had received different training, or if she had another orientation, or if that were more her specialty, or if she had different skills, or perhaps if she were someone else.

For example, the patient demands that the therapist hold her, give her advice, tell her she is special, or reassure her that she will get better. Perhaps the patient has a friend whose therapist holds her. Perhaps the patient was given answers or made to feel special by a previous therapist. Perhaps the patient was given guarantees in a previous treatment.

But, inevitably, the patient will find herself wanting the very thing that the therapist is not comfortable giving. Theoretically, the therapist could hold her, could give her advice, could tell her she is special, or could reassure her that she will get better. But, as it happens, these are things the therapist does not feel in a position to offer—and the patient comes to know this but insists even so.

Or the patient demands that the therapist be her advocate with the welfare department, write her a letter of recommendation, testify on her behalf in court, get her husband to recognize the ways in which he is wronging her, or side with her against a previous therapist.

Again, these are things that the therapist could conceivably offer but, for whatever the reasons, does not—and here, too, the patient knows this but will not take the therapist's no for an answer.

Ordinarily, a patient who has been told no must confront the pain of her disappointment and come to terms with it. In other words, she must grieve. In fact, it is this grieving, this confronting of reality, this mastering of disappointment, that is thought to constitute the therapeutic action in some deficiency-compensation models.

As mentioned earlier, growing up (the task of the child) and getting better (the task of the patient) have to do with coming to terms with the disappointment and the pain that come with the recognition of just how imperfect the world really is—optimal disillusionment.

With respect to the treatment situation, in the process of making her peace with just how disappointed she feels, the patient internalizes the good that she had experienced in the relationship with her therapist prior to being failed. Structural growth and the filling in of deficit result from the experience of having had, of having lost, and then of having worked through the grief accompanying that loss.

But a patient who is relentlessly hopeful does something other than confront the pain of her grief. She refuses to confront the pain of her disappointment; she refuses to grieve—because deep within her she feels entitled to a yes.

It is the relentlessness with which the patient pursues her quest and the intensity of her outrage in the face of its being denied that demonstrate the defensive nature of her desire and speak to her need to defend herself against the pain of her disappointment. The patient is unable to tolerate the disappointment experienced in the face of the object's failure of her. Unable to bear the pain of her heartache, she pursues the object with a vengeance, absolutely insisting that the answer be yes.

For the therapist who is the recipient of a patient's relentless entitlement, the challenge is great. And if it is not handled well, there may be weeks or even months of agonized torture for both patient and therapist before there is any resolution. The patient may act out by terminating prematurely, or the therapist may act out by letting her go.

The situation is even further complicated by the fact that, as I suggested earlier, the therapist often shares not only the patient's illusion that she (the therapist) can make up the difference to the patient, but also the patient's conviction that she (the therapist) should make up that difference. The therapist may believe that since the problem arose in the context of the mother's early-on failure, then it stands to reason that the therapist (a stand-in for the patient's mother) should come through for the patient now—the relationship with the therapist a compensation for the early-on failed relationship with the mother. The therapist, as well as the patient, may be convinced that the therapist should be able to gratify the patient's infantile longing to have the therapist be the patient's perfect mother.

And so the therapist may well want to say yes to the patient's insistence that the therapist be the good mother the patient never had, but the therapist must say no. Much as the therapist might wish to be able to make up the difference to the patient, the therapist will never really be able to compensate the patient entirely for the damage sustained early on—and both patient and therapist will eventually have to grieve this sobering reality.

For the therapist to believe that she can, and should, be the good mother the patient never had is to rob the patient of the opportunity to confront the grief she harbors deep inside about her actual mother. The therapist will be colluding with the patient's defensive need not to know the truth about her mother—thereby perpetuating the patient's refusal to grieve.

But if the therapist can tolerate being in the position of breaking the patient's heart every now and again, then the patient will have a chance to do now what she could not possibly do as a child—namely, to grieve.

Within the context of safety provided by her relationship with the therapist, the patient will be able, finally, to feel the pain against which she has spent a lifetime defending herself.

She must be able to confront the heartrendingly painful reality of just how flawed and how imperfect her mother really was and of just how great a price she has paid for that. She must be able, at last, to grieve—to access her devastation and her outrage that her mother really was not good enough and that she has been deeply scarred because of that.

As the patient gains an awareness of the extent to which she protects herself against her grief by way of clinging to her relentless hope, it becomes more and more difficult for her to maintain her attachment to the defense and to deny the truth about the infantile object. Belatedly, she grieves on behalf of the vulnerable little child she once was, a little child whose heart was broken by her mother. The patient confronts, at last, the reality of just how starved that small child was for recognition, understanding, appreciation, and love.

As part of the grieving she must do, the patient must come to accept the fact that she is ultimately powerless to do anything to make her objects, both past and present, different. She must feel, to the very depths of her soul, her anguish and her outrage that her mother was as she was, her therapist is as she is, and her other love objects are as they are. Such is the work of grieving and making one's peace with reality.

Until the patient can confront these excruciatingly painful realities, then she will be destined to be feeling ever frustrated and ever helpless. As long as she locates the responsibility for change within others (and not within herself), as long as she experiences the locus of control as external (and not as internal), then she will be consigning herself to a lifetime of chronic frustration and angry dissatisfaction with respect to each of her relationships.

Ultimately, the patient's relentless hope is worked through by way of resolving the idealizing transference; in other words, the patient begins to relent as she dares to confront the reality of her disillusionment with her therapist (a stand-in, of course, for her mother) and becomes able to master her outrage and her pain.

As the patient's transferential need to have her objects be better than who they are is gradually worked through, such a need becomes transformed into the capacity to accept her objects as they are. Infantile need becomes transformed into mature capacity by way of working through disruptions of the positive transference (in other words, optimal disillusionment); and infantile hope becomes transformed into mature hope as the patient, at last, faces the truth about her love objects and grieves.

Clinical Vignette—Helplessly Hoping

By way of illustrating the defense of relentless hope, I offer now the case of Lin, a young woman who presented recently to treatment with a chief complaint of concern about her husband's insensitivity to her needs and, more generally, his lack of emotional availability. As her story has unfolded, it has become clear that Lin is looking to her husband to be the good mother she never had and, to the extent that he does not do this, she is in an absolute rage at him.

Lin's mother was an extremely narcissistic woman who was relatively impervious to her daughter's needs; in fact, she insisted that her daughter accommodate to her own (the mother's) needs. Lin was never able to feel that she really mattered to her mother and was instead left with the feeling that she was invisible. Throughout her life, it has been extraordinarily important to Lin to be able to feel that the important people in her world are able to hold her in their mind, even when she is elsewhere.

As it happens, her husband, Paul, is a very decent man who loves his wife deeply and is devoted to her. Instead of telling her how much he loves her, however, he shows her—in a million little ways and many big ways as well. He wants very much to make her happy and tries hard to accommodate himself to her needs as best he can.

But, over the years, Lin has found herself feeling increasingly frustrated by Paul's "withholding" of verbal expressions of his caring for her. It makes her so angry whenever he forgets to ask her how she is feeling, or does not think to draw her out, or does not remember from one conversation to the next the issues with which she is most concerned. Furthermore, Lin becomes very upset when Paul is not attuned to her internal state and is not able to "intuit" exactly what she wants.

Although Paul demonstrates his love for her and his commitment to her by way of doing all kinds of things for her, admittedly he is not as adept at being empathically attuned and emotionally responsive to her. Each time he lets pass an opportunity to make up to her for what she never had as a child, Lin finds herself feeling devastated and therefore redoubles her efforts to extract from him the love she feels she must have.

The evidence would suggest that even though Paul is many things, he will never be the kind of man who will be able to "talk about feelings" or to "engage in deep conversation." Nonetheless, Lin continues to hope, hoping against hope, that Paul will eventually become someone who will be able to "talk deeply."

Over time, in the face of Paul's "refusal" to change, Lin has become increasingly outraged, dissatisfied, and resentful. She feels that she cannot live with Paul unless he can be available to her in the ways that she needs him to be; she feels entitled to such availability and tells herself (and him) that it is not unreasonable for her to be expecting this of him.

Lin's relentless efforts to persuade Paul that he ought to be someone he is not are fueled by her refusal to accept that he is, basically, the way he is. Unable to recognize the part she plays by way of her unrelenting desire, Lin holds fast to her conviction that the problem lies within him and derives from his unwillingness to relent.

As long as Lin clings to her desperate desire to have her love objects provide for her in the ways that her mother should have provided for her but did not, then she will be consigning herself to a lifetime of frustration, disappointment, and anger. Eventually, if Lin is ever to get better, she must be able to confront the intolerably painful reality that her objects (whether her husband, her therapist, or the other people in her world) are never going to be exactly who she would have wanted them to be.

In the transference, it will be the therapist's inevitable failures (recreating for Lin her mother's early-on failure of her) that will offer Lin the opportunity to achieve belated mastery of her heartbreak. When the therapist begins to fail her as her mother once failed her, all the old pain, all the old hurt, will be revived.

But within the context of her relationship with a therapist who understands how devastated she feels and has the capacity to see her through it, Lin will have the opportunity to do now what she could not possibly do as a child. In other words, Lin will be able to confront the reality of just how limited her mother really was and to feel whatever she needs to feel so that she can move on—sadder, perhaps, but no longer consumed by the relentlessness of her infantile desire.

It will be by way of grieving that Lin will eventually be able to let go of her illusions and of her entitlement. As Lin confronts the pain of her heartache, she will gradually replace her illusion that her love objects must be for her the good mother she never had with a reality—

namely, that she will have to become for herself that good mother. Her need for illusion and her entitlement will be replaced by a capacity to experience and to accept reality as it is.

More generally, although the patient's contention may be that her pain will not go away until her needs have been gratified, my belief is that the patient's pain will not go away until her need for good mothering has been frustrated (optimally frustrated) against a backdrop of gratification.

In other words, the patient must have the experience of working through her optimal disillusionment, of working through the devastation and the outrage that she feels as she begins to confront, head-on, her object's limitations (whether the object is her parent, her therapist, or a significant other). The patient must grieve such limitations and master them.

Ultimately, the patient must move beyond the need to have reality be a certain way, having transformed such a need into the capacity to know and to accept reality as it is, the hallmark of mental health. Once the patient has made her peace with the fact that reality is as it is, then she will be able to let go of her relentless hope and to move on to a deeper and a richer enjoyment of her life and of her relationships.

Clinical Vignette—Please Hold Me

I would like now to develop a clinical example that speaks to the therapist's benevolent containment of a patient's relentless hope.

I worked for a number of years with Meg, a very depressed young woman who, over time, became absolutely insistent that I be willing to hold her when she was feeling frightened and alone. Meg was the only child of a profoundly depressed, narcissistic, and alcoholic mother who loved her daughter but was so caught up with both her drinking and her misery that she was unable to be emotionally available to Meg, who—in order to comfort herself—would retreat to her room and to her stuffed animals, all of whom had special names and elaborate histories.

Over the course of our first several years, Meg, initially withdrawn and herself inaccessible, gradually dared to entrust herself to the relationship with me. It was a deeply fulfilling experience for me to bear witness to her coming more and more into her own, as she became enlivened through her connection with me.

But there came a time in our work when Meg began to feel that she needed the experience of actually being held by me. She said that she was so starved for physical contact in her life that she felt she might die without it. (Meg had friends but no romantic involvements and lived alone.) Over and over Meg told me that she had come to feel so close to me, yearned so to be my little baby, and longed so for me to be the comforting mother she had never had.

My heart would break as she pleaded with me to hold her, promising that one good hug would last her an awfully long time. For me, it was excruciatingly painful and heartrending; it troubled me deeply that I was causing her such anguish.

On the one hand, I wanted to be able to hold her. I was very much aware of the fact that it was through the relationship with me that she had come alive; it was easy to understand why she would now be finding herself looking to me for actual physical contact as well. I felt very close to her. I did love her. And I knew how much it would mean to her were I to hold her. I also knew that she had been starved for that kind of contact as a child and was now starved for that kind of contact as an adult.

On the other hand, my immediate gut response to her request to be held was one of discomfort; it made me very anxious to think about actually hugging her. In my psychoanalytic training, I had been taught to avoid physical contact with patients. It had been made very clear to me that the appropriate response to a patient's request for physical contact was to look at why the need (for the physical contact) and not to provide actual gratification of that need. I had been warned about the dangers of becoming physically intimate with a patient, of stirring the patient up in ways that were inappropriately stimulating and potentially seductive. I had been taught about the dangers of fostering too profound a regression through gratification of the patient's physical needs.

I was truly conflicted about Meg's request. But, at least initially, I was aware of feeling more anxious and confused than anything else—and of not wanting to have to hug her.

As time went on and Meg continued to plead with me to hug her, ever striving to convince me that it would be so healing for her to get that hug, I found something shifting inside me. I began to allow myself to enter more fully into her experience and to join with her as the subject—and not the object—of her desire (Schwaber 1981). I was now able to listen more empathically—and less defensively.

Although with time Meg had become increasingly insistent that she get that hug, at least initially her wish to be held had arisen from her desire for contact. Meg had not wanted to make me uncomfortable; she had not been trying to be difficult. Meg had simply been feeling the need to be touched and held by someone she experienced as her good mother.

So although my initial response had been one of anxiety, confusion, and reluctance, upon further reflection I found myself reconsidering. I was now able to recognize that certainly a part of me wanted very much to embrace Meg, to hold her close, to comfort her with my physical presence. I began to entertain the possibility of hugging her, imagined what it would be like to have her in my arms, holding her, comforting her, soothing her, perhaps stroking her gently, perhaps rocking her—and it felt good.

But I was also aware that it did still make me feel anxious, very anxious. It really did seem to me that holding Meg might create a confusing blurring of boundaries between us. Not only was it the party line that touching was verboten because it could be so easily misconstrued, but I was aware of feeling—deep within me—my own discomfort at the thought of crossing that boundary. Perhaps it was my training, deeply ingrained; but though my heart was willing to consider a yes, my gut was telling me that, bottom line, to give Meg a hug would not be quite right.

I was also aware that part of my reluctance to accommodate her need for the contact had to do with the annoyance I was beginning to feel in the face of her demanding insistence that the hug was her due. And I wanted to be sure that my discomfort with giving Meg what she so desperately wanted was not an acting out of any anger I might be feeling in relation to her.

It did also seem to me that were I to gratify her need, we would then be losing an opportunity to understand what was fueling both the intensity of her need and the relentlessness with which she was pursuing me. As painful as it might be, it did seem to me that here was a chance for Meg to come to terms with the fact that her objects (first her mother and now me) might not always be able to give her what she was wanting.

I knew from her history that in each significant relationship, Meg would inevitably come up against something in the other person that was deeply disappointing to her. And she would end up feeling dissatisfied, frustrated, and miserable. Ultimately, all her objects failed her.

By denying Meg the hug, I would now be just like all the others from whom Meg had wanted something that was being withheld. But by denying Meg the hug, I would also now be in a position to help her come to terms with some painful realities about her objects (both present and past).

Meg had never really mourned her mother's unavailability but would now have an opportunity to grieve in relation to me (a stand-in for her mother). Although I had offered her many things in my time, I would ultimately not be able to give her the hug she so desperately sought. She, in coming to terms with the excruciatingly painful reality of that, would be doing some important—even if belated—grieving.

So what did I do with Meg? I decided, finally, to share with her the dilemma with which I was struggling. I told her that, on the one hand, I wanted very much to hold her and to comfort her but that, on the other hand, I did not feel completely comfortable with the idea of actual physical contact, because it felt to me like the crossing of a boundary—and I was not willing to risk doing that to her.

I knew that no matter how I explained it, a no was a no. But my hope was that by sharing with Meg both my wish to be able to respond to her need for contact and my concern about how confusing such gratification might be, I would be enabling her to understand my frustration of her need in its context.

It was hard to say the actual no; but as I became more comfortable with that position, I began to see how my refusal to oblige was a necessary catalyst for the grieving Meg would have to do before she would be able to relinquish her infantile need for her objects to be something they were not. As I came to see ever more clearly the opportunity Meg would have to do some belated grieving, it became a little easier for me to be in the position of thwarting her desire. I recognized that the therapeutic action involved Meg's dealing with the disappointment, the hurt, and the outrage she felt in the face of my frustration of her.

It was very difficult to tell Meg no; but as I was doing it, I became aware of feeling a little bit hopeful as well—hopeful about being able to offer her the opportunity to discover that she could survive the experience of her heartbreak.

The work was not easy and took several more years to get done; but once I became clear that I was not comfortable gratifying Meg's need to be held, she was able to begin grieving. She cried for the hungry little girl she had once been and cried for the starved woman she had then become.

But there did come a time when Meg began to make her peace with the reality of what we were now both able to describe as my limitations—that I was a pretty good mother but, even so, had some very real limitations because I was kind of "uptight" about offering patients physical contact.

As Meg came to understand and to accept the disillusioning reality that I was probably not someone who would ever feel comfortable offering a patient a hug, she began to relent. It still made her sad that I was this way, but she decided finally that she would just have to live with the knowledge that I was not all that she would have wanted me to be—though I was many other good things.

Once Meg was able to relent, she was then freed up to direct her energies toward the realization of some of her more realistic dreams.

As Searles (1979) so poignantly notes, mature hope arises in the context of surviving disappointment. It is by way of facing the reality of her disillusionment—and discovering she survives—that the patient will be able to find her way to hope based on realistic aspirations, not unrealistic pipe dreams. As the patient confronts the pain of her grief about her mother, pain against which she has spent a lifetime defending herself, then it is that she will be able, at last, to relinquish her relentless entitlement—replacing her infantile hope with mature, realistic hope.

SADOMASOCHISTIC INTERACTIVE DYNAMICS

As we will now see, it is the patient's longing for the bad object to be good and her hatred of the object for being bad that fuels the relentlessness with which she pursues her objects—and that also gives rise to sadomasochistic interactive dynamics.

Although Fairbairn's (1954) claim is that he is writing about schizoid personalities (people whose attachments are to internal, not external, objects), I believe that the way he conceptualizes the "endopsychic situation" of schizoid personalities captures, in a nutshell, the psychodynamics of patients with underlying sadomasochism.

Let me begin by suggesting that masochism and sadism always go hand in hand: masochism (in which the patient's libidinal ego is desperate with desire for the exciting object) and sadism (in which the patient's antilibidinal ego is consumed with hatred for the rejecting object). In my formulation, I do not limit sadomasochism to the sexual arena.

Masochism is, I believe, about hope, relentless hope—the hoping against hope that perhaps someday, somehow, someway, if one were but good enough, tried hard enough, and suffered long enough, one might eventually be able to extract from the object (a stand-in for the heartbreaking parent) the love one was denied as a child. I believe, therefore, that the investment of the sadomasochist is not so much in the suffering per se as it is in the hope, the illusion, that, perhaps this time . . .

Sadism is then the response of the sadomasochist to the loss of hope. Instead of confronting the reality of her disillusionment, grieving it, and letting go of her relentless need to extract love from her contemporary objects, she does something else. With the dawning recognition that she is not going to be rewarded for her unstinting efforts, the sadomasochist responds with the unleashing of a torrent of abuse directed either toward herself (for having failed to get what she so desperately wanted) or toward the disappointing object (for having failed to give it to her). She alternates between enraged protests at her own inadequacy and angry reproaches against the object for having betrayed her.

In the treatment situation, when a patient is in the midst of an outpouring of hostility and rage toward the therapist, it behooves the therapist to ask the patient the specific question, "How have I failed you?" Please recall that the question is not "How do you feel that I have failed you?" This latter suggests that (1) the therapist sees the problem as lying exclusively within the patient and the patient's tendency to misconstrue reality and (2) the therapist is not open to learning about how she (the therapist) might indeed have failed the patient.

In any event, by asking the patient to address specifically the issue of how the therapist has actually failed her, the therapist is signaling her willingness to consider that the patient's devastation and outrage is co-created—a story about both the patient's vulnerability to injury and the therapist's actual failure of her. The patient is also being given a way both to give voice (more directly) to her disappointment and to understand the intensity of her outrage and her devastation as a reaction to the thwarting of her desire in relation to the therapist (a stand-in for her mother).

Whereas the masochistic stance is characterized by hope and feelings of omnipotence (that one will be able, eventually, to extract the goodies from the object), the sadistic stance is characterized by hopelessness and feelings of helplessness.

The cycle is repeated if the (seductive) object throws the person a few crumbs. The sadomasochist, a real sucker for such crumbs, is once again hooked and reverts to her original stance of suffering, sacrifice, and surrender in a repeat attempt to get what she so desperately wants and feels she must have.

CHAPTER

26

The Therapist's Unwitting Seductiveness

I would like to begin by explaining how I became interested in therapists who are unwittingly seductive. It arose out of my interest in patients who are relentlessly hopeful. Such patients, as we have seen, refuse to grieve—that is, they refuse to confront the reality that they are never going to be able to get exactly what they would have wanted from their objects. Their refusal to deal with the pain of their disappointment fuels the relentlessness with which they pursue their objects—both the relentlessness of their entitled sense that something is their due and the relentlessness of their outrage in the face of its being denied.

Until fairly recently, I had conceived of the patient's relentless hope as primarily a story about the patient (and the patient's refusal to grieve). I had believed that when a patient got caught up, say, in her desire for a hug from her therapist (a therapist who had made it perfectly clear that she was not someone who gave hugs), such desire spoke to the patient's refusal to accept the reality that her therapist was not, and would never be, someone who gave hugs.

Over time, however, I have come to understand that when a patient is in the throes of her relentless hope, it is usually not only a story about the patient but also a story about the therapist. The patient's contribution has to do, admittedly, with her refusal to take no for an answer; but the therapist may also contribute by way of her unwitting seductiveness, whereby she initially offers (whether explicitly or implicitly) the enticing promise of a yes—only later to say no.

It is important that the therapist, in order to avoid being seductive, strive as best she can to be consistent and to beware of promising more than she can realistically provide over the long haul—although, as we will soon see, it is inevitable, necessary, and therefore even desirable that the therapist (in some way or another) allow herself to be drawn into participating countertransferentially as a seductive (that is, exciting/rejecting) object in the patient's transferential enactments.

Relational-conflict theorists believe, as we know, that patients with internalized traumas have the need—aspects of which are unhealthy, aspects of which are healthy—to be now failed as they were once failed. More specifically, the patient who had an exciting/rejecting mother will attempt to re-create in the relationship with her therapist this early-on traumatic failure situation of seduction and then betrayal.

In fact, unless the patient has this opportunity to enact with the therapist her early-on experience of heartbreak—a therapist who actually participates (albeit unwittingly) as an exciting/rejecting object—the patient may never have occasion to confront the pain of her grief about the mother's betrayal of her. Unless the patient is able to deliver her compulsive repetitions into the here-and-now engagement with a therapist who allows herself to become a participant in the patient's dramatic re-enactment, then the patient may be robbed of the opportunity to rework her relentless desire.

Again, although the therapist must attempt to withstand the patient's efforts to draw her into participating countertransferentially in the patient's transferential enactments, it is extremely important that when the inevitable "crunch" (Russell 1980) does finally occur, the therapist have the capacity to recognize the role she has played (by way of her unwitting seductiveness) in first stoking the flames of the patient's desire and then breaking the patient's heart—when it turns out that the therapist is not all that the patient had had every reason to believe that she could be.

Clinical Vignette—Paradise Lost and Never Refound

I would like to present the case of Melinda, a 52-year-old married woman who, broken and desperate, came to me last year for a consultation after the devastatingly traumatic breakup of an eight-year-long intensive psychotherapy with a local psychoanalyst. I offer this case because it speaks so poignantly to the issue of a patient's relentless pursuit of her analyst as a story about not only the patient's refusal to let go but also the analyst's unwitting seductiveness.

Melinda was the only child of two alcoholics, both of whom were verbally and emotionally abusive to her. After their divorce when she was 4, Melinda lived alone with her mother, a horrid experience that she described as stifling and sickening. But she has little more to say about her childhood years, except that she learned, from an early age, to be strong and to endure.

Melinda feels that her life began only after she entered treatment in 1989 with Dr. Sloan, a psychoanalyst who (at least initially) was extremely kind to her, listened to her very attentively, and invited her to trust him. He would encourage her to sit close to him; sometimes he would hold her hand or hug her. Indeed, over time, Melinda opened up her heart to him and felt loved, cherished, and understood in a way that she had never before felt.

But after two years, Dr. Sloan began to pull back. Melinda, immediately sensing the change, was utterly devastated; she confronted him about his retreat and he, after consulting with a senior analyst, acknowledged that he had indeed pulled back once he had become aware that he was sexually attracted to her.

Although he reiterated his desire to be able to work with her and, on the surface of things, the situation improved for a while, it was never really the same between them after that; and, over the course of the next six years, the therapy slowly and progressively deteriorated.

As time went on, Melinda became increasingly frantic with desire for him and desperately intent upon winning him back. The more relentless Melinda became in her pursuit of him, the more distant and unavailable Dr. Sloan became. The more frenzied and desperate Melinda became, the more shaming, the more punitive, and the more cruel Dr. Sloan became.

During the last years of their relationship, Dr. Sloan would tell her that she had become a bad, difficult patient. But Melinda just couldn't let go; she felt she needed to be able to understand what had happened between them, why things had changed, why Dr. Sloan was now so remote.

Meanwhile, Melinda was feeling increasingly awful about herself: "I could barely tolerate sitting in front of him; I would feel as if I were covered with maggots." She felt fat, ugly, disgusting, loathsome. The more Dr. Sloan rejected her, the more frantically insistent and unrelentingly demanding Melinda became.

The situation deteriorated to the point where Dr. Sloan (a year ago) refused to see her altogether; when Melinda insisted (even so) that she had to be able to see him, Dr. Sloan took out a restraining order against her.

When Melinda came to me several months later for a consultation (about nine months ago), she was profoundly depressed, confused, and in great despair. She said again and again: "I don't want to be shut out of his life. I can't bear to think that he no longer wants me."

In our sessions, Melinda has talked repeatedly about how shattered and destroyed she feels by Dr. Sloan's betrayal of her. "At the beginning of our work, he would tell me, 'Everything you're doing is fine. I'm right here. Everything will be okay.' And then crash—he totally wiped me out. Because it really wasn't okay, even though he had said it was." With incredulity and anguish (but not nearly enough outrage) Melinda tells me, "He knew that his dumping me would kill me—but he did it anyway."

Even to this day, Melinda refuses to confront the reality that Dr. Sloan no longer wants to see her; instead, she clings tenaciously to her love for him. Even as there are moments when she is filled with horror at what he did to her, she is nonetheless desperate with desire to see him again.

In sum, Melinda's heartbreak is a story about both her own relentless need and her therapist's unintentional seductiveness.

THE PATIENT'S HOPE AS CO-CREATED

More generally, my belief is that the patient's unrelenting brokenheartedness is co-created, with contributions from both the patient (in the form of her refusal to grieve) and the therapist (in the form of her unwitting seductiveness). In fact, it is the therapist's unwitting seductiveness that reinforces the patient's need and stokes the flames of the patient's desire, inciting the patient to pursue her therapist all the more relentlessly.

As we know, the patient who, devastated and broken, pursues her therapist with a vengeance (intent upon extracting that which she feels she must have in order to survive) is a patient who has never been able to make her peace with the reality of her mother's limitations. As we have seen, Fairbairn (1943, 1954, 1958) helps us understand what fuels the patient's relentless hope (and underlying sadomasochism).

But as I mentioned earlier, I have come to believe that the patient's thwarted desire and heartache in relation to her therapist may also be fueled by the therapist's unwitting seductiveness. The therapist may end up breaking the patient's heart because she first excites by offering the patient (either implicitly or explicitly) the possibility of a yes and then devastates by rescinding the offer. In essence, the therapist unwittingly becomes an exciting/rejecting object as she allows herself to be drawn into participating countertransferentially in the patient's transferential enactments, thereby creating a mutual enactment.

And so it is that the patient's expectation and desire may be co-constructed. The patient's contribution, as we have seen, has to do with her refusal to take no for an answer; and the therapist's contribution, as we will now see, may have to do with her initial offer of a yes followed by a no.

Alternatively, we might say that the relentlessness with which the patient pursues the therapist is a story about both the patient (what she brings in the form of her vulnerability and her desire) and the therapist (what she brings in the form of her need to offer her patient the promise of restitution—a promise she ultimately breaks).

In other words, both patient and therapist participate in the creation of the patient's relentless hope.

THE THERAPIST AS SEDUCTIVE

I believe that most therapists, at some point or another, are inadvertently seductive with their patients—that is, they offer the exciting promise of something that they then break.

Particularly at risk are those therapists who strongly identify with their patients (particularly the "needy" ones), those therapists who have an intense desire to rescue their patients, and those therapists who pride themselves on having the exquisite attunement and emotional availability of a good mother.

As I noted earlier, the therapist's unwitting seductiveness is not only inevitable but also necessary and, therefore, desirable—because unless the therapist allows herself to be drawn into participating in the patient's internal dramas and ends up failing the patient in ways specifically determined by the patient's early-on experience of seduction and betrayal at the hands of her mother, the patient may never have a chance to confront the pain of her grief about the limitations of her objects (both her therapist and, before that, her mother). In other words, unless the patient has the opportunity to play out (in the here-and-now engagement with her therapist) her early-on experience of seduction and betrayal, then she may never be able to move on in her life and will be destined instead to be ever re-creating with her contemporary objects the early-on situation of heartache and despair.

I am therefore suggesting that—inevitably, necessarily, and desirably—the therapist must first offer her patient the promise of restitution (necessary if the patient is to be engaged at all) and must then be available to the patient to help her deal with her devastation and her outrage when the therapist breaks that promise (necessary if the relentlessness of the patient's desire is to be contained).

In other words, the patient who has relentless hope because of her refusal to grieve early-on losses may be unable to engage in the treatment process unless the therapist enacts some kind of promise for restitution—a promise that is the result of both her own need to make reparation to the patient and the patient's need to be so met.

But if all goes well, the therapist will (in time) fail the patient in the way that the patient needs to be failed; in other words, the therapist will renege on her original promise—the breaching of which is the result of both her own inability to sustain the level of her engagement with the patient and the patient's need to be so failed.

As we will see, for there to be resolution of what might otherwise be an unresolvable therapeutic impasse, the therapist must have the ability to recognize how she has been participating in the patient's dramatic re-enactments. Not only must she realize that she has failed the patient by way of her unwitting seductiveness, but also she must be able to utilize that understanding to further the analytic endeavor.

In fact, it could be said that if the patient is ever to be able to relinquish her relentlessness, the therapist must likewise have the capacity to relent—and to do it first.

Once the therapist has been able to recognize and to acknowledge—certainly to herself, perhaps to the patient as well—her contribution to the stalemated situation (in the form of her unwitting seductiveness), then patient and therapist can go on to look at the patient's contribution to the stalemated situation (in the form of her refusal to accept her therapist's limitations). Patient and therapist will be able to wend their way out of their mutual enactment by grieving together the reality that, much as both would have wished that it could have been otherwise, the therapist will never be able to make up the difference to the patient nor be the good mother both would have wished she could have been.

With respect to the therapist's unwitting seductiveness: sometimes therapists (usually with the best of intentions) unwittingly offer more than they can deliver, because they want so desperately to be able to make up the difference to the patient. It is crucial that the therapist know her limitations well enough that she can be realistic regarding what she offers the patient; otherwise, she will be in the untenable position of seductively offering the patient the enticing promise of a certain kind of availability that she must later renege upon.

And so it is that the therapist must be ever aware of how important it is that she be reliable, that she be consistent, that she sustain the level of her commitment to (and involvement with) the patient, and that she always follow through. If she offers the patient an unusually early appointment hour or makes herself available to the patient for weekend contact, then she must recognize that she is encouraging the patient to expect this kind of flexibility and this kind of availability for the duration. Or if the therapist runs over at the end of an hour, she must recognize that here, too, she will be fostering the expectation that the patient will get extra time in the future.

What is important is that the therapist at least try to maintain her consistency—even as she recognizes that, inevitably, she will find herself in the position of having failed her patient by way of being inconsistent.

If the therapist offers to make a phone call on the patient's behalf or to track down some information for the patient, it is crucial that the therapist do as she has promised. If the therapist agrees to read something the patient has given her, it is imperative that she do so. If the therapist is not prepared to be absolutely trustworthy and to honor every single one of her promises to the patient, then far better that she never have offered her availability in the first place. To commit to doing something for the patient and then not to follow through can be devastating for a patient who has finally allowed herself to have expectation and desire in relation to her therapist.

Or imagine, for example, the situation of a therapist who, wanting to give the patient something extra, offers a home phone number and invites the patient to initiate telephone contact between sessions (should the patient so desire). If the therapist offers a patient the option of calling her at home between appointments, then the therapist must be prepared to be available in that way for as long as the patient needs her to be. Otherwise the patient may have the excruciatingly painful experience of being drawn in—only then to have the door slammed in her face.

Nor is it fair to the patient for the therapist initially to offer the phone contact at no charge and then, when she finds herself becoming resentful of the patient's escalating demands for telephone time, to ask that the patient pay for such contact. Much better that the therapist know (and accept) her limitations in advance and that she be comfortable with imposing clear limits from the start—or the patient may feel (and rightly so) that she has been deeply betrayed.

Nor is it right for the therapist to agree to touch base with the patient at a particular time on a particular day, only then to forget to call. Much better never to have offered at all than to offer—and then to end up not making good on the offer.

Or if patient and therapist know from the start that they will not have much time to work together, then the therapist should make every effort to avoid being in the untenable position of allowing herself to be enlisted as a new good object—only then to have to withdraw that availability prematurely because of the time constraints. Such an abrupt withdrawal may well be traumatizing for the patient.

Alternatively, if patient and therapist agree to do twice-weekly sessions for the summer (because the patient is in need of more regular contact and the therapist's schedule permits), then the therapist must be prepared to continue the twice-weekly sessions for as long as the patient wants, even though the original agreement might have been time-limited.

Again, the therapist wants to avoid being in the position of committing to something that she will not be able to sustain over time—even as it is inevitable that, ultimately, the therapist will fall into the trap of offering more than she can realistically deliver for the duration.

Even when the therapist does not explicitly offer the patient something, the mere fact that she listens, remembers, understands, accepts, and cares, may generate longing within the patient's heart for the good mothering she never experienced consistently and reliably early on. It is therefore important that the therapist both recognize and appreciate the seductive pull of her empathic presence. In fact, the therapy setting (which is consistent, reliable, and regression-promoting) by its very nature gives rise to expectation and stokes the flames of the patient's desire.

Consider the situation of a patient whose therapist has offered her the emotional accessibility and the understanding acceptance that had been so sorely lacking for the patient in her earlier relationship with her mother. It is not difficult to understand how such a patient might find herself hoping for a hug from her therapist or, even, feeling entitled to such a hug—or hoping/expecting to hear that her therapist loves her.

Or consider the situation of a patient who has developed a very close, intimate relationship with her therapist. Here as well it is not too difficult to see how such a patient might find herself longing for some kind of relationship with her therapist outside the room and unable to make sense of her therapist's "boundaries." Or if such a patient understands that there can be no relationship outside the room while the therapy is in progress, the patient may hope that, upon termination, the therapist will be open to the possibility of a relationship.

Again, by its very nature, the therapy relationship produces expectation and creates desire—of which the therapist must never lose sight.

Another instance of unwitting seductiveness on the therapist's part occurs when the therapist, initially willing to offer the patient empathic understanding, becomes impatient and (over time) finds herself wanting to hold the patient ever more accountable for her behavior. If the therapist now reverses herself in midstream by becoming more confrontational, the patient may be devastated.

In such situations the patient, caught by surprise, may protest all the more vehemently her need for the therapist to be, simply, the way she used to be. Perhaps the patient acts out her desperation in impulsive, destructive ways. Such a patient will then appear to be relentlessly entitled and manipulative (even borderline) when, in fact, her demanding behavior is to some extent an understandable response to the therapist's abrupt withdrawal of support.

Therapeutic impasses develop when the therapist experiences the patient as unrelentingly demanding and does not recognize her own seductiveness in relation to the patient. In such situations, it may not just be that the patient is unrealistically expectant; it may also be that the therapist (by way of offering the patient a certain kind of relatedness that she later withdraws) has fueled the patient's infantile need by reawakening her desire.

In other words, it is not just the patient's entitlement but also the therapist's seductiveness that can create a therapeutic impasse. Although the therapist is insistent that the patient relent, it may well be she who must first relent.

Or let us think about the situation of a therapist who offers her patient conflicting messages about the degree to which she is prepared to be available to the patient when the latter is, say, in crisis. Although the therapist may have some clarity in her own mind about the limits of her availability, to the extent that these limits are never explicitly communicated to the patient, then the patient may find herself innocently requesting something that the therapist (unbeknownst to her) has decided is off limits.

If the therapist refuses to recognize the part she has played in creating confusion in the patient's mind about what does and what does not constitute acceptable behavior on the patient's part, then the therapist may unfairly misinterpret the patient's behavior as demanding and as entirely a story about the patient and her refusal to accept certain limits—when, in fact, the patient's "demandingness" is an understandable response to the therapist's conflicting messages.

Again, although the patient brings her own need (and, perhaps, her own refusal to confront certain realities), if the therapist participates in an ambiguous or a confusing fashion, the patient's infantile desires may be reinforced by the therapist's inadvertently seductive behavior—and the therapist must come to recognize this.

Finally, consider this point. Most therapists imply that if the patient commits herself to coming regularly to treatment, invests herself in the work, allows herself to become vulnerable, exposes her desire, shares intimate details about her life, expresses her feelings, deals with her sexuality and her aggression, explores her past, reports her dreams, and works in the transference, then (in time) she will get better. And so the patient tries hard to do all these things, with the expectation that (over time) she will begin to experience some improvement. But when, despite her best efforts, she begins to feel not better but worse—as deep-seated issues become therapeutically reactivated—the patient will understandably feel confused, upset, angered, and betrayed.

Here the therapist's promise may be implicit, but it is offered nonetheless—and, ultimately, here (as in the examples cited above) the therapist must have both the wisdom to recognize and the integrity to acknowledge (certainly to herself and quite possibly to the patient as well) her unwitting participation in the patient's heartbreak.

If the therapist is not "on to herself" and never "comes clean" about the extent to which she has failed the patient by implicitly offering the promise of more than she is ultimately prepared to deliver, then the patient may never have the opportunity to work through her grief about her therapist's (and, before that, her mother's) very real limitations. As long as the therapist denies her participation in the patient's heartbreak, then the patient may never be able to relinquish her infantile yearnings and her compulsive repetitions.

But if the therapist has the capacity to confront the reality that she may unwittingly have misled the patient by stirring up expectation and desire within the patient's heart, then the patient may herself begin to confront the reality that her therapist (a stand-in for her mother) will never be all that the patient would have wanted her to be. As the patient confronts that horrid truth and grieves it, she may at last be able to relinquish her tie to the infantile object and, in the process, the relentlessness with which she pursues her contemporary objects.

In sum, my contention will be that it is not so much the therapist's unwitting seductiveness (which is both inevitable and quite possibly necessary) that interferes with the therapeutic work; rather, it is the therapist's need to disavow her seductiveness that can have devastating consequences for the patient.

Parenthetically, I believe that there are some therapists who have such a highly refined sensitivity that they are more likely than their less exquisitely attuned colleagues to have patients who clamor for gratification of their infantile needs. The mere fact that such therapists are so emotionally available may be part of what ignites the patient's desire for ever more recognition.

Although the therapist's finely tuned empathic sensitivity may enable the work to go deeper, it is also a potential problem—at least to the extent that it generates desire in the patient's heart and draws her into having the infantile expectation that her therapist will turn out to be the source of unending gratification.

For this and many other reasons, it behooves all therapists to be rigorously honest with themselves so that they can become aware of how their particular subjectivity shapes the patient's experience of them and affects what unfolds in the continuously evolving intersubjective field.

Clinical Vignette—What Becomes of the Brokenhearted?

I would like now to present the case of Helen, a Ph.D. psychologist whom I have known for a long time. Many years ago, Helen came to me for a one-shot consultation, at which time she presented with many borderline features and a dreadful early history of multiple traumas. But most striking was Helen's desperate desire to get better.

Twelve years later Helen returned to me for another consultation, reporting that in the interim she had been in treatment with a superb clinician, Dr. Rose, with whom she had worked intensively for ten years—and whom she still saw intermittently. They had done extraordinarily good work—they were obviously an excellent match and deeply committed to their work together. Over the course of the years, Helen had gained considerable insight, had learned to tolerate intense affect and internal conflict, and, over all, had developed a much more solid sense of herself and of her own capacity.

But Helen reported that her world had been shattered when, eight and a half years into their treatment, Dr. Rose had announced that in six months she would be returning to school for several years of post-graduate education, a time-consuming proposition that would require her both to cut back on their sessions from twice to once a week and, more generally, to be less available to Helen between sessions.

They did the best they could to plan for the disruption to their work. But once Dr. Rose's rigorous training program began and she found herself consumed with her many new clinical responsibilities, Helen began to come undone. In her desperation, she frantically reached out to her therapist for help—just as she would have done in the past when in crisis. Dr. Rose attempted as best she could to respond to Helen's pleas for help but eventually, as Helen's demands continued to escalate, Dr. Rose—simply unable to devote either the time or the energy—became more and more defensive, angry, and withholding.

Dr. Rose told Helen that she would need to face the reality that she could simply no longer be available to Helen in the ways that she had once been; she suggested that Helen's relentlessness spoke to Helen's refusal to confront the reality of this—and that Helen needed to let go of her unrealistic expectations.

But Helen, unable to contain either her devastation or her outrage, had had ten hospitalizations over the course of the next year (for alcohol and drug abuse and, sometimes, suicidality)—continuing, all the while, her private practice of psychotherapy (admittedly with frequent interruptions).

It was in this context (and with the blessing of her therapist) that about six months ago Helen—broken, frantic, enraged, confused, and desperate—returned to me after twelve years for a consultation, which has turned out to be an extended consultation. Although Helen is in a rage at Dr. Rose and in excruciating pain, it has been obvious to both Helen and me how much she grew as a result of the hard work she and Dr. Rose did together.

In our work, it has become clear (over time) that Helen's outrage at this point has to do not so much with the fact of Dr. Rose's decreased availability as with Dr. Rose's reluctance to recognize (1) the extent to which she has, probably somewhat self-protectively, shut down in the face of Helen's unrelenting outrage and (2) the devastating impact on Helen of Dr. Rose's defensive shutdown. Whereas Dr. Rose's interpretive efforts are directed primarily to Helen's relentlessness, Helen's enraged protest is that what she most wants is for Dr. Rose to acknowledge that she is no longer lovingly available in the way that she had once been.

In Helen's journal, she writes of her heartbreak as follows:

I remember your telling me that it would be safe to deliver to you what I feared the most.
I remember your saying over and over again so many times, "I'm not going anywhere; I am here to see you through all of this."
You said I would never again have to cry alone.
You made the space between us so safe that I could deliver to you what so badly needed to be said and experienced.
You wrote me notes that I could carry with me if I forgot that you were there.
You said I could call, especially when the pain got to be too much.
But then came all the changes. I lost my balance and fell.
All of a sudden I couldn't hold on to you anymore. And the depression and the terror went so deep that I kept ending up in the hospital.
People didn't understand why I couldn't just leave my therapy. "Simple," they said. "If it causes pain and it isn't working, then leave!"
But I couldn't forget how it had once worked. I couldn't forget about all the time, the energy, and the effort that had gone into our therapy.

But now I can't find you anymore. I don't know who you are or where you went.
I have pulled inside and don't reach out to you anymore. And you don't lean forward in your seat to listen to me anymore.
I do cry alone—I cry because of all the pain. You promised that you would always be there for me, but you aren't.
I am so worn out and panicked that you, as I knew you, are never coming back. I tear apart inside trying to get back to the place where we once were. I keep trying to find you but you are not there. I cry out—but you no longer listen.
I am broken and my heart is shattered.
Are you gone from me? Trust me, this is not something casual—this is something so serious. It is the core of the work that needs to be done—but you are nowhere to be found.

Again, it is not so much Dr. Rose's initial loving availability followed by its withdrawal that has broken Helen's heart and shattered her world as it is Dr. Rose's difficulty acknowledging the reality that her heart has indeed now closed to Helen. Helen beseeches Dr. Rose: "Please just tell me that you are never coming back the way you once were, so that I can get on with my life and my healing. Don't pretend, that's torture. Please just tell me the truth that it is all over."

In order for Helen to be able to confront (and grieve) the reality of Dr. Rose's limitations, she needs Dr. Rose herself to be able to confront the reality of those limitations.

MALIGNANT REGRESSION

Balint (1968), whom we discussed earlier, writes about the salutary effects of benign regression and the traumatogenic effects of malignant regression.

In fact, Balint's distinction between benign regression and malignant regression is akin to Kris's (1958) distinction between "regression in the service of the ego" and "regression that overwhelms the ego."

And Balint's suggestion that empathic recognition fosters benign regression whereas instinctual gratification promotes malignant regression is akin to Winnicott's (1965) suggestion that the patient's ego needs must be recognized and responded to whereas her id needs must be thwarted.

Some years before Balint, Ferenczi (1930) had observed in some of his patients a re-activation, during treatment, of infantile yearnings for understanding, comfort, and reparation. Ferenczi wondered if the usual analytic stance of neutrality might not further traumatize patients such as these who had experienced either neglectful or indifferent parents.

In fact, in those situations where classical technique had not yielded therapeutic results, Ferenczi began to experiment with a more indulgent stance—to which he referred as his "relaxation technique."

Ferenczi did, however, encounter some difficulties with its use, noting that in some patients there was regression to a very primitive state characterized by raging mistrust, venomous aggression, and suicidal despair. Furthermore, the patient's demands for ever-increasing gratification sometimes became endless. In such cases, the results were disastrous. In fact, Ferenczi's advocacy of this approach is one of the reasons that he and Freud parted ways.

There was little further study of regression in the therapeutic setting until the work of Balint and Winnicott (about whom we will have much more to say later).

Balint studied the effects of regression in the treatment, carefully exploring both its dangerous underside and its potential value.

Balint was deeply convinced that the patient with a basic fault (what we have been describing as structural deficit) needs to have the experience of regressing in the therapeutic setting to the point where the environmental disruption originally occurred, so that there can be a new beginning and the patient can recover her hope that she will someday get better.

Balint believed that the therapist can foster such a regression by providing empathic understanding. The patient needs to be able to feel that she is being recognized and responded to as a person in her own right. She is thought to ask of her therapist simply that the therapist appreciate the existence of her internal life and her own unique individuality.

In benign regression, the regression is aimed at empathic recognition of who the patient is and what she is feeling.

It is only when the patient's libidinal aims are gratified, Balint suggested, that the patient may be catapulted into a dangerous malignant regression in which her ego becomes overwhelmed by unmanageable anxiety. In other words, the therapist's indiscriminate instinctual gratification of the patient can foster a dangerous regression in which the patient's infantile longings begin to escalate out of control. Such a situation is potentially catastrophic and clearly countertherapeutic.

I believe that both Melinda and Helen (in the two clinical vignettes cited earlier) were catapulted into a malignant regression not because they were instinctually gratified but because they encountered therapists who, having initially offered empathic recognition and understanding acceptance of their patients' ego needs, subsequently withdrew such support—and without acknowledging that they had done so.

In other words, I am suggesting that malignant regression is the result not just of the therapist's gratifying the patient's id needs but of the therapist's refusal to be held accountable for having promised more than she could ultimately deliver and her refusal, therefore, to recognize her contribution to the patient's distress.

In fact, my contention is that it is the therapist's refusal to relent that transforms what might otherwise have been a powerfully corrective relational experience (made possible by the therapist's ability to create a safe space within which the patient could regress to the point of the original disruption so that she could begin anew) into a catastrophically retraumatizing experience (that leaves the patient devastated and overwhelmed by unmanageable anxiety because of the therapist's refusal to take responsibility for her part in breaking the patient's heart).

To repeat, it is the therapist's refusal to relent, her refusal to appreciate the devastating impact on the patient of her (the therapist's) unacknowledged breach of faith, that almost destroys the patient—and converts what would have been a health-promoting benign regression into a dangerously destructive malignant regression.

THE THERAPIST'S ACCOUNTABILITY

Ultimately, it is the therapist who must be held accountable for what transpires at the intimate edge between patient and therapist. Although, as we have seen, both players have their parts and both contribute to the interactive dynamic that gets played out, it is the therapist who, in the final analysis, is responsible. It is the therapist who (in assuming the significance of the original parent) has the power both to break and to heal the patient's heart.

For a patient to be able to relinquish her relentlessly hopeful stance, the therapist must have both the capacity to confront the reality of her unintended (but necessary) failures of the patient by way of her unwitting seductiveness and the ability to help the patient work through the pain of her heartbreak and her grief that her objects may not always be exactly as she would have wanted them to be.

CHAPTER

27

The Patient's Behavior as Inviting

Sometimes, as we have just seen, when the patient transferentially enacts her need for new good she encounters a no.

But what is involved when the patient attempts to enlist the therapist as the good parent she never had and the therapist responds in the affirmative to such pressure?

We will now focus our attention on those situations (of displacive identification) in which the therapist responds positively to the patient's need for her to be the good parent the patient never had—that is, those situations in which the patient, by way of her inviting behavior, is able to draw the therapist into participating countertransferentially as a new good object.

By way of overview: my contention is that the therapist's responsiveness to the patient's need for new good may be necessary if the patient is to be fully engaged in the treatment and is to have the opportunity to relinquish her need for infantile gratification.

At least initially, the therapist's willingness to allow herself to be responsive to the patient's inviting behavior is deeply gratifying to a patient who was denied such responsiveness in the early-on relationship with her mother.

But when the patient signals her readiness, the therapist must be able to step back from her participation in the patient's enactment. Stepping back from such participation enables the therapist (1) to recover her objectivity and (2) to bring to bear her capacity to process, in collaboration with the patient, what had been mutually enacted in the relationship between them.

As we will later see, the patient must ultimately grieve the experience of having had and then of having lost (with respect to both her therapist and her mother). Such grieving is done against the backdrop of loving support provided by a therapist whom the patient knows (1) understands her need and (2) has even been willing to do the best she (the therapist) could do in order to satisfy that need.

The therapeutic action in situations of displacive identification lies in the therapist's ability, first, to offer the patient the experience of securing, at least for a while, gratification of her previously unmet need to find the good mother she never had and, then, to make herself available to the patient as the patient confronts, at last, the pain of her grief about her objects' very real limitations—at the same time internalizing that which *was* there for her.

This process by which patient and therapist work through the patient's need for new good in the context of their here-and-now engagement is akin to the process by which patient and therapist work through the patient's need for old bad.

As we know, the therapist's responsiveness to the patient's need to be failed may be necessary if the patient is to be fully engaged in the treatment. At least initially, the therapist's ability to allow herself to be responsive to the patient's provocative behavior may be necessary if the patient is to have the opportunity of being contained.

But here, too, the therapist, once she has been drawn into participating countertransferentially as the old bad object, must be able to step back from her participation in the patient's enactment. Stepping back from such participation enables the therapist (1) to recover her objectivity and (2) to bring to bear her capacity to process, in collaboration with the patient, what had been mutually enacted in the relationship between them.

Once the therapist recovers her ability to understand and is no longer involved in enacting, then she recovers her status as a new good object.

The therapeutic action in situations of projective identification lies in the therapist's ability, first, to respond to the patient's need to recreate the early-on traumatic failure situation in the here-and-now engagement with her therapist and, then, to wend her way out of the mutual enactment so that she can recover her goodness—thereby affording the patient the corrective relational experience of bad-become-good.

Of note is that in situations of projective identification, it falls to the therapist to be the one who must first relent, which then enables the vicious cycle (of mutual enactment) to be broken. As we will see, in contradistinction to this are situations of displacive identification, wherein it may well be the patient who (when ready by virtue of a "maturational thrust") first relents.

THE THERAPIST'S NECESSARY INVOLVEMENT

In any event, once the therapist finds herself drawn into participating as a new good object, she may find herself doing things with this particular patient that she would never contemplate doing with other patients. For example, perhaps she finds herself "making exceptions" or "breaking the rules" for the patient. Perhaps she decides not to raise the patient's fee. Or maybe she offers the patient an appointment at a time when she would not ordinarily be seeing patients. Perhaps she agrees to see the patient on weekends. Maybe she decides to give the patient her home phone number in the event that the patient wants to reach her between sessions. Whenever the therapist goes on vacation, perhaps she agrees to stay in touch with the patient—either by way of phone or by way of letters and postcards.

Although some of the therapist's behaviors might appear to be motivated by the therapist's wish to avoid the patient's anger or her fear of provoking the patient's anger, I mean to be speaking now to those situations in which the therapist finds herself wanting to offer the patient an extra special something and wanting to do whatever she can to accommodate the patient.

Or maybe the therapist finds herself offering the patient more advice, more guidance, and more answers that she would ordinarily offer. Maybe she helps the patient write the essays for her college application. Perhaps she aids the patient in preparing a curriculum vitae or designing a logo for her business cards. Maybe the therapist decides to give the patient the name of her own lawyer or her own internist. Perhaps the therapist lends the patient some of the magazines from her waiting room or some of the books from her personal library because she thinks they will be of particular interest to the patient.

Although the therapist's introduction of these outside "parameters" (Eissler 1958) could be very costly to the patient, I believe that there are times when the therapist's willingness to make exceptions on the patient's behalf may be necessary if the patient is to be reached at all and when the therapist's holding fast to a more neutral stance robs the patient of the opportunity to feel truly met.

In each of the above situations, the therapist makes a more-or-less conscious decision to be available to her patient as a gratifying object. Even so, the therapist is often uncomfortable sharing with her colleagues the specifics of her countertransferential participation in the patient's transferential enactments. In other words, for the most part, the therapist keeps to herself the details of what she is doing.

The therapist recognizes that what she is delivering of herself into the here-and-now engagement with her patient (that is, what the therapist is enacting in the relationship) is unorthodox. Indeed, the therapist recognizes that what she is offering the patient in the form of her participation as the good mother the patient never had is different from standard operating procedure—different also from her own modus operandi.

But the therapist continues to respond to the patient's enactment of her need for special consideration because the therapist is convinced that what she is offering is what the patient, for now, most needs in order to get better. Deep within the therapist's soul, she feels that what she is doing is clinically indicated—that what she is doing is necessary in order to reach the patient.

Part of what fuels the therapist's reluctance to go public with the details about the extent of her involvement with the patient is the confusion that exists, as I earlier noted, in the Model 2 literature about (1) what exactly constitutes the therapeutic action when the therapist is said to offer the patient a corrective experience and (2) what is actually involved when the therapist is said to participate as a new good object.

Furthermore, because the whole topic is so verboten, there is little support for the therapist who dares to make herself available to the patient as the recipient of the patient's displacements. The therapist's willingness to respond to the patient's need for good is a particularly charged topic because of the omnipresent danger that the therapist's involvement could go too far, could get out of hand, or could cross over into actual boundary violations.

In situations involving displacive identification, there is so much potential for something to go terribly wrong, particularly if the therapist behaves irresponsibly. But, by the same token, there is so much potential for incredible gain when the therapist allows the patient to have an impact on her—when she allows the patient to draw her into participating in the very ways the patient most needs in order to get better.

I believe that, at any given point in time, most therapists have one or two patients to whom they give special consideration. In other words, most therapists find themselves having a favorite patient or two—which I am here suggesting speaks to the therapist's participation as a new good object in response to the patient's inviting behaviors.

These are the patients whom the therapist talks about all the time with her colleagues and presents often in her supervision; these are the patients whose first names are known by the therapist's family members. In fact, more generally, whenever the patient fairly routinely exerts interpersonal pressure on her therapist by way of either inviting (as above), entitled, or provocative behaviors, the therapist's colleagues, supervisors, and family members usually come to know about it because of how engaged the therapist is with her patient—and, at times, how preoccupied as well.

Of graver concern than these situations in which the therapist makes a more-or-less conscious choice to be responsive to the patient's need for new good are those situations in which the therapist becomes unconsciously caught up in participating as a good mother and is oblivious to the potentially destructive impact on the patient of her willingness to make exceptions for the patient and to break the rules on the patient's behalf.

In fact, I believe that the therapist is being bombarded all the time by the patient's interpersonally inviting, entitled, and provocative behaviors and that unless the therapist makes a concerted effort to focus her attention on the here-and-now engagement between herself and her patient, the therapist will find herself unwittingly participating in the patient's enactments with no witting understanding of the potential consequences.

When the therapist finds herself becoming a participant in the patient's dramatic re-enactments, it is therefore crucial that she do her best to remain exquisitely attuned to those aspects of her subjectivity that are shaping, and are being shaped by, the patient's behavior.

Although there are aspects of the therapist's subjectivity that may make it difficult to resolve a mutual enactment (for example, the therapist's sadistic reaction to a patient's interpersonally provocative behavior), I believe that the therapist's need to disavow this countertransferential reaction is much more dangerous. So, too, if a therapist promises more than she can ultimately deliver, she may be inadvertently stoking the flames of a patient's desire—all the while unaware that her unwittingly seductive behavior is fueling the relentlessness with which the patient is pursuing her.

But even though the patient may be retraumatized if the therapist is not able to be honest with herself about her own activity/reactivity, there is tremendous potential for gain if she is able to use herself to engage, and to be engaged by, the patient. It is my belief that the therapist who is able to work effectively with the patient's displacive identifications and projective identifications will be able to offer the patient a much richer therapeutic experience than either the therapist who refuses to become a participant in the patient's transferential enactments or the therapist who becomes a participant in the patient's internal dramas and then is unable to relent.

Unwitting enactment with no witting understanding can admittedly have catastrophic results, but enactment accompanied by understanding can open up a world of therapeutic possibilities.

Again, my belief is that the therapist is continuously responding—whether wittingly or unwittingly—to pulls from the patient to participate as both a new good object and the old bad object. In other words, the therapist is ever busy participating—whether consciously or unconsciously—in both displacive identifications and projective identifications. My intent is not to prescribe a particular behavior for the therapist; rather, it is to describe the mutual enactments that I believe take place all the time at the intimate edge between patient and therapist (Greenberg 1981).

My aim here is to offer the therapist a way to conceptualize the interactive dynamic that unfolds when the therapist allows herself to be shaped by the patient's need. By providing this conceptual framework, my wish is to create the opportunity for transformation of mutual enactments that might otherwise have gone unrecognized and remained unprocessed into profoundly transformative corrective relational experiences for the patient.

CHAPTER

28

Displacive Identification

I would like now to highlight some of the similarities as well as some of the differences between projective identification and displacive identification.

I will be suggesting that displacive identification is to positive transference and the filling in of structural deficit as projective identification is to negative transference and the reworking of pathogenic structures.

Both projective identification and displacive identification involve actualization of the transference (by way of the patient's transferential enactment and the therapist's responsiveness to that enactment).

Both projective identification and displacive identification have two phases: The induction phase results in the therapist's participation in the patient's enactment as either a bad object or a good object; the recovery phase involves the therapist's resumption of a more neutral stance, which affords the patient the corrective relational experience either of bad-become-good (in situations involving projective identification) or of relinquishment-of-infantile-need (in situations involving displacive identification).

PROJECTIVE IDENTIFICATION AND STRUCTURAL CHANGE

When we are dealing with situations involving the internal absence of good (in the sense of missing structure and impaired capacity), the patient must be given the opportunity to deliver (by way of displacement) her need for external good into the transference. Gradual internalization of the good encountered there will be the process by which the patient's internal absence of good is corrected for.

When we are dealing with situations involving the internal presence of bad (in the form of pathogenic introjects that are the internal records of early-on traumatic interactions), it is not enough that the patient have the experience of external good and an opportunity to internalize it—because the internal pathogenic structures will still be there.

Rather, within the context of the here-and-now engagement with her therapist, the patient must be able to detoxify the actual pathogenic structures.

As we know, projective identification is the process by which the patient (1) delivers her pathology, in the form of her introjective configurations, into the relationship with her therapist; (2) re-creates in that relationship the interactive dynamic that had characterized the earlier, traumatogenic relationship with her parent; (3) encounters, eventually, a response different from (and better than) the original parental response; and (4) re-introjects an amalgam (part old, part new), such that her pathogenic structures do indeed become detoxified over time.

In the final analysis, in situations involving projective identification, the therapeutic action involves the therapist's ability first to respond to the patient's need to be failed and then to introduce aspects of her own capacity into the mix, such that what the patient re-internalizes will be a somewhat less toxic version of the original projection. By way of a series of these salutary interactions, the patient's internal bad objects will be gradually reworked over time, so that what the patient externalizes on each successive round will be ever less pathogenic.

Eventually, by way of the therapist's containment, the patient's compulsive need to re-create the early-on traumatic failure situation will become transformed into a healthy capacity to accept her objects as they are, uncontaminated by her need for them to be otherwise.

The induction phase of a projective identification involves re-creation of the old bad object situation—the patient exerting pressure on the therapist to lose her objectivity, to accept the patient's projections, and to assume the role assigned her. The therapist becomes, in fact and not just in the patient's fantasy, the old bad object—and the patient feels deeply engaged.

The recovery phase of the projective identification involves "correction" of the traumatogenic situation by virtue of the therapist's capacity—a capacity that enables the therapist (1) to wend her way out of what has become a mutual enactment, (2) to lend aspects of her own healthy functioning to a psychological processing of the patient's disavowed psychic contents, and (3) to return to the patient for re-internalization a modified version of what the patient had originally extruded.

As a result, first, of the therapist's responsiveness to the patient's need for her to be the old bad object and, then, of the therapist's ability to recover her status as a new good object, the therapist offers the patient the mutative experience of bad-become-good. Furthermore, when patient and therapist are able to process the dysfunctional interactive dynamic that has unfolded between them, the patient is afforded an opportunity to gain further understanding of what she enacts in her relationships.

In other words, as we mentioned in Part I, the net result for the patient of being contained by a therapist (who can first allow herself to be made bad and can then recover her goodness) may involve both knowledge and experience—that is, enhanced knowledge of her relational dynamics and the corrective relational experience of bad-become-good.

Repeated success in resolving the patient's projective identifications results ultimately in transformation of the patient's need to be failed by her objects into a capacity to engage them healthily in relationship.

In the induction phase of the projective identification, it is the therapist's capacity to respond to the patient's need to be failed that enables her to participate as she must if the patient is to be fully engaged. In the recovery phase of the projective identification, it is the therapist's capacity to contain the patient's projection (by introducing aspects of her own, more mature ego functioning) that enables her to give the patient the experience of being contained.

For a projective identification to be effective, both the induction and the recovery phases must take place.

(1) If the induction phase never occurs (that is, if the therapist refuses to participate as the old bad object), then the patient may never have an opportunity to achieve mastery of her internal demons because she will never be able to engage her therapist as a container for, and metabolizer of, those internal demons.

In other words, if the therapist never responds to the patient's interpersonally provocative behavior, then there may be a failure of engagement.

(2) If only the induction phase occurs (that is, if the therapist is unwittingly drawn into participating countertransferentially in the

patient's transferential enactments and then gets stuck in the mire), the patient will be retraumatized—because the therapist's participation as the old bad object will be an all-too-painful recapitulation for the patient of what had been traumatic for her early on.

In other words, if the therapist responds to the patient's interpersonally provocative behavior but remains entangled, then there may be a failure of containment.

(3) But if the patient can have the experience first of bad and then of bad-become-good (that is, if the therapist participates initially as the old bad object and then has the capacity to relent), the patient will have a corrective relational experience that involves both engagement and containment. Ultimately, such experience will enable her to detoxify her pathogenic structures and, in the process, to banish her internal demons—structural change.

DISPLACIVE IDENTIFICATION AND STRUCTURAL GROWTH

When the patient enacts in the transference her need to find the good mother she never had and the therapist (responding to the patient's inviting behavior) allows herself to be drawn into participating as that good mother, the patient comes to depend on the therapist in much the way that a young child depends on her caregiving mother.

The induction phase of a displacive identification involves the creation of a new object relationship—the patient exerting pressure on the therapist to lose her objectivity, to accede to the patient's invitation, and to assume the role of good parent assigned her. The therapist becomes, in fact and not just in the patient's fantasy, the good mother the patient never had; and, under the sway of the patient's need, the therapist finds herself willing (and even wanting) to make exceptions for the patient, to break the rules, to treat her as a "special" patient. As a result, the patient feels truly met.

The recovery phase of the displacive identification involves "correction" of a potentially traumatogenic situation by virtue of the therapist's "capacity"—a capacity that enables the therapist (1) to step back from her participation in the patient's enactment, (2) to recover her more neutral stance, and (3) to stop offering the patient special consideration.

Successful resolution of the patient's displacive identification results ultimately in transformation of the patient's infantile need to find a good mother into a capacity to engage in more adult relationships.

In the induction phase of the displacive identification, it is the therapist's capacity to respond to the patient's need for gratification that enables her to participate as she must if the patient is to be met. In the recovery phase of the displacive identification, it is the therapist's capacity to recognize when the patient is no longer needing to be gratified that enables the therapist to facilitate the process by which the patient is gradually able to relinquish her infantile need.

For a displacive identification to be effective, both the induction and the recovery phases must take place.

(1) If the induction phase never occurs (that is, if the therapist refuses to participate as a new good object), then the patient may never have an opportunity to modulate the intensity of her infantile desire because she will never be able to use the here-and-now engagement with her therapist to tame that desire.

In other words, if the therapist never responds to the patient's interpersonally inviting behavior, then there may be a failure of engagement.

(2) If only the induction phase occurs (that is, if the therapist allows herself to be enlisted as a new good parent and is never able to revert to her original—more neutral—stance), then the patient may be catapulted into a full-blown regression that could be very costly for her. As we will later see, what had begun as a benign regression may give way to a malignant regression, characterized by venomous aggression, heartrending despair, and escalating demands for ever more gratification.

In other words, if the therapist responds to the patient's interpersonally inviting behavior by allowing herself to become a source of endless gratification for the patient, then there may be a failure of containment—and the results will be disastrous.

(3) If the induction phase of the displacive identification occurs (that is, if the therapist allows herself to be responsive to the patient's need for new good) and then the therapist—too abruptly—withdraws that support, here, too, the price may be very costly for the patient. The therapist may have unwittingly recapitulated for the patient her early-on experience of being drawn in by a seductive parent and then slammed—seduced and then betrayed.

As we will later see, this can happen when the therapist, made anxious by the degree of her involvement with the patient, suddenly pulls out. Or it can happen when the therapist, in response to pressure from the patient for ever deeper involvement, abruptly withdraws because she is feeling coerced.

(4) But if the patient can have the experience first of good and then, when the time is right, of something more neutral (that is, if the therapist participates initially as a new good object and then is able to retract that support gradually as the patient needs it less and less), the patient will have the opportunity to consolidate her self and to fill in her deficits—structural growth.

It is, however, only when the patient signals her readiness to relinquish the need for her therapist to participate as a new good object that the therapist can revert to her original stance.

But does that time ever come? If the therapist allows herself to be enlisted as a good mother, does the patient's need ever become satisfied or does it simply escalate out of control?

As we will later discuss, I believe that the patient's need can spiral out of control if the therapist behaves seductively. But if the therapist behaves in a responsible fashion, promising only that which she will be able to deliver, then the therapist's willingness to participate as a new good object may prove to be profoundly transformative for the patient.

In fact, my experience has been that if things are allowed to run their natural course, then there does indeed come a time when the patient's appetite is sated and she no longer has the same need for her therapist to be the good mother she never had.

Relinquishment of Infantile Need

I would like now to explore the issue of what prompts the patient to relinquish her infantile need. Is it that something shifts within her? Is it that something shifts within the therapist? Or is it that something shifts in the intersubjective field between them such that the patient no longer has the same need to convert her objects into the good mother she never had?

I would like to draw upon Winnicott's (1963a,b) concept of the child's developmental progression—from a stage of absolute dependence through a stage of relative dependence to a stage of autonomy—to shed light on the process by which the patient transitions from a state of infantile need to a state of decreased need and greater self-reliance.

Winnicott's Developmental Progression

Winnicott (1960, 1963a,b) posits a series of maturational stages through which the infant advances en route to the achievement of more autonomous functioning.

How does Winnicott understand the impetus for such progression? Is it because the child is able to internalize aspects of the maternal care such that she comes to need her mother less and less? Or is it because the child has within her an inborn maturational thrust toward autonomy?

Interestingly, Winnicott's (1958) emphasis is on the latter. In fact, as noted in Part I, Winnicott believes that the good mother cannot be internalized until the child has come to recognize the fact of mother's otherness, the fact of her existence as outside the sphere of the child's omnipotence. Such recognition comes only with achievement of the third, and final, stage of development—that is, only with the child's attainment of autonomy. Prior to this point, the child is unable to use, in the sense of internalize, the mother. Thus it is not because the child internalizes aspects of maternal care that she comes to need her mother less and less. Rather, as we will see, it is the child's inborn thrust toward autonomy that, if unimpeded, provides the impetus for the child's relinquishment of her attachment to the infantile object.

I believe that the stage of absolute dependence corresponds in many ways to the situation that accrues once the therapist, in response to the patient's invitation, allows herself to be drawn into participating as the patient's good mother. If the holding environment provided by the therapist is sufficiently facilitative, then the patient will be able (of her own accord) to advance toward autonomy, simultaneously letting go of her need for the therapist to be her good mother.

I would like, therefore, to present some of Winnicott's ideas about the child's developmental progression from absolute dependence on the mother toward autonomy—a progression that I am suggesting parallels in important ways what happens when the patient, after delivering her infantile need into the therapy relationship, comes in time to need less and less for the therapist to recognize and respond to her every need.

Absolute Dependence

At the stage of absolute dependence, the mother is a "subjective object," experienced by the infant as indistinguishable from the self. Because the subjective object is not recognized as a separate object, there is no impetus for its internalization; in other words, the infant cannot yet use mother (that is, internalize various aspects of the maternal provision) because she has not yet come to be experienced as external to the infant's self.

In contradistinction to object usage (the term Winnicott employs to characterize the third, and final, stage of the young child's development) is the term object relating, which Winnicott uses to describe the way in which the infant, during this first stage of her development, engages the mother.

Winnicott (1958, 1965), as we know, introduced the concept of the good-enough mother who provides a holding environment that protects the infant from impingement and facilitates the coming into being of the infant's true self. As such, she serves as a protective envelope within which the child's inherited potential can become actualized.

During the first months of her infant's life, when her infant is absolutely dependent upon her, the good-enough mother is so attuned to her infant that she is able to recognize and respond to her infant's every need. The good-enough mother meets the omnipotence of the infant and, in so doing, reinforces the infant's illusions of omnipotence and her belief in the goodness of the world.

An infant needs to have had the experience, at least for a while, of being able to create her world. And the good-enough mother will be able to give such an experience to her infant.

So, too, I believe, a good-enough therapist will be able to offer this experience to those of her patients who, never having had such an experience early on, would seem to need that experience now.

Winnicott goes on to explain that when all goes well during the stage of absolute dependence, the child's little peapod true self is able to develop unhampered, in its own way, and at its own pace. With the care that she receives from her devoted mother, the child is able to have a personal existence and begins to build up a continuity of being.

When the patient enlists the therapist as the good mother she never had, the patient is given the opportunity to feel that she can relax into being absolutely dependent on someone who will recognize and respond to her on her own terms. It is when the patient is completely dependent on a therapist who is comfortable with being related to in this way that the patient will have the powerfully mutative experience of being able to feel that she can make a difference, that she can have an impact. The patient's sense of personal agency will be reinforced by the good-enough therapist's ability (and willingness) to be shaped by the patient's need.

Relative Dependence

Winnicott (1963a,b) believes that there inevitably comes a time when the child, secure in her knowledge that she deeply matters to someone, will begin to abrogate some of her omnipotence. Of her own accord and in response to maturational forces within her, the child will come to require less and less that her mother be perfectly adaptive to her every need. The child's willingness to relinquish some of her illusions of omnipotence will usher in the next stage—the stage of relative dependence.

This stage is characterized by the mother's graduated failure of adaptation, her failure, little by little, to shape the world according to her child's demands—as she senses that her child needs less and less for her to do so.

Where the earlier stage involved the mother's meeting of (that is, her recognition and response to) the child's every need, now the child—motivated by an innate maturational thrust—is thought to be able to tolerate ever less gratification and ever more frustration. Where once the child needed to have her mother's accommodation, now the child can more easily deal with being a little more separate.

It is the stage of relative dependence that is characterized by the child's use of transitional objects, animate and inanimate. These objects exist in the realm of illusion, having elements of both internal and external reality. The transitional object is in the creative area between the subjective and the objective; it is given life and meaning by the subject, but it exists as an object in the outer world. It is therefore part created and part found, part imagined and part real.

So, too, with respect to the patient. Where once the patient had needed the therapist to be perfectly attuned to her every need, I believe there comes a time when the patient—having already had the experience of being met in this way—can more easily tolerate the experience of being failed every now and again by a therapist who is not always perfectly attuned—but attuned-enough.

Toward Autonomy

Winnicott's (1963a,b) final stage involves the child's abrogation of her omnipotence, her acceptance of the limits of her power, and her awareness of the independent existence of others. In this third and final stage, the child comes to recognize the separateness of her mother. No longer a subjectively conceived object (as she was during the stage of absolute dependence) and no longer a transitional object (as she became during the stage of relative dependence), the mother is now an objectively perceived object.

Only now, once the mother's externality has been established, can the child begin to internalize different aspects of her.

With respect to the relationship between internalization and the attainment of separation, please note a subtle distinction between Winnicott and Kohut (Kohut 1966, Kohut and Wolf 1978). For Winnicott, as we have just seen, once separation is achieved, internalization is possible. For Kohut, internalization is the means by which separation is achieved—that is, as the child internalizes aspects of the good mother, she comes to need less and less for her mother to perform as a selfobject (that is, as a narcissistic extension of herself).

In any event, according to Winnicott, one of the ways the child comes to recognize the existence of her mother as a separate subject is through mother's survival of the child's efforts to destroy her. When the mother demonstrates resilience and nonretaliatory durability, the child is forced to become aware of the mother's existence as outside the sphere of her omnipotence; the child is confronted with both the reality of how limited her own power is and the reality of her mother's separateness, the recognition of which is accompanied by a mixture of tremendous frustration and extreme relief.

Winnicott believes it is the child's dawning awareness of the mother as having an independent center of initiative that prompts the child to internalize those aspects of her mother that the child will need in order to come truly into her own and to achieve her autonomy.

So, too, with respect to the patient, for whom there may be no incentive to internalize aspects of her therapist until the latter's existence can be recognized as outside her sphere of omnipotent control.

To review, Winnicott would seem to be suggesting that when a child has had the opportunity to be absolutely dependent on someone who makes the child the center of her world—at least for as long as the child needs it—then the child, in time and of her own accord, will begin to direct her energies elsewhere. It is an inborn maturational thrust toward autonomy that provides the impetus for the child to progress from a stage in which the mother is experienced as a part of the child's self to a stage in which the mother is experienced as separate from the self.

The Patient's Separation from the Infantile Object

Drawing upon Winnicott's (1963a,b) ideas about the child's progression from a stage of absolute dependence on the mother, to a stage of relative dependence on the mother, to a stage of independence from the mother, I therefore propose the following for the patient who has drawn the therapist into participating countertransferentially in the patient's transferential enactment of her infantile need for a good mother.

My claim will be that if the patient is able to have the experience of being important, of really mattering, of being special to her therapist, then there will inevitably come a time when the patient will no longer have the same need to have such an impact on her therapist.

Furthermore, when the patient (in response to her inborn maturational thrust toward autonomy) comes to recognize the independent existence of her therapist, this realization will provide the impetus for the patient to internalize various aspects of her therapist, in order to preserve internally a piece of the original experience of external goodness.

Accordingly, as the patient (by way of internalizing aspects of the therapist's corrective provision) acquires new psychic structure and fills in deficit, she will transform her need for the therapist to be her good mother into a capacity to be that good mother unto herself—and no longer will she have the same need for her therapist to be the good mother she never had.

The Role of Grieving

To what extent is grieving involved? Whenever something is relinquished, it is always accompanied by some grief. And, certainly, once the patient finds herself no longer needing what she had once needed from her therapist, it is a loss experienced by both—and a loss that must be grieved by both.

But when the patient is given whatever time she needs to transition from a stage of absolute dependence on her therapist to a stage of autonomy, I believe that the transition can sometimes be accomplished fairly smoothly. Just as a small child will one day, of her own accord, simply lose interest in her tattered blankie or her stuffed teddy bear with its one eye (transitional objects that had served as reminders of her mother), so, too, the patient will one day, by her own choice, simply let go—without much ado, once she no longer needs her therapist to function as her good mother.

The Therapist as a Facilitating Environment

Not all patients who were deprived of a good mother early on will be able to "overcome their dread of surrender to resourceless dependence" (Khan 1969) in the here-and-now engagement with their therapist, but neither will all such patients have an opportunity to regress to absolute dependence on their therapist. If the therapist is not able to tolerate the experience of being enlisted as her patient's good mother, then the patient will not have the profoundly transformative experience of finding someone upon whom she can be absolutely dependent. Or if the therapist is not able to tolerate the process whereby her patient, having regressed to the stage of absolute dependence on her "mother," begins to abrogate her need for such a mother, then the patient may be robbed of the opportunity to develop her own capacity to be a good mother unto herself.

A lot is required of the therapist who dares to be responsive to pressure from the patient to participate as the good mother the patient never had. The therapist must initially be able to tolerate being drawn into participating countertransferentially in the patient's transferential enactments and must then be able (when the patient signals that the time is right) to step back from such involvement in order to give the patient the freedom to get on with her life.

Some therapists (for a variety of reasons) are reluctant to respond to the patient's infantile needs for gratification; they will then be unable to give the patient the experience of knowing that she really matters to them, that she is special, that she can have an impact and can make a difference in their lives. Other therapists, readily responsive to being enlisted as the patient's new good mother, may become so invested in that position that they are unable to tolerate it when the time comes that the patient no longer needs them to serve in that way.

In other words, the therapist must allow herself to be utilized by the patient as a facilitating environment. She must first respond to the patient's invitation to be her good mother and must then step back when the patient no longer needs her to participate in that capacity. If the therapist can allow her moves to be choreographed by the patient, if she can allow herself to be first drawn in and then dismissed, the patient's displacive identifications will be successfully resolved, her infantile desire modulated, and the integrity of her self consolidated.

Clinical Vignette—Strong at the Broken Places

I worked for many years with Karen who, never having had the experience of being the center of her mother's world, found herself, over time, yearning to get that kind of recognition from me. Although initially she either kept me at bay or fought me tooth and nail, over the course of our years together she came to trust me deeply and to depend upon me absolutely.

During our first years together, I offered her numbers of interpretations, the intent of which was to make her more aware of her internal dynamics. She came to see, for example, that in order not to feel the emptiness of her relationship with her mother and the pain of her loneliness, she had thrown herself from an early age into developing her intellect and excelling academically. Karen also came to understand that although she had felt loved by her father, he was also a big disappointment to her because his work had always been his top priority.

Karen found such interventions useful because they enabled her to feel more grounded and more in control of her life.

In our relationship, however, Karen initially struggled to convince me that I was not to be trusted, that I was not reliable. In fact, during much of our early time together, she was relentless in her insistence that I could not possibly care, that I could not possibly be invested in her.

Karen was not at first aware that she had also experienced her mother as unreliable. But by virtue of what she found herself playing out with me in the transference, it gradually became clear to her that she must be re-enacting with me the dynamic that had characterized that earlier relationship.

And there were numbers of times when despite my best efforts to avoid being drawn in, I would find myself failing her in the very ways she had known I would—namely, I demonstrated my untrustworthiness. As an example, one time I forgot the details of something important that she had shared with me months earlier—to her, this was proof that I really didn't care; I was horrified that I had forgotten—and she was devastated and outraged.

But with much effort we would manage, somehow, to wend our way out of these mutual enactments—I would usually apologize for my contribution to the impasse and then we would look at the part she had played in provoking me to fail her. Karen began to understand that because she had experienced her mother as so unavailable, she now had not only the expectation that I too would be unavailable but also the need to be so failed—because that was all she had ever known. She came to see that she played this dynamic out in all her important relationships—so that she was always feeling misunderstood, not met, not cared about, alone.

As Karen gained insight into both her internal dynamics (by way of our work in Model 1) and her relational dynamics (by way of our work in Model 3), she gradually began to let me in and to trust me. Eventually there even came a time when she was able to let herself experience me as someone who cared about her and carried her inside of me when I was not with her.

There also came a time when I found myself thinking of her as one of my favorite patients—a special patient for whom I was willing to make some exceptions. For example, I lent her some of my jigsaw puzzles; I taught her a card game that had always been a favorite of mine; I called her up on her birthday to let her know I was thinking of her; I gave her my home phone number (something I rarely do with my patients); and I made myself available to her for Sunday appointments in order to help her get through her lonely weekends.

In other words, I found myself participating as the good mother Karen had never had, both in response to pressure from Karen to participate in that way and because of my own desire to be available to her in that way. In essence, a displacive identification was taking place in which I was being enrolled as a loving mother who held a special place in my mind and in my heart for Karen.

Once Karen had dared to let me really matter to her, it became very important to her that I not fail her. When I would inadvertently fail her even so, it was crucial to her that I be able to demonstrate my indestructibility in the face of her outrage and her devastation—crucial that I bear with her until she had had a chance to recover her equilibrium.

For almost two years, we continued to have our periodic Sunday sessions. But there came a time when Karen—secure in the knowledge that I would be pleased to make myself available were she to ask—no longer needed me to be available every Sunday because, as she was coming to know that she mattered to me (and, by extension, that she could matter to others as well), her relationships were developing a depth and her life was developing a richness that she had never before experienced.

As she came to see that she really could have an impact on somebody, she began to find that she had less of a need to see me on Sundays. Karen made it clear that it was still important to her to know that she had the option of asking for time on a Sunday—but rarely did she now avail herself of that option.

With Karen, the transition (from her dependence on me to her independence of me) was accomplished almost effortlessly—even though it was bittersweet for both of us when she realized that she no longer needed me to be her good mother. She now had a relationship with a man (whom she later married) and, though I still meant the world to her, she was no longer as absolutely dependent on me as she had once been and no longer needed me to make exceptions on her behalf or to do things a little differently for her. It was clear to us both that it had been my willingness to allow myself to be enlisted as her good mother that had enabled her to consolidate enough of a self and enough of a sense of personal agency that she no longer needed to feel special.

Early in our work, Karen had brought in a potted plant. It was a beautiful plant, but Karen, with scissors in hand, had cut half of each leaf off, angrily declaring that this symbolized what her mother had done to stunt her own (Karen's) growth. When she departed at the end of the session, she left the poor little plant, injured and pathetic-looking, on my hearth. Unbeknownst to Karen, I had taken the plant and had put it in another room with some of my own plants. Over the years, in an effort to bring it back to life, I had carefully nurtured and groomed it.

When Karen (some years later) terminated her work with me, I surprised her by giving her back her plant—now flourishing and more robust than ever. She was deeply touched that I had been willing to invest my energies in nursing it back to health. She and I both agreed that the plant, although somewhat unusual looking because of its battle scars, had nonetheless grown strong at the broken places—and was now more beautiful than ever.

In order for a successful displacive identification to occur, the therapist must be able to tolerate (1) first being called upon by the patient to participate as a good mother with boundless resources and (2) then being cast off when the patient's need has been satisfied. In fact, my experience has been that most patients, in time, are able to relinquish this aspect of their engagement with the therapist once they have had the opportunity to know that they can have an impact on someone whom they have come to depend upon absolutely.

As noted earlier, the patient may then be able to let go of the object in much the same way that a small child discards her transitional object—with never a backward glance. But the infantile longing cannot be relinquished unless the patient has had the opportunity to know that she had once been at the center of someone's world, at least for a while.

As with any mutual enactment, the stakes are high—but so, too, are the potential gains.

DISPLACIVE IDENTIFICATION: MODEL 2 OR MODEL 3?

In which model of therapeutic action is there a place for the concept of displacive identification—that is, the patient's exerting of pressure on the therapist to participate as a new good object?

In Model 2, the therapeutic action is thought to revolve around the patient's experience of the therapist as a new good object. As we noted earlier, self psychologists emphasize the patient's experience of the therapist as a new good object; and Model 2 object relations theorists emphasize the therapist's actual participation as that new good object.

But nowhere in Model 2 does there seem to be interest in the patient's exerting of pressure on the therapist to participate as a new good object and the therapist's responsiveness to that pressure. Nor, as we have seen, is there even a name in Model 2 for such an enactment.

It is to Model 3 object relations theorists that we must look if our interest is in the patient's exerting of pressure on the therapist to participate in a certain way (as happens, say, with projective identification) and the therapist's responsiveness to that pressure.

Model 3 object relations theorists, however, concern themselves with relational conflict and not with structural deficit. In other words, their interest is in the patient's enactment of her need for old bad (projective identification) and not in the enactment of her need for new good. In Model 3, the focus is on the patient's recreation of old bad and not on her creation of new good.

And other Model 3 theorists (like those who embrace contemporary relational theory) focus, more generally, on each participant in the intersubjective field as an authentic subject—the subjectivity of each influencing, and influenced by, the other's subjectivity.

But nowhere in Model 3 is there specific interest in the patient's exerting of pressure on the therapist to participate as a new good object and the therapist's responsiveness to that pressure. Nor, as we have seen, is there even a name in Model 3 for such an enactment.

So which model of therapeutic action most comfortably accommodates what I am here describing as displacive identification? I would like to suggest that neither Model 2 nor Model 3 fills the bill; neither Model 2 nor Model 3 theorists speak directly to the patient's (often unconscious) efforts to invite the therapist to participate as a new good object.

Model 2 is about the therapist's participation as a new good object, but not about the patient's exerting of pressure on the therapist to participate in that way. Model 3 is about the patient's exerting of pressure on the therapist to participate as the old bad object, but not about the therapist's participation as a new good object.

Displacive identification, therefore, falls into the province of neither Model 2 nor Model 3. Rather, it would seem to lie somewhere between the two models of therapeutic action: On the one hand, displacive identification has elements that are compatible with Model 2 (which concerns itself with the therapist's participation as a new good object); on the other hand, it has elements that are compatible with Model 3 (which concerns itself with the patient's enactment of need and the impact of that enactment on the therapist's participation).

For some time now theorists have been writing about the patient's need to be failed in ways specifically determined by her developmental history. In other words, their interest has been in the patient's provocative behavior as speaking to her (often unconscious) need for the old bad object so that she can achieve belated mastery of her internalized traumas. And when clinicians experience the patient's exerting of such pressure and find themselves responding to such pressure, it is understood that projective identification is implicated.

But there has been much less attention paid to the patient's need for infantile gratification—a need deriving specifically from traumatic thwarting of her early-on desire for a good mother. In other words, there has been relatively little interest in the patient's inviting behavior as speaking to her (perhaps unconscious) need for a new good object so that she can have a chance to begin anew. And yet I think clinicians experience the patient's exerting of such pressure and find themselves responding to such pressure all the time. Unfortunately, there has been no specific term used to describe this interpersonal event.

Just as it has taken time for theorists to recognize that the patient enacts her need for the old bad object and that the process of working through what happens as a result of such an enactment can be powerfully transformative, so, too, it may take time for theorists to recognize that the patient also enacts her need for a new good object and that the process of working through what happens as a result of this enactment can be profoundly healing. Both projective identification and displacive identification are powerful therapeutic resources that deepen the here-and-now engagement between patient and therapist and facilitate development of the patient's capacity for healthy, authentic relatedness.

References

Abend, S. M. (1989). Countertransference and psychoanalytic technique. *Psychoanalytic Quarterly* 58:374–395.

Akhtar, S. (1994). *Tethers, orbits, and invisible fences: developmental, clinical, cultural, and technical aspects of optimal distance.* Paper presented in the Guest Lecture Series sponsored by Three Ripley Street, Newton Centre, MA, September.

Alexander, F. (1946). The principle of corrective emotional experience. In *Psychoanalytic Therapy: Principles and Application*, ed. F. Alexander and T. French, pp. 66–70. New York: Ronald.

——— (1948). *Fundamentals of Psychoanalysis*. New York: Norton.

Aron, L. (1991). The patient's experience of the analyst's subjectivity. *Psychoanalytic Dialogues* 1(1):29–51.

——— (1992). Interpretation as expression of the analyst's subjectivity. *Psychoanalytic Dialogues* 2(4):475–508.

——— (1996). *A Meeting of Minds: Mutuality in Psychoanalysis*. Hillsdale, NJ: Analytic Press.

Atwood, G., and Stolorow, R. (1984). Intersubjectivity: I. the therapeutic situation. In *Structures of Subjectivity: Explorations in Psychoanalytic Phenomenology*, pp. 41–64. Hillsdale, NJ: Analytic Press.

Balint, M. (1949). Early developmental states of the ego: primary object love. *International Journal of Psycho-Analysis* 30:265–273.

——— (1950). Changing therapeutical aims and techniques in psychoanalysis. *International Journal of Psycho-Analysis* 31:117–124.

——— (1952). On love and hate. *International Journal of Psycho-Analysis* 33:355–362.

——— (1968). *The Basic Fault: Therapeutic Aspects of Regression*. New York: Brunner/Mazel.

Beebe, B., and Lachmann, F. M. (1988). Mother–infant mutual influence and precursors of psychic structure. *Progress in Self Psychology* 3:3–25.

Benjamin, J. (1988). *The Bonds of Love: Psychoanalysis, Feminism, and the Problem of Domination*. New York: Pantheon.

——— (1992). Recognition and destruction: an outline of intersubjectivity. In *Relational Perspectives in Psychoanalysis*, ed. N. Skolnick and S. Warshaw, pp. 43–60. Hillsdale, NJ: Analytic Press.

Bion, W. R. (1959). Attacks on linking. *International Journal of Psycho-Analysis* 40:308–315.

——— (1967). *Second Thoughts*. New York: Basic Books.

Bird, B. (1972). Notes on transference: universal phenomenon and hardest part of analysis. *Journal of the American Psychoanalytic Association* 20:267–301.

Blechner, M. (1988). Differentiating empathy from therapeutic action. *Contemporary Psychoanalysis* 24:301–310.

Bollas, C. (1987). Expressive uses of the countertransference: notes to the patient from oneself. In *The Shadow of the Object: Psychoanalysis of the Unthought Known*, pp. 200–235. New York: Columbia University Press.

Brenner, C. (1955). *An Elementary Textbook of Psychoanalysis*, lst ed. New York: International Universities Press.

Carpy, D. (1989). Tolerating the countertransference: a mutative process. *International Journal of Psycho-Analysis* 70:287–294.

Casement, P. (1985). Forms of interactive communication. In *On Learning from the Patient*, pp. 72–101. London and New York: Tavistock.

Davies, J. M. (1994). Love in the afternoon: a relational reconsideration of desire and dread in the countertransference. *Psychoanalytic Dialogues* 4(2):153–170.

Davison, W. (1984). Reflections on the mutative interpretation, defence analysis and self analysis. *International Review of Psycho-Analysis* 11:143–150.

Dicks, H. (1967). *Marital Tensions*. New York: Basic Books.

Ehrenberg, D. B. (1974). The intimate edge in therapeutic relatedness. *Contemporary Psychoanalysis* 10:423–437.

——— (1984). Psychoanalytic engagement, II: affective considerations. *Contemporary Psychoanalysis* 20:560–599.

Eissler, K. R. (1958). Remarks on some variations in psychoanalytical technique. *International Journal of Psycho-Analysis* 39:222–229.

Epstein, L. (1979). The therapeutic function of hate in the countertransference. In *Countertransference: The Therapist's Contribution to the Therapeutic Situation*, ed. L. Epstein and A. Feiner, pp. 213–234. New York: Jason Aronson.

Fairbairn, W. R. D. (1943). The repression and the return of bad objects. In *An Object-Relations Theory of the Personality*, pp. 59–81. New York: Basic Books, 1954.

——— (1954). *An Object-Relations Theory of the Personality*. New York: Basic Books.

——— (1958). On the nature and aims of psycho-analytical treatment. *International Journal of Psycho-Analysis* 39:374–385.

Ferenczi, S. (1930). The principle of relaxation and neocatharsis. *International Journal of Psycho-Analysis* 11:428–443.

Fishman, G. (1998). *Love in the afternoon revisited: when should a therapist profess her love—or ever?* Paper presented at the annual meeting of Division 39 of the American Psychological Association, Boston, MA, April.

Freud, S. (1905). Fragment of an analysis of a case of hysteria: part 4, postscript. *Standard Edition* 7:112–122.

——— (1912). Recommendations to physicians practising psycho-analysis. *Standard Edition* 12:109–120.

——— (1914). Remembering, repeating and working-through. *Standard Edition* 12:146–156.

——— (1923). The ego and the id. *Standard Edition* 19:1–66.

Friedman, L. (1985). Toward a comprehensive theory of treatment. *Psychoanalytic Inquiry* 5:589–599.

Geist, R. (1995). *Resistance: safeguarding the healthy self.* Paper presented at a conference sponsored by the Harvard Medical School, Boston, MA, March.

Gill, M. (1982). *Analysis of Transference*, vol. 1. New York: International Universities Press.

——— (1987). The analyst as participant. *Psychoanalytic Inquiry* 7:249–259.

Gray, P. (1973). Psychoanalytic technique and the ego's capacity for viewing intrapsychic activity. *Journal of the American Psychoanalytic Association* 21:474–494.

——— (1994). *The Ego and Analysis of Defense*. Northvale, NJ: Jason Aronson.

Greenberg, J. R. (1981). Prescription or description: therapeutic action of psychoanalysis. *Contemporary Psychoanalysis* 17:239–257.

——— (1986a). The problem of analytic neutrality. *Contemporary Psychoanalysis* 22:76–86.

——— (1986b). Theoretical models and the analyst's neutrality. *Contemporary Psychoanalysis* 22:87–106.

——— (1991). Countertransference and reality. *Psychoanalytic Dialogues* 1(1):52–73.

Greenberg, J., and Mitchell, S. (1983). Harry Guntrip. In *Object Relations in Psychoanalytic Theory*, pp. 209–219. Cambridge, MA: Harvard University Press.

Greenson, R. R. (1967). *The Technique and Practice of Psychoanalysis*, vol. 1. New York: International Universities Press.

Grotstein, J. (1985). The nature of projective identification. In *Splitting and Projective Identification*, pp. 132–133. Northvale, NJ: Jason Aronson.

Guntrip, H. (1961). *Personality Structure and Human Interaction*. London: Hogarth.

——— (1969). *Schizoid Phenomena, Object-Relations, and the Self*. New York: International Universities Press.

——— (1973). *Psychoanalytic Theory, Therapy, and the Self*. New York: Basic Books.

Heimann, P. (1956). Dynamics of transference interpretations. *International Journal of Psycho-Analysis* 37:303–310.

Herzog, J. (1984). Fathers and young children: fathering sons and fathering daughters. In *Frontiers of Infant Psychiatry*, vol. 2, ed. J. Caul, E. Galenson, and R. Tyson, pp. 335–342. New York: Basic Books.

Hirsch, I. (1987). Varying modes of analytic participation. *Journal of the American Academy of Psychoanalysis* 15(2):205–222.

Hoffer, A. (1985). Toward a definition of psychoanalytic neutrality. *Journal of the American Psychoanalytic Association* 33:771–795.

——— (1991). The Freud–Ferenczi controversy: a living legacy. *International Review of Psycho-Analysis* 18:465–472.

Hoffman, I. (1983). The patient as interpreter of the analyst's experience. *Contemporary Psychoanalysis* 19:389–422.

——— (1992). Some practical implications of a social-constructivist view of the psychoanalytic situation. *Psychoanalytic Dialogues* 2(3):287–304.

Khan, M. M. R. (1969). On the clinical provision of frustrations, recognitions, and failures in the analytic situation: an essay on Dr. Michael Balint's researches on the theory of psychoanalytic technique. *International Journal of Psycho-Analysis* 50:237–248.

Klein, M. (1964). *Contributions to Psychoanalysis 1921–1945*. New York: McGraw-Hill.

Kohut, H. (1966). Forms and transformations of narcissism. *Journal of the American Psychoanalytic Association* 14:243–257.

——— (1968). The psychoanalytic treatment of the narcissistic personality disorders: outline of a systematic approach. *Psychoanalytic Study of the Child* 23:86–113. New York: International Universities Press.

——— (1971). *The Analysis of the Self.* New York: International Universities Press.

——— (1982). Introspection, empathy, and the semi-circle of mental health. *International Journal of Psycho-Analysis* 63:395–407.

——— (1984). *How Does Analysis Cure?* Chicago and London: University of Chicago Press.

Kohut, H., and Wolf, E. (1978). The disorders of the self and their treatment: an outline. *International Journal of Psycho-Analysis* 59:413–425.

Kopp, S. (1969). The refusal to mourn. *Voices*, Spring, pp. 30–35.

Kris, E. (1958). Writings of Ernst Kris. *Psychoanalytic Study of the Child* 13:562–573. New York: International Universities Press.

Lacan, J. (1977). *Ecrits: A Selection*. New York: Norton.

Langs, R. (1979). Interventions in the bipersonal field. *Contemporary Psychoanalysis* 15:1–54.

——— (1988). *A Primer of Psychotherapy*. New York: Gardner.

Levenson, E. A. (1988). Show and tell: the recursive order of transference. In *How Does Treatment Help?*, ed. A. Rothstein, pp. 135–143. Madison, CT: International Universities Press.

——— (1991). *The Purloined Self: Interpersonal Perspectives in Psychoanalysis*. New York: Contemporary Psychoanalysis Books—William Alanson White Institute.

Loewald, H. (1960). On the therapeutic action of psychoanalysis. *International Journal of Psycho-Analysis* 41:16–33.

Mahler, M. S. (1967). On human symbiosis and the vicissitudes of individuation. *Journal of the American Psychoanalytic Association* 15:740–763.

Malin, A., and Grotstein, J. (1966). Projective identification in the therapeutic process. *International Journal of Psycho-Analysis* 47:26–31.

McLaughlin, J. T. (1991). Clinical and theoretical aspects of enactment. *Journal of the American Psychoanalytic Association* 39:595–614.

Meissner, W. W. (1974). Correlative aspects of introjective and projective mechanisms. *American Journal of Psychiatry* 131:176–180.

——— (1976). Psychotherapeutic schema based on the paranoid process. *International Journal of Psychoanalytic Psychotherapy* 5:87–113.

——— (1980). The problem of internalization and structure formation. *International Journal of Psycho-Analysis* 61:237–248.

Miller, J. B. (1988). Connections, disconnections and violations. *Work in Progress, No.* 33. Wellesley, MA: Stone Center Working Paper Series.

Miller, J. B., and Stiver, I. P. (1991). *A relational reframing of therapy*. Paper presented in the Stone Center Colloquium Series, Wellesley, MA, June.

Mitchell, S. (1988). *Relational Concepts in Psychoanalysis*. Cambridge, MA: Harvard University Press.

Modell, A. (1965). On having the right to a life: an aspect of the superego's development. *International Journal of Psycho-Analysis* 46:323–331.

——— (1975). A narcissistic defense against affects and the illusion of self-sufficiency. *International Journal of Psycho-Analysis* 56:275–282.

____ (1980). Affects and their non-communication. *International Journal of Psycho-Analysis* 61:259–268.

——— (1984). *Psychoanalysis in a New Context*. New York: International Universities Press.

Morrison, A. (1994). The breadth and boundaries of a self-psychological immersion in shame: a one-and-a-half-person perspective. *Psychoanalytic Dialogues* 4(1):19–35.

Ogden, T. (1979). On projective identification. *International Journal of Psycho-Analysis* 60:357–373.

——— (1982a). The concept of projective identification. In *Projective Identification and Psychotherapeutic Technique*, pp. 11–37. New York: Jason Aronson.

——— (1982b). Issues of technique. In *Projective Identification and Psychotherapeutic Technique*, pp. 39–74. New York: Jason Aronson.

——— (1983). The concept of internal object relations. *International Journal of Psycho-Analysis* 64:227–242.

Ornstein, A. (1974). The dread to repeat and the new beginning: a contribution to the psychoanalysis of the narcissistic personality disorders. *The Annual of Psychoanalysis* 2:231–248.

Ornstein, P. (1974). On narcissism: beyond the introduction—highlights of Kohut's contribution to the psychoanalytic treatment of narcissistic personality disorders. *The Annual of Psychoanalysis* 2:127–149.

Pick, I. B: (1985). Working through in the countertransference. *International Journal of Psycho-Analysis* 66:157–166.

Pine, F. (1990). *Drive, Ego, Object, and Self: A Synthesis for Clinical Work*. New York: Basic Books.

Powers, T. (1984). What's it about? *Atlantic Monthly*, January.

Racker, H. (1953). A contribution to the problem of countertransference. *International Journal of Psycho-Analysis* 34:313–324.

Renik, O. (1993). Analytic interaction: conceptualizing technique in light of the analyst's irreducible subjectivity. *Psychoanalytic Quarterly* 62:553–571.

Rogers, C. (1961). *On Becoming a Person*. Boston, MA: Houghton Mifflin.

Russell, P. (1980). The theory of the crunch (unpublished manuscript).

——— (1982). Beyond the wish: further thoughts on containment (unpublished manuscript).
——— (1995). Ownership, boundaries, and psychic structure. *Psychotherapy Forum* 1(2):1–4.
Sandler, J. (1976). Countertransference and role-responsiveness. *International Review of Psycho-Analysis* 3:43–48.
——— (1987). *From Safety to Superego: Selected Papers of Joseph Sandler*. New York: Guilford.
Schafer, R. (1968). *Aspects of Internalization*. New York: International Universities Press.
Schwaber, E. A. (1979). On the "self" within the matrix of analytic theory—some clinical reflections and reconsiderations. *International Journal of Psycho-Analysis* 60:467–479.
——— (1981). Narcissism, self psychology, and the listening perspective. *The Annual of Psychoanalysis* 9:115–132. New York: International Universities Press.
——— (1983). Psychoanalytic listening and psychic reality. *International Review of Psycho-Analysis* 10:379–392.
——— (1992). Countertransference: the analyst's retreat from the patient's vantage point. *International Journal of Psycho-Analysis* 73:349–361.
Searles, H. (1979). The development of mature hope in the patient–therapist relationship. In *Countertransference and Related Subjects: Selected Papers*, pp. 479–502. New York: International Universities Press.
Stark, M. (1994a). *Working with Resistance*. Northvale, NJ: Jason Aronson.
——— (1994b). *A Primer on Working with Resistance*. Northvale, NJ: Jason Aronson.
Stern, D. (1985). *The Interpersonal World of the Infant*. New York: Basic Books.
Stern, S. (1994). Needed relationships and repeated relationships: an integrated relational perspective. *Psychoanalytic Dialogues* 4(3):317–345.
Stiver, I. P. (1990). *Movement in therapy*. Paper presented at the annual meeting of the American Psychological Association, Boston, MA, August.
Stolorow, R. (1978). The concept of psychic structure: its metapsychological and clinical psychoanalytic meanings. *International Review of Psycho-Analysis* 5:313–320.
——— (1988). Epistemology: ways of knowing in psychoanalysis. *Contemporary Psychoanalysis* 24:331–338.
Stolorow, R., Brandchaft, B., and Atwood, G. (1987). Principles of psychoanalytic exploration. In *Psychoanalytic Treatment: An Intersubjective Approach*, pp. 1–14. Hillsdale, NJ: Analytic Press.

Stolorow, R., and Lachmann, F. (1980). Developmental arrests and the psychoanalytic situation. In *Psychoanalysis of Developmental Arrests: Theory and Treatment*, pp. 171–191. New York: International Universities Press.

Stone, L. (1954). The widening scope of indications for psychoanalysis. *Journal of the American Psychoanalytic Association* 2:567–594.

Strachey, J. (1934). The nature of the therapeutic action of psycho-analysis. *International Journal of Psycho-Analysis* 15:127–159.

Tansey, M., and Burke, W. F. (1989). *Understanding Countertransference: From Projective Identification to Empathy*. Hillsdale, NJ: Analytic Press.

Wachtel, P. (1980). Transference, schema, and assimilation: the relevance of Piaget to the psychoanalytic theory of transference. *The Annual of Psychoanalysis* 8:59–76.

——— (1982). Vicious circles. *Contemporary Psychoanalysis* 18:259–272.

——— (1986). On the limits of therapeutic neutrality. *Contemporary Psychoanalysis* 22:60–70.

Winnicott, D. W. (1947). Hate in the countertransference. In *Collected Papers: Through Paediatrics to Psycho-Analysis*, pp. 194–203. New York: Basic Books, 1958.

——— (1955). Metapsychological and clinical aspects of regression within the psycho-analytic set-up. *International Journal of Psycho-Analysis* 36:16–26.

——— (1958). *Collected Papers: Through Paediatrics to Psycho-Analysis*. New York: Basic Books.

——— (1960). The theory of the parent–infant relationship. In *The Maturational Processes and the Facilitating Environment*, pp. 37–55. New York: International Universities Press, 1965.

——— (1963a). From dependence to independence in the development of the individual. In *The Maturational Processes and the Facilitating Environment*, pp. 83–99. New York: International Universities Press, 1965.

——— (1963b). Dependence in infant-care, in child-care, and in the psychoanalytic setting. In *The Maturational Processes and the Facilitating Environment*, pp. 249–259. New York: International Universities Press, 1965.

——— (1965). *The Maturational Processes and the Facilitating Environment*. New York: International Universities Press.

——— (1969). The use of an object. *International Journal of Psycho-Analysis* 50:711–716.

Index